COMPETITION MATHEMATICS
(PART 2)

R. C. HAESE	B.Sc.
S. H. HAESE	B.Sc.
B. WEBBER	M.Sc., Dip.Ed.
M. BRUCE	B.Ed.

HAESE & HARRIS PUBLICATIONS

HAESE & HARRIS PUBLICATIONS

27 Simcock Street, West Beach   SA 5024

Phone: (08) 8356 9203

Fax: (08) 8235 9110

National Library of Australia Card Number & ISBN   0-9586951-4-8

© Haese & Harris Publications

Published by **Raksar Nominees Pty Ltd**, 27 Simcock Street, West Beach SA 5024

First Edition   1982
Second Edition 1998

Typeset in Australia by Susan Haese (Raksar Nominees).

Artwork by Joanna and Piotr Poturaj.

FOREWORD

This book is not an ordinary textbook but one in which a number of important topics in mathematics have been selected and an abundant number of problems given which will enable students to expand and deepen their knowledge of mathematics.

We would hope that students who rejoice in the challenge of a problem will find this book stimulating and motivating and that it will enable them to be better prepared, not only for mathematics competitions, but for any future course in mathematics they may take. We would also hope that teachers will encourage their students to rise beyond the security offered by prefabricated exercises and experience the creative vitality of the problems given in this book.

This book should appeal to a broad range of readers from students in schools, student teachers in training and the teachers of these students. As a supplement to a standard textbook it will act as a most valuable resource.

We acknowledge the work done by the various groups who have made significant contributions to the development of this book and to mathematics education in this State:

- ◆ the authors who have put together a most valuable resource for teachers,
- ◆ the many students and teachers who have helped in the preparation of
- ◆ questions for the MASA Mathematics Competition for IBM Prizes,
- ◆ IBM without whose financial support over the past 30 years none of this might have happened.

Keith Hamann
President – MASA (1998)

ACKNOWLEDGEMENTS

The authors/editors would like to sincerely thank

- **John Finger** for assisting with proof reading and checking,
- **John van der Hoek** – Editor of '*Trigon*' for many years,
- the many teachers and students who have constructed questions for the student magazine '*Trigon*' and the MASA Mathematics Competitions over a period of nearly 30 years.

CONTENTS

PYTHAGORAS

THE PROBLEMS

1.1 A *median* of a triangle is a line joining a vertex to the midpoint of the opposite side.

In a right-angled triangle, the medians from the acute angles have length 3 cm and 4 cm respectively.

Find the length of the hypotenuse.

1.2 3 circles touch each other externally and have a common tangent, as illustrated.

If the radii of the larger circles are 4 cm and 1 cm respectively, find the radius of the smallest circle.

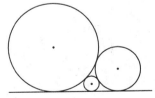

1.3

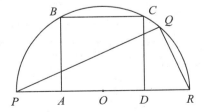

$ABCD$ is a square inscribed in a semicircle.
PQR is a triangle with the same area as the square.
Locate the poition of Q.

1.4 ABC is a right angle. The three circles touch each other as illustrated and touch $\overline{AB}$ and $\overline{BC}$. If the smallest circle has radius 1 cm, find the radii of the two larger circles.

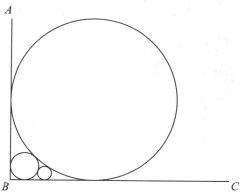

1.5 Two people watch the sun setting over the ocean on a calm day. One is 10 m above sea level, and the other is on a cliff top 30 m above the first.

How long after the first does the second observe the instant of sunset? [The circumference of the earth is 40 000 km.]

1.6 A square-based pyramid has all edges of length a cm, and a sphere of radius r cm is inscribed within it. Find the relationship between r and a.

1.7 Two pipes of diameters 2 m and 1 m respectively are to be placed inside a semicircular tunnel. The pipes touch the floor at X and Y , the roof of the tunnel at B and C and each other at A. Find the height of the tunnel.

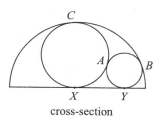

cross-section

1.8

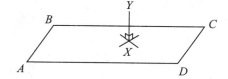

$ABCD$ is a rectangular plane. X is any point within the rectangle. $\overline{XY}$ is normal to the plane. If $YA = 6$ m, $YB = 4$ m and $YC = 3$ m, find the length of $\overline{YD}$.

1.9 3 edges of a tetrahedron meet at a vertex so that a right angle is formed between each pair of edges. Prove that the triangle formed by the remaining 3 edges cannot be right angled.

1.10 A sphere of radius R fits snugly into the corner of a rectangular box. A smaller sphere of radius r fits exactly into the space remaining in the corner. Find the relationship between R and r.

PROBLEM SOLVING

THE PROBLEMS

2.1 A and B are at a distance of 85 km. A motorist and a cyclist leave A and B at the same time and travel towards each other for an hour at uniform speeds. Their distance apart at the end of the hour is 27 km. The cyclist rests for 15 minutes, then continues, and the two meet 90 minutes after their start from A and B. Find the speed of each and their meeting point. Illustrate with a graph.

2.2 A bus route leads up a hill along a uniformly sloping path from terminus G at the bottom to terminus H at the top. A bus A leaves G at 8.12 am, and a bus B leaves H at 8.18 am. The two meet exactly midway. Bus B arrives at G and stays there for a few minutes before starting upwards. Bus A arrives at H, turns, and starts downwards immediately. The two buses meet again at 8.44 am at a point M, the distance HM being twice the distance GM.

Find the duration of the ascent and the descent, and find the resting time at G.

2.3 Between midnight and noon the minute-hand and the hour-hand of a clock sometimes

    a   coincide,

    b   point in opposite directions.

By *drawing graphs,* show how all such times may be found.

2.4 A train departs from the Adelaide railway station between ten and eleven o'clock. After travelling for eight kilometres the driver noticed that the minute hand of his watch was directly over the hour hand. If the average speed for the eight kilometres was 33 kmph, at what time did the train leave Adelaide?

2.5 Two ships, an ocean liner and an oil tanker, pass each other on the high seas. If it would take twice as long for the liner to *overtake* the tanker as it does to pass the tanker when they travel in opposite directions, give a comparison of their speeds.

2.6 An aeroplane flies from X to Y and back again, the speed of the motors being constant. Neglecting the turn-around time of the plane, will the total time of the flight be more if a wind is blowing at a constant speed from X to Y than if no wind blows?

2.7 Jack and Mack run a 10 lap race around a housing block. For the first 5 laps Jack ran at an average of 2 kmph faster than Mack. For the last 5 laps Jack ran at an average of 2 kmph slower than Mack. Who won the race?

2.8 Once a jolly swagman had walked $\frac{3}{8}$ of the way onto a high one-lane bridge when he heard behind him a stampede of cattle coming towards the bridge at 20 kmph. He could just save his life by running to a coolibah tree at either end of the bridge. How fast could he run?

2.9 After a good season my Uncle Fred, a wheat farmer, enlarged his rectangular farm by buying the square farm next door, on the longer side of his farm.

As he drew up the plans of his new farm, he was amazed to find that the sides were in the same proportions as were the sides of his original farm.

Several years later, he bought another adjacent farm - again it was square, and along his longer boundary. His plan now looked like this:

"Jeff," he said, "D'you think the farm is still in the same proportions as it was when it was smaller?"

"I'm sure it is - in fact if you keep buying farms in the same patterns, I can prove that you'll keep the same proportions forever."

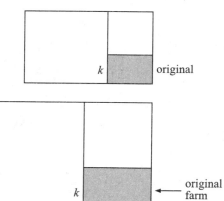

(I was getting confident!) Further, I offered to calculate the area of his farm before he did any more buying, if he could tell me the length of the shorter side of his original farm.

I wonder if you could have solved these three problems for Uncle Fred, that is

a that the farm after the first two additions (see diagram) is in the same proportions as the original farm,

b prove that continuing the pattern will continue the proportions,

c find an expression for the area of the largest farm, as described by the diagram, given the shorter side is $\underline{k}$ kilometres.

2.10 Each hand of a clock is exactly on a minute mark, and the angle between the hands measures $36°$. What is the time?

2.11 6 cows take 3 days to eat a field of grass. 3 cows would take 7 days to eat the same field. How long would 1 cow take?

2.12   To fill a swimming pool it would take either:
2 days using pipe A,   3 days using pipe B,   4 days using pipe C,   6 days using pipe D.

If the pool is filled using all four pipes working at once, each delivering water at the same rate as before, how long would it take to fill the pool (in hours and minutes)?

2.13   The 25 students of class 5B are seated in a square array of 5 rows and 5 columns. Mr Jones, the teacher, requests that every student changes seats by either going to the seat in front, back, right or left but no other way. Fred, the chess champion, argued that this was impossible. Do you support Fred's statement?

2.14   Water can be supplied to a tank through either or both of two pipes. Using the smaller pipe alone, the tank takes two hours longer to fill than if the larger pipe is used alone. Using both pipes, the tank is filled in $1\frac{7}{8}$ hours. How long does it take to fill the tank by each pipe (separately)?

2.15   Two machines, an old and new one, are used simultaneously to complete a job. The new machine, if used on its own, can complete the work in 2 hours less time than the old one. However, after 7 hours work, the new machine breaks down partially and is slowed down to half speed. The job is completed in 9 hours counted from commencement. How long would the old machine take to complete the job on its own?

2.16   "Last year," said the mounted policeman to his mathematical daughter, "Johnnies' Christmas Pageant was two kilometres long. I was on line patrol (you know, riding up and down the procession checking that none of the little kids came over the line on to the road, in the way of the oncoming parade). Well, last year was a remarkable year: there were no holdups at all, the procession moved constantly from beginning to end."
"Gee," said the Kid.
"Yes," went on Father, "I had to begin from the tail end, just as it started to move and ride at a steady pace right along the Pageant to the front and then back again to the end. You know, by the time I got back to the end of the procession, they were $1\frac{1}{2}$ kilometres from where they had started."
"Big deal," said the Kid.
"Look, enough lip, Kid. What I want you to tell me is how far did I travel on that patrol? Come on, I've got to put in this claim for new horse-shoes - so I'll have to tell them how far I've travelled, so come on, eh, ... please tell me, how far did I travel?"

2.17   Three motorists A, B and C often travel on a certain highway, and each motorist always travels at a constant speed. A is the fastest of the three and C the slowest.

One day when the three travel in the same direction, B overtakes C, five minutes later A overtakes C and in another three minutes A overtakes B. On another occasion when they again travel in the same direction, A overtakes B first then, nine minutes later, overtakes C. When will B overtake C?

MEASURE

THE PROBLEMS

3.1 A cardboard circle is cut along a diameter and a cone is formed out of one of the semicircular pieces. Now suppose that another cardboard circle is fitted to the base of the cone. This base circle is then cut along a diameter and a cone formed from one of the halves.

What is the ratio of volumes of the two cones?

3.2

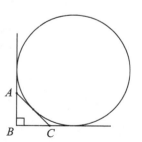

In the given figure, the circle shown touches $\overrightarrow{BA}$ and $\overrightarrow{BC}$ and the side $\overline{AC}$.

Show that the diameter of the circle is equal to the perimeter of the triangle.

3.3 $ABCD$ is a parallelogram; P is a point such that no point of the [whole] line $\overline{PA}$ lies inside the parallelogram. Prove that the area of the triangle PAC is the sum of the areas of the triangles PAB, PAD.

3.4 Leningrad and Anchorage lie approximately on the $60°$ latitude line, and their difference in longitudes is approximately $180°$. Show that the air-route over the pole between them is approximately $\frac{2}{3}$ of the length of the route around the same latitude.

3.5 Show that the ratio of the perimeter of a triangle to the circumference of the inscribed circle is the same as the ratio of the areas of the two figures.

Can the theorem be extended to a polygon and the circle inscribed in it?

3.6

Use your 'compass' to reproduce the given figure.

Which curve is longer, the one shown with thick outline or the outermost circle?

Prove your statement.

3.7 The shaded crescents are obtained by drawing semicircles on the 3 sides of a right-angled triangle ABC. Show that the sum of their areas is equal to the area of $\triangle ABC$.

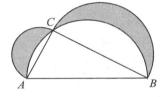

3.8

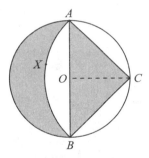

In the figure shown, $\overline{AB}$ is the diameter of a circle with centre O. $\overline{OC}$ is perpendicular to $\overline{AB}$ and arc AXB is the arc of a circle with centre C. Prove that the areas of the two shaded regions are equal.

3.9 $ABCD$ is a square with centre O. Circles are drawn about A, B, C and D as centres with equal radii AO, BO, CO, DO respectively. The circles intersect at P, Q, R and S.

Prove that the shaded area determined by these 5 circles is equal to twice the area of square $ABCD$.

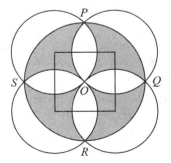

3.10 Three perpendicular planes meet in a fixed point inside a fixed sphere. Prove that the sum of the areas of the three circles of intersection remains constant, as the positions of the three planes are varied.

3.11 Two circles of radii r_1 and r_2 respectively meet at right angles. This means that the tangents at either point of intersection are at right angles.

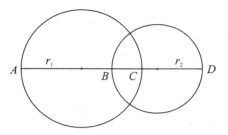

Let the straight line through the centres of the circles meet them at A, B, C and D, as shown.

If $AD = l$ and $BC = s$, show that $ls = 2r_1r_2$.

3.12 Given the two regular decahedrons $ABCDEFGHIJ$ and $AHEBIFCJGD$ as shown, prove that the difference in side lengths of these figures is equal to the common radius of their circumscribed circles.

[**Hint:** Show that, $HE - AB = r$.]

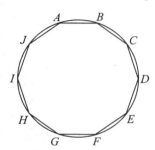
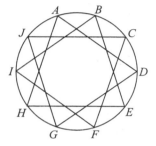

3.13 a ABC is a given equilateral triangle and P a point inside the triangle. Perpendiculars are drawn from P to the sides, the feet of the perpendiculars being X, Y, Z respectively. Prove that $PX + PY + PZ$ is constant for all postions of P.

b Show that this theorem can be extended to any convex regular polygon. (Some perpendiculars may meet the sides produced.)

c Is the converse of the theorem also true, i.e., if the sum of the lengths of the perpendiculars to the sides of a convex polygon is constant, are the sides of the polygon necessarily equal?

If the converse theorem is true, prove it; if it is not, give an example to show why it is false.

3.14 The circumference of a circle is divided into n equal arcs and the points of division are joined to the centre.

A semi-circle is drawn on each of the radii shown to obtain the pattern shown.

Is it possible to choose n so that the dark shaded area (of the flower) is equal to the lightly shaded area of the edge?

3.15 Using as centres the vertices of

  a a regular hexagon,

  b a square,

circular arcs are drawn, each of radius equal in length to the side.
Find in each figure the area of the shaded 'flower'. [Take each side to be of unit length.]

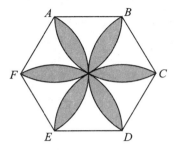

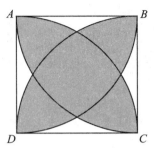

3.16 The radius of the larger circle is R.

Form 4 smaller circles of radius $\dfrac{R}{2}$, each one

intersecting the large one as shown (while they do not overlap with each other).

Show that the shaded areas outside the larger circle are equal in sum to the dotted area inside the circle.

Can you generalize this result?

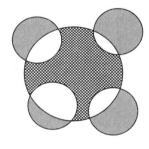

3.17

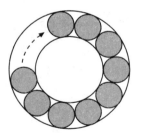

Two concentric circles have radii r and R respectively.

A sequence of equal circles is drawn as shown in the figure such that they touch each other externally, the larger circle internally and the smaller circle externally.

If r is fixed, how should R be chosen if the circles inside the annulus form a closed chain?

Show that there are an infinite number of values of R.

3.18 A circular wooden frame with cross-section in the shape of an isosceles triangle is to be covered by metal foil.

The dimensions of the frame are given in the diagram.

Determine the shape (giving dimensions) of the piece which must be cut out from the sheet of foil in order to cover smoothly the frame.

[The base of the frame is not to be covered and no provisions are to be made for flaps.]

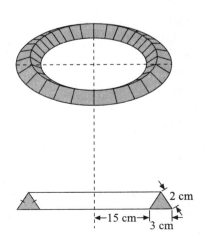

3.19 h_1, h_2 and h_3 are the altitudes of $\triangle ABC$. r is the radius of the inscribed circle and r_1, r_2, r_3 are the radii of the escribed circles.

[h_1 is the altitude from A to $\overline{BC}$ and r_1 is the radius of the circle "outside" $\overline{BC}$, etc.]

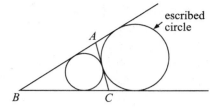

Prove that

a $\dfrac{1}{r} = \dfrac{1}{h_1} + \dfrac{1}{h_2} + \dfrac{1}{h_3}$

b $\dfrac{1}{r_1} = \dfrac{1}{h_2} + \dfrac{1}{h_3} - \dfrac{1}{h_1}$

c $\dfrac{1}{r} = \dfrac{1}{r_1} + \dfrac{1}{r_2} + \dfrac{1}{r_3}$

GEOMETRY

THE PROBLEMS

4.1 Find the angle between the planes *AFH* and *EFGH*.

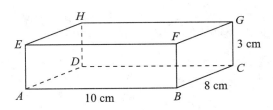

4.2 Triangle *ABC* is isosceles with $AB = AC$. If *X* is any point on $\overline{BC}$, show that the circles circumscribing triangles *ABX* and *ACX* have the same diameter.

4.3

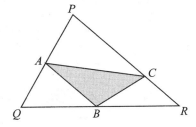

A is the midpoint of $\overline{PQ}$.
B divides $\overline{QR}$ in the ratio 1 : 2.
C divides $\overline{RP}$ in the ratio 1 : 3.
What fraction of triangle *PQR* is occupied by triangle *ABC* ?

4.4 A triangle has angles *A*, *B* and *C* such that $A < B < 90^o < C$.
The bisectors of the exterior angles at *A* and *C* meet $\overline{BC}$ and $\overline{AB}$ produced at *X* and *Y*. If $\overline{AX}$ and $\overline{CY}$ have the same length as $\overline{AC}$, what is the size of the angle *A*?

4.5 *X*, *Y* are the centres of the square on the sides $\overline{AB}$, $\overline{AC}$ of the triangle *ABC* right angled at *A*. If *M* is the mid-point of $\overline{BC}$, prove that triangle *XMY* is isosceles and right angled at *M*.

4.6   The bisectors of angle B and angle C of the triangle ABC meet the opposite sides at X and Y respectively. The line through Y drawn parallel to $\overline{BX}$ and the line through X drawn parallel to $\overline{CY}$ meet the external bisector of angle A at P and Q respectively. Prove that the points B, C, P and Q are concyclic.

4.7   Any three points A, B and C are located on a circle. The three tangents at A, B and C meet at P and Q. Prove that the measure of angle CAB is the average of the measure of the angles at P and Q.

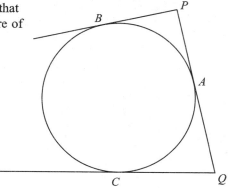

4.8 $ABCD$ is a cyclic quadrilateral and $\overline{AC}$ is a diameter. From A and C perpendiculars are drawn to $\overline{BD}$ meeting $\overline{BD}$ at X and Y respectively. Prove that $BY = XD$.

4.9   Consider a line l joining the two midpoints of a pair of opposite edges of a cube. A cube has four diagonals; show that l is perpendicular to two and only two of them.

4.10 $ABCD$ is a cyclic quadrilateral. The edges $\overline{AB}$, $\overline{DC}$ produced intersect in R and $\overline{DA}$, $\overline{CB}$ produced in S.

Prove that the bisectors of angle BRC and ASB are perpendicular.

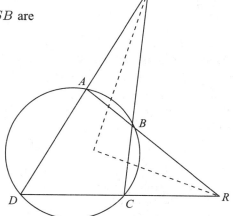

4.11   Prove that in an isosceles triangle the sum of the distances from any point on the base to the other two sides is a constant.

4.12 M is the midpoint of side $\overline{BC}$ of $\triangle ABC$. Show that if $AM : BC = 3 : 2$ then the medians from B and C are perpendicular to each other. ($\overline{AM}$ is an example of a median.)

4.13 The smallest square on a pegboard has unit area. The diagram shows how to construct squares of area 1, 2, 4, 5 square units using pegs and rubber bands.

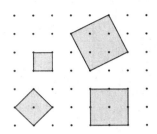

    a Show how to construct squares of area

        i 8 square units,

        ii 10 square units, on the pegboard.

    b Prove that it is impossible to construct a square with area $A = 4p + 3$ square units where p is an integer.

4.14

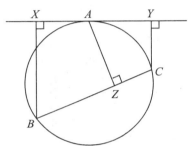

B and C are any two points on a circle. X and Y are the feet of the perpendiculars from B and C to a tangent at a third point A. Z is the foot of the perpendicular from A to $\overline{BC}$.

Show that AZ is the geometric mean of BX and CY. i.e., $AZ = \sqrt{BX.CY}$.

4.15 You are given a triangle PQR and X is a point on $\overline{QR}$. Circles are inscribed inside triangles PQX and PRX and these circles touch at Y on $\overline{PX}$. Let the lengths of $\overline{PQ}$, $\overline{PR}$, $\overline{QR}$ be r, q and p respectively.

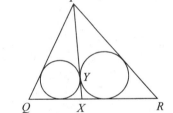

    a Find the length of $\overline{QX}$ in terms of r, q and p.

    b Show that if the inscribed circle of triangle PQR touches $\overline{QR}$ at Z, then Z is at X.

4.16 Prove that the vertex of a parabola is the point on the parabola which is closest to the focus.

4.17 An infinite number of chords $\overline{AB}$ can be drawn on the parabola $y^2 = 4x$ which subtend a right-angle at the origin O. Show that all such chords are concurrent.

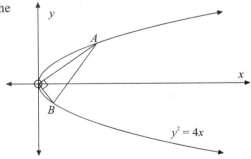

4.18 ABC is an equilateral triangle and P is a point on the circumference of its circumcircle. Prove that one of the distances PA, PB and PC is the sum of the other two.

4.19 O is a point inside the triangle ABC. Let K, L, M be the mid-points of the sides $\overline{BC}$, $\overline{CA}$, $\overline{AB}$ respectively, and let X, Y, Z be the midpoints of $\overline{OA}$, $\overline{OB}$, $\overline{OC}$ respectively. Prove that the lines $\overline{KX}$, $\overline{LY}$, $\overline{MZ}$ are concurrent.

4.20 ABC is a triangle such that the difference between the angles B and C is $90°$. Show that the line through A perpendicular to $\overline{BC}$ is a tangent to the circumcircle of the triangle.

4.21 ABC is an acute angled triangle. ABZ, BCX and CAY are equilateral triangles such that the points X, Y, Z are outside the triangle ABC. Prove that

    a the circumcircles of the three equilateral triangles intersect in a common point,

    b the centres of the three circles form another equilateral triangle. (Napoleon's Theorem.)

4.22 ABC is an acute angled triangle, and $\overline{AD}$, $\overline{BE}$, $\overline{CF}$ are its altitudes. P, Q, R, S are the feet of the perpendiculars from D on the lines $\overline{BA}$, $\overline{BE}$, $\overline{CF}$, $\overline{CA}$. Show that the points P, Q, R, S lie on one straight line.

4.23 Prove that the angle bisectors of a triangle are concurrent.

4.24 V the apex and O the centre of the base of an isosceles triangle VAB are fixed, while the vertices A, B are varying points on the fixed line l which is perpendicular to $\overline{OV}$. If M is the point of intersection of the altitudes of the triangle VAB and $ABCD$ is a rectangle such that M is on $\overline{CD}$, show that the points C and D lie on a fixed parabola.

4.25 $\overrightarrow{OX}$, $\overrightarrow{OY}$ are fixed perpendicular rays (or half-lines) through the point O. The points A, B move on the rays $\overrightarrow{OX}$, $\overrightarrow{OY}$ respectively in such a way that the sum of the reciprocals of their distances from O,

$$\frac{1}{OA} + \frac{1}{OB} \quad \text{remains constant.}$$

Show that, for all positions of A and B, the line $\overleftrightarrow{AB}$ passes through a fixed point.

[**Note:** Any point P on the line l divides l into two parts called rays or half-lines.]

4.26 P is a point on the circumference of a circle of radius r which touches a circle of radius $2r$ from the inside. If the small circle rolls without slipping along the circumference of the large circle, show that the locus of P is a straight line segment.

4.27 Two small circles, centres A and B touch each other at C, and touch the largest circle, centre O, at X and Y as shown. $\overline{XC}$ is extended to D and $\overline{YC}$ is extended to E.
Prove that $\overline{DE}$ is a diameter of the largest circle.

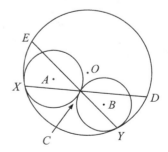

4.28

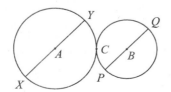

$\overline{XY}$ and $\overline{PQ}$ are parallel diameters of two circles which touch at C as shown.
What can be deduced about $\overline{QX}$ and $\overline{PY}$?

4.29 The triangle ABC has a right angle at vertex C. The line $\overline{AD}$ bisects the angle at A and intersects the side $\overline{BC}$ at D. The midpoint of the line segment $\overline{AD}$ is E. Prove that the line $\overline{CE}$ intersects the *external* bisector of the angle A on the circumcircle of triangle ABC.

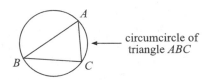

circumcircle of triangle ABC

4.30

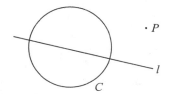

Let the line l include a diameter of a circle C. If P is a point not on C or l, use a *ruler only* to show how it is possible to construct the perpendicular from P to the line l.
[A proof that you have done this is essential.]

4.31 A triangle has sides in the ratio 5:6:7. A circle is drawn through the vertices of the triangle. Find the radius of the circle.

4.32 Triangle ABC is right-angled at B and $AB = BC$. P is any point on $\overline{AC}$. Prove that $(AP)^2 + (CP)^2 = 2(BP)^2$.

4.33 Three non-collinear holes are drilled through the top of a table. Through each hole a thread is passed with a weight hanging from it below the table. Above, the three threads are all tied together and released. If the three weights are equal, where will the knot come to rest?

4.34 Show that the edges $\overline{AD}$, $\overline{BC}$ of a tetrahedron $ABCD$ are mutually perpendicular if and only if $(AB)^2 + (CD)^2 = (AC)^2 + (BD)^2$.

4.35 All six faces of a polyhedron are cyclic quadrilaterals. Show that the vertices lie on a sphere.

4.36 The opposite vertices of a square have coordinates (a, b) and (c, d) respectively. Determine the coordinates of the other two vertices.

4.37 Prove that the diagonals of a trapezium and the line joining the centres of the parallel sides meet in a common point.

4.38

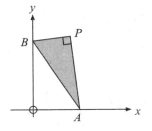

A wooden right-angled triangle moves on a plane so that the vertices of its acute angles A and B move along the x-axis and the y-axis as shown.
How does the vertex P at the right-angle of the triangle move?
[**Hint:** Experiment a little.]

4.39 $\overline{AB}$ is a painting on a wall. E is the eye of an observer who is walking towards the wall. Show how to maximise the angle of view of the painting (i.e., angle θ) without using calculus.

[**Hint:** Draw a circle through A, B and E.]

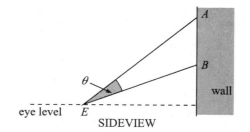

4.40

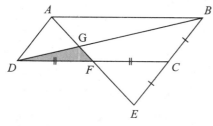

$ABCD$ is a parallelogram. $\overline{BC}$ is produced to E such that $BC = CE$. F is the midpoint of $\overline{DC}$. $\overline{AF}$ and $\overline{DB}$ intersect at G. What fraction of the parallelogram is occupied by triangle DFG?

4.41 A square $PQRS$ is inscribed in the acute-angled triangle ABC. Prove that the area of the square is less than half the area of the triangle.

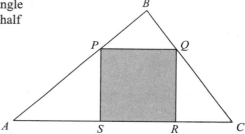

4.42

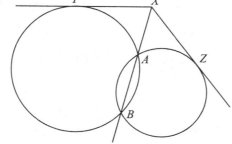

Two circles intersect at A and B. The common chord $\overline{AB}$ is extended and X is a point on it. Tangents $\overline{XY}$ and $\overline{XZ}$ are drawn from X to the circles meeting them at Y and Z respectively. Prove that $\overline{XY}$ and $\overline{XZ}$ are always equal in length.

4.43 ABC is a right-angled triangle and $\overline{CD}$ is the altitude to the hypotenuse. In each of the triangles ABC, ADC and BDC a circle is inscribed. Show that the sum of the radii of these three circles is equal to the length of $\overline{CD}$.

4.44 The rectangle has sides in the ratio $2 : 1$. B is the midpoint of the shorter side, and A is a point of trisection of the opposite side. What fraction of the rectangle is shaded?

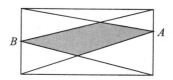

4.45 The incircle of triangle ABC touches its sides $\overline{AB}$, $\overline{BC}$ and $\overline{CA}$ at points M, N and P respectively, and it is known that $\overrightarrow{AN} + \overrightarrow{BP} + \overrightarrow{CM} = \mathbf{0}$. Prove that triangle ABC is equilateral.

4.46 $\overline{OA}$, $\overline{OP}$ are two radii of a circle perpendicular to each other at $t = 0$ $(t = \text{time})$.
A tangent-line $\overline{AX}$ is fixed to the circle which rotates uniformly (with constant speed) in an anticlockwise direction about O.

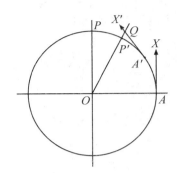

At the same time the line $\overline{OP}$ rotates in a clockwise direction at the same rate as the circle.
Suppose Q is the point where $\overline{OP'}$ and $\overline{A'X'}$ intersect, where $\overline{OP'}$, $\overline{A'X'}$ are the positions taken up by $\overline{OP}$, $\overline{AX}$ at a certain time instant. Express the coordinates of Q in terms of the angle of rotation and hence find the equation of Q. Sketch the locus.

4.47

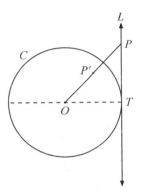

The centre of a circle C is O and its radius is of length r. Let P be a point in the plane distinct from O. Let P' be a point on the ray $\overrightarrow{OP}$ (i.e., on $\overrightarrow{OP}$ or on $\overrightarrow{OP}$ produced) such that $OP.OP' = r^2$.

$[OP, OP'$ denote the *lengths* of segments $\overline{OP}$, $\overline{OP'}$, respectively.]

We call the point P' the **inverse** of point P with respect to the circle C. If the point P describes a line L, then we call the set of inverses P', the inverse of the line L.

a Let L be a straight line tangent to the circle C at the point T (see figure). Find the nature of the locus of P', the inverse of the line L.

b A regular n-sided polygon is circumscribed to the circle C, i.e., the sides of the polygon are tangents of C. Sketch the inverse of the polygon and show that the perimeter of the inverse is independent of n.

4.48 A container with the rectangular base $ABCD$ has a transparent semi-cylindrical cover. A thin elastic thread joining the diametrically opposite vertices A and C is stretched over the cover - it may be assumed that the thread takes up a position such that its length is minimised. Vertical light rays cast a shadow of the thread upon the base. Determine the shape of the shadow.

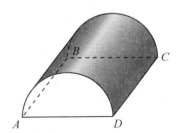

4.49 S is a point inside the triangle ABC such that the areas of the triangles SAB, SBC, SCA are equal. Show that S is the centroid of the triangle.

4.50 Show that it is possible to cut a hole of square cross-section in a wooden cube C, through which can be passed a wooden cube slightly larger than C. (Prince Rupert's Cube)

4.51 Three circles with centres A, B and C touch externally in pairs at the points X, Y and Z. Prove that the circle through X, Y and Z is the inscribed circle of the triangle ABC.

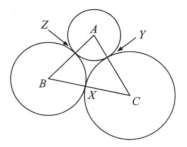

4.52 To an astronaut at a point P in space, the earth and the moon appear equally large.

    a What can be said about the ratio $\dfrac{PE}{PM}$ where E, M are the centres of the earth, moon respectively?

    b Describe the nature of the orbit of the spacecraft.

ALGEBRA

THE PROBLEMS

5.1 Find the value of the continued fraction:

$$1 + \cfrac{1}{2 + \cfrac{1}{1 + \cfrac{1}{2 + \cfrac{1}{1 + \cfrac{1}{2 + \cfrac{1}{1 + \cfrac{1}{2 + ...}}}}}}}$$

5.2 The cubic equation $x^3 + px^2 + qx + r = 0$ has roots a^2, b^2 and c^2 where $a^2 + b^2 = c^2$. Find the relationship connecting p, q and r.

5.3 $x^2 + ax + bc = 0$ and $x^2 + bx + ca = 0$ where $a \neq 0$, $b \neq 0$, $c \neq 0$, have a single common root. Prove that the other roots satisfy $x^2 + cx + ab = 0$.

5.4 Find a function $f(x)$ which statisfies $f(f(x)) = 4x^2$.

5.5 A function $f(x, y)$ is defined for all pairs of natural numbers (x, y) by

$$f(x, x) = x$$
$$f(x, y) = f(y, x)$$
$$(x + y)f(x, y) = yf(x, x + y).$$

Find the value of
  a $f(2, 4)$,
  b $f(30, 40)$.

5.6   Solve the equation $3^x + 4^x = 5^x$.

5.7   Find all real quadratic expressions $f(x) = ax^2 + bx + c,\ a \neq 0$ such that $f(a) = c,\ f(b) = b$ and $f(c) = c$.

5.8   When Joan's age in years and John's age in years are written down one after the other they form a four digit number. [Each of them is over 10 years of age.] The resulting number is a perfect square. In 31 years time, if they write their ages down in the same order once again the four digit number which results is a perfect square. What are their present ages?

5.9   If $x = a^{\frac{1}{3}} + b^{\frac{1}{3}}$,   show that $x^3 = 3(ab)^{\frac{1}{3}} x + (a + b)$.
Hence, find all real solutions of the equation $x^3 = 6x + 6$.

5.10   A rectangular prism has dimensions 2 cm by 4 cm by 6 cm. Its volume is 48 cm³ and the total length of its 12 edges is 48 cm, that is, its volume is numerically equal to the total length of its edges. Find all other rectangular prisms for which the volume and total edge length are numerically equal.

5.11   Find all positive integers a and b satisfying the equation $a^2 = 3.2^b + 1$.

5.12   Find the exact value of $\sqrt{3 + \sqrt{5}} - \sqrt{3 - \sqrt{5}}$ without using logarithms or a calculator.

5.13   Solve for x: $8.9^x + 3.6^x - 81.4^x = 0$.

5.14   Simplify $\sqrt[3]{2 + \sqrt{5}} + \sqrt[3]{2 - \sqrt{5}}$.

5.15   Find $\sqrt{8 - 4\sqrt{3}}$ giving your answer in the form $\sqrt{a} - \sqrt{b}$ where a and b are integers.

5.16   Sketch the graphs of
  a $f(x) = [x]$ **b** $f(x) = x - [x]$
  [**Reminder:** $[x]$ reads "the integer part of x".]

5.17   Find all integer solutions to the simultaneous equations
$$|x| + |y| = 3,$$
$$|x - y| = 3.$$

5.18   Solve the equation $|x| + |x - 1| = a$ where $a > 0$.
Plot the solutions x against a on a graph.

5.19

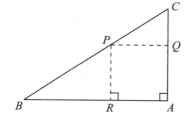

Triangle ABC has fixed sides of length a, b and c units. P lies on hypotenuse $\overline{BC}$ and is free to move anywhere along $\overline{BC}$. Rectangle $PQAR$ is inscribed within the triangle with Q on $\overline{AC}$ and R on $\overline{AB}$. Find the position of P which maximises the area of rectangle $PQAR$.

5.20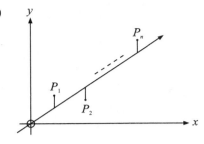

The points $P_1(a_1, b_1)$, $P_2(a_2, b_2)$, ..., $P_n(a_n, b_n)$ obtained in a science experiment are observed to lie close to a straight line through the origin. We define the **line of best fit** through the origin as the one for which $(P_1M_1)^2 + (P_2M_2)^2 + ... + (P_nM_n)^2$ is a minimum, where $\overline{P_iM_i}$ is the vertical line from P_i to the line. Determine the slope of the line of best fit in terms of $a_1, a_2, ..., a_n, b_1, b_2, ..., b_n$.

5.21 Solve simultaneously,
$$x = 16y$$
$$\log_y x - \log_x y = \tfrac{8}{3}.$$

5.22 Find all values of m for which the quartic equation $x^4 - (3m + 2)x^2 + m^2 = 0$ has 4 real roots in arithmetic progression.

5.23 Simplify $\dfrac{1}{\sqrt{3 + 2\sqrt{2}}} - \dfrac{1}{\sqrt{3 - 2\sqrt{2}}}$ without using a calculator.

5.24 If $x^2 + \dfrac{1}{x^2} = 7$, find the values of $\sqrt{x} + \dfrac{1}{\sqrt{x}}$.

5.25 If $x > 0$ and $x + \dfrac{1}{x} = 3$, find the value of $x^{\frac{3}{2}} + x^{-\frac{3}{2}}$.

5.26 Infinitely many squares are placed on the x-axis with one vertex on the curve with equation $y = x^{-1}$. Find the sum of the areas of these squares.

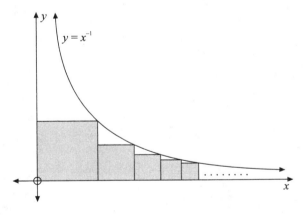

5.27 Given a function $f(x)$ with the property that $f(a + b + ab) = f(a) + f(b) + f(ab)$ for all a and b. Show that $f(x + y) = f(x) + f(y)$ for all x and y.

5.28 a, b, c and d are rational numbers in which $a + b\sqrt{2} + c\sqrt{3} + d\sqrt{6} = 0$. Deduce that $a = b = c = d = 0$.

5.29 p, q and r are non-zero real numbers and each is a solution of $x^3 + qx = px^2 + r$. Find the values of p, q and r.

5.30 If the equation $x^3 + ax^2 + bx + c = 0$ has roots p, q and r,

    a   find a, b and c in terms of p, q and r.

    b   Determine $p^2q^2 + q^2r^2 + r^2p^2$ in terms of a, b and c.

    c   Solve the system of equations,

$$p + q + r = 3\tfrac{1}{2}$$
$$pq + qr + rp = -2$$
$$pqr = -2.$$

5.31

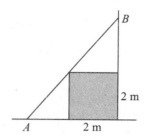

A ladder of length $3\sqrt{5}$ m is placed against a vertical wall with foot A on horizontal ground. When the ladder is in a certain position a 2 m cube-shaped box fits exactly under the ladder as illustrated.

How high up the wall does the ladder reach?

5.32 Determine the least value of the function
$$f(x) = (x - a - b)(x - a + b)(x + a - b)(x + a + b)$$ where a, b are real constants.

5.33 A function f is not defined for $x = 0$, but for non-zero real numbers x, $f(x) + 3f(\dfrac{1}{x}) = 2x$.
Show that $f(-x) = -f(x)$,   for all x,   i.e., $f(x)$ is an odd function.

5.34 An antinuclear demonstration, 1400 m long, marches at a constant speed. A policeman on a motor bike rides, at constant speed, from the rear of the procession to the head of the procession and then immediately returns to the rear again. During this time the procession had advanced 700 m. How far did the policeman travel?

5.35 α and β are two of the roots of $x^3 + ax^2 + bx + c = 0$.
Prove that $\alpha\beta$ is a root of $x^3 - bx^2 + acx - c^2 = 0$.

5.36 Solve the equation $abc + 4(a + b + c) = 8 + 2(ab + bc + ca)$.

5.37 If $a^2 + b^2 + c^2 = ab + bc + ca$,   prove that $a = b = c$.

5.38 $\sqrt[3]{26 - 15\sqrt{3}} = a + b\sqrt{3}$ where a and b are rational. Find a and b.

5.39 Find rational numbers a, b, c and d such that
$$\frac{1}{1 + \sqrt{2} + 2\sqrt{3} - \sqrt{6}} = a + b\sqrt{2} + c\sqrt{3} + d\sqrt{6}.$$

5.40 $*$ is a binary operation defined on the set of all integers and satisfying

    a $0 * a = a$,   for all integers a,

    b $(a * b) * c = c * ab + a * c + b * c - 2c$.

By considering $1 * a$, deduce that $a * 0 = a$,   for all integers a.
Hence, prove that $a * b = a + b + ab$.

5.41 x and y satisfy the equations $x^2 - 3xy + 9 = 0$ and $y^2 + y - 1 = 0$.
Solve for x given that x is real.

5.42 Consider the example: $f(x, y) = x^2 + 3xy$ $\therefore$ $f(1, 2) = 1^2 + 3.1.2 = 7$ and
$$f(3, -2) = 3^2 + 3.3.(-2) = -9.$$

Find a new function, $g(x, y)$, such that: $g(1, 1) = 1$
$$g(1, 2) = 2$$
$$g(1, 3) = 3$$
$$g(1, 4) = 4$$
$$g(2, 1) = 5$$
$$g(2, 2) = 6$$
$$g(2, 3) = 7$$
$$g(2, 4) = 8.$$

5.43 Let $f(x)$ be a function which satisfies the conditions

a $f(-x) = -f(x)$ for all x,   [i.e., $f(x)$ is an **odd function**.],

b   there exists a real number r such that $f(r - x) = f(r + x)$ for all x.

Prove that $f(x)$ is a **periodic function**,   i.e., that there exists a positive number p such that
$f(x + p) = f(x)$ for all x.

[e.g., $f(x) = \sin x$ satisfies **a** and **b** as $\sin(-x) = -\sin(x)$ and

$\sin(\frac{\pi}{2} + x) = \sin(\frac{\pi}{2} - x)$ for all x.]

5.44

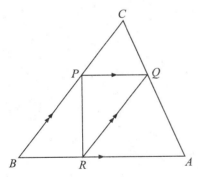

ABC is a given triangle. P is a point which can move along $\overline{AC}$. $\overline{PQ}$ is drawn parallel to $\overline{AB}$ and then $\overline{QR}$ is drawn parallel to $\overline{AC}$. Locate the position of P such that triangle PQR has maximum area.

5.45 Let f be the continuous function such that $f(x)$ is defined for $x > 0$ and
$$f[(x + y)^2] = f[x^2] + f[y^2]   \text{ and }   f(1) = 1.$$

Show that

a $f(0) = 0$,

b $f[(nx)^2] = n f[x^2]$,   for all positive integers n.

5.46 For any real number x,
let $[x]$ denote the largest integer less than or equal to x, and
let $\{x\}$ denote the fractional part of x.
Notice that $\{x\} = x - [x]$.

(e.g., $[3\frac{1}{4}] = 3$, $\{3\frac{1}{4}\} = \frac{1}{4}$, $[-2\frac{1}{4}] = -3$, $\{-2\frac{1}{4}\} = \frac{3}{4}$, $[4] = 4$, $\{4\} = 0$.)

Let m and n be non-negative integers, and a, b and c be any real numbers which satisfy $ma + nb = c$.

Show that
a $m[a] + n[b] \leq [c]$,
b $m\{a\} + n\{b\} - \{c\}$ is a non-negative integer.

5.47 a   If q is a prime number, show that $a + b\sqrt{q} = 0$ implies that $a = b = 0$, for rationals a and b.

b   Let f be a function whose domain is the set of all real numbers and f has the properties:
  i $f(a + b) = f(a) + f(b)$ for all real a and b,
  ii $f(ab) = f(a).f(b)$ for all real a and b,
  iii $f(a) = a$ for all rationals a.

If p and q are distinct primes, show that there do not exist rational numbers a and b such that
$f(a + b\sqrt{p}) = \sqrt{q}$.

5.48 b represents an integer which is not a perfect cube. Determine a cubic equation with integral coefficients which has $\sqrt[3]{b} + \sqrt[3]{b^2}$ as a root. Show that this equation has no other real root.

5.49 a   Solve the system of equations, i.e., find x_1, x_2, x_3, ... , x_{100}.

$$x_1 + x_2 + x_3 = 0$$
$$x_2 + x_3 + x_4 = 0$$
$$x_3 + x_4 + x_5 = 0$$
$$\vdots$$
$$\vdots$$
$$x_{99} + x_{100} + x_1 = 0$$
$$x_{100} + x_1 + x_2 = 0$$

b   For the n simultaneous equations in unknowns x_1, x_2, x_3, ..., x_n:

$$x_1 + x_2 + x_3 = 0$$
$$x_2 + x_3 + x_4 = 0$$
$$\vdots$$
$$\vdots$$
$$x_{n-1} + x_n + x_1 = 0$$
$$x_n + x_1 + x_2 = 0$$

  i   find the values of n when the equations have a unique solution,
  ii   find the most general solution when the equations do not have a unique solution.

5.50 **a** Factorize $x^4 + 2x^3 - 2x - 4$, and hence write down the real roots of the equation
$x^4 + 2x^3 - 2x - 4 = 0$.

b

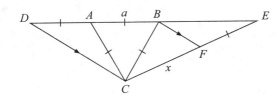

In the figure shown, triangle ABC is equilateral, the length of the sides being a. Base $\overline{AB}$ is produced in both directions to D and E respectively such that $AD = AB = a$, while E is the intersection of $\overline{AB}$ produced and the line $\overline{CFE}$ where $\overline{BF}$ is parallel to $\overline{DC}$ and the length of $\overline{EF}$ is again a.

Show that the length x of $\overline{CF}$ is $a.\sqrt[3]{2}$.

5.51 Suppose $(1 + \sqrt{2})^n = a_n + b_n\sqrt{2}$.
    a Find the values of a_n and b_n for $n = 1, 2, 3, 4$.
    b Prove that a_n is the integer nearest to $b_n\sqrt{2}$.
    c Show that $(1 + \sqrt{2})^n$ is very close to integer values when n is sufficiently large.

5.52 a and b are two of the roots of $x^3 - x + 1 = 0$.
Show that ab is a root of $x^3 + x^2 - 1 = 0$.

5.53 Prove that if the quadratics $ax^2 + bx + c$ and $cx^2 + bx + a$ (where $a \neq c$, $a \neq 0$, and $c \neq 0$), have a common linear factor, then $(a + b + c)(a - b + c) = 0$.

5.54 a and b are real numbers such that $a + b \neq -1$ and $b \neq 0$.

Prove that, if there is one and only one solution of the equation $x^2 + ax + b = 0$ between 0 and 1, then the equation

$$\frac{1}{x + 2} + \frac{a}{x + 1} + \frac{b}{x} = 0, \quad \text{has one, and only one, positive solution.}$$

5.55 The symbol [ ] stands for: *"integer part of"*.

Compare the three numbers $[2x]$, $2[x]$, $[x + \frac{1}{2}] + [x - \frac{1}{2}]$.

Can all three be equal? Can all three be different from each other?

5.56 Prove that for any number x,

$$[x] + [x + \frac{1}{n}] + [x + \frac{2}{n}] + \ \ldots\ldots\ + [x + \frac{n-1}{n}] = [nx].$$

5.57 The function f is defined for all real numbers, and satisfies the inequalities $f(x) \leqslant x$ and $f(x + y) \leqslant f(x) + f(y)$.

Prove that
    a $f(0) = 0$, and
    b $f(x) = x$ for all x.

    [Jozef Kurschak - Hungarian Mathematics competition 1979.]

5.58 Problem due to **Issai Schur**:

"If $a_1, a_2, a_3, \ldots\ldots, a_n$ are distinct integers where $n \geqslant 1$ and
$f(x) = (x - a_1)(x - a_2)(x - a_3) \ldots\ldots (x - a_n) - 1$ for every real number x, show that there do not exist monic polynomials $g(x)$ and $h(x)$ of degree at least 1 with integer coefficients such that $f(x) = g(x).h(x)$.

[A *monic* polynomial has leading coefficient 1.]

[**Hint:** Consider $k(x) = g(x) + h(x)$ and use a contradiction argument.]

5.59 Find all polynomial functions, $f(x)$, with real coefficients, such that
$$f(x).f(x + 1) = f(x^2 + x + 1).$$

5.60 Solve for x: $\dfrac{1}{x} + \dfrac{1}{a} + \dfrac{1}{b} = \dfrac{1}{x + a + b}$ where a, b and $a + b$ are non-zero.

5.61 Prove that $1.2^{n-1} + 2.2^{n-2} + 3.2^{n-3} + \ldots\ldots + (n - 1).2 + n.1 = 2^{n+1} - 2 - n$ for all positive integers n.

PIGEON HOLE PRINCIPLE

THE PROBLEMS

6.1 Let T be an equilateral triangle, each side of which has length 2.

    a If five points are randomly chosen in T, show that at least two of them are within a distance of 1 of each other.

    b If seventeen points are randomly chosen in T, show that at least two of them are within a distance $\frac{1}{2}$ of each other.

    c Generalize.

6.2 An equilateral triangle and a square are inscribed in the same circle in such a way that no vertices of the triangle and square coincide. Show that amongst the seven circular arcs thus obtained there will always be one which is no longer than $\frac{1}{24}$th of the circumference of the circle.

6.3 Using the identity $\quad \tan(A - B) = \dfrac{\tan A - \tan B}{1 + \tan A . \tan B}$

show that, from any 7 real numbers, it is always possible to select 2 of them, x, y say, which satisfy the inequality,

$$0 < \frac{x - y}{1 + xy} < \frac{1}{\sqrt{3}}.$$

6.4 Ten teams have completed part of the football season, where every team is to play each team only once, though matches are not necessarily all played on the same day of the week.
Show that at least two teams have played the same number of matches, given that all teams have played at least one match.

SEQUENCES, SERIES & PRODUCTS

THE PROBLEMS

7.1   **a**   Find the value of the sum,

$$\frac{1}{1+\sqrt{2}} + \frac{1}{\sqrt{2}+\sqrt{3}} + \frac{1}{\sqrt{3}+\sqrt{4}} + \dots + \frac{1}{\sqrt{99}+\sqrt{100}}.$$

$$\left[\textbf{Hint}: \quad \frac{1}{1+\sqrt{2}} = \frac{1}{1+\sqrt{2}} \cdot \frac{\sqrt{2}-1}{\sqrt{2}-1} = \sqrt{2}-1 \right]$$

  b   Can you make any generalizations of **a**?

7.2   The large square has been cut up into smaller squares as shown. Assuming that the large square measured 6 units by 6 units, we can calculate the area of the square by adding up the areas of the smaller squares.

What formula can you deduce in this case?

Can you generalize it?

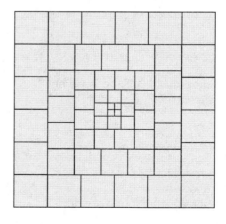

7.3 Show that every perfect cube can be written down as the difference between two perfect squares.

7.4 n points inside a triangle and the 3 vertices (no three of which are collinear) are connected by non-intersecting line segments until the triangle is partitioned into smaller triangular regions. Obtain and prove a formula for the number of triangular regions so formed. Can you state the analogue in 3 dimensions?

7.5 Three numbers, x, y and z are such that $x > y > z > 0$.

Show that if $\dfrac{1}{x}$, $\dfrac{1}{y}$ and $\dfrac{1}{z}$ are in arithmetic progression, then $x - z$, y and $x - y + z$ are the lengths of the sides of a right-angled triangle.

7.6 Find P in simplest form if $P = (1 + 2)(1 + 2^2)(1 + 2^4)(1 + 2^8) \text{ ...... } (1 + 2^{2^n})$.

7.7 Prove that the numbers 49, 4489, 444889, ... obtained by inserting 48 in the middle of the preceeding number are all perfect squares.

7.8 Show that if the sequence of real numbers $a_1, a_2, a_3, a_4, \text{ ...... }$ is strictly increasing, i.e., $a_1 < a_2 < a_3 < a_4 \text{ .... }$, then the sequence of numbers $b_1, b_2, b_3, b_4, \text{ .... }$ defined

by $b_k = \dfrac{a_1 + a_2 + a_3 + \text{ ...... } + a_k}{k}$ is also strictly increasing.

7.9 Show that $\underbrace{(111111......1)}_{2n \text{ 1's}} - \underbrace{(22222......2)}_{n \text{ 2's}}$ is a perfect square.

[For example: $11 - 2 = 9 = 3^2$ and $1111 - 22 = 1089 = 33^2$.]

7.10 **a** A line drawn on a plane divides it into 2 parts. Two intersecting lines divide the plane into 4 parts. Three intersecting lines (but not concurrent) divide the plane into 7 parts, as you may convince yourself by drawing a sketch.

Find the number of parts into which a plane is divided by n lines, given that no two of the lines are parallel and no three of them are concurrent.

b n circles are drawn in the plane so that every two distinct circles meet in exactly two points, and no set of 3 circles has a common point. Let R_n be the number of regions that the plane is divided into by the n circles. Give a formula for R_n, and prove that your formula is correct.

7.11 A sequence is defined by the recurrence relationship

$$a_1 = 1 \quad \text{and} \quad a_{n+1} = \tfrac{1}{2}\left[a_n + \frac{2}{a_n}\right] \quad \text{when} \quad n \geq 1, \quad n \text{ a positive integer.}$$

Show that

a $\dfrac{a_n - \sqrt{2}}{a_n + \sqrt{2}} = \left(\dfrac{1 - \sqrt{2}}{1 + \sqrt{2}}\right)^{2^{n-1}}$ and hence, that

b for n sufficiently large a_n is very close to $\sqrt{2}$.

7.12 n points are placed inside a convex quadrilateral. The quadrilateral is then partitioned into triangles with vertices being the internal points and the vertices of the given triangle. No added lines cross each other. P_n is the number of partitioned triangles for the case of n points.

e.g., $P_3 = 8$    Find and prove a formula for P_n.

7.13   Each summer 10% of the trees on a certain plantation die out, and each winter, workmen plant 100 new trees. At the end of the winter 1980 there are 1200 trees in the plantation.
How many living trees were there at the end of winter in 1970? What happens to the number of trees in the plantation during the 21st century providing the conditions remain unchanged?

7.14   It takes two seconds for a dropped "superball" to hit the ground and at each successive bounce it takes $\frac{9}{10}$ of the time of the previous fall. How long will it take for the ball to stop bouncing?

7.15   Given an arithmetic progression and a geometric progression with positive terms. The first two terms of these progressions coincide. Show that any other term of the arithmetic progression does not exceed the corresponding term of the geometric progression.

7.16   **a**   I wish to borrow $20000 for 10 years at 12% p.a. where the interest is compounded quarterly and I intend to pay off the loan in quarterly instalments. How much do I pay back each quarter?

   b   Find a formula for calculating the repayments R if the total amount borrowed is P, for n years at r% p.a. if there are to be m equal payments at equal intervals each year.

7.17   Consider the sequence of curves C_1, C_2, C_3, C_4 ....

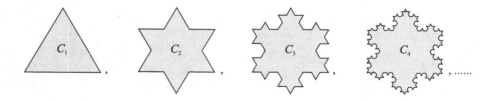

Each successive curve is obtained from the previous one by trisecting a side and adding an equilateral triangle to the middle section of it, as illustrated.

If the perimeter of C_1 is P_1 and its area is A_1,
   a   find a formula for P_n, the perimeter of the nth curve, C_n,
   b   find a formula for A_n, the area of the nth curve, C_n,
   c   show that as n increases indefinitely the perimeter of the curve becomes infinitely large but it contains finite area.

What about the sequence of curves on the next page?

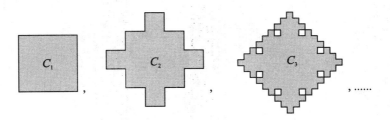

7.18 $S_1 = \frac{1}{1} = 1$

$S_2 = \frac{1}{1} + \frac{1}{2} + \frac{1}{1.2} = 2$

$S_3 = \frac{1}{1} + \frac{1}{2} + \frac{1}{3} + \frac{1}{1.2} + \frac{1}{2.3} + \frac{1}{3.1} + \frac{1}{1.2.3} = 3$

$\vdots$

a Show that $S_4 = 4$.

b Prove that $S_n = n$.   [**Note:** $S_4 = S_3 + \frac{1}{4} + \frac{1}{4}S_3$]

7.19 **a** A sequence has a recurrence relationship $a_{n+1} = r.a_n + s$ and $a_1 = a$.

$$\text{Show that } \quad a_n = r^{n-1}.a + s.\left(\frac{1 - r^{n-1}}{1 - r}\right) \quad \text{for } n \geq 1.$$

b

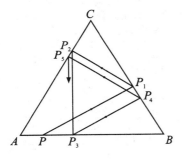

Triangle ABC is equilateral and P is any point on $\overline{AB}$. P_1 is the foot of the perpendicular from P to $\overline{BC}$. P_2 is the foot of the perpendicular from P_1 to $\overline{AC}$. P_3 is the foot of the perpendicular from P_2 to $\overline{AB}$, etc.

Show that the triangle $P_n P_{n+1} P_{n+2}$ as n increases indefinitely is tending to become equilateral.

[**Hint:** let $BP_1 = x_1$, $CP_2 = x_2$, $AP_3 = x_3$, $BP_4 = x_4$, etc.and find a recurrence relationship for the sequence of x's.]

c

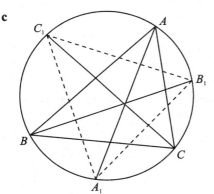

A, B and C are the vertices of a triangle inscribed in a circle. The bisectors of the angles at A, B and C are produced to meet the circle at A_1, B_1, and C_1. In a similar way the angle bisectors of triangle $A_1 B_1 C_1$ are produced to cut the circle at A_2, B_2 and C_2 and this process is continued indefinitely defining points A_n, B_n, and C_n in terms of A_{n-1}, B_{n-1} and C_{n-1}.

What can be said about triangle $A_n B_n C_n$ for large n ?

DIFFERENT BASES

THE PROBLEMS

8.1 For what positive integers a and b is it true that $215_a = 341_b$?

$[5234_7 = 5.7^3 + 2.7^2 + 3.7 + 4]$

8.2 Insects have six legs, so we would expect that if intelligent insects develop a number-system similar to our own, the base will be 6 and not 10. Assuming that the insects also discover a "sextimal" point corresponding to our decimal point, state the conditions under which the sextimal fractions will terminate.

    a Write $(\frac{1}{8})_{10}$ as a sextimal in base 6.

    b Write

        i $(0.\overline{a})_6$,

        ii $(0.\overline{ab})_6$, as fractions in base 10.

    c Write $(\frac{1}{5})_{10}$ and $(\frac{1}{7})_{10}$ as sextimals in base 6.

8.3   **a** Show that, whenever a and n are positive integers, then a^n and a^{n+4} always end in the same digit in the decimal system.

    b What can you say if the number system has base 6?

8.4   **a** Show that the numbers $12, 102, 1002, 10002, \ldots\ldots$ and so on, are all divisible by 6.

    b If the above digits represent numbers in a number system of base n instead of base 10 $(n \geq 3)$, for what values of n are the numbers still divisible by 6?

8.5 Determine the positive integers a, b and c if abc_{10} represents an odd number in the decimal system, divisible by 9, and abc_9 represents a number in the system of base 9, divisible by 10.

8.6 **a** If x is divisible by 3, prove that when x is written in binary form the difference between the number of 1's standing in the odd numbered places and the number of 1's standing in the even numbered places is divisible by 3.

b Prove that if the binary form of a number x has the property described above, then x is divisible by 3.

COUNTING

THE PROBLEMS

9.1 9 points are fixed in a plane so that no 3 are collinear.
How many triangles are determined by these points?

9.2

```
                    1
                1   1   1
            1   2   3   2   1
        1   3   6   7   6   3   1
    1   4   10  16  19  16  10  4   1
```

In the number triangle, each number is the sum of 3 neighbouring numbers in the previous row.
[If a number has less than 3 neighbouring digits above it, 0 is used in the sum.]

Establish an expression for the sum of the numbers in the nth row.

Prove that your expression is correct.

9.3 How many different ways are there of seating 4 married couples at a circular table with men and women in alternate positions and no wife next to her husband?

[Two seating arrangements are the *same* if each person has the same right and left hand neighbours.]

9.4 $\dbinom{n}{r} = \dfrac{n!}{r!(n-r)!}$ is the general binomial coefficient.

Prove the relations,

a $r\dbinom{n}{r} = n\dbinom{n-1}{r-1}$,

b $\dbinom{n}{0} + \dbinom{n}{1} + \dbinom{n}{2} + \ldots\ldots + \dbinom{n}{n} = 2^n$,

[i.e., the sum of the elements in the nth row of Pascal's triangle is 2^n.]

c $1\dbinom{n}{1} + 2\dbinom{n}{2} + 3\dbinom{n}{3} + \ldots\ldots + r\dbinom{n}{r} + \ldots\ldots + n\dbinom{n}{n} = n.2^{n-1}$.

[**Hint:** In **c** use **a** and **b**.]

9.5 How many integers are of the form: $a_1a_2a_3\ldots\ldots a_{n-1}a_na_{n-1}\ldots\ldots a_3a_2a_1$

where $0 < a_1 < a_2 < a_3 <\ldots\ldots < a_{n-1} < a_n$ and $n \geq 2$?

[In words: the numbers are symmetrical, having more than one digit, none of the digits is zero and the digits are strictly increasing towards the centre.
Examples: 151,   23732,   135696531.]

9.6 A rectangle is divided by m lines parallel to one pair of opposite sides and n lines parallel to the other pair. How many rectangles are there in the figure obtained?

9.7 A group of 20 people is to be seated at a long table, 10 each side. There are 7 people who wish to sit on one side of the table and 6 people who wish to sit on the other side.
How many seating arrangements are possible?
Generalize this result.

9.8 The numbers   123456,   234165,   512346, ...   are constructed by using the digits 1, 2, 3, 4, 5 and 6.

    a How many such numbers exist?

    b How many of these numbers are divisible by 3?

    c How many of them are divisible by 9?

    d How many of them are divisible by 11?

9.9 A rook (castle) on a chess board may move either horizontally or vertically. In travelling from one corner square to the diagonally opposite corner square numerous paths are possible.
How many paths require exactly 7 moves?

[One such move is illustrated.]

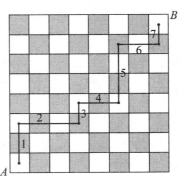

9.10 **a** 4 medical tests A, B, C and D are carried out within 14 days on a patient. A must precede B and B must precede C and D. On the days when A and B are carried out the patient must not undergo any other test, but C and D can be carried out on the same day or on different days in any order.
In how many ways can the days for the test be chosen?

    b By solving the problem in **a** by two different methods, prove that:
$$1.(n-2)^2 + 2(n-3)^2 + 3(n-4)^2 + \ldots\ldots + (n-2)^2.1 = \frac{n(n-1)^2(n-2)}{12}.$$

9.11   Prove the following facts about the binomial coefficient $\binom{n}{r}$:

    a $\binom{n}{r}$ is an integer,

    b $\binom{n}{r}$ is never prime for $r = 2, 3, 4, 5, \ldots, n-2$,

    c $\binom{n}{r}$ is odd if $n = 2^m - 1$, m a positive integer,

    d $\binom{n}{r}$ is even if $n = 2^m$, m a positive integer.

9.12   **a**   Prove Pascal's rule: $\binom{n}{r} + \binom{n}{r+1} = \binom{n+1}{r+1}$.

    b   Prove that $\binom{n}{r} - \binom{n}{r-1} + \binom{n}{r-2} - \binom{n}{r-3} + \ldots + (-1)^r . \binom{n}{0} = \binom{n-1}{r}$.

    c   Prove that $\binom{r}{r} + \binom{r+1}{r} + \binom{r+2}{r} + \ldots + \binom{r+n}{r} = \binom{r+n+1}{r+1}$.

9.13   I put 62 stones on an ordinary 8×8 chess board with one stone on each square but leaving two opposite corner squares vacant. I now remove stones from the board by jumping two at a time and removing the two jumped over. Jumps may be horizontal or vertical but not diagonal. Prove that if I keep jumping until there are just 2 stones left, they must be on squares of the same colour.

[From the Wisconsin Math. Engineering and Science Talent Search.]

9.14   **a**   Schools A and B each preselect 11 members for a team to be sent interstate. However, circumstances allow only a combined team of 11 to be sent away.
In how many ways can a team of 11 be selected and a captain be chosen if the captain must come from A?

    b   Prove that, $1. \binom{n}{1}^2 + 2. \binom{n}{2}^2 + 3. \binom{n}{3}^2 + \ldots + n. \binom{n}{n}^2 = n \binom{2n-1}{n-1}$.

9.15   Lottery tickets are numbered $1, 2, 3, 4, \ldots, n$.
r numbers are drawn in such a way that *no two consecutive numbers* are amongst those drawn.
Prove that there are $\binom{n-r+1}{r}$ ways in which this can happen.

9.16   Prove that $\binom{2}{3}\binom{4}{2}\binom{6}{2} \ldots \binom{2n-2}{2}\binom{2n}{2} = n!.1.3.5.7.\ldots(2n-1) = \dfrac{(2n)!}{2^n}$.

Interpret the equalities by a combinational meaning.
[**Hint:**   consider pairing off $2n$ players in a tennis tournament.]

9.17   Suppose that each of 5 people knows exactly one piece of information, and all 5 pieces of information are different. Every time person A phones person B, A tells B everything he knows, while B tells A nothing.

What is the minimum number of phone calls between pairs of people needed for everyone to know everything?

What is the answer for n people?

9.18 5 birds sit near one another on 4 telegraph
wires. How many different arrangements
are possible?

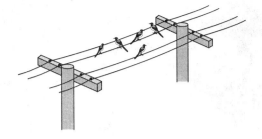

(Consider:
- how many arrangements have 4 on one line, and 1 on another,
- how many arrangements have 3 on one line, 1 on another, 1 on another, etc.)

IRRATIONALS

THE PROBLEMS

10.1 Prove that the solution of $2^x = 3$ is irrational.

10.2 Show that
    a $\log_{10} 2$,
    b $\log_{\frac{1}{2}} 12$, are irrational.

10.3 If a and b are unequal integers, prove that $\log(2^a 5^b)$ is irrational.

10.4 Prove that
    a if x^2 is divisible by 3, then so is x,
    b $\sqrt{3}$ is irrational,
    c if a, b, c and d are rational and $a + b\sqrt{3} = c + d\sqrt{3}$, then $a = c$ and $b = d$.

10.5 Prove that $\sqrt{2}$, $\sqrt{3}$ and $\sqrt{5}$ cannot be terms of a single arithmetic progression.

10.6 Prove that
    a $\sqrt{5} - \sqrt{2}$ is irrational,
    b $\log 5$ is irrational.

10.7 **a** If a, b, c are integers and $ax^2 + bx + c = 0$ has a rational root of $\dfrac{r}{s}$ where r and s are coprime, show that

  i s is a factor of a, and

  ii r is a factor of c.

  b Hence, show that $\sqrt{p}$ is irrational for p a prime number.

  [**Hint:** $\sqrt{p}$ is a root of $x^2 - p = 0$]

10.8 Show that $\tan(5^o)$ is irrational.

  [**Hint:** prove that $\tan^2(5^o)$ is irrational, first of all.]

10.9 The coordinates of three points A, B, C in the plane are all integers. By considering areas, or otherwise, prove that triangle ABC cannot be equilateral.

10.10 Triangle ABC is right-angled and isosceles.
When folded along $\overline{AD}$, B moves to B' on $\overline{AC}$.
Use this figure to prove that $\sqrt{2}$ is irrational.

  [**Hint:** $\sqrt{2} = \dfrac{AC}{AB} = \dfrac{DC}{B'C}$.]

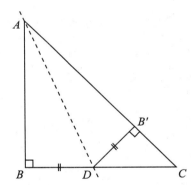

10.11 Prove that $\sqrt[3]{9}$ is irrational.

DIOPHANTINE EQUATIONS

THE PROBLEMS

11.1 A cylindrical tank has a bottom but no top, a radius of 3 m and height 3 m. It is noticed that its volume is 27π m^3 and its outer surface area is 27π m^2, i.e., the numerical values of its volume and its surface area are the same.

Show that there is one and only one *other* cylindrical tank with radius and height a whole number of metres long which has this property.

11.2 Show that the equation $\sqrt{x} - \sqrt{11} = \sqrt{y}$ has an infinite number of solutions where x and y are integers. Find the solution where the ratio $\dfrac{x}{y}$ has the greatest possible value.

11.3 Find all 3-digit integers m such that $2m$ is the original m with its digits in the reverse order.

11.4 In a charity drive it is suggested that each child should donate one full set of coins (1-cent, 2-cent, 5-cent, 10-cent, 20-cent and 50-cent). By a misunderstanding, some contributors donated a full set of 'silver' coins (5-cent, 10-cent, 20-cent and 50-cent) only. The money raised turns out to be exactly $20. Find the number of contributors.

11.5 Find all positive integers x and y such that $x^3 = 2^y + 1$.

11.6 Show that no integers a, b, and c satisfy the equation $a^2 + b^2 = 8c + 6$.

11.7 Show that the equation $x^2 - 2y^2 = -1$ has an infinite number of integer solutions x, y and write down four of these solutions.

DIVISIBILITY

THE PROBLEMS

12.1 Prove that whenever n is an integer, $n^3 + 11n$ is divisible by 6.

12.2 Prove that if p and q are odd numbers then $p^2 - q^2$ is divisible by 8.

12.3 How many perfect cubes leave a remainder of
    a 5 when divided by 7,
    b 9 when divided by 12?

12.4   **a** Any three digit number "abc" is divisible by 7 if and only if $2a + 3b + c$ is divisible by 7. Why is this so?

    b The sum of the digits of a three digit number n written down in the decimal system of notation is equal to 7. Prove that the number n is divisible by 7 if and only if the last two digits are equal.
[For example, the number 133 is such a number, $1 + 3 + 3 = 7$ and the last two digits are equal. Indeed $133 = 7 \times 19$.]

12.5 If n is an integer greater than 1, show that $n^6 - n^2$ is divisible by 60.

12.6 Prove that $p^2 - 1$ is divisible by 24 if p is a prime not less than 5.

12.7   **a** Prove that a 5 digit integer is divisible by 3 provided that the sum of the digits is divisible by 3.

    b Let n be a positive integer. Show that the number formed by placing the digits of the numbers 2^n and 2^{n+1} side by side in either order is divisible by 3.
[For example: If $n = 6$, $64\,128$ and $12\,864$ are both multiples of 3.]

12.8 Show that if n is not divisible by 7, then either $n^3 + 1$ or $n^3 - 1$ is divisible by 7.

12.9 It is known that $x^n + y^n$ is divisible by $x + y$ for all odd integers n.
Use this result to find prime divisors of $2^{35} + 3^{35}$.

12.10 Let x and y be integers such that

$$\frac{x}{y} = 1 - \tfrac{1}{2} + \tfrac{1}{3} - \tfrac{1}{4} + \cdots\cdots + \tfrac{1}{1321} - \tfrac{1}{1322} + \tfrac{1}{1323}\;.$$

Prove that x is divisible by 1985.

12.11 Show that if x, y and z are positive integers such that $x^4 + y^4 = 5z + 1$, then x or y is divisible by 5.

12.12 a and b are positive integers such that $a + b$ and $a^2 + b^2$ are both divisible by 7.
Prove that a and b are both divisible by 7.

Is the statement still valid if each 7 is replaced by 49?

12.13 The number $N = 12$ has divisors (factors): 1, 2, 3, 4, 6 and 12. The sum of the divisors of 12 is
$1 + 2 + 3 + 4 + 6 + 12 = 28$ and the sum of the reciprocals of the divisors of 12 is

$$\tfrac{1}{1} + \tfrac{1}{2} + \tfrac{1}{3} + \tfrac{1}{4} + \tfrac{1}{6} + \tfrac{1}{12} = \tfrac{28}{12}\;.$$

If the sum of the divisors of a number N is 5 times the number, i.e., $5N$, find the sum of reciprocals of the divisors.

12.14 Prove that $11^{10} - 1$ is divisible by 100. Can you generalize this result?

12.15 Show that if none of the integers a, b and c is divisible by 5, then the product
$(a^2 - b^2)(a^2 - c^2)(b^2 - c^2)$ is a multiple of 60.

12.16 **a** Show that if $3^{2m} - 1$ is divisible by 2^r, where m and r are positive integers, then one of the numbers $3^m + 1$ or $3^m - 1$ must be divisible by 2^{r-1}.

b Deduce that $3^k - 1$ is divisible by 2^k for $k = 1, 2$ and 4 and for no other positive integer k.

12.17 **a** Show that if a and d are two positive integers not divisible by 3, then one of $a + d$, $a + 2d$ is divisible by 3.

b If p is a prime number and a and d are positive integers not divisible by p, then one of the numbers $a + d,\ a + 2d,\ a + 3d,\ \ldots\ldots\ ,\ a + (p-1)d$ is divisible by p. Justify?

12.18 **a** a and b are positive integers and p divides both $a + b$ and $a^2 + b^2$.
Prove that p divides both a and b.

b p is a prime number greater than 3 and a, b and c are positive integers such that p divides each of $a + b + c$, $a^2 + b^2 + c^2$ and $a^3 + b^3 + c^3$.
Prove that p divides each of a, b and c.

12.19   **a**   Observe Pascal's triangle:

$$
\begin{array}{ccccccccccccccc}
 & & & & & & & 1 & & 1 & & & & & \\
 & & & & & & 1 & & 2 & & 1 & & & & \\
 & & & & & 1 & & 3 & & 3 & & 1 & & & \\
 & & & & 1 & & 4 & & 6 & & 4 & & 1 & & \\
 & & & 1 & & 5 & & 10 & & 10 & & 5 & & 1 & \\
 & & 1 & & 6 & & 15 & & 20 & & 15 & & 6 & & 1 \\
 & 1 & & 7 & & 21 & & 35 & & 35 & & 21 & & 7 & & 1 \\
\end{array}
$$

In a prime row of Pascal's triangle, e.g., $p = 7$ it seems that

$$\binom{p}{1}, \binom{p}{2}, \binom{p}{3}, \ \ldots\ldots\ , \ \binom{p}{p-1} \quad \text{are all divisible by } p.$$

Prove or disprove?

b   If p is a prime number, prove that $\displaystyle\binom{p-1}{r} - (-1)^r$ is divisible by p.

12.20 Prove that if n and m are positive integers then $(mn)!$ is divisible by $(m!)^n$.

NUMBER
THEORY

THE PROBLEMS

13.1 Let p be the smallest prime factor of an integer n, and suppose that $p > \sqrt[3]{n}$.

Show that $\dfrac{n}{p}$ is also prime.

13.2 Prove that the sum of the squares of 3 consecutive integers cannot be the cube of a positive integer.

13.3 I have two different integers (whole numbers) greater than 1. I inform Sam and Pam of this fact and I tell Sam the sum of my two numbers and I tell Pam their product. The following dialogue then occurs:

Pam: I can't determine the numbers.
Sam: The sum is less than 25.
Pam Now I know the numbers.
Sam: Now I know the numbers too.

What are the numbers?

13.4 Is 111111111 .... 11111, consisting of 121 ones, a prime number?

13.5 3, 5 and 7 are prime numbers. Are there any other triplets of prime numbers of the form n, $n+2$ and $n+4$?

13.6 Prove that for integral $m > 1$, $n > 1$, $m^4 + 4n^4$ is never prime.

13.7 $27 = (13 + 14)$ $22 = (4 + 5 + 6 + 7)$.

    a Which other numbers from 1 to 30 can also be written as the sum of two or more consecutive integers?

    b Only one number between 1000 and 2000 *cannot* be written in such a way. Which number?

c What can you conjecture from **a** and **b**? Prove your statement.

13.8 Show that, if a, b and c are such that $ax^2 + bx + c$ is an integer when $x = 0$, 1, 2, then $ax^2 + bx + c$ is an integer whenever x is an integer.

13.9 **a** Find all 3 digit numbers of the form "aba" which are perfect squares.

  b How many 4 digit numbers of the form "$abab$" are perfect squares?

13.10 Show that $n(n + 1)(n + 2)$ is never a perfect cube for n a positive integer.

13.11 Find the smallest positive integer a such that $a^3 + a = b^2$, where b is also a positive integer.

13.12 A perfect number is a positive integer n which is the sum of all its *factors* other than itself. e.g., $6 = 1 + 2 + 3$ is the smallest perfect number.

Prove that if $p = 1 + 2 + 2^2 + \ldots + 2^n$ is prime, then $2^n p$ is a perfect number.

13.13 How many distinct divisors does the number $18\,000$ have (including 1 and $18\,000$)?

Determine the sum of these divisors of $18\,000$.

[**Hint:** Consider the product $(1 + 2 + 2^2 + 2^3 + 2^4)(1 + 3 + 3^2)(1 + 5 + 5^2 + 5^3)$.]

13.14 **a** If n is composite, show that $2^n - 1$ is composite.

  b Show that if $2^n - 1$ is a prime, then n must also be prime.
  (The converse is not true. e.g., $2^{11} - 1 = 2047 = 23 \times 89$.)

13.15 Prove that, if the lowest common multiple of two numbers is equal to the square of their difference, then the highest common factor of the two numbers is the product of two consecutive integers.

13.16 Find the last 4 digits of 7^{1000}.

13.17 Show that all integers of the form $M = 11111 \ldots\ldots 112222 \ldots\ldots 225$ where there is one more 2 digit appearing than digit 1, are perfect squares. e.g., 1225, $112\,225$, $11\,122\,225$, $\ldots\ldots$

Find the form of $\sqrt{M}$.

13.18 Show that for every real number x, the numbers

$$x^2 - 2x + 3,$$
$$x^4 - 2x^3 + 3x^2 - 4x + 5,$$
$$x^6 - 2x^5 + 3x^4 - 4x^3 + 5x^2 - 6x + 7,$$
$$x^8 - 2x^7 + 3x^6 - 4x^5 + 5x^4 - 6x^3 + 7x^2 - 8x + 9,$$

are all different from zero.

13.19 **a** The integers a and b are coprime (that is, they have no common divisors other than 1 and -1).
  Prove that $a + b$ and ab are coprime.

  b The sum of two integers is 216 and their lowest common multiple is 480.
  Determine the integers.

13.20 Find the set of three unequal positive integers such that the sum of any two is divisible by the third one and the sum of the three is equal to 96.

13.21 Given that $2^n + 1$ is a prime number, prove that n is a power of 2.
The converse is not true (e.g., $2^{32} + 1 = 641 \times 6700417$).

13.22 If a and b are integers and b is odd, prove that the equation $x^2 + 2ax + 2b = 0$ has no rational roots.

13.23 There are just three proper fractions with denominators less than a hundred which may be reduced to lowest terms by illegitimately cancelling a digit. One of these is

$$\frac{26}{65} = \frac{2\cancel{6}}{\cancel{6}5} = \frac{2}{5}$$

Find the other two and confirm the statement that there are no others.

13.24 Show that there are exactly two integers x such that $x^2 + x + 11$ is a perfect square.

13.25

		4	a	b	
	$\times$		3	c	
	3	6	d	e	
f	g	7	i		
j	k	3	l	m	

where a, b, c, ... , m, are missing (unknown) digits.
Find the values of all the missing digits.

13.26 If $2^{2^{2^{2^2}}}$ is written in integer form, how many digits would it contain?

13.27 a, b, c and d are positive integers such that $ab = cd$.
Prove that $a^2 + b^2 + c^2 + d^2$ cannot be a prime number.

13.28 Show that the sum of the squares of two odd integers cannot be a perfect power.
[A perfect power has form m^n where m and n are integers and $n \geqslant 2$.]

13.29 Is it possible to find real numbers x, y and z such that $x + y + z = 2$ and $xy + yz + zx = 2$?

13.30 If $n = 2^k$, k a positive integer, and $1 \leqslant r \leqslant n - 1$,
show that the binomial coefficient $\binom{n}{r}$ is even whilst $\binom{n-1}{r}$ is odd.

13.31 If n is a positive integer, show that $2^n - 1$ cannot be a perfect power.
(i.e., of the form a^k where a, k are positive integers and a, $k \geq 2$.)

13.32 Let n be a natural number. Show that n^k can be represented as the sum of n consecutive odd numbers, for any integral value of k greater than 1.
(For example, $3^2 = 1 + 3 + 5$, $3^3 = 7 + 9 + 11$, $3^4 = 25 + 27 + 29$, etc.)

13.33 Determine the last 6 digits of 7^{1000}.

13.34 If p is an odd prime, and integers x, y, z can be found such that $x^p + y^p = z^p$, prove that z cannot be a prime number.

13.35 We are given 15 different positive integers n_1, n_2, ... n_{15}, listed in increasing order. Assume that $n_r.n_s = n_{rs}$ whenever $r \neq s$ and $rs \leqslant 15$.
(Thus we know for instance that $n_2.n_6 = n_{12}$, $n_3.n_5 = n_{15}$ but we do not know that $n_3{}^2 = n_9$ and we have no information about $n_3.n_7$.)

  a Show that $n_3 < n_2{}^2$.

  b If $n_2 = 2$, show that $n_{15} = 15$.

13.36 Each letter stands for a different non-zero digit in the addition shown. What are your *PLANS*?

$$
\begin{array}{ccccc}
M & A & K & E \\
S & A & F & E \\
\hline
P & L & A & N & S
\end{array}
$$

PROBABILITY

THE PROBLEMS

14.1 Two different numbers are randomly chosen out of the set $\{1, 2, 3, 4, 5, \ldots, n\}$, where n is a multiple of four. Determine the probability that one of the numbers is

  a four times larger than the other,

  b a multiple of the other if $n = 12$.

14.2 A hundred seeds are planted in ten rows of ten seeds per row. Assuming that each seed independently germinates with probability $\frac{1}{2}$, find the probability that the row with the maximum number of germinations contains at least 8 seedlings.

14.3 Consider a randomly chosen n child family, where $n > 1$. Let A be the event that the family has at most one boy, and B be the event that every child in the family is of the same sex.
For what values of n are the events A and B independent?

14.4 Two marksmen, A and B, fire simultaneously at a target. If A is twice as likely to hit the target as B, and if the probability that the target does get hit is $\frac{1}{2}$, find the probability of A hitting the target.

14.5 A quadratic equation $ax^2 + bx + c = 0$ is copied by a typist. However, the numbers standing for a, b and c are blurred and she can only see that they are integers of one digit.
What is the probability that the equation she types has real roots?

14.6 Two people, X and Y, agree to meet each other at the corner of two city streets between 1 pm and 2 pm, but neither will wait for the other for more than 30 minutes. If each person is likely to arrive at any time during the one hour period, determine the probability that they will in fact meet.

14.7 n fair dice are simultaneously rolled. Find the probability that the *product* of the integers thus generated is a multiple of 6.

14.8 A bag contains $2r$ red marbles and some others of a different colour. If the contents of the bag are placed in two bags such that each contains r red marbles, show that the probability of drawing a red marble from one of these bags, chosen at random, is not less than that of drawing a red marble from the single bag.

14.9 A wardrobe closet contains n pairs of shoes. If $2r$ shoes are chosen at random (with $2r < n$), what is the probability that there will be no complete pair?

14.10 An urn contains $2n$ tickets, marked $1, 2, 3, \ldots\ldots, 2n$. Three tickets are drawn in succession without replacement. What is the probability that the sum of the numbers on

   a two of the tickets equals the number on the third ticket,

   b the *first* two tickets drawn equals the number on the third ticket?

14.11 Tickets marked with $1, 2, 3, 4, \ldots\ldots, N$ where $N = 2^n$ (n an integer greater than 1) are placed inside a hat. The players are each to draw two tickets, read them and replace them. Prize winners are those who draw two numbers the ratio of which is 2. However, if the ratio is some other power of 2 (i.e., not 2^1), then they get their entry money refunded.
What is the probability of

   a a win,

   b a refund?

GEOMETRICAL
CONSTRUCTIONS

THE PROBLEMS

15.1 Construct a triangle given the size of two of its angles and the length of the bisector of the third angle.

15.2 Find a construction to surround a given circle by 8 equal circles, each touching the given circle and its other two neighbours.

15.3 P is a fixed point inside a fixed angle, ABC. A line through P completes a triangle XBY, and this line can rotate about P.

Show how to construct $\overline{XY}$ so that triangle XBY has least perimeter.

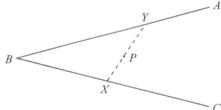

15.4 Given two straight lines which are not parallel but do not meet on the sheet of paper on which they are drawn, make a construction on the paper for the bisector of the angle between them.

15.5 A and B are two points on the same side of a line l. Find a point M on l such that $\overline{MB}$ bisects the angle between $\overline{MA}$ and l. Is the construction always possible?

15.6 A, B are fixed points on the same side of a straight line l. Determine the position of two points M, N on l such that MN is a given distance, and the path $AM + MN + NB$ is as short as possible.

15.7 If we are given any square, we can easily construct a triangle enclosing it so that one of the square's sides is on a side of the triangle and the other vertices of the square lie on the other sides of the triangle - see diagram 1.

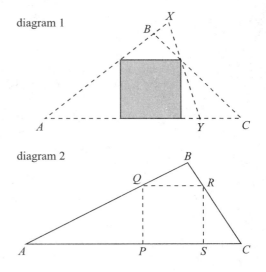

Obviously several triangles will do, e.g., ABC, AXY, etc.

The reverse problem is not so simple (and the solution is unique!), that is, given any triangle, find a square enclosed by, but touching, all sides of the triangle - see diagram 2.

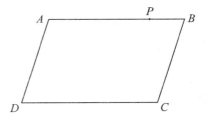

Describe a construction which will do this. (Write the steps in a numbered list.)

15.8 P and Q are two points inside the triangle ABC. Determine S and T on the sides $\overline{AB}$ and $\overline{AC}$ respectively, to make the path $PSTQ$ as short as possible.

15.9 A is one of the points of intersection of two circles. Show how to find a straight line through A which intersects the two circles giving equal chords.

15.10 $ABCD$ is a parallelogram; P is a point on the side $\overline{AB}$. Construct a rectangle $PQRS$ with vertices Q, R, S on the sides $\overline{BC}$, $\overline{CD}$, $\overline{DA}$ respectively.

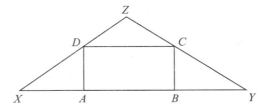

15.11 Given a triangle XYZ, show how to construct a 2 by 1 rectangle $ABCD$ with A and B on $\overline{XY}$, C on $\overline{ZY}$ and D on $\overline{XZ}$. [AB is twice BC].

15.12 Construct a triangle if you are given the length of a side, an angle adjacent to that side and the sum of the lengths of the other two sides.

15.13 Triangle XYZ is given. Find the point P in the plane for which $PX + PY + PZ$ is as small as possible.

[**Hint:** Label $\triangle XYZ$ in an anticlockwise direction and put P in an arbitrary position. Rotate P, X, Z about Y through $60°$ in an anticlockwise direction to new positions P', X', Z' respectively. Now consider the length of the path $X'P'PZ$.]

15.14 On a sheet of paper there are a point P and two (straight) lines l and m. The lines l and m intersect in a point Q which does not lie on the paper. You are given a straightedge (ungraduated ruler) and a pair of compasses. State and justify a construction which determines the line $\overline{PQ}$.

15.15 Construct a rhombus $ABCD$ given the angle DAB and the sum of the lengths of the diagonals $\overline{AC}$ and $\overline{BD}$.

15.16 You are given a solid sphere, a compass, a ruler and a sheet of paper. You are allowed to make marks on the surface of the sphere. Use your tools and the sheet of paper to determine the diameter of the sphere.

15.17 In the diagram, the two perpendicular lines represent the wall and floor of a room, B and A represent the highest and lowest points of a picture on the wall, and OM, the height of a man. $PM' = OM$.

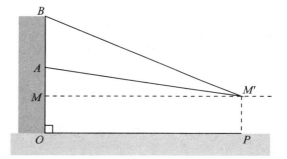

Give a ruler and compass construction to find the point P on the floor so that the man has the best view of the picture when he stands at P (i.e., so that the angle $AM'B$ is as large as possible).

INEQUALITIES

THE PROBLEMS

16.1 Given that $a \geqslant b$ and $x \leqslant y$, prove that $\dfrac{ax + by}{2} \leqslant \dfrac{a + b}{2} \cdot \dfrac{x + y}{2}$.

16.2 Prove that if a, b, c and d are positive where $\dfrac{a}{b} < \dfrac{c}{d}$, then $\dfrac{a}{b} < \dfrac{a + c}{b + d} < \dfrac{c}{d}$.

16.3 Prove that $\dfrac{a^3 + b^3}{2} \geqslant (\dfrac{a + b}{2})^3$ for all positives a and b.

16.4 Consider the perfect square $(\sqrt{x} - \sqrt{y})^2$ where x and y are positive.
Prove that

a $\dfrac{x + y}{2} \geqslant \sqrt{xy}$ (i.e., their arithmetic mean is not less than their geometric mean.),

b if a, b and c are positives then $(a + b)(b + c)(c + a) \geqslant 8abc$.

16.5 a, b and c are the lengths of the sides of a triangle.
Prove that $a(b - c)^2 + b(c - a)^2 + c(a - b)^2 + 4abc > a^3 + b^3 + c^3$.

16.6 An infinite number of rectangles $ABCD$ can
be inscribed inside a right-angled triangle with
legs 10 cm long, such that $\overline{AB}$ lies on the
hypotenuse. Find the position of A to
maximise the area of $ABCD$.

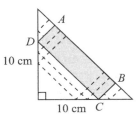

16.7 If $a > 0$, $b > 0$, $c > 0$ and $s = a + b + c < 1$,

show that $1 + s < (1 + a)(1 + b)(1 + c) < \dfrac{1}{1 - s}$.

16.8 Prove that for all real numbers a, b and c not equal to zero,

$$\frac{a}{b} + \frac{b}{c} + \frac{c}{a} \leqslant \tfrac{1}{2}\left(a^2 + b^2 + c^2 + \frac{1}{a^2} + \frac{1}{b^2} + \frac{1}{c^2}\right).$$

For what values of a, b, and c is the equal sign valid?

16.9 Prove that for all real x, $\dfrac{x^3 - 1}{3} \leqslant \dfrac{x^4 - 1}{4}$.

16.10 If a, b, c and d are positive with sum S, prove that $(ab + bc + cd) < \dfrac{S^2}{4}$.

16.11 We are given a finite set of weights: w_1, w_2, w_3, ... , w_n. The total weight of the set is 1 kilogram. Show that for some number k, the weight of w_k is heavier than $\dfrac{1}{2^k}$ kilograms.

16.12 Tiddle ball is a three player game. In each round the winner gets a points, the runner-up gets b points and the loser gets c points, where $a > b > c$ are positive integers. One day Anne, Bill and Claire played some Tiddle ball and the final score was:
Anne - 20, Bill - 10, Claire - 9. Bill won the second round.
Who won the first round and how many points did Claire get in the last round?

16.13 x, y and z are integers, not all zero.
Prove that $3(x^2 + y^2 + z^2) - 2(xy + yz + zx) \geqslant 3$.

16.14 **a** By considering the function $f(x) = (ax - d)^2 + (cx - b)^2$ whose graph never goes below the x-axis, prove that $|ad + bc| \leqslant \sqrt{a^2 + c^2}.\sqrt{b^2 + d^2}$, the **Cauchy-Schwarz inequality.**

b Consider the figure below where $OA = a$, $OB = b$, $AC = c$, $BD = d$ units.

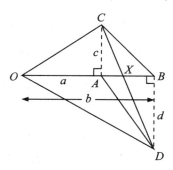

Prove that
  i area $\triangle OCD$ = area $\triangle OAD$ + area $\triangle OBC$,
  ii area $\triangle OCD \leq \tfrac{1}{2}\sqrt{a^2 + c^2}.\sqrt{b^2 + d^2}$.
  iii Using **i** and **ii**, show that, $|ad + bc| \leqslant \sqrt{a^2 + c^2}.\sqrt{b^2 + d^2}$ for a, b, c and d being positive.
  [A geometric proof of **a**.]

16.15 For how many positive ingeters n is $(n+1)^n$ greater than n^{n+1}?

16.16 x, y and z are positive real numbers with sum 1. Prove that $\dfrac{1}{x} + \dfrac{1}{y} + \dfrac{1}{z} \geqslant 9$.

16.17 If a, b, c and d are positive numbers, prove that
$$4(ab + bc + cd + da) \leqslant (a + b + c + d)^2.$$

16.18 5 integers a, b, c, d and e exist such that $0 < a \leqslant b \leqslant c \leqslant d \leqslant e$ and their sum is equal to their product.

Find all possible solutions (a, b, c, d, e).

16.19 Prove that for any positive integer n, $n! < \left(\dfrac{n+1}{2}\right)^n$, by using

$\dfrac{x+y}{2} \geqslant \sqrt{xy}$ for $x > 0$ and $y > 0$.

16.20 Show that for all integers $n > 2$, $2^{\frac{n(n-1)}{2}} > n!$

16.21 If b_1, c_1, b_2 and c_2 are real numbers such that $b_1 b_2 = 2(c_1 + c_2)$, show that at least one of the equations $x^2 + b_1 x + c_1 = 0$ and $x^2 + b_2 x + c_2 = 0$ has two real roots.

16.22 If a, b and c are real numbers and $a^2 + b^2 + c^2 = 1$, show that $-\frac{1}{2} \leqslant ab + bc + ca \leqslant 1$.

16.23 If a_1, a_2, a_3, ..., a_n are each greater than 1, prove that
$$a_1 a_2 a_3 a_4 ...... a_n > a_1 + a_2 + a_3 + a_4 + ... + a_n + 1 - n.$$

16.24 If a, b and c are positive, prove that $\dfrac{a}{b+c} + \dfrac{b}{c+a} + \dfrac{c}{a+b} \geqslant \dfrac{3}{2}$.

16.25 Prove that $a + b + c \leqslant \dfrac{a^2 + b^2}{2c} + \dfrac{b^2 + c^2}{2a} + \dfrac{c^2 + a^2}{2b}$ for all positive numbers a, b and c.

16.26 Prove that $x^2 + y^2 + z^2 \geqslant \frac{2}{3}(xy + yz + zx)$ for all real numbers x, y and z.

16.27 **a** If x and y are positive real numbers such that $xy = 1$, show that $x + y \geqslant 2$.

b Use **a** to show that if $xy = k$ where x, y and k are positive then $x + y \geqslant 2\sqrt{k}$.

c Let $f(S) = S^2 + \dfrac{2}{S}$. Show that $f(S) - 3 = \dfrac{(S-1)^2(S+2)}{S}$.

d Let $g(t) = t + \dfrac{2}{\sqrt{t}}$ for $t > 0$. Use **c** to show that $g(t) \geqslant 3$ for $t > 0$.

e Use the information in **b** and **d** to show that if x, y and z are positive and $xyz = 1$, then $x + y + z \geqslant 3$.

f Use **e** to prove that for positives x, y and z: $\dfrac{x + y + z}{3} \geqslant \sqrt[3]{xyz}$
called the **arithmetic-geometric means inequality**.

16.28 **a** By considering the expression $(a-b)^2 + (b-c)^2 + (c-a)^2$, prove that
$a^2 + b^2 + c^2 \geqslant ab + bc + ca$ for all real a, b and c.

b Simplify the product $(a+b+c)(a^2+b^2+c^2-ab-bc-ca)$.

c Using **a** and **b**, prove that "for all positives x, y and z, $\dfrac{x+y+z}{3} \geqslant \sqrt[3]{xyz}$
with equality when $x = y = z$."

d Hence, show that, amongst all rectangular boxes of equal surface area, the cube has greatest volume.

16.29 Using the arithmetic-geometric means inequality for two positive numbers only, prove the arithmetic-geometric means inequality for 4 positive numbers:
$$\frac{a+b+c+d}{4} \geqslant \sqrt[4]{abcd}$$
with equality occuring when $a = b = c = d$.

16.30 x, y and z are non-zero integers, not necessarily all different.
Determine 3 numbers such that $x \leqslant x+y+z \leqslant y \leqslant xyz \leqslant z$.

16.31 a, b and c are three real numbers and m is the smallest of the numbers $|a-b|$,
$|b-c|$, $|c-a|$.
[i.e., m is the smallest of the distances between a, b and c.]

Show that
a $3(a^2+b^2+c^2) \geqslant (a-b)^2 + (b-c)^2 + (c-a)^2$, and hence that,
b $m^2 \leqslant \frac{1}{2}(a^2+b^2+c^2)$.

16.32 Let f be a non-negative function which satisfies the inequality
$$f\left(\frac{x_1+x_2}{2}\right) < \tfrac{1}{2}[f(x_1)+f(x_2)] \quad \text{whenever } x_1 \neq x_2.$$
Show that

a $f\left(\dfrac{s_1+s_2+s_3+s_4}{4}\right) < \tfrac{1}{4}[f(s_1)+f(s_2)+f(s_3)+f(s_4)]$ for s_1, s_2, s_3 and s_4 not all equal, and hence that,

b $f\left(\dfrac{a+b+c}{3}\right) < \tfrac{1}{3}[f(a)+f(b)+f(c)]$ for a, b and c not all equal.

[**Hint:** select values of s_1, s_2, s_3 and s_4 in terms of a, b and c.]

16.33 The graph alongside is that of the function whose equation is given by $y = \dfrac{1}{x}$, $x > 0$.

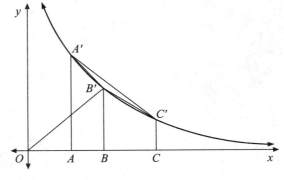

A, B and C are three points on the x-axis such that $\dfrac{OB}{OA} = \dfrac{OC}{OB}$.

Show the following:

a $\overline{OB'}$ produced bisects the chord $\overline{A'C'}$,

b   triangle $A'B'C'$ is the triangle of largest area which has base the chord $\overline{A'C'}$ and vertex on the curve $A'C'$,

c   use **b** to show that the tangent to the curve at B' is parallel to $\overline{A'C'}$.

GEOMETRIC INEQUALITIES

THE PROBLEMS

17.1 ABC is an acute angled triangle with sides a, b and c, and altitudes h_a, h_b, h_c.

Prove that $\frac{1}{2} < \dfrac{h_a + h_b + h_c}{a + b + c} < 1$.

17.2 **a** $\triangle PQR$ has sides of length p, q and r (the usual notation).
Show that if P is acute, then, $p^2 < q^2 + r^2$,
and if P is obtuse, then, $p^2 > q^2 + r^2$.

b A cyclic quadrilateral has sides a, b, c and d.
What can be said about the shape of the quadrilateral if $a^2 + b^2 = c^2 + d^2$?

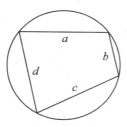

17.3 **a** Two numbers a and b are such that $a \leqslant 1$ and $b \geqslant 1$. If S is the sum of a and b, and P is their product, prove that S and P differ by more than 1.

b If the product of two positive numbers is 1, show that their sum cannot be less than 2.

c Use **b** to prove that "amongst all right-angled triangles of equal area, the isosceles triangle has the shortest hypotenuse".

17.4 Two farmers at A and B wish to place a pipeline connecting one another. The pipeline must connect the two roadways at points C and D. Show how to locate C and D so that the total length of pipe is a minumum. Prove your answer.

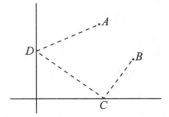

17.5 Four friends buy a kilometre square parcel of land on which they build their homes. The land is bordered on the north and south by parallel highways. They desire to connect their homes by driveways to a road (or roads) parallel to the edges of their parcel joining both highways.
Show that at most $2\frac{1}{2}$ km of roadway (including driveways) need be made (no matter where the houses are situated).
The figure shows a possible driveway system.

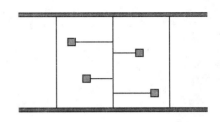

17.6 A square $ABCD$ has sides of length a and diagonals of length d. $\triangle APQ$ is drawn such that P is on side $\overline{BC}$ and Q is on side $\overline{CD}$. $AP = AQ$. Let the triangle have perimeter p.
Prove that

   a $p > 2d$

   b $p < 4a$

   c $p \leqslant 2a + d$.

17.7 ABC is an acute-angled triangle and X a fixed point on the base $\overline{BC}$.

   a By reflecting $\triangle ABC$ in the lines $\overline{AB}$ and $\overline{AC}$, determine points Y and Z on $\overline{AC}$ and $\overline{AB}$ respectively such that the perimeter of $\triangle XYZ$ is as small as possible.

   b Show that the perimeter in **a** is $2l \sin A$ where $l = AX$.

   c Deduce the position of 3 points P, Q and R if $\triangle PQR$ has minimum perimeter and is inscribed in $\triangle ABC$.

17.8 $\overline{AB}$, $\overline{BC}$ and $\overline{AC}$ are three chords of a circle. Prove that the sum of the areas of the three segments of the circle outside the triangle is always more than half the area of the circle.

17.9 A and B are diametrically opposite points of a circle, centre O and radius r. The point P moves on a larger circle with radius R and same centre O.
Show that for all positions of P, $R^2 - r^2 \leqslant PA.PB \leqslant R^2 + r^2$.
[**Hint:**   Let A be $(0, r)$, B be $(0, -r)$, P be $(R\cos\theta, R\sin\theta)$.]

17.10 A general is to defend 'square island', an island which is indeed a square. Where would he station whole platoons of men to defend the island from attack if each platoon had to stay together and distances to be travelled have to be kept to a minimum, if he has at his disposal

   a 2 platoons,

   b 3 platoons

   c 4 platoons?

17.11 Locate the position of point P within triangle ABC such that $(AP)^2 + (BP)^2 + (CP)^2$ is minimal.

17.12 $\triangle ABC$ has perimeter P, circum-radius R and in-radius r. Show that

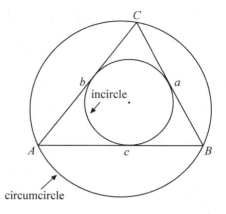

circumcircle

a $\sin A = \dfrac{a}{2R}$,

b the area of $\triangle ABC = \dfrac{abc}{4R}$,

c the area of $\triangle ABC = \frac{1}{2}r(a + b + c)$, and hence show that

d $P \geqslant 3.\sqrt{6Rr}$.

17.13 Heron's formula:

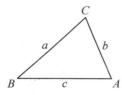

The area of a triangle with sides of length a, b and c is given by,

$$A = \sqrt{s(s - a)(s - b)(s - c)} \quad \text{where}$$

$$s = \frac{a + b + c}{2}.$$

a Prove Heron's formula using the cosine rule.

b Prove that "amongst triangles of given perimeter, the equilateral triangle has the largest area".

17.14 Find conditions which ensure that a rectangular mat, a metres by b metres can be laid in a square room of sides c metres.

17.15 An ellipse may be defined as the locus of all points P such that $PF_1 + PF_2$ is a constant where F_1 and F_2 are fixed points called foci.

a Explain how to construct an ellipse using two pegs and a piece of string.

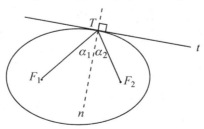

b If t is a tangent line and T is the point of contact with the ellipse and Q is another point on t, show that $TF_1 + TF_2 < QF_1 + QF_2$.

c Hence, show that TF_1 and TF_2 enclose equal angles with the normal n at T. i.e., $\alpha_1 = \alpha_2$.

[This is called the **optical property** of an ellipse: with a light source at F_1, the light is reflected on the elliptical mirror and passes through F_2.]

17.16 **a**   If P, Q and R are angles which have a sum of 180°,

show that $\cos 2P + \cos 2Q + \cos 2R = -1 - 4\cos P . \cos Q . \cos R.$

b   3 points A, B and C lie on a circle whose radius is 1 unit.

Show that $a^2 + b^2 + c^2 \leqslant 9$ square units.

[$a = BC$, etc., the usual notation]

TRIGONOMETRY

THE PROBLEMS

18.1 A circular cake is divided into two portions by a straight line cut across the circle.

Where should the cut be made to divide the cake in the ratio 2 : 1?

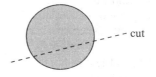

18.2 Find the area of the shaded region.

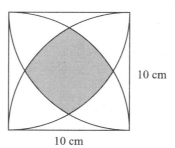

10 cm

10 cm

18.3 A truncated, conical vase has dimensions as shown. A thin elastic band is placed on its outer surface. Points A and B are in the same vertical plane. Find the shortest distance from A to B along the elastic band line.

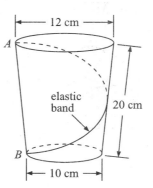

18.4   **a**   A function $f(x)$ has the property $f(a) + f(b) \leqslant 2f\left(\dfrac{a+b}{2}\right)$ for every pair of numbers a

and b in the domain of $f(x)$, with equality occuring when $a = b$.

Prove that $f(a) + f(b) + f(c) \leqslant 3f\left(\dfrac{a+b+c}{3}\right)$ for every a, b and c in the domain

of $f(x)$, with equality occuring when $a = b = c$.

b   If A, B and C are the angles of a triangle, find the maximum value of
$\sin A + \sin B + \sin C$ and state the nature of the triangle when this maximum occurs.

18.5   Use the figure alongside to show that $\cos 36^o = \dfrac{1 + \sqrt{5}}{4}$.

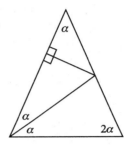

18.6   If the acute angle between the diagonals of a quadrilateral is θ, and the diagonals have length a and b units, find the area of the quadrilateral in terms of a, b and θ. The two diagonals of three quadrilaterals have the same length but the acute angles between the diagonals are 30°, 45°, and 60° respectively. Determine the ratio of the areas of the three quadrilaterals.

18.7   **a**   Two cylindrical rods of radii 10 cm and 30 cm are placed side by side and bound together by a thin wire which will go round them once.
Find the length of the wire.

b   If the wire has length L and the rods have radii R and r, find L in terms of R and r.

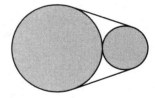

18.8 ABC is a right-angled triangle, right-angled at A.
The hypotenuse $\overline{BC}$ is trisected at M and N.

a   If triangle ABC is isosceles, determine the size of angle NAM.

b   If triangle ABC is not necessarily isosceles and $AM = a$ units and $AN = b$ units, find the length of $\overline{MN}$ in terms of a and b.

18.9

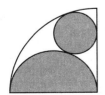

In a quarter circle a semi-circle and a small circle are inscribed (as illustrated). If the quarter circle has a radius of 10 cm, find the radius of the small circle.

18.10 A parallelogram timber frame with diagonals a and b is pushed into the shape of a rectangle.
Find, in terms of a and b, the length of the diagonals of the rectangle.

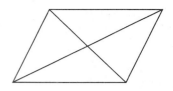

18.11 In triangle ABC, if angle A has size θ and angle B has size 2θ, and the sides $\overline{BC}$, $\overline{CA}$ and $\overline{AB}$ have lengths a, b and c respectively, show that $b^2 = a(a + c)$.

18.12 Find α:

  a   **b**

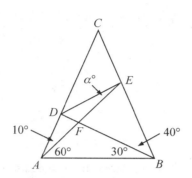 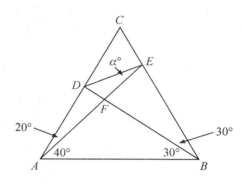

        [Hint: let $AB = x$ in each case.]

18.13 One side of a triangle is divided into segments of length a and b by the inscribed circle of radius r.
Prove that the area of the triangle is $\dfrac{abr(a + b)}{ab - r^2}$.

18.14   **a**   If A, B and C are the angles of a triangle, show that
$$\tan A + \tan B + \tan C = \tan A.\tan B.\tan C.$$
      b   For A, B, C not necessarily the angles of a triangle, what can be deduced about $A + B + C$ if $\tan A + \tan B + \tan C = \tan A.\tan B.\tan C$?

18.15 Find the possible values of θ:

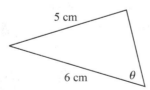

18.16 Prove that $2\tan^{-1}\left(\tfrac{1}{3}\right) + \tan^{-1}\left(\tfrac{1}{7}\right) = \dfrac{\pi}{4}$.

18.17 A sphere fits snugly into a regular tetrahedron with sides 10 cm.
Find the radius of the sphere.

18.18 ABC is a fixed triangle and point P moves on side $\overline{AB}$. $\overline{PQ}$ is parallel to $\overline{BC}$ and $\overline{QR}$ is parallel to $\overline{AB}$. Thus $\triangle PQR$ can change shape. Where must P be located so that $\triangle PQR$ has maximum area?

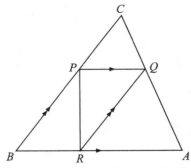

18.19

(View from above)

4 identical metal spheres of radius 1 cm are placed so that 3 of them are on a horizontal table just touching one another and the fourth on top of them to form a stable stack. Find the height of the stack above the horizontal table.

18.20 A cyclic quadrilateral has sides with length a, b, c and d. Show that the area of the cyclic quadrilateral is given by $\sqrt{(s-a)(s-b)(s-c)(s-d)}$ where $2s = a + b + c + d$.

18.21

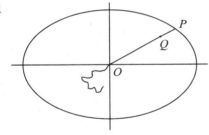

The boundary fence at Football Park is in the shape of a perfect ellipse. The groundsman has to mark out a white line for an Aussie Rules match. He decides on the following method:

"Use a rope $\overline{OQP}$, O being the centre of the elliptical playing field. Place a knot at Q so that $\overline{PQ}$ is 10 m long. P moves around the fence keeping the rope tight. The path of Q is to be the boundary line."
Does Q trace out an ellipse?

18.22 $\overline{BC}$ is twice as long as $\overline{AC}$.
$\overline{AB}$ is three times as long as $\overline{AD}$.
Prove that $\overline{CD}$ is twice as long as $\overline{AD}$.

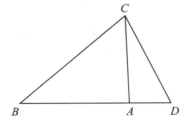

18.23 Points A, B and C lie on a circle. Prove that $(AB)^2 + (BC)^2 + (CA)^2 \leqslant 9$ if the circle has radius 1 unit.

18.24 Find the length of $\overline{AB}$.

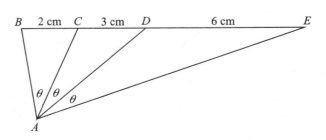

18.25 If $PR = PQ$, show that $RQ = QS + SP$.

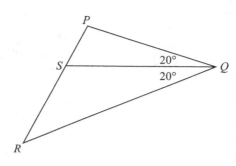

18.26 P, Q and R lie on $\overline{BC}$, $\overline{AC}$ and $\overline{AB}$ respectively.

If $\dfrac{BP}{BC} = \dfrac{CQ}{CA} = \dfrac{AR}{AB} = \dfrac{\text{area } \triangle PQR}{\text{area } \triangle ABC}$, locate

the exact positions of P, Q and R.

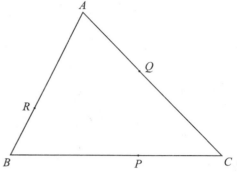

18.27 An ellipse with centre $(0,0)$, x-intercepts $\pm a$, y-intercepts $\pm b$ has Cartesian equation

$\dfrac{x^2}{a^2} + \dfrac{y^2}{b^2} = 1.$

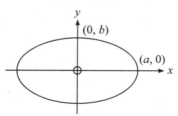

  a   Show that $P(a\cos\theta,\, b\sin\theta)$ is a general point on the ellipse for varying θ.

  b   An ellipse is inscribed in a rectangle $KLMN$. The sides of the rectangle are parallel to the axes of symmetry of the ellipse. Another rectangle $PQRS$ with sides parallel to the first rectangle, is inscribed in the ellipse.

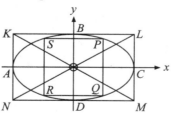

     i   Find the coordinates of P for the rectangle inscribed in the ellipse to have maximum area and indicate exactly where P is located.

    ii   Find the coordinates of P if $PQRS$ is to have maximum perimeter.

18.28 Prove that for acute angles A and B, $\tan A + \tan B + 2 \leqslant \sqrt{2}(\sec A + \sec B)$.

18.29 The graph of $y = \sin\theta$, $0 \leqslant \theta \leqslant 2\pi$ is drawn on a strip of paper which is then wrapped around a cylinder of unit radius so that the points $(0,0)$ and $(2\pi, 0)$ on the graph paper are superimposed. Prove that the sine curve now lies on a plane and hence determine the shape of the plane figure that the sine curve has become.

18.30 M is the midpoint of $\overline{AB}$ and angle ACM is twice as large as angle MCB. Find the measure of angle MCB.

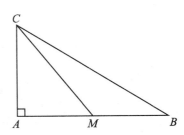

18.31

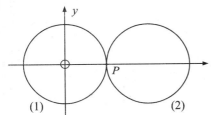

Circle (1) is fixed with constant radius r. Circle (2), of the same radius, initially touches (1) at P where P is a fixed point on circle (2). Circle (2) rolls around (1) without slipping and P traces out a path. Find the Cartesian equation of the path traced out by P, and sketch the path of P relative to Circle (1).

18.32 In triangle ABC, $\sin C = \cos A + \cos B$. Show that the triangle has a right angle.

18.33 A mountain is perfectly conical in shape. The base is a circle of radius 2 km, and the steepest slopes leading up to the top are 3 km long.
From a point A on the southernmost point of the base a path leads up on the side of the mountain to B a point on the northern slope and 1.2 km up the slope from C. [A and C are diametrically opposite.]

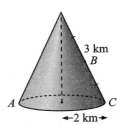

If AB is the shortest distance from A to B along the mountainside, find

   a   the length of the path from A to B (i.e., distance AB.),

   b   the length of the part of the path from P to B where P is a point on the path where it is horizontal.

18.34 If A, B and C are the angles of a triangle, prove that

   a $\sin A + \sin B + \sin C = 4\cos\left(\dfrac{A}{2}\right)\cos\left(\dfrac{B}{2}\right)\cos\left(\dfrac{C}{2}\right)$,   and hence

   b   the sum of the sines of the angles is more than half the product of the sines.

18.35   **a** M, N and K are positive constants such that $K \leqslant M+N$, and $M\cos\theta + N\cos\phi = K$. Find the maximum value of $M\sin\theta + N\sin\phi$ in terms of M, N and K.

   b $ABCD$ is a quadrilateral in which the lengths of the sides are fixed. Show that the quadrilateral has maximum area when it is cyclic.
   [**Hint:**   Let one angle be θ and its opposite angle be $180^o - \phi$.]

18.36 From a one metre diameter log, three beams are
to be cut as shown in the diagram.
What sized beams should be cut in order to
minimise waste?

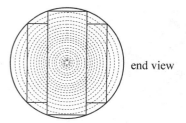

end view

18.37

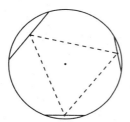

A circle has 3 non-overlapping arcs which all subtend
angles of $60°$ at the circle's centre. End points of these
arcs are joined by straight lines. Prove that the
midpoints of these 3 chords are the vertices of an
equilateral triangle.

18.38 Find the value of α.

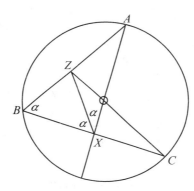

18.39 Instead of using Cartesian coordinates (x, y) to specify the position of a point in the plane, we will
use **polar coordinates** $P(r, \theta)$ where r is the distance from the origin O to P, and θ is the angle
$\overrightarrow{OP}$ makes with the horizontal line $\overrightarrow{OR}$.

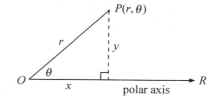

a   State equations which connect r, θ, x and y.

b   Without converting to Cartesian equations,
sketch the graphs of

    i $r = 2$,

    ii $r = \dfrac{\theta}{\theta + \pi}$, $\theta \geqslant 0$.

    iii $r = 1 + \cos\theta$, $0 \leqslant \theta \leqslant 2\pi$,

    iv $r^2 = 4\sin^2 2\theta$.

c   **i** The Cartesian equation of the curve H is $xy = 1$.
      Determine the shortest distance from the origin to the curve.

      The equation of the curve L is $(x^2 + y^2)^2 = 4xy$.

    ii Let $\overrightarrow{OPQ}$ be the ray from O cutting curve L in P and curve H in Q.
      Find a relationship between OP and OQ and hence sketch the graph of L.

PYTHAGOREAN
TRIPLES

THE PROBLEMS

19.1 **a** Write down the expression $(ax - by)^2 + (ay + bx)^2$ as a product of two factors.

b The number triples 15, 8, 17 and 5, 12, 13 can each represent the lengths of sides of a right-angled triangle as you may check by applying Pythagoras's theorem. A third right-angled triangle has hypotenuse of length 221 units and its two smaller sides have integer lengths. Find these lengths.

19.2 The lengths of the side of a right-angled triangle are integers. If the length of one side is 12, find the lengths of the remaining sides.

19.3 The triples 3, 4, 5; 5, 12, 13; 7, 24, 25 respectively represent sides of right-angled triangles.
In each of these the length of the smallest side is a **prime** number.
Is it possible to find an infinite number of such triples?
(It is well known that there are infinitely many prime numbers.)
List three more examples.

19.4 Find all right-angled triangles which have sides of integral measure and the lengths of the sides form

a an arithmetic progression,

b a geometric progression.

19.5 **a** Show that the integral sides of a right-angled triangle are in the ratio
$2rs : r^2 - s^2 : r^2 + s^2$ for positive integers r and s, where $r > s$.

b Show that the area of a right-angled triangle with integer sides is an integer.

c Show that if a, b and c are Pythagorean integers (i.e., $a^2 + b^2 = c^2$),
then abc is divisible by $a + b + c$.

19.6 A Pythagorean triple is a triple of 3 *positive* integers a, b and c which satisfy $a^2 + b^2 = c^2$.
Such a triple $a : b : c$ is called **primitive** if a, b and c have no factors in common (other than the factor 1). For example $3 : 4 : 5$ is primitive, whilst $6 : 8 : 10$ is not.

    a Show that every odd number greater than 1 is the smallest member of some primitive Pythagorean triple.

    b If $c - b$ is an odd prime, show that $a : b : c$ is *not* primitive.
       If $c - b = 2$,   then give 4 *primitive* Pythagorean triples.

19.7   **a** Show that if three integers form a Pythagorean triple,   i.e., they satisfy the equation
$a^2 + b^2 = c^2$,   then at least one of them is divisible by 3, at least one of them (not necessarily distinct from the first) is divisible by 4, and at least one of them (again not necessarily distinct from the first two) is divisible by 5.

    b Show that the area of a right-angled triangle with integer side lengths is divisible by 6.
    [For example: for $3 : 4 : 5$ the area $= 6$,   for $7 : 24 : 25$ the area $= 84$.]

19.8 Three positive integers a, b, c are the lengths of the sides of a rectangular box, and the positive integer d is the length of its diagonal. Investigate all possible values of a, b, c, d such that

    a the numbers a, b, c, d fall into two pairs of consecutive integers;

    b they include three consecutive integers.

MISCELLANEOUS

THE PROBLEMS

20.1 At Flinders University there are 1000
student lockers in the locker room.
On the first day of term, student 0001
opens every locker.
Then student 0002 closes every
second locker.
Student 0003 changes every third
locker (i.e., opens it if it was closed
and closes it if it was opened).
Student 0004 does the same with each
fourth locker.
Student 0005 does the same with each
fifth locker and so on until student
1000 changes only the 1000 th locker.
How many lockers are now open?

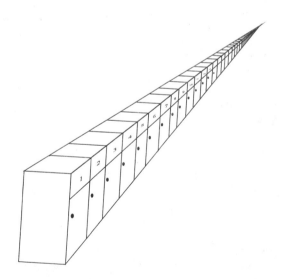

20.2 A four digit number has two digits the same and ends in 5. If the number is divisible by both 9 and
11, what is the number?

20.3

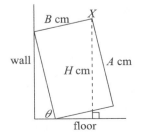

An A cm by B cm rectangular refrigerator leans at an angle
of θ to the floor against a wall.

a Find H in terns of A, B and θ.

b Explain how the figure can be used to prove that
$$A \sin \theta + B \cos \theta \leqslant \sqrt{A^2 + B^2}$$
with equality when $\tan \theta = \dfrac{A}{B}$.

20.4　A chess board (as illustrated) has 64 unit squares. 31 tiles are made, each one being 2 units by 1 unit. The tiles must not be cut or folded.

Can you find a tiling arrangement on the board so that all but two opposite corner squares remain uncovered.

20.5　Find all integers x and y such that $2x + y^3 = xy$.

20.6

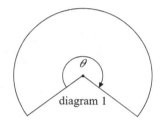

diagram 1

is formed into the cone

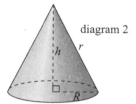

diagram 2

a　Explain why $R = \dfrac{r\theta}{2\pi}$.

b　What angle θ (in degrees) must be used to maximise the cone's volume given that the radius of the sector is fixed.

20.7

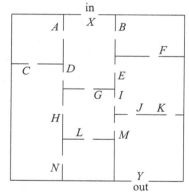

Farmer Brown has 8 paddocks with gates A, B, C, D, ..., M and N with the main gates at X and Y. She believes that she can find a way through the property going into it at gate X and leaving at gate Y and by going through each gate on the property *once only*.

However, she discovered that she had missed out one gate.

a　Which gate did she miss?

b　Explain why this gate was missed without actually working out her path.

20.8　A class room contains 5 desks per row and there are 5 rows. Now every student is required to move to a different *adjacent* desk, but must move left or right or front or back and *not diagonally.* Peta says it is possible. Paula doubts that it can be done. Which one is correct?

20.9　**The Butterfly Problem**

A circle centre O has chord $\overline{AB}$, (not the diameter). M is the midpoint of $\overline{AB}$. $\overline{EF}$ and $\overline{CD}$ are any two chords containing M. $\overline{CE}$ and $\overline{FD}$ intersect $\overline{AB}$ at points Q and P, respectively. Prove that $MP = MQ$.

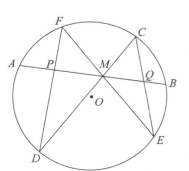

20.10 Partition a square into the smallest possible number of acute-angled triangles.

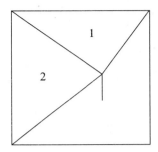

20.11 When $\begin{array}{r} AB \\ \times\, CD \\ \hline \end{array}$ is performed the answer is the same as that obtained when doing $\begin{array}{r} BA \\ \times\, DC \\ \hline \end{array}$.

How many possible solutions are there for A, B, C and D, given that they represent different digits?

20.12

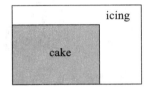

A rectangular slice of 'cake' has cake and icing as shown.

Show how to make a single straight line, knife cut to divide the 'cake' into two portions each containing equal amounts of cake and icing.

20.13 A right-angled triangle has integer length sides. The triangle has area and perimeter numerically equal. Find the triangles dimensions.

20.14

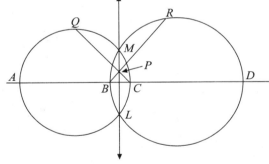

Two circles intersect at L and M. $\overleftrightarrow{ABCD}$ is the common diameter. If P is any point on $\overleftrightarrow{LM}$, $\overleftrightarrow{CP}$ produced and $\overrightarrow{BP}$ produced meet the circles at Q and R respectively, show that $\overrightarrow{AQ}$, $\overrightarrow{DR}$ and $\overleftrightarrow{LM}$ are concurrent.

20.15 Two circles with centres X and Y touch each other externally at Z. The circles also touch a larger circle, centre O, at P and Q respectively. $\overline{PZ}$ is produced to meet the large circle at A. $\overline{QZ}$ is produced to meet the large circle at B.

Prove that $\overline{AB}$ is a diameter of the large circle.

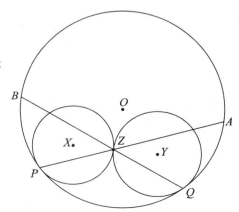

1983 MASA SENIOR MATHEMATICS COMPETITION

Time 3 hours

1 **a** Can the natural numbers from 1 to 30 be arranged in a 5×6 rectangular array (5 rows, 6 columns) in such a way that all **columns** have the same sum?

   b Can the natural numbers from 1 to 30 be arranged in a 5×6 rectangular array (5 rows, 6 columns) in such a way that all **rows** have the same sum?

2 A party of tourists decided to sit on a number of buses in such a way that each bus would contain the same number of tourists. At first they tried to sit 22 on each bus, but it turned out that one tourist was left over. But, by leaving one bus empty, the tourists were able to divide themselves equally among the remaining buses. If each bus held fewer than 45 people, how many buses and how many tourists were there originally?

3 Observe that: $6^3 - 6 = 210$
$$7^3 + 7 = 350$$
$$8^3 + 8 = 520$$

   Prove that if n is any positive integer, then either $n^3 + n$ or $n^3 - n$ ends with the digit zero.

4 Nine points are randomly selected in a square whose side has length one unit. Show that three of these points are the vertices of a triangle of area at most $\frac{1}{8}$ of a square unit.

5 $PABC$ is a triangular pyramid with 'vertex' at P and base ABC. We suppose that

   • ABC is an equilateral triangle, and
   • the angles PAB, PBC, PCA are equal.

   Show that $PA = PB = PC$.

6 Let S be a set consisting of 10 real numbers with the property that each of the numbers is greater than the sum of all the others.

   a Show that S contains at least one negative number.

   b Show that S contains at least three negative numbers.

   c Give an example of such a set S which contains 10 elements of which 7 are positive, 3 negative.

1984 MASA SENIOR MATHEMATICS COMPETITION

Time 3 hours

1 $100! = 100.99.98......3.2.1.$ sure is a big number.

    a In exactly how many zeros does it end?

    b What is the last non-zero digit equal to?

    c How many digits does it have?

2 If $x_1, x_2, x_3, ..., x_n$ are positive numbers, prove that

$$(x_1 + x_2 + x_3 + ... + x_n)(\frac{1}{x_1} + \frac{1}{x_2} + \frac{1}{x_3} + ... + \frac{1}{x_n}) \geqslant n^2.$$

3 A number is said to be **perfect** if the sum of its factors, including 1 but not the number itself, is equal to the number. For example, 6 is perfect since $6 = 1 + 2 + 3$.
Check also that 28 is perfect.

    a If p is an odd prime number, n is an integer, under what conditions will $2^n p$ be perfect?
       Use this to find another perfect number.

    b Are there perfect numbers of the type $3^n q$ where q is a prime number?
       Give reasons for your answer.

       [You may use the formula, $1 + x + x^2 + x^3 + ... + x^n = \dfrac{x^{n+1} - 1}{x - 1}$ in this question.]

4   **a** Prove that $\cos^3\phi - \frac{3}{4}\cos\phi - \frac{1}{4}\cos3\phi = 0.$

    b Solve $x^3 - 3x + 1 = 0$ [**Hint:** let $y = mx$]

    c Show that the equation $x^3 - 3px + q = 0$ has 3 real roots if and only if both

        i $p \geqslant 0,$ and

        ii $-2p^{\frac{3}{2}} \leqslant q \leqslant 2p^{\frac{3}{2}}.$

       Use this to give the general procedure for solving $x^3 - 3px + q = 0$ if this has 3 real roots.
       Your answer should indicate where you have used this fact.

5 What is the smallest square in which 5 identical squares with sides of unit length can be placed?
There is to be no overlapping of the unit squares.
[**Hint:** in proving reasons for your answer it may help to divide the covering square into 4 equal squares and decide that one of these must contain the centres of at least 2 of the 5 unit squares. What is the smallest possible area of this square?]

1985 MASA SENIOR MATHEMATICS COMPETITION

Time 3 hours

1 $7 = 4^2 - 3^2$

    a Express each **odd** integer between 0 and 10 as the difference between the squares of two integers.

    b Prove that **every** odd integer can be expressed as the difference between the squares of two integers.

    c Is a similar result true for even integers? If not, what can be said about the even integers?

2 The angles ACB, DCB and ADC are right angles in a tetrahedron $ABCD$. What is the maximum number and what is the minimum number of right angles between intersecting edges of this tetrahedron?

3 A number of simple checks in arithmetic are based on adding the digits of the numbers involved. Two examples will illustrate these checks.

    a Addition

$$
\begin{array}{r}
2356 \\
+\ 4781 \\
\hline
7137
\end{array}
$$

    Check: $2 + 3 + 5 + 6 = 16, \quad 1 + 6 = 7$
                $4 + 7 + 8 + 1 = 20, \quad 2 + 0 = 2$
                $7 + 1 + 3 + 7 = 18, \quad 1 + 8 = 9$

We have reduced all the numbers involved to single digits and $7 + 2 = 9$. This completes the check.

    b Multiplication

$$
\begin{array}{r}
62\,027 \\
\times\ 124 \\
\hline
7\,692\,348
\end{array}
$$

    Check: $6 + 2 + 0 + 2 + 7 = 17, \quad 1 + 7 = 8$
                  $1 + 2 + 4 = 7, \qquad\qquad 7,$
        $7 + 6 + 9 + 2 + 3 + 4 + 8 = 39, \quad 3 + 9 = 12, \quad 1 + 2 = 3.$

$8 \times 7 = 56$ and, since this is not a single digit, add $5 + 6 = 11$ and add the digits again to get $1 + 1 = 2$.

But $2 \neq 3$ and hence the answer is **wrong**.

    i Complete the multiplication **b** correctly, and show that the check works for this corrected example.

    ii Explain why the check for multiplication works. However, it is possible that a check might *work* for an incorrect multiplication. Can you give an example of this?

    iii Make up a similar check for long division and illustrate with an example which has a remainder.

4

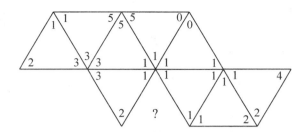

A trimino is a tile in the shape of an equilateral triangle. On each of the three corners on the face is a number from (0, 1, 2, 3, 4, 5). The back of the tile is blank. The game of triminoes is similar to dominoes. The first player places a tile face up on the table. For a tile to be played it must have at least one edge in common with the tiles already played, and all adjoining corners must have the same numbers. The above diagram shows a game in progress.

[**Note:**   No two triminoes in a set are the same.]

   a Explain why the space marked with ' ? ' in the above diagram cannot be filled for the given game.

   b How many "different" triminoes are there?

   c What is the sum of all the numbers on all the triminoes?

   d In dominoes the numbers run from 0 to 6. Why do you think they only go from 0 to 5 in triminoes?

> Dominoes are rectangular in shape and on each end is a number from 0 to 6 (example illustrated). In a game of dominoes pieces are added by each player in turn to either end of the line of pieces in such a way that the joining numbers are the same.

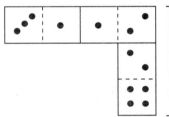

5 O is the centre of a unit circle. OAB is an equilateral triangle with sides of unit length. P is any point on the circumference of the circle. The lengths PA and PB are a and b units respectively. Show that $3(a^4 + b^4 + 2) = (a^2 + b^2 + 2)^2$.

Can you generalise this result?

1986 MASA SENIOR MATHEMATICS COMPETITION

Time 3 hours

1   **a** Try to use the digits of 1986 in the given order and the basic operations $+$, $-$, $\times$, $\div$ and exponentiation to produce all the integers from 1 to 12.

For example: $1^{986} = 1$ and $(1 + 9 + 8) \div 6 = 3$ are okay, but the following two are not:

$$(9 - 8) \times 1^6 = 1 \quad \text{(as order of digits is wrong)}$$
$$1 \times (\sqrt{9})^{(8-6)} = 9 \quad \text{(as } \sqrt{9} \text{ is not allowed)}$$

    b Using the above rules what is the biggest number you can make? How many digits does this number have?

2 On a certain day a 2 m rod was placed in a vertical position in Birdsville and an identical one in Adelaide. The shortest lengths cast by the rods on a horizontal plane were measured.
In Birdsville the length was 0.968 m.
In Adelaide the length was 1.396 m.
For the purpose of this question, Birdsville is 1010 km north of Adelaide.

    a Suppose the earth is a sphere and that the sun's rays are all parallel.
Use the above information to find the radius of the earth. (See diagram below).

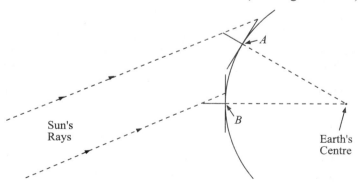

    b Suppose the earth is **flat** and that the sun is a single **point**. Use the above information to find the vertical distance of the sun from the surface of the earth.

3 Consider right angled triangles for which the lengths of all sides are integers. Find all such triangles which have their areas numerically equal to their perimeter. Your answer should include an explanation of why your list is complete.

4 **a** A square with sides of length 'n' units has one diagonal drawn across it from one corner to the opposite one. The square is divided into n^2 unit squares. How many of these unit squares do not have a diagonal drawn on them? Use this to find a formula for
$$1 + 2 + 3 + \ldots\ldots + n.$$

  b n lines are drawn in the plane so that no pair is parallel, and no three meet in a single point. Find

   i the number of regions into which the plane is divided,

   ii the number of these regions which do **not** extend to infinity.

5 Two rectangles will be called 'comparable' if one can be placed on top of the other such that

  • corresponding sides are parallel, and
  • one of the rectangles does not overlap the other.

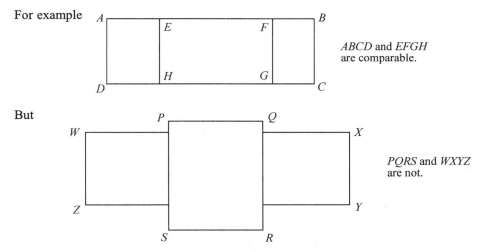

For example $ABCD$ and $EFGH$ are comparable.

But $PQRS$ and $WXYZ$ are not.

  a How many rectangles are there such that no pair is comparable?

  b Prove or disprove: "If two rectangles are **not** comparable, then one cannot be placed on top of the other without overlapping."

It should be clear that if any rectangle is cut into two rectangles, then the two rectangles are comparable.

  c **Prove** that if a rectangle is cut into three rectangles, at least two of these three rectangles are comparable.

   [**Hint:** one of the three smaller rectangles contains **two** corners of the original rectangle.]

  d Is a similar statement true if we cut a rectangle into four rectangles?

  e What if we cut a rectangle into five rectangles?
   [You should include an explanation in your answers.]

1987 MASA SENIOR MATHEMATICS COMPETITION

Time 3 hours

1 **a** A calculator represents numbers, as ten digits and a two digit exponent, in standard form   (i.e., scientific notation). How many different numbers can this calculator represent?

   b Find the exact value of $(33......37)^2$ where there are 1987 "3"s.

2 The following is problem 41 from the Egyptian Rhind papyrus.

   Problem 41:   Find the volume of a cylindrical granary of diameter 9 and height 10.

   Solution: Take $\frac{1}{9}$ of 9, namely 1 (from 9):   8 remains

                      Multiply 8 times 8:   it makes 64

                      Multiply 64 times 10:   it makes 640 cubed cubits.

   a Solve Problem 42 of the Rhind papyrus in a similar manner.

   Problem 42:   Find the volume of a cylindrical granary of diameter 10 and height 10.

   b What fraction did the Egyptians use to approximate π?

   c Replace the $\frac{1}{9}$ in the solution given to Problem 41 by a fraction $\dfrac{p}{q}$, with q as small as possible, to give a better approximation to the volume of the cylinder.

3 **a** Prove Pythagoras' theorem.
       [**Note:**   Neither the cosine rule nor the fact that $\sin^2\theta + \cos^2\theta = 1$ may be used without first proving these identities.]

   b Prove that the sum of the areas of the equilateral triangles on the two smaller sides of a right angled triangle is equal to the area of the equilateral triangle on the hypotenuse.

   c Show that the result in **b** is not true if the words "equilateral triangles" are replaced by "similar triangles".
       Under what conditions will the result be true for similar triangles? Give reasons for your answer.

   d Can this be generalised for "similar quadrilaterals"?

4 A manufacturer of balls buys rectangular slabs of rubber with dimensions 66 cm by 210 cm by 462 cm. To produce the balls the manufacturer cuts the slabs into cubes and then cuts the cubes into spheres. All the balls must be of the same size and have a diameter of at least $2\frac{1}{2}$ cm.
   In order of priority the manufacturer also wants to

   a minimise the amount of rubber wasted,

   b have the balls as big as possible (and at least $2\frac{1}{2}$ cm diameter as stated before).

What size balls should he produce? Give reasons for your answer.

5 An integer, m, is **abundant** if the sum of its factors, not including m, is larger than m.

   For example 12 has factors 1, 2, 3, 4 and 6.

   Since $1 + 2 + 3 + 4 + 6 = 16 > 12$,   12 is abundant.

   a Find another four numbers that are abundant.

   b Show that p^k where k is an integer and p is a prime number, cannot be abundant.

   c Find an odd integer which is abundant.

   [**Hint:** Calculate $\frac{1}{3} + \frac{1}{5} + \frac{1}{7} + \frac{1}{9} + \frac{1}{11} + \frac{1}{13} + \frac{1}{15}$]

   d Find an odd integer less than 2000 which is abundant.

1988 MASA SENIOR MATHEMATICS COMPETITION

Time 3 hours

1 Express 1988 as the sum of consecutive positive integers in as many different ways as you can.

2

$$
\begin{array}{r}
T\ W\ E\ N\ T\ Y \\
T\ W\ E\ N\ T\ Y \\
+\quad T\ H\ I\ R\ T\ Y \\
\hline
S\ E\ V\ E\ N\ T\ Y
\end{array}
$$

Each different letter represents a different digit from 0 to 9 and, of course, neither S nor T is to be zero. Find all possible solutions.

3 **a** Why does the angle of a regular polygon of n sides have measure $(n-2).\dfrac{180^o}{n}$?

    b Find all the regular polygons that tesselate the plane. The word **tesselate** merely means that figures of the same size and shape can be fitted together like tiles leaving no gaps between them.
    [**Hint:** what can you say about the sum of the angles about any vertex?]

    c Bees measure length in a unit called a "b", 1 square b being a comfortable area for a cell. The latest buzz amongst the new generation bees is for cells with the shape of equilateral triangles instead of the old fashioned hexagonally shaped cells. Not only do they reckon the shape is really something, but you can join these cells together into the shape of a large equilateral triangle bounded by straight edges and that's something you can't do with hexagons. No matter how bees shape a flat frame using hexagons, the edges can never be straight, but must be serrated. So the new bees argue that you would get a better shape *and* use less wax. Now, the old fuddy duddies don't care much about the new fangled shape, but the economy argument sets them thinking and they grudgingly agree to a trial.

    The agreement is that each group will construct a frame of 169 cells. Each cell will have an area of 1 square b. The new bees will form their cells into a large equilateral triangle while the oldies will form their cells into a regular hexagon.

    Which of the two frames uses the lesser amount of wax, and what is the difference?

4 If x and y are real numbers show that $(x^2 - y^2)^2 + (2xy)^2 = (x^2 + y^2)^2$.

Hence, or otherwise, find at least 4 Pythagorean triplets, i.e., integers m, n and p which are the lengths of 3 sides of a right angled triangle.

Examine the product of the triplets you have found. What do you observe? Will this be true for all Pythagorean triplets? Give reasons for your answer.

5 **a** Consider the equation $x^4 + ax^3 + bx^2 + cx + d = 0$.

This can be changed into an equation in y by letting $x = y + k$ where k is some constant. How should k be selected to change the equation to one of the form

$$y^4 + By^2 + Cy + D = 0,$$

i.e., a polynomial equation without the y^3 term?

b A 4 m ladder is leaning against a wall while one point of the ladder just touches a cubic box which is pushed against the wall and has edges of 1 m. See diagram.

Find the distance between the top of the ladder and the point of contact with the box.

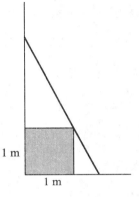

1 m

1 m

1989 MASA SENIOR MATHEMATICS COMPETITION

Time 3 hours

1 Which of the two expressions is of greater numerical value,

$$1989^{1989} \quad \text{or} \quad 1988^{1989} + 1989^{1988}?$$

2 X and Y are two motorists, driving in opposite directions from the South Australian city A and the Victorian city B respectively. The distance along the highway between the two cities is 670 km.

The two motorists meet at a service station on the road, and begin a conversation.

X looking at his watch, tells Y:

'This is interesting. It is just mid-day now. This is my first stop. I left A on the hour, and I have kept a pretty steady 110 kmph speed.'

'I have also left on the hour', laughs Y, 'but I have travelled only at 100 kmph'.

'You may have driven more slowly, but you have an advantage, because Victorian time is half an hour ahead of South Australian time', answers X.

What time did each of the drivers start, and how far is the service station from A?

3 A solid pyramid shaped monument has a square $ABCD$ of side 40 m long for its base, and equilateral triangles for its sloping faces. The top of the monument is T. What is the height of T above ground-level?

A sculpture is to be placed at P, the *centre* of the face TBC. An external stairway leading from A to P is also proposed. It is to lead along the faces TAB and TBC, intersecting the edge $\overline{TB}$ at E, and must be of the *shortest possible length*.

Find this length. Also find the angle, α, between $\overline{AE}$ and $\overline{AB}$.

Now find a better estimate than α for the steepness of the stairway at A. Comment on the section $\overline{EP}$ of the stairway.

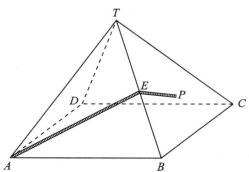

4 Beginning with an arbitary triangle ABC, we construct a sequence of nested triangles in the following manner.

    a *Going inwards:* Let the incircle of the triangle ABC touch the sides $\overline{BC}$, $\overline{CA}$, $\overline{AB}$ in I_1, J_1, K_1 respectively.

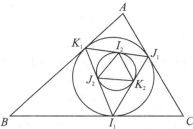

    Next construct the incircle of $\Delta I_1 J_1 K_1$, touching at I_2, J_2, K_2 the sides $\overline{J_1 K_1}$, $\overline{K_1 I_1}$, $\overline{I_1 J_1}$ respectively.

    We continue in the same manner, constructing the incircle of $\Delta I_2 J_2 K_2$ obtaining the triangle $I_3 J_3 K_3$ at the points of contact on the sides of $\Delta I_2 J_2 K_2$, and so on.

    b *Going outwards:* Construct the circumcircle of ΔABC and let the tangents to the circumcircle at A, B and C intersect at the points Z_1, X_1 and Y_1 respectively.

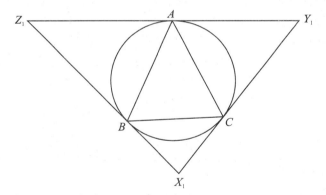

    We continue, by drawing the circumcircle of $\Delta X_1 Y_1 Z_1$ and find the triangle $X_2 Y_2 Z_2$ at the intersections of the tangents to the second circumcircle $X_1 Y_1 Z_1$, and so on.

      i Consider, as an example, a triangle with angles 40°, 60°, 80°.
      Determine as accurately as you can the angles of $I_5 J_5 K_5$.

      ii Can we continue indefinitely our constructions **a** and **b**, provided that we have an ideally large drawing board, and ideally fine drawing instruments?

      iii Can we obtain an equilateral triangle by continuing the procedures **a** or **b**?

Justify your answers algebraically.

5 The well known Pascal triangle

$$
\begin{array}{ccccccccccccc}
&&&&&& 1 &&&&&& \\
&&&&& 1 && 1 &&&&& \\
&&&& 1 && 2 && 1 &&&& \\
&&& 1 && 3 && 3 && 1 &&& \\
&& 1 && 4 && 6 && 4 && 1 && \\
& 1 && 5 && 10 && 10 && 5 && 1 & \\
1 && 6 && 15 && 20 && 15 && 6 && 1
\end{array}
$$

makes the calculations of the binomial coefficients easy.

[To refresh your memory: the binomial coefficient, $\dbinom{n}{r} = \dfrac{n(n-1)(n-2)\ldots\ldots(n-r+1)}{1.2.3\ldots\ldots r}$

gives the number of ways in which a team of r members can be chosen out of a set of n people.]

The construction of the Pascal array is based on the identity

$$\binom{n}{r} = \binom{n-1}{r-1} + \binom{n-1}{r}.$$

We can use a similar array for evaluating combinatorial expressions of a different type.

Let $S(n, r)$ denote the number of ways in which *a set of n persons can be divided into r subsets so that each person belongs to exactly one subset, and each subset contains at least one person.*

Thus $S(1, 1) = 1$ and $S(2, 1) = S(2, 2) = 1$ since there is exactly one way in which 2 persons can be assigned to one set, and one way in which 2 persons can be divided into two subsets.

It is easily seen that $S(3, 1) = 1$, $S(3, 2) = 3$, $S(3, 3) = 1$.

More interesting is the example $S(4, 2) = 7$.

To see this, regard the set a, b, c, d. The ways to divide it into two subsets are:

a	bcd
b	acd
c	abd
d	abc
ab	cd
ac	bd
ad	bc

It follows from the meaning of $S(n, 0) = S(n, n+1) = 0$ for all n.

You should be ready now to answer the following questions:

a Prove that $S(n, r) = S(n-1, r-1) + r\,S(n-1, r)$ ...... (*)
for all $n \geqslant 2$ and all r where $1 \leqslant r \leqslant n$.

b Using (*) we can construct the array for evaluating $S(n, r)$. The first rows of the array are

$$
\begin{array}{lccccccc}
n=1 & & & & 1 & & & \\
n=2 & & & 1 & & 1 & & \\
n=3 & & 1 & & 3 & & 1 & \\
n=4 & 1 & & 7 & & 6 & & 1
\end{array}
$$

Find the values of $S(5, 2)$ and $S(6, 3)$.

c Prove that $S(n, 2) = 2^{n-1} - 1$ and $S(n, n-1) = \dbinom{n}{2}$, for all $n \geqslant 2$.

1990 MASA SENIOR MATHEMATICS COMPETITION

Time 3 hours

1   Fifteen people meet at a chess club. Everyone plays at least one game of chess but never twice against the same opponent. Show the following:

   a   There are at least two people in the club who play the same number of games.

   b   If every participant plays the same number of games, then that number is even.

   c   Suppose that each player has to play one game against everyone else, but the meeting is too short for this, so they have to continue another time. Show that the number of games played on the two occasions cannot be equal.

2   What are the last four digits (in the decimal system) of 5^{1990}?

   Finding the answer is good. Showing your method is even better. Giving complete justification is excellent.

3   Triangle ABC is isosceles with $AB = AC$.
   The angle at vertex A is 36°.
   The base $\overline{BC}$ is produced to D so that $CD = AB$.
   A semicircle is drawn with $\overline{BD}$ as diameter.
   E is a point on the semicircle such that $BE = AB$.

   Show that $\overline{EC}$ is perpendicular to $\overline{BD}$.

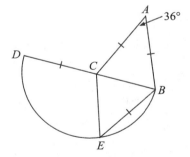

4 It is known that all natural numbers can be written in the binary system, using only 0 and 1 as digits.

For example, $[11011001]_2 = 2^7 + 2^6 + 2^4 + 2^3 + 2^0 = 217$.

This means that all natural numbers can be represented uniquely as sums of *different* powers of 2.

The question now is the following: If (-2) is used as a *base* instead of 2, can *all* integers (negative or positive) be expressed as a sum of different powers of (-2)?

Examples:

$$[1011001]_{(-2)} = (-2)^6 + (-2)^4 + (-2)^3 + (-2)^0 = 73$$
$$[11011001]_{(-2)} = (-2)^7 + (-2)^6 + (-2)^4 + (-2)^3 + (-2)^0 = -55.$$

a What can you say about an integer in this sytem if its number of digits is even?
b Can all integers be represented as sums of different powers of (-2)?
c If a number can be represented as a sum of different powers of (-2), is the representation unique?

---

5 $\overline{XY}$, $\overline{YZ}$ and $\overline{ZX}$ are the sides of an acute angled triangle. The centres of the sides are C, A, B respectively.

Using the triangle ABC for base, fold the other three triangles up so that X, Y and Z meet in a common vertex, named V, forming a tetrahedron $VABC$.

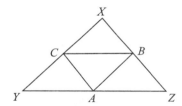

a What can you say about the pairs of opposite edges of this tetrahedron (e.g., $\overline{AB}$ and $\overline{VC}$)?
b Show that the line segments joining the midpoints of each pair of opposite edges bisect each other perpendicularly.

1991 MASA SENIOR MATHEMATICS COMPETITION

Time 3 hours

1 For what values of n can $2^n + 1$ be a perfect square?

2 In triangle ABC, angle $ABC = 75^o$ and angle $BAC = 45^o$. The altitude drawn from vertex A meets side $\overline{BC}$ at D and the altitude from C meets $\overline{AB}$ in F. The line through F, perpendicular to $\overline{AC}$ meets $\overline{AC}$ in G.

Prove $AG = GD$.

3 Prove that $\sqrt{\underbrace{1111........11}_{2n \text{ digits}} - \underbrace{22......2}_{n \text{ digits}}} = \underbrace{33......3}_{n \text{ digits}}$

i.e., prove that a positive integer written in the decimal system by n digits, all equal to 2, subtracted from another positive integer consisting of $2n$ digits, all equal to 1, is the square of a positive integer of n digits, all equal to 3.

4 $PQRS$ is a trapezium where $\overline{PQ}$ is parallel to $\overline{RS}$ and the length of the side $\overline{QR}$ is equal to the sum of the parallel sides. Let T be the midpoint of side $\overline{SP}$.

Find the size of angle QTR.

5 Solve the system of equations:
$$x_1 + 2x_2 + 3x_3 + 4x_4 = 10$$
$$x_2 + 2x_3 + 3x_4 + 4x_1 = 10$$
$$x_3 + 2x_4 + 3x_1 + 4x_2 = 10$$
$$x_4 + 2x_1 + 3x_2 + 4x_3 = 10$$

6 The sum of seven distinct positive integers is 100.
Show that the sum of the three largest of these integers is at least 50.

1992 MASA SENIOR MATHEMATICS COMPETITION

Time 3 hours

1   What is the sum of the coefficients in the expansion of the following polynomial?

$(w^1 - 9x^9 + 9y^9 - 2z^2)^{1992}$

2   The fire alarm at Melbourne Grammar goes off at 6.39 pm precisely. The distance between Melbourne Grammar and the Metropolitan Fire Station is 4.40 km. The fire alarm travels at the speed of sound through air (330 ms^{-1}). The firefighters are notified in 50 times the time it took the message to reach the station. Each of the five firefighters goes into the dressing room in turn and gets changed, each fire fighter taking 5 seconds less than the previous one. Then it takes 7 times the fourth fire fighter's changing time to get the fire engine out onto the road. They travel with an average speed of 42.3 km/hr. They reach Melbourne Grammar at 7:06 pm (on the same evening!) to find a worried looking boy who is about to burst into tears. How long did it take the second firefighter to get changed?

3   **a**   Solve the following set of 3 equations, $xy = 1$
$$xz = 4$$
$$yz = 9$$

     b   Solve this set of 4 equations, $pqr = 1$
$$pqs = 4$$
$$prs = 9$$
$$qrs = 16$$

     c   Now solve the general set of n equations, $a_2a_3a_4\ldots\ldots a_n = 1^2$
$$a_1a_3a_4\ldots\ldots a_n = 2^2$$
$$\vdots \qquad\qquad \vdots$$
$$a_1a_2a_3\ldots\ldots a_{n-1} = n^2$$

4   A quadrilateral-shaped frame has pivots at its corners and can move freely. Show that, if its diagonals are ever at right angles, then they are always at right angles.

5   **a** Given a circle, centre O, radius r, with chords $\overline{RS}$ and $\overline{UT}$ intersecting externally at P, prove that $PS.PR = PT.PU = PO^2 - r^2$.

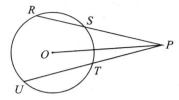

   b In the following diagram (not to scale), $AO = OE$,

prove that $\dfrac{AB}{CD} = \dfrac{DE}{AB} = \dfrac{BC}{DE}$.

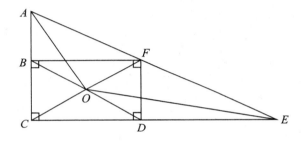

1993 MASA SENIOR MATHEMATICS COMPETITION

Time 3 hours

1   If 4 points are marked on a circle, 6 chords can be drawn joining the points.

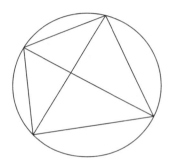

   a   How many chords can be drawn when there are:

   i   5 points,
   ii   10 points,
   iii n points.

   b   In the preliminary round of a netball competition, each team plays each other team once. If 66 games are played, how many teams are entered?

2   A colony of fairy penguins is to be relocated. Fairy penguins always travel by bus and they insist that the same number of fairy penguins travel on each bus. Initially 36 get on each bus, but they find that there are five penguins left over. They get one more bus and discover that they can divide themselves equally onto each bus with none left over. How many fairy penguins are in the colony?

3   You are given 6 balls, which appear identical except that 1 is white and 5 are black. You are also told that the white and 4 of the black balls are of the same weight, while the remaining black ball is of a different weight. All you have available is a balance (i.e., a pair of scales) which can be used to compare the weights of two sets of balls, but cannot be used to find their actual weights. Show how to work out which is the black ball with different weight in just two weight comparisions.

   Does your method enable you to distinguish which balls are heavier/lighter? If not, can you suggest two comparisons that will do this?

4   The following diagram represents five identical adjacent squares.

   Show that $\alpha = \beta$.

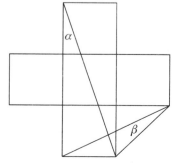

5   An oil slick in the ocean is observed to be a convex pentagon. The next day each edge has moved 40 metres outwards.

Prove that the area of the slick has increased by at least 5000 square metres.

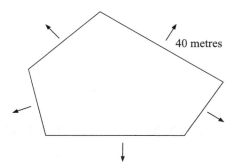

40 metres

6   If n is a non-negative integer,

    a   prove that 3^n has a remainder of either 1 or 3 when divided by 8,

    b   prove that the number $3^n + 2 \times 17^n$ is never a perfect square.

7   Scratch the kitten is playing with a spherical ball when it rolls into the corner of the room. Scratch's owner then places another larger ball in the same corner such that both balls are touching both walls (and the floor, of course) and they are also touching each other.

What is the radius of the kitten's ball, if the larger ball has a radius of 20 cm?

1994 MASA SENIOR MATHEMATICS COMPETITION

Time 3 hours

1 None of the digits in 1994 are prime.

Using each of the four digits only once and using the operations of addition, subtraction, multiplication and division as often as you like, how many different prime numbers can you make?
[For example, $9 - 9 + 4 + 1 = 5$.]

[**Note:** Brackets may be used, but numbers like 99 or 941, etc., may not.]

2 Triangle ABC has point P lying anywhere on $\overline{BC}$. Suppose the circle through A, P and C has centre M, and the circle through A, P and B has centre N.

Prove

    a triangles ANM and PNM are congruent,

    b triangles PNM and ABC are similar.

3   **a** Find the smallest number k that gives a remainder of 1 when divided by 2, a remainder of 2 when divided by 3 and a remainder of 3 when divided by 4.

    b Find the smallest number n such that:

      n gives a remainder of 1 when divided by 2,
      n gives a remainder of 2 when divided by 3,
      n gives a remainder of 3 when divided by 4,

$$\vdots \qquad \vdots \qquad \vdots \qquad \vdots$$

      n gives a remainder of 8 when divided by 9.

4 Show, without using a calculator, that $\sqrt{2 + \sqrt{2}} + \sqrt{2 - \sqrt{2}} < 2\sqrt{2}$.

5 The function f satisfies:

$$f(x + f(y)) + f(f(x)) + y, \quad \text{for all real numbers } x \text{ and } y, \text{ and } f(0) = c, \quad \text{a constant.}$$

Find $f(x)$ for all real x.

6 **a** Show that for some real number p

$$1 + p + p^2 + p^3 + \ldots\ldots + p^k = \frac{p^{k+1} - 1}{p - 1}.$$

b For prime number p, the sum of the factors of p^k is given by

$$\sigma(p^k) = 1 + p + p^2 + \ldots\ldots + p^k$$

[For example, $\sigma(3^4) = 1 + 3 + 9 + 27 + 81$]

If p and q are prime numbers show that: $\sigma(p^k q) = \sigma(p^k).\sigma(q)$

c For the distinct primes $p_1, p_2, p_3, \ldots, p_k$, $\sigma(n) = \sigma(p_1{}^{a_1}).\sigma(p_2{}^{a_2})\ldots\ldots\sigma(p_k{}^{a_k})$
where $a \geqslant 1$.

Prove that $\sigma(n) = \left(\dfrac{p_1{}^{a_1+1} - 1}{p_1 - 1} \right) \left(\dfrac{p_2{}^{a_2+1} - 1}{p_2 - 1} \right) \ldots\ldots \left(\dfrac{p_k{}^{a_k+1}}{p_k - 1} \right).$

7 Given two lengths a and b, we construct a triangle AOB as shown, with $AO = a$, $OB = b$ and $\angle AOB = \theta$.

An equilateral triangle ABC is constructed on $\overline{AB}$.

What value at θ maximizes the length OC, and what is its maximum length?

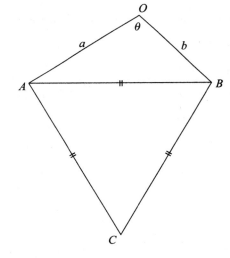

1995 MASA SENIOR MATHEMATICS COMPETITION

Time 3 hours

1   **a**   Find all the factors of 1995.

  b   Any positive integer $P \geqslant 1$ can be represented in prime factor form as

$$p_1{}^a \times p_2{}^b \times p_3{}^c \times \ \ldots\ldots$$

where p_1, p_2, p_3,...... are different prime numbers and a, b, c, ... are positive integers.
Explain why the number of factors of P is $(a+1)(b+1)(c+1)$......

  c   Find all the numbers less than 400 which have exactly 16 factors (including themselves and 1).

2   The quadrilateral $ABCD$ is cyclic, i.e., it can be inscribed in a circle as shown. The diameter of the circle is $\overline{CD}$. If $AB = BC = 15$ and $CD = 50$, find the length of $\overline{AD}$.

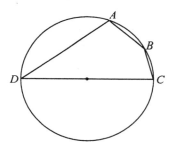

3   Suppose a is a positive odd number and n is any positive integer.

Let $N = a^{2^n} - 1$.

Prove that

  a 2^{n+1} divides N,

  b 2^{n+2} divides N.

4   Each term in the Fibonnacci sequence is obtained by adding the previous two terms, where the first two terms are both 1:

$$1,\ 1,\ 2,\ 3,\ 5,\ 8,\ 13,\ 21,\ 34,\ 55,\ 89,\ \ldots\ldots$$

Show that

  a   every third number is even;

  b   every fourth number is divisible by three;

  c   every fifth number is divisible by five.

5 **a** Find all the solutions in positive integers x and y, to the equation:

$$1xy + 9x + 9y + 5 = 1995.$$

    b Show that there is no solution, in integers x and y, to the equation:

$$\frac{1}{xy} + \frac{1}{9x} + \frac{1}{9y} + \frac{1}{5} = 1.$$

6 **a** From an 8×8 chessboard we remove two diagonally opposite corner squares. Show that it is not possible to cover exactly (i.e., without gaps or overlap) the resulting shape with dominoes, each the same size as two chessboard squares.

    b In general, given an $m \times n$ chessboard with two opposite corner squares removed, when is it possible to cover exactly the resulting shape with dominoes?
[You may assume m and $n \geqslant 2$.]

7 **a** Let a regular pentagon have edges of length 2.

    Show that it has diagonals of length $2\,\tau$, where $\tau = \dfrac{1 + \sqrt{5}}{2}$

    b Find the volume of a regular dodecahedron which has edges of length 2 units.
(A regular dodecahedron has 12 regular pentagonal faces, 3 meeting at each vertex.)

> Hint: A cube can be embedded in the dodecahedron as shown (one of the faces of the cube is shaded). Then the volume of the dodecahedron is the volume of the cube plus the volumes of the six identical caps which have been added to the faces of the cube.]

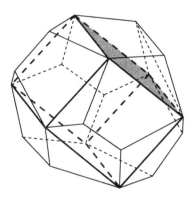

SOLUTIONS
TO PROBLEMS

I. PYTHAGORAS

1.1 Let M, N be midpoints of $\overline{AB}$ and $\overline{BC}$ respectively.

In $\triangle ABN$, $(2c)^2 + a^2 = 9$

i.e. $a^2 + 4c^2 = 9$........(1)

Also in $\triangle MBC$, $4a^2 + c^2 = 16$........(2)

adding (1) and (2), $5a^2 + 5c^2 = 25$

$\therefore a^2 + c^2 = 5$........(3)

Now $(AC)^2 = (2a)^2 + (2c)^2$

$= 4(a^2 + c^2)$

$= 20$ {using (3)}

$\therefore$ the hypotenuse is $\underline{\sqrt{20}}$ cm (or $2\sqrt{5}$ cm) long.

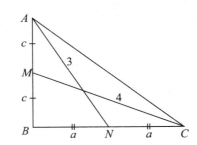

1.2 In $\triangle ABD$,

i.e. $BD = 4$ cm

$\therefore EF = 4$ cm also.

But in $\triangle AEC$,

$EC = \sqrt{(4+r)^2 - (4-r)^2}$

$= \sqrt{16r}$

$= 4\sqrt{r}$

and in $\triangle CBF$

$CF = \sqrt{(1+r)^2 - (1-r)^2}$

$= \sqrt{4r}$

$= 2\sqrt{r}$

Thus as $EF = EC + CF$

then $4 = 4\sqrt{r} + 2\sqrt{r}$

i.e., $\sqrt{r} = \frac{2}{3}$

$\therefore r = \frac{4}{9}$.

$\therefore$ the smallest circle has radius $\underline{\frac{4}{9}}$ cm.

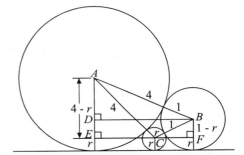

1.3 Let Q have y-coordinate y, and the circle have radius r.
Now if the square has sides of length $2a$,
then in $\triangle OCD$,

$a^2 + (2a)^2 = r^2$ {Pythagoras}

$\therefore 5a^2 = r^2$

But $(2a)^2 = \frac{1}{2}.2r.y$ {equating areas}

$\therefore 4a^2 = ry$

$\therefore \frac{ry}{4} = \frac{r^2}{5}$ {equating a^2's}

$\therefore y = \frac{4r}{5}$ {as $r \neq 0$}

$\therefore$ x-coordinate of $Q = \pm\frac{3r}{5}$ {as $x^2 + y^2 = r^2$}

$\therefore Q$ is at $\left(\frac{3r}{5}, \frac{4r}{5}\right)$ or at $\left(-\frac{3r}{5}, \frac{4r}{5}\right)$

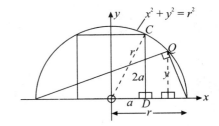

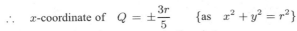

1.4 **a** $(R+1)^2 = y^2 + (R-1)^2$

$$\therefore \quad y^2 = (R+1)^2 - (R-1)^2$$
$$= [R+1+R-1][R+1-R+1]$$
$$= 2R.2$$
$$= 4R$$
$$\underline{y = 2\sqrt{R}}$$

Likewise

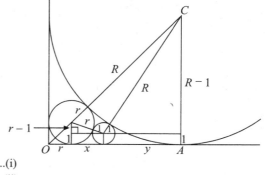

b $(r+1)^2 = x^2 + (r-1)^2$

$$\therefore \quad \underline{x = 2\sqrt{r}}$$

But $r + x + y = R$ (length of OA)..........(i)

and $R + r + \sqrt{2}r = \sqrt{2}R$ (length of OC)..........(ii)

In (i) $r + 2\sqrt{r} + 2\sqrt{R} = R$

$$\therefore \quad 2(\sqrt{R} + \sqrt{r}) = R - r$$
$$\therefore \quad 2(\sqrt{R} + \sqrt{r}) = (\sqrt{R} + \sqrt{r})(\sqrt{R} - \sqrt{r})$$
$$\therefore \quad \sqrt{R} - \sqrt{r} = 2 \qquad \{\text{as} \quad \sqrt{R} + \sqrt{r} \neq 0\}$$

Thus in (ii) $r(1 + \sqrt{2}) = R(\sqrt{2} - 1)$

$$\therefore \quad \frac{R}{r} = \frac{1+\sqrt{2}}{\sqrt{2}-1} \frac{R}{r} = \left(\frac{1+\sqrt{2}}{\sqrt{2}-1}\right)\left(\frac{\sqrt{2}+1}{\sqrt{2}+1}\right) = (1+\sqrt{2})^2$$

$$\therefore \quad \sqrt{R} = (1+\sqrt{2})\sqrt{r} \quad ....(*)$$

Thus $(1+\sqrt{2})\sqrt{r} - \sqrt{r} = 2$

$$\therefore \quad \sqrt{2r} = 2$$
$$\therefore \quad 2r = 4$$
$$\therefore \quad r = 2$$

Thus in * $\sqrt{R} = 2 + \sqrt{r} = 2 + \sqrt{2}$

$$\therefore \quad R = (2+\sqrt{2}) = 6 + 4\sqrt{2}$$

$\therefore$ larger circle has radius $\underline{(6+4\sqrt{2})\text{ cm}}$ and smaller circle has radius $\underline{2\text{ cm}}$.

1.5 Since $C = 2\pi r = 40000$

then $r = \dfrac{20000}{\pi} \approx 6366 \text{ km}$

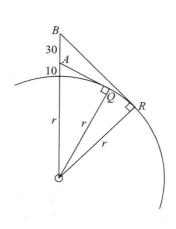

Now $(AQ)^2 = (r + \frac{1}{100})^2 - r^2$

$$= \frac{r}{50} + \frac{1}{10000} \approx \frac{r}{50}$$

$$\therefore \quad AQ \approx 11.28 \text{ km}......(1)$$

Likewise, $(BR)^2 = (r + \frac{4}{100})^2 - r^2$

$$\therefore \quad (BR)^2 \approx \frac{2r}{25}$$

$$\therefore \quad BR \approx 22.56 \text{ km}......(2)$$

Thus, from (1) and (2),   arc $QR \approx BR - AQ$

$$\approx \underline{11.28 \text{ km}}$$

Now in 1 day $(24 \times 60 \times 60 \text{ secs})$,   earth spins through 40000 km.

$\therefore$ it takes $\dfrac{24 \times 60 \times 60}{40000}$ secs to spin through 1 km.

$\therefore$ time delay of sunset $= \dfrac{24 \times 60 \times 60}{40000} \times 11.28 \text{ secs} \approx \underline{24.36 \text{ secs}}$

1.6 $\dfrac{AT}{r} = \dfrac{\frac{\sqrt{3}a}{2}}{\frac{a}{2}} = \sqrt{3}$ {$\triangle ATE$ and $\triangle ACB$ are similar}

$\therefore \quad \underline{AT = \sqrt{3}r}$

Thus in $\triangle ABC$

$$(\sqrt{3}r + r)^2 + \left(\frac{a}{2}\right)^2 = \left(\frac{\sqrt{3}a}{2}\right)^2$$

$\therefore \quad (\sqrt{3}+1)^2 r^2 = \dfrac{3a^2}{4} - \dfrac{a^2}{4} = \dfrac{a^2}{2}$

$\therefore \quad (\sqrt{3}+1)r = \dfrac{a}{\sqrt{2}}$

$\therefore \quad r = \dfrac{a}{\sqrt{6}+\sqrt{2}} \cdot \dfrac{\sqrt{6}-\sqrt{2}}{\sqrt{6}-\sqrt{2}}$

$\therefore \quad \boxed{r = a\left[\dfrac{\sqrt{6}-\sqrt{2}}{4}\right]}$

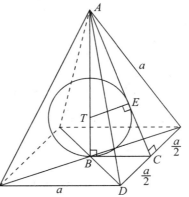
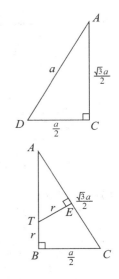

1.7 $OX = \sqrt{(x-2)^2 - 2^2}$ {Pythagoras}

$OY = \sqrt{(x-1)^2 - 1^2}$

$\therefore \quad \sqrt{x^2 - 4x} + \sqrt{x^2 - 2x} = \sqrt{8}$ {see $\triangle PQR$}

$\therefore \quad \sqrt{x^2 - 4x} = \sqrt{8} - \sqrt{x^2 - 2x}$

which, on squaring and simplifying twice gives

$\qquad 8(x^2 - 2x) = 16 + 8x + x^2$

$\therefore \quad 8x^2 - 16x - 16 - 8x - x^2 = 0$

$\therefore \quad 7x^2 - 24x - 16 = 0$

$\therefore \quad (x-4)(7x+4) = 0$

$\therefore \quad x = 4 \text{ or } -\frac{4}{7}$

$\therefore \quad$ height is $\underline{4 \text{ m}}$

Note: This occurs when larger pipe is in centre of tunnel. i.e. $\underline{X \text{ is at } O}$.

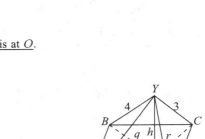

1.8 AX, BX, CX, DX in this diagram
are the shadows of AY, BY, CY, DY
on plane $ABCD$.

By Pythagoras' Theorem, $\begin{cases} p^2 = a^2 + c^2 \\ q^2 = a^2 + d^2 \\ r^2 = b^2 + d^2 \\ s^2 = b^2 + c^2 \end{cases}$

$\therefore \quad p^2 + r^2 = q^2 + s^2$ {as both $= a^2 + b^2 + c^2 + d^2$}

Now $\begin{cases} x^2 = s^2 + h^2 \\ 3^2 = h^2 + r^2 \\ 4^2 = h^2 + q^2 \\ 6^2 = h^2 + p^2 \end{cases}$

$\qquad$ But $p^2 + r^2 = q^2 + s^2$

$\therefore \quad 36 - h^2 + 9 - h^2 = 16 - h^2 + x^2 - h^2$

$\therefore \qquad 45 = 16 + x^2$

$\therefore \qquad 29 = x^2$

$\therefore \qquad x = \sqrt{29} \text{ as } x > 0.$

$\therefore \quad DY$ is $\underline{\sqrt{29} \text{ cm}}$.

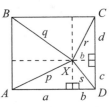

[View from above]

1.9 Suppose it is right-angled at B.

$$\therefore \quad b^2 = a^2 + c^2$$
$$\text{But} \quad a^2 = q^2 + r^2$$
$$b^2 = p^2 + r^2$$
$$c^2 = p^2 + q^2$$
$$\text{Thus} \quad p^2 + r^2 = q^2 + r^2 + p^2 + q^2$$
$$\therefore \quad 2q^2 = 0$$
$$\therefore \quad q = 0 \quad \text{which is a contradiction as} \quad q > 0$$

$\therefore \quad B$ cannot be right-angled.
Likewise A and C <u>cannot be right-angled.</u>

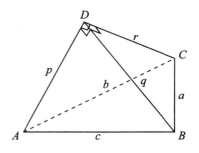

1.10 C_1 lies on a line joining A to the opposite
vertex of a cube with sides r units.

$$\therefore \quad AC_1 = \sqrt{r^2 + r^2 + r^2} \quad \text{\{3-D Pythagorean formula.\}}$$
$$\therefore \quad AC_1 = \sqrt{3}r$$
$$\text{Likewise} \quad AC_2 = \sqrt{3}R$$
$$\text{Now} \quad AC_2 = AC_1 + C_1C_2$$
$$\therefore \quad \sqrt{3}R = \sqrt{3}r + R + r$$
$$\therefore \quad (\sqrt{3} - 1)R = (\sqrt{3} + 1)r$$

$$\therefore \quad R = \frac{\sqrt{3}+1}{\sqrt{3}-1}r$$

$$\therefore \quad R = \left(\frac{\sqrt{3}+1}{\sqrt{3}-1}\right)\left(\frac{\sqrt{3}+1}{\sqrt{3}+1}\right)r = \left(\frac{4+2\sqrt{3}}{2}\right)r = \underline{(2+\sqrt{3})r}$$

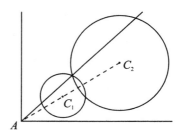

2. PROBLEM SOLVING

2.1 Let the motorist leave A at m kmph,
the cyclist leave B at c kmph.
At the end of 1 hour, the motorist has travelled
m km and the cyclist, c km.

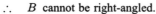

$$\therefore \quad m + 27 + c = 85 \qquad \therefore \quad m + c = 58 ....(1)$$

After   90 mins $= 1\frac{1}{2}$ hours,   the motorist has travelled $\frac{3m}{2}$ km   and the cyclist $\frac{5c}{4}$ km.

Thus $\frac{3m}{2} + \frac{5c}{4} = 85 \qquad \therefore \quad 6m + 5c = 340 ....(2) \quad \{\times 4\}$

Solving (1) and (2) simultaneously, $m = 50$, $c = 8$. Thus the <u>motorist</u> is travelling at <u>50 kmph</u>
and the <u>cyclist</u> at <u>8 kmph</u>, and they meet at a point <u>10 km from B.</u>

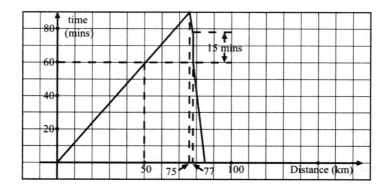

2.2 Let t minutes be the duration of the ascent.

A travels for $\frac{t}{2}$ mins., and B for $\frac{t}{2} - 6$ mins. before they meet.

Since they meet half way, B travels again for $\frac{t}{2} - 6$ mins. before arriving at G

Hence the duration of descent is $2\left(\frac{t}{2} - 6\right) = t - 12$ mins.

A travels continuously from the start to the second meeting, and this takes him 32 minutes.

Since $HM = 2GM$, then $HM = \frac{2}{3}GH$

and $32 = t + \frac{2}{3}(t - 12)$

$\therefore \quad 96 = 3t + 2t - 24$

$\therefore \quad 120 = 5t$

$\therefore \quad t = 24$

Thus the time for descent is 12 min, and looking at the time B takes to travel from his start to the second meeting at M,

$26 = 12 + \frac{1}{3}(24) + r$

$\therefore \quad 26 = 20 + r$

$\therefore \quad r = \underline{6\,\text{mins.}}$

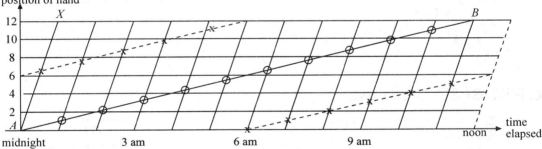

2.3 position of hand

The 12 steep lines parallel to $\overline{AX}$ give the minute hand's position.
$\overline{AB}$ gives the position of the hour hand.
Points $\odot$ occur when the hands coincide, $\times$ occur when they point in opposite directions.

2.4 During a 12 hour period, the minute and hour hands of a watch correspond exactly 11 times. Thus, since the time is between 10 and 11 o'clock, and the hands correspond, the time is $\quad$ 10 hours $+ \frac{10}{11}(60)$ minutes

and the train left Adelaide $\frac{8}{33}$ hours prior to this

$$= \frac{8 \times 60}{33} \text{ mins.}$$

$$\begin{cases} \text{speed} = \dfrac{\text{dist.}}{\text{time}} \\[2mm] \therefore \text{ time} = \dfrac{\text{dist.}}{\text{speed}} \end{cases}$$

$\therefore$ the train left at $\quad \dfrac{10 \times 60}{11} - \dfrac{8 \times 60}{33} \quad$ minutes past 10 o'clock.

$$= \frac{60}{33}\left[30 - 8\right]$$

$$= \frac{60}{33} \times 22$$

$$= 40 \text{ min,} \qquad \text{i.e., the train left at } \underline{10:40}.$$

2.5 Let the speed of the oil tanker be t, and that of the liner be l, the length of the tanker be m and the length of the liner be n.

We know that that $\text{speed} = \dfrac{\text{distance}}{\text{time}}, \quad \therefore \text{ time} = \dfrac{\text{distance}}{\text{speed}}.$

We know that that $\text{speed} = \dfrac{\text{distance}}{\text{time}}$, $\therefore$ $\text{time} = \dfrac{\text{distance}}{\text{speed}}$.

When they are travelling in the same direction,
the speed of the liner relative to the tanker is $l - t$.

$\therefore$ time to overtake $= \dfrac{m + n}{l - t}$

When they are travelling in opposite directions, the
speed of the liner relative to the tanker is $l + t$.

$\therefore$ time to overtake $= \dfrac{m + n}{l + t}$

thus $\dfrac{m + n}{l - t} = \dfrac{2(m + n)}{l + t}$

$\therefore$ $(m + n)(l + t) = 2(m + n)(l - t)$

$\therefore$ $l + t = 2l - 2t$ $\quad \{$as $(m + n) \neq 0\}$

$\therefore$ $3t = l$ and $\therefore$ <u>the liner is 3 times faster than the tanker.</u>

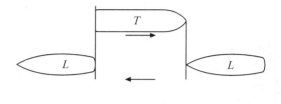

2.6 $\text{speed} = \dfrac{\text{dist.}}{\text{time}}$ $\quad \therefore$ $\text{time} = \dfrac{\text{dist.}}{\text{speed}}$

<u>No wind blows.</u> Total time $= 2\left(\dfrac{s}{v}\right)$

$w =$ speed of wind
$\therefore$ $v + w =$ speed of plane with wind
$\quad\; v - w =$ speed of plane against wind.

<u>With wind blowing X to Y</u>

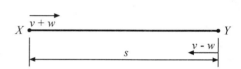

$\text{Total time} = \dfrac{s}{v + w} + \dfrac{s}{v - w}$

$= \dfrac{sv - sw + sv + sw}{(v + w)(v - w)}$

$= \dfrac{2sv}{v^2 - w^2}$

$> \dfrac{2sv}{v^2}$ $\quad \{$as $w^2 > 0\}$

i.e., $> \dfrac{2s}{v}$

i.e., $>$ <u>total time without wind.</u>

2.7

1st 5 laps	speed	dist.	time
Jack	$(x + 2)$ kmph	D km	$\dfrac{D}{x + 2}$ hrs.
Mack	x kmph	D km	$\dfrac{D}{x}$ hrs.

2nd 5 laps	speed	dist.	time
Jack	$(x - 2)$ kmph	D km	$\dfrac{D}{x - 2}$ hrs.
Mack	x kmph	D km	$\dfrac{D}{x}$ hrs.

Jack's total time $= \dfrac{D}{x + 2} + \dfrac{D}{x - 2}$

$= D\left(\dfrac{1}{x + 2} + \dfrac{1}{x - 2}\right)$

$= D\left(\dfrac{2x}{(x + 2)(x - 2)}\right)$

$= \dfrac{2Dx}{x^2 - 4}$ hrs.

Mack's total time $= \dfrac{D}{x} + \dfrac{D}{x}$

$= \dfrac{2D}{x}$

$= \dfrac{2Dx}{x^2}$ hrs

$<$ Jack's total time

$\therefore$ <u>Mack wins.</u>

2.8 Because he could save his life only just by running to the end where the bulls were, the bulls reach the bridge in the time it takes him to cross $\frac{3}{8}$ of the bridge.

Because he could also save his life by running to the other end, the bulls could run one bridgelength further in the time he takes to run $\frac{5}{8}$ of the bridge.

Therefore in the time it takes him to run $\frac{2}{8} = \frac{1}{4}$ of the bridge, the bulls could run the length of the bridge. Therefore he can run $\frac{1}{4}$ as fast as the bulls, or <u>5 kmph</u>.

2.9 **a** We are given that $\dfrac{x+k}{x} = \dfrac{x}{k}$

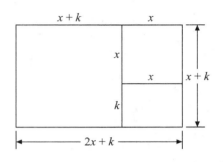

Now $\dfrac{2x+k}{x+k} = \dfrac{(x+k)+x}{x+k}$

$$= \left[\dfrac{\frac{x^2}{k} + x}{x+k} \right] \cdot \dfrac{k}{k} \qquad \{x+k = \tfrac{x^2}{k}, \text{ given}\}$$

$$= \dfrac{x^2 + kx}{k(x+k)}$$

$$= \dfrac{x(x+k)}{k(x+k)}$$

$$= \dfrac{x}{k}$$

b Consider the pattern of successive forms:

First	x by k
Second	$x+k$ by x
3rd	$2x+k$ by $x+k$
4th	$3x+2k$ by $2x+k$
5th	$5x+3k$ by $3x+2k$
6th	$8x+5k$ by $5x+3k$
$\vdots$	$\vdots$
In general	$(a+b)x+ak$ by $ax+bk$

Now $\dfrac{(a+b)x+ak}{ax+bk} = \dfrac{a(x+k)+bx}{ax+bk}$

$$= \left[\dfrac{a\frac{x^2}{k} + bx}{ax+bk} \right] \cdot \dfrac{k}{k} \qquad \{x+k = \tfrac{x^2}{k}, \text{ given}\}$$

$$= \dfrac{ax^2 + bkx}{k(ax+bk)}$$

$$= \dfrac{x(ax+bk)}{k(ax+bk)}$$

$$= \dfrac{x}{k}$$

where $\dfrac{x+k}{x} = \dfrac{x}{k}$

$\therefore \quad x^2 - kx - k^2 = 0$

$\therefore \quad x = \dfrac{k \pm \sqrt{k^2 - 4(1)(-k^2)}}{2} = \dfrac{k \pm k\sqrt{5}}{2} = \underline{k \left(\dfrac{1+\sqrt{5}}{2} \right)} \qquad \{as\ x > 0\}$

c Area = length × breadth
$$= (2x + k)(x + k)$$
$$\therefore \quad \text{Area} = \left(2 + \sqrt{5}\right)\left(\frac{3 + \sqrt{5}}{2}\right)k^2$$
$$= \left(\frac{11 + 5\sqrt{5}}{2}\right)k^2$$

2.10 Each minute mark is $6°$ apart, $\therefore$ there are 6 units (minutes) in $36°$.
When the time is h hours m minutes, $(60h + m)$ minutes, the hour hand stands at
$$\frac{60h + m}{12}, \quad 0 \le h < 12, \quad \text{and the minute hand at } m.$$
Thus $\quad \dfrac{60h + m}{12} - m = \pm 6$

$\therefore \quad \dfrac{60h - 11m}{12} = \pm 6$

$\therefore \quad 60h - 11m = 72 \quad \text{or} \quad 60h - 11m = -72$

Case (i) $\quad 60h - 11m = 72$

$\qquad \therefore \quad 12(5h - 6) = 11m$

$\qquad \therefore \quad 5h - 6 = 11t \quad \text{and} \quad m = 12t \qquad \{11, 12 \text{ are coprime, } t \text{ in } Z\}$

$\qquad \therefore \quad h = \dfrac{6 + 11t}{5} \quad \text{where} \quad t = 0, 1, 2, 3, 4. \qquad \{\text{as} \quad 0 \le m < 60\}$

$\qquad \therefore \quad h = 10, \quad m = 48 \qquad \{\text{when } t = 4, \text{ the only integral solution}\}$

Case (ii) Similarly, $\quad h = 1, \quad m = 12$
Thus the time is either $\quad \underline{1 : 12 \text{ or } 10 : 48}$.

2.11 Assume that the field has originally G units of grass on it, and that the growth rate of grass is g units/day. Let each cow eat at the same rate of c units/day.
Now if 6 cows are on the field for 3 days,
$$G + 3g - 18c = 0 \ldots\ldots(1)$$
and if 3 cows are on the field for 7 days,
$$G + 7g - 21c = 0 \ldots\ldots(2)$$

thus $\quad \begin{array}{ll} 3g - 18c = -G & \times 7 \\ 7g - 21c = -G & \times -3 \end{array}$

$\therefore \quad \begin{array}{l} 21g - 126c = -7G \\ -21g + 63c = 3G \end{array}$

(adding), $\qquad -63c = -4G \quad \therefore \quad c = \dfrac{4G}{63} \quad \text{and} \quad g = \dfrac{G}{21}$

If one cow takes x days, then $\qquad G + xg - xc = 0$

$\qquad\qquad\qquad \therefore \quad x(c - g) = G$

$\qquad\qquad\qquad \therefore \quad x\left(\dfrac{G}{63}\right) = G \qquad \text{and so,} \qquad \underline{x = 63 \text{ days}}$

2.12 In 1 day,
pipe A fills $\frac{1}{2}$ of the pool,
pipe B fills $\frac{1}{3}$ of the pool,
pipe C fills $\frac{1}{4}$ of the pool,
pipe D fills $\frac{1}{6}$ of the pool.

$\therefore$ together, in 1 day, they fill
$\frac{1}{2} + \frac{1}{3} + \frac{1}{4} + \frac{1}{6}$ of the pool
i.e. $1\frac{1}{4}$ of the pool.
Thus, in 1 day the pipes fill $\frac{5}{4}$ of the pool.
$\therefore$ it would take $\frac{4}{5}$ day to fill the pool.
i.e. $\quad \underline{19 \text{ hours and } 12 \text{ minutes}}$.

2.13 Let the seating be seen as
on a 5×5 chess board.
There are 25 squares.
13 are black and 12 white, say.
If a student is on a black
square, he or she must go to a white square
and this is clearly impossible as there is one less white square.
Therefore <u>Fred is correct</u>.

2.14 Let the tank hold L litres and be filled by the larger pipe in h hours.

The tank would be filled by the smaller pipe in $(h+2)$ hours.

The combined rate of flow is $\dfrac{L}{h} + \dfrac{L}{h+2}$ litres/hour.

$$\text{Thus} \quad \frac{L}{h} + \frac{L}{h+2} = \frac{L}{1\frac{7}{8}}$$

$$\therefore \quad \frac{1}{h} + \frac{1}{h+2} = \frac{8}{15}$$

$$\therefore \quad \left[\frac{1}{h} + \frac{1}{h+2}\right] h(h+2) = \frac{8}{15} h(h+2)$$

$$\therefore \quad 15(h+2+h) = 8h(h+2)$$

$$\therefore \quad 30h + 30 = 8h^2 + 16h$$

$$\therefore \quad 8h^2 - 14h - 30 = 0$$

$$\therefore \quad (h-3)(8h+10) = 0$$

$$\therefore \quad h = 3 \qquad \{\text{as } h \text{ is positive.}\}$$

Using the <u>smaller pipe we would take 5 hours</u> and <u>using the larger one, 3 hours</u>.

2.15 Let the new machine take t hours to complete the job working on its own.

$\therefore$ the old machine takes $(t+2)$ hours on its own.

It follows that in 1 hour, the new machine does $\dfrac{1}{t}$ of the work on its own,

and the old machine does $\dfrac{1}{t+2}$ of the work on its own.

Hence after 7 hours with 2 machines used simultaneously $\dfrac{7}{t} + \dfrac{7}{t+2}$ of the work

is done, and in the next 2 hours the new machine does $2\left[\dfrac{1}{2t}\right] = \dfrac{1}{t}$ of the work

and the old machine $\dfrac{2}{t+2}$ of the work.

$$\therefore \quad \frac{8}{t} + \frac{9}{t+2} = 1$$

$$\therefore \quad 8(t+2) + 9t = t(t+2)$$

$$\therefore \quad t^2 - 15t - 16 = 0$$

$$\therefore \quad (t-16)(t+1) = 0$$

$$\therefore \quad t = 16 \qquad \{\text{as } t > 0\}$$

$\therefore$ the old machine would take <u>18 hours</u> to do the job on its own.

2.16 Suppose the pageant moves at x kmph and the policeman at y kmph.

Let $t_1 = $ time to go from end of pageant to start,

and $t_2 = $ time to go from start to the end of the pageant.

$$\therefore \quad t_1 = \frac{2}{y-x} \quad \text{and} \quad t_2 = \frac{2}{y+x}$$

$$\left\{ \begin{aligned} \text{speed} &= \frac{\text{dist.}}{\text{time}} \\ \text{time} &= \frac{\text{dist.}}{\text{speed}} \end{aligned} \right.$$

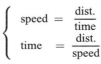

$$\begin{cases} y - x & \text{is the policeman's speed relative to the pageant when in same direction.} \\ y + x & \text{is the policeman's speed relative to the pageant when in opposite direction.} \end{cases}$$

But $\quad t_1 + t_2 = \dfrac{\text{distance pageant travels}}{\text{speed of pageant}} = \dfrac{1\frac{1}{2}}{x}$

$$\therefore \quad \frac{2}{y-x} + \frac{2}{y+x} = \frac{3}{2x}$$

$$\therefore \quad \frac{2y + 2x + 2y - 2x}{y^2 - x^2} = \frac{3}{2x}$$

$$\therefore \quad 8xy = 3y^2 - 3x^2$$

$$\therefore \quad 3x^2 + 8xy - 3y^2 = 0$$

$$\therefore \quad (3x - y)(x + 3y) = 0$$

$$\therefore \quad 3x = y \qquad \text{\{the other solution is meaningless\}}$$

$\therefore \quad$ the policeman travels 3 times as fast as the pageant, and so covers $4\frac{1}{2}$ km.

2.17 Let speeds of A, B, C be a, b, c. $a > b > c$.

1st occasion
Thus $\quad 5b - 5c = 3a - 3b$

$$\frac{a-b}{b-c} = \frac{5}{3} \quad \dots\dots\dots \quad (1)$$

2nd occasion
Thus $\quad 9a - 9b = (x-9)b - (x-9)c$

$$\therefore \quad 9(a-b) = (x-9)(b-c)$$

$$\therefore \quad \frac{a-b}{b-c} = \frac{x-9}{9} \quad \dots\dots\dots \quad (2)$$

Comparing (1) and (2), $\quad \dfrac{x-9}{9} = \dfrac{5}{3}$

$$\therefore \quad 3x - 27 = 45$$

$$\therefore \quad 3x = 72$$

$$\therefore \quad x = 24$$

$\therefore \quad$ B overtakes C, 15 minutes later.

1st Occasion

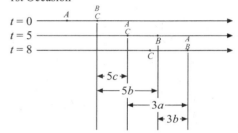

2nd Occasion

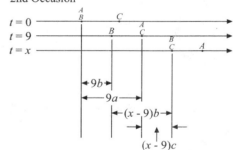

---

3. MEASURE

3.1 Circumference of circular base is $2\pi r$

$$\therefore \quad 2\pi r = \pi R \quad \text{and so} \quad r = \frac{R}{2}$$

Likewise, circumference of circular base, $C = 2\pi x$

$$\therefore \quad 2\pi x = \pi \left(\frac{R}{2}\right) \quad \text{and so} \quad x = \frac{R}{4}$$

We have similar figures, with dilation factor $\frac{1}{2}$.

$$\therefore \quad \frac{V_{\text{small}}}{V_{\text{large}}} = \left(\frac{1}{2}\right)^3 \quad \text{and so} \quad V_{\text{small}} : V_{\text{large}} = \underline{1 : 8}$$

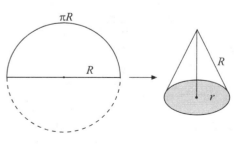

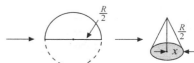

3.2 Diameter of circle
$$= 2r$$
$$= PB + BR$$
$$= (PA + AB) + (BC + CR)$$
$$= (PA + CR) + AB + BC$$
$$= (AQ + QC) + AB + BC \qquad \{\text{tangents from an}$$
$$= AC + AB + BC \qquad\qquad \text{external point theorem}\}$$
$$= \underline{\text{perimeter of } \triangle ABC.}$$

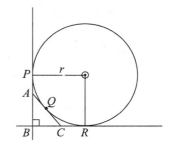

3.3 Let X, Y, Z be feet of the perpendiculars from B, C, D to
the line $\overleftrightarrow{PA}$ and let O be the foot of the perpendicular
from B to $\overline{CY}$.

Then $BX = OY$ and $DZ = CO$
{because $OBXY$ is a rectangle and $\triangle$s DZA, COB are congruent.}

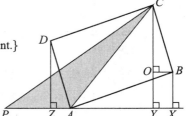

$$\therefore \quad \text{Area } \triangle PAC$$
$$= \tfrac{1}{2}(PA)(CY)$$
$$= \tfrac{1}{2}(PA)(CO + OY)$$
$$= \tfrac{1}{2}(PA)(CO) + \tfrac{1}{2}(PA)(OY)$$
$$= \tfrac{1}{2}(PA)(DZ) + \tfrac{1}{2}(PA)(BX)$$
$$= \text{area } \triangle PAD \;+\; \text{area } \triangle PAB.$$

3.4 Route over pole
$$\doteq \tfrac{1}{6} 2\pi r$$
$$\doteq \tfrac{\pi}{3} r \quad \{r \text{ is the radius of the earth}\}$$

Route around same latitude
$$\doteq \tfrac{1}{2} 2\pi \left(\tfrac{r}{2}\right)$$
$$\doteq \tfrac{\pi r}{2}$$

$$\therefore \quad \frac{\text{Route over pole}}{\text{Route, same latitude}} \doteq \frac{\tfrac{\pi r}{3}}{\tfrac{\pi r}{2}} \doteq \tfrac{2}{3}$$

i.e., Route over pole $\doteq \tfrac{2}{3}$ (Route, same latitude).

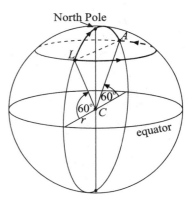

3.5 $$\frac{\text{Perimeter of } \triangle}{\text{Circumference of Circle}} = \frac{2a + 2b + 2c}{2\pi r} = \frac{a+b+c}{\pi r} \dots\dots(1)$$
{tangents from external point theorem}

Also $$\frac{\text{Area } \triangle}{\text{Area circle}} = \frac{\tfrac{1}{2}(a+b)r + \tfrac{1}{2}(b+c)r + \tfrac{1}{2}(c+a)r}{\pi r^2}$$
$$= \frac{\tfrac{1}{2}r(2a + 2b + 2c)}{\pi r^2}$$
$$= \frac{a+b+c}{\pi r} \dots\dots(2)$$

thus proving the statement on triangles.
The theorem can be established in the same way
for a circle inscribed in any n-sided polygon. $(n \geqslant 3)$
Try proving it for a quadrilateral.

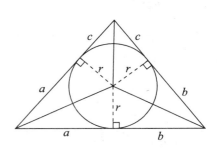

3.6 Let R and r be the radii of the large and small circles respectively.

then $R = 2r$ ....(1)

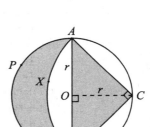

Now the length of the thick boundary

$\quad$ = 6 [length of one of its arcs]

$\quad$ = $6.[\frac{1}{3}$ perimeter of small circle]

$\quad$ = $2.2\pi r$

$\quad$ = $4\pi r$

$\quad$ = $2\pi(2r)$

$\quad$ = $2\pi R$ $\qquad$ {from (1)}

$\quad$ = length of outer circle.

3.7 Area (1) + Area (2)

$\quad$ = area of semicircle $\overline{AC}$ + area of semicircle $\overline{BC}$

$\qquad$ − area of semicircle $\overline{AB}$ + area of $\triangle ABC$

$\quad$ = $\frac{1}{2}\pi\left(\frac{a}{2}\right)^2 + \frac{1}{2}\pi\left(\frac{b}{2}\right)^2 - \frac{1}{2}\pi\left(\frac{c}{2}\right)^2 +$ area $\triangle ABC$

$\quad$ = $\frac{\pi}{8}(a^2 + b^2 - c^2)+$ area $\triangle ABC$

$\quad$ = Area $\triangle ABC$ $\qquad$ {as $a^2 + b^2 = c^2$, Pythagoras}

3.8 Let r be the radius of the circle.

$\quad\therefore\quad AC = \sqrt{2}r$ $\qquad$ {Pythagoras}

Now area of crescent shape shaded

$\quad$ = area semicircle APB − area sector $CAXB$ + area $\triangle ABC$

$\quad$ = $\frac{1}{2}\pi r^2 - \frac{1}{4}\pi(\sqrt{2}r)^2 +$ area $\triangle ABC$

$\quad$ = $\frac{1}{2}\pi r^2 - \frac{1}{2}\pi r^2 +$ area $\triangle ABC$

$\quad$ = area $\triangle ABC$

3.9 Let the sides of square $ABCD$ be x units long.

$\quad\therefore\quad OB = \dfrac{x}{\sqrt{2}}$ $\qquad$ {Pythagoras, in $\triangle AOB$}

and $\quad OQ = AB = x$ units

Thus the shaded area

$\quad = \left[\begin{array}{c}\text{area of large circle}\\\text{of radius } OQ\end{array}\right] - [8. \text{ area segment}$

$\quad = \pi x^2 - 8\left[\frac{1}{4}\pi\left(\dfrac{x}{\sqrt{2}}\right)^2 - \frac{1}{2}\cdot\dfrac{x}{\sqrt{2}}\cdot\dfrac{x}{\sqrt{2}}\right]$

$\quad = \pi x^2 - 8\left[\dfrac{\pi x^2}{8} - \dfrac{x^2}{4}\right]$

$\quad = \pi x^2 - \pi x^2 + 2x^2$

$\quad = 2[\text{area of square } ABCD]$

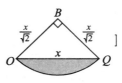

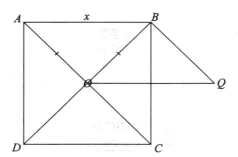

3.10 Let C be the centre of the sphere and O be the
point of intersection of the 3 perpendicular planes.
Also let the 3 circles of intersection have radii r_1, r_2, r_3.

Now $OC = \sqrt{x^2 + y^2 + z^2}$ {distance formula in 3-D}

$\therefore$ $(OC)^2 = x^2 + y^2 + z^2$

Now sum of areas of circles

$= \pi r_1{}^2 + \pi r_2{}^2 + \pi r_3{}^2$

$= \pi(R^2 - x^2) + \pi(R^2 - y^2) + \pi(R^2 - z^2)$

$= 3\pi R^2 - \pi(x^2 + y^2 + z^2)$

$= 3\pi R^2 - \pi(OC)^2$,   which is constant as both
$\qquad\qquad\qquad\qquad$ O and C are fixed points
$\qquad\qquad\qquad\qquad$ within the sphere.

Thus the <u>area remains unchanged</u> for varying
positions of the 3 planes.

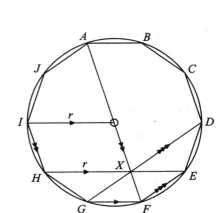

3.11 Each tangent at P is at right angles to the radius
at P.

Thus both tangents pass through the centres O_1
and O_2. Let $O_1O_2 = k$

Now $l = AO_1 + O_1O_2 + O_2D$

$\therefore$ $l = r_1 + k + r_2$........(1)

Also $s = O_1C - O_1B$

$\therefore$ $s = r_1 - (k - r_2)$

$\therefore$ $s = r_1 + r_2 - k$........(2)

Thus $ls = (r_1 + r_2 + k)(r_1 + r_2 - k)$

$= (r_1 + r_2)^2 - k^2$

$= (r_1 + r_2)^2 - (r_1{}^2 + r_2{}^2)$

$= r_1{}^2 + 2r_1r_2 + r_2{}^2 - r_1{}^2 - r_2{}^2$

$= \underline{2r_1r_2}$

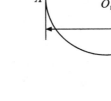

3.12 $\overline{HE}$ has the same length in both figures.

$\therefore$ $\underset{\text{(fig 2)}}{HE}\ -\ \underset{\text{(fig 1)}}{AB}$

$=\ \underset{\text{(fig 1)}}{HE}\ -\ \underset{\text{(fig 1)}}{AB}$

$=\ \underset{\text{(fig 1)}}{HE}\ -\ \underset{\text{(fig 1)}}{GF}$

$=\ HX + XE - GF$ (fig 1)

$=\ HX$ $\qquad$ {as $XE = GF$,   opposite sides of
$\qquad\qquad\qquad\qquad$ parallelogram $EFGX$}

$=\ IO$ $\qquad$ {opposite sides of parallelogram $IOXH$}

$=\ \underline{r}$

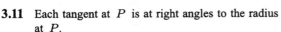

3.13   **a** Join $\overline{AP}$, $\overline{PB}$, $\overline{PC}$, and let the equal sides be a units long.

Area $\triangle ABC =$ area $\triangle ABP +$ area $\triangle BCP +$ area $\triangle CAP$

$= \tfrac{1}{2}AB.PX + \tfrac{1}{2}BC.PY + \tfrac{1}{2}CA.PZ$

$= \tfrac{1}{2}a.PX + \tfrac{1}{2}a.PY + \tfrac{1}{2}a.PZ$

$= \tfrac{1}{2}a[PX + PY + PZ]$

Since $\triangle ABC$ is fixed, both a and its area are constants.

$\therefore$ $\underline{PX + PY + PZ}$ is constant for all positions of P.

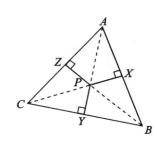

b   For an n-sided regular polygon, we let the vertices
be $A_1, A_2, A_3, \ldots, A_n$.
The area of the polygon

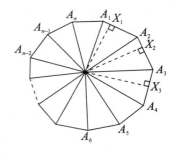

$$= \text{area } \triangle A_1 A_2 P + \text{ area } \triangle A_2 A_3 P + \ldots + \text{ area } \triangle A_n A_1 P$$

$$= \tfrac{1}{2} A_1 A_2 . P X_1 + \tfrac{1}{2} A_2 A_3 . P X_2 + \ldots + \tfrac{1}{2} A_n A_1 . P X_n$$

where $X_1, X_2, \ldots, X_n$ are the feet of the
perpendiculars from P to $\overline{A_1 A_2},\ \overline{A_2 A_3},\ \ldots,\ \overline{A_n A_1}$
(or the line segments produced.)

$$= \tfrac{1}{2} a (P X_1 + P X_2 + \ldots + P X_n)$$

{if equal sides are a units long}

Thus $\underline{P X_1 + P X_2 + P X_3 + \ldots + P X_n}$ is constant for all P.

c   The converse is <u>false</u>.   e.g.   rectangle
Sum of distances $P X_1 + P X_2 + P X_3 + P X_4$
   $= a + b$,   which is a constant,
but the figure is <u>not a regular polygon</u>.

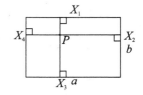

3.14 $D + A = $ area of semicircle $= \tfrac{1}{2} \pi \left(\dfrac{r}{2} \right)^2$

i.e. $D + A = \dfrac{\pi r^2}{8} \ldots\ldots(1)$

Also $A + L = $ area sector OXY

$$= \dfrac{\theta}{2\pi} \cdot \pi r^2 \quad \text{(where } \theta \text{ is in radians, } 2\pi = 360°)$$

$$= \tfrac{1}{2} r^2 \theta$$

If there are n such semicircles, then $\theta = \dfrac{2\pi}{n}$

$\therefore \quad A + L = \tfrac{1}{2} r^2 \left(\dfrac{2\pi}{n} \right)$

i.e. $A + L = \dfrac{\pi r^2}{n} \ldots\ldots(2)$

Thus when $D = L$, $\dfrac{\pi r^2}{8} = \dfrac{\pi r^2}{n}$,   and $\therefore$ $n = 8$.

Thus if we divide the original circle into <u>8 arcs</u>, the shaded areas are equal.

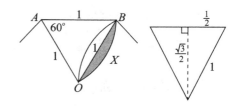

3.15 a   Shaded area $=$ area of sector $ABXO-$ area $\triangle ABO$.

$$= \tfrac{1}{6} \pi \times 1^2 - \dfrac{\sqrt{3}}{4}$$

$$= \dfrac{\pi}{6} - \dfrac{\sqrt{3}}{4}$$

Total area of 'flower' $= 12 \left(\dfrac{\pi}{6} - \dfrac{\sqrt{3}}{4} \right)$

$$= \underline{(2\pi - 3\sqrt{3}) \text{ units}^2}$$

b   Shaded area

$= $ area of square $ABCD-$ area $\triangle PCD - 2$ area sector PBC

$= 1 - \dfrac{\sqrt{3}}{4} - 2[\tfrac{1}{12}.\pi.1^2]$

$= 1 - \dfrac{\sqrt{3}}{4} - \dfrac{\pi}{6}$

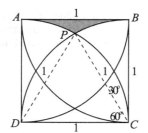

$\therefore$ total area of flower $= 1 - 4[1 - \frac{\sqrt{3}}{4} - \frac{\pi}{6}]$

$\qquad\qquad\qquad\qquad = 1 - 4 + \sqrt{3} + \frac{2\pi}{3}$

$\qquad\qquad\qquad\qquad = (\sqrt{3} + \frac{2\pi}{3} - 3) \text{ units}^2$

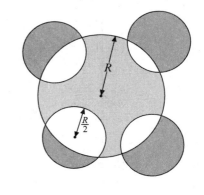

3.16 Total outside area

$$= p\pi \left(\frac{R}{2}\right)^2 + q\pi \left(\frac{R}{2}\right)^2 + r\pi \left(\frac{R}{2}\right)^2 + s\pi \left(\frac{R}{2}\right)^2$$

where p, q, r, s are real numbers between 0 and 1

$$= \frac{\pi R^2}{4}(p + q + r + s)........(1)$$

Total inner shaded area

$$= \pi R^2 - \left[(1-p)\pi \left(\frac{R}{2}\right)^2 + (1-q)\pi \left(\frac{R}{2}\right)^2 + (1-r)\pi \left(\frac{R}{2}\right)^2 + (1-s)\pi \left(\frac{R}{2}\right)^2\right]$$

$$= \pi R^2 - \frac{\pi R^2}{4}[1 - p + 1 - q + 1 - r + 1 - s]$$

$$= \frac{\pi R^2}{4}[4 - 4 + p + q + r + s]$$

$$= \frac{\pi R^2}{4}(p + q + r + s)........(2)$$

Thus the <u>total outer area $=$ total inner area.</u>

Generalization: If we form n^2 small circles, each of radius $\dfrac{R}{n}$, and each is intersecting the large circle, while they do not overlap each other, then the sum of the outer areas is equal to the remaining inner area.

3.17 Let $\angle BOD = \theta$.

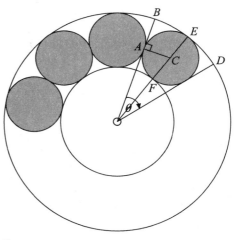

Now $OC = \dfrac{R+r}{2}$ {average of the radii}

and $AC = \dfrac{R-r}{2}$ {$AC = CE = \frac{1}{2}(EF)$}

$\therefore$ in $\triangle OAC$, $\sin\dfrac{\theta}{2} = \dfrac{AC}{OC} = \dfrac{R-r}{R+r}$

But if the little circles form a closed chain,

then $\theta = \dfrac{2\pi}{n}$,   where n is a positive integer, $n \geqslant 3$.

n is the number of little circles.

Thus $\dfrac{R-r}{R+r} = \sin\left(\dfrac{\pi}{n}\right)$,

which on rearranging   gives $R = r\left[\dfrac{1 + \sin\left(\dfrac{\pi}{n}\right)}{1 - \sin\left(\dfrac{\pi}{n}\right)}\right]$ ....(1)

For a given $n \geqslant 3$, R can always be found using
(1), and as there are infinitely many values of
n that can be used, there are <u>infinitely many values of R.</u>

3.18

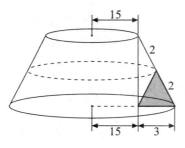

The surface covered is actually part of a conical surface. This top part is folded on the heavily dotted line, to form the required shape.

Thus the "development" is:

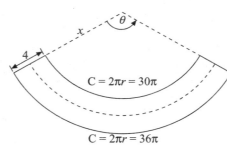

where x and θ are to be determined.

Now $\theta = \dfrac{30\pi}{x} = \dfrac{36\pi}{x+4}$

$\therefore\ 30\pi(x+4) = 36\pi x$

$\therefore\ 5(x+4) = 6x$

$\therefore\ \underline{x = 20}$ and $\therefore \theta = \dfrac{3\pi}{2}$

The actual development is thus:

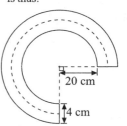

3.19 Let O and O_1 be the centres of the two circles, as shown. Let $AB = c$, $BC = a$, $AC = b$.
Notation: let "area of triangle ABC" be "ΔABC".

a Now $\Delta ABC = \Delta OAB + \Delta OBC + \Delta OCA$

$\qquad = \frac{1}{2}cr + \frac{1}{2}ar + \frac{1}{2}br$

$\qquad = \frac{1}{2}r(a+b+c)$

$\therefore\ a+b+c = \dfrac{2.\Delta ABC}{r}$

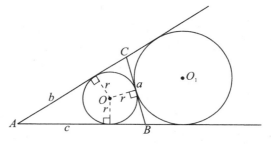

But $\Delta ABC = \frac{1}{2}ah_1 = \frac{1}{2}bh_2 = \frac{1}{2}ch_3$

$\therefore\ \dfrac{2.\Delta ABC}{r} = \dfrac{2.\Delta ABC}{h_1} + \dfrac{2.\Delta ABC}{h_2} + \dfrac{2.\Delta ABC}{h_3}$ $\quad \left\{ \text{since } a = \dfrac{2.\Delta ABC}{h_1}, \text{ etc} \right\}$

$\therefore\ \dfrac{1}{r} = \dfrac{1}{h_1} + \dfrac{1}{h_2} + \dfrac{1}{h_3}$ $\quad$ {dividing by $2.\Delta ABC$}

b Similarly $\Delta ABC = \Delta O_1AB + \Delta O_1AC - \Delta O_1BC$

$\qquad = \frac{1}{2}cr_1 + \frac{1}{2}br_1 - \frac{1}{2}ar_1$

$\qquad = \frac{1}{2}r_1(b+c-a)$

$\therefore\ b+c-a = \dfrac{2.\Delta ABC}{r_1}$

$\therefore\ \dfrac{2.\Delta ABC}{r_1} = \dfrac{2.\Delta ABC}{h_2} + \dfrac{2.\Delta ABC}{h_3} - \dfrac{2.\Delta ABC}{h_1}$

$\therefore\ \dfrac{1}{r_1} = \dfrac{1}{h_2} + \dfrac{1}{h_3} - \dfrac{1}{h_1}$

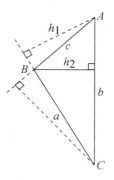

c Likewise, $\dfrac{1}{r_2} = \dfrac{1}{h_1} + \dfrac{1}{h_3} - \dfrac{1}{h_2}$

$\qquad \dfrac{1}{r_3} = \dfrac{1}{h_2} + \dfrac{1}{h_1} - \dfrac{1}{h_3}$ $\quad$ {by considering the other escribed circles}

Adding these last 3 equations we get

$\dfrac{1}{r_1} + \dfrac{1}{r_2} + \dfrac{1}{r_3} = \dfrac{1}{h_1} + \dfrac{1}{h_2} + \dfrac{1}{h_3} = \dfrac{1}{r}$

4. GEOMETRY

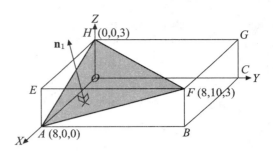

4.1 $\overrightarrow{HF} = [8, 10, 0]$ and $\overrightarrow{HA} = [8, 0, -3]$

$\mathbf{n_1} = \overrightarrow{HF} \times \overrightarrow{HA}$

$$= \left[\begin{vmatrix} 10 & 0 \\ 0 & -3 \end{vmatrix}, \begin{vmatrix} 0 & 8 \\ -3 & 8 \end{vmatrix}, \begin{vmatrix} 8 & 10 \\ 8 & 0 \end{vmatrix} \right]$$

$$= [-30, \ 24, \ -80]$$

$$= -2[15, \ -12, \ 40]$$

The angle between the two planes is the acute angle between their normals.

Now $\mathbf{n_1} \cdot \mathbf{n_2} = |\mathbf{n_1}| \, |\mathbf{n_2}| \cos \theta$

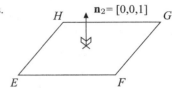

$\therefore$ $[0, \ 0, \ 1] \cdot [15, \ -12, \ 40] = 1 \cdot \sqrt{225 + 144 + 1600} \cos \theta$

$\therefore$ $\cos \theta = \frac{40}{\sqrt{1969}}$

$\therefore$ $\theta \doteqdot \underline{25.65^o}$.

4.2 Triangle ABC is isosceles with $AB = AC$.

$\therefore$ $\alpha_1 = \alpha_2$ {base angles are equal}

But $\angle APX = 2\angle ABX$ {angle at centre theorem}

$= 2\alpha$

Likewise $\angle AQX = 2\angle ACX = 2\alpha$

Since $\triangle$'s APX, AQX are isosceles,

$\angle PAX = \angle PXA = 90^o - \alpha$ and

$\angle QAX = \angle QXA = 90^o - \alpha$

Thus, $\triangle$'s APX, AQX are equiangular and therefore similar. But they share common corresponding side $\overline{AX}$. Consequently, the two triangles are congruent, $\therefore$ $AP = AQ$ i.e., <u>same radius and $\therefore$ same diameter.</u>

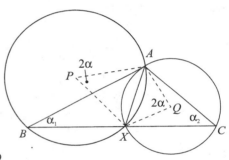

4.3 Let the triangle PQR have area a units^2.

(1) <u>Consider $\triangle AQB$</u> ; altitude $\frac{1}{2}h$, base $\frac{1}{3}b$

Area $= \frac{1}{2}$ base $\times$ altitude

$= \frac{1}{2} \cdot \frac{1}{3} b \cdot \frac{1}{2} h$

$= \frac{1}{6}(\frac{1}{2} bh)$

$= \frac{1}{6} a$

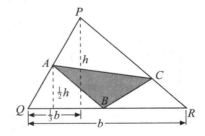

(2) <u>Consider $\triangle BCR$</u> ; altitude $\frac{1}{4}h$, base $\frac{2}{3}b$

$\therefore$ Area $= \frac{1}{2} \cdot \frac{1}{4} h \cdot \frac{2}{3} b$

$= \frac{1}{6}(\frac{1}{2} bh)$

$= \frac{1}{6} a$

$\therefore$ $\dfrac{\text{Area } ABC}{\text{Area } PQR} = \left[\dfrac{a - \frac{1}{6}a - \frac{1}{6}a - \frac{3}{8}a}{a} \right] \dfrac{24}{24}$

$= \dfrac{24a - 4a - 4a - 9a}{24a}$

$= \underline{\dfrac{7}{24}}$

(3) <u>Consider $\triangle APC$</u>

(see diagram below)

Area $= \frac{1}{2} \cdot \dfrac{B}{2} \cdot \frac{3}{4} H$

$= \frac{3}{8}(\frac{1}{2} BH)$

$= \underline{\frac{3}{8} a}$

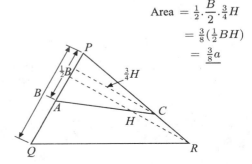

4.4 Let the angle bisectors of A and C bisect in angles of α and β respectively.

Now $\angle XCA = \angle CXA = 2\beta$ {base angles of isosceles $\triangle$}

Also $\angle ACB = 180° - 2\beta$

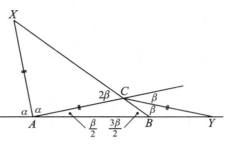

$\therefore$ $\angle CAY = \angle CYA = \dfrac{180 - (180 - 2\beta) - \beta}{2} = \dfrac{\beta}{2}$

Thus $\alpha + 4\beta = 180°$ {sum of angles of $\triangle AXC$}

and $2\alpha + \dfrac{\beta}{2} = 180°$ {sum of angles on a line at A}

Solving for $\dfrac{\beta}{2}$: $2\alpha + \dfrac{\beta}{2} = 180°$

$\underline{-2\alpha - 8\beta = -360°}$

adding $-\dfrac{15\beta}{2} = -180°$

$\therefore$ $\angle A = \dfrac{\beta}{2} = \dfrac{180°}{15} = \underline{12°}$

4.5 $\angle BAX = 45°$ and $\angle CAY = 45°$ $\Rightarrow$ $\angle YAX = 180°$

$\therefore$ $\overline{XY}$ passes through A.

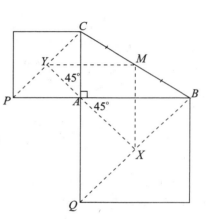

In $\triangle CPB$, Y is the midpoint of $\overline{CP}$

M is the midpoint of $\overline{CB}$

$\therefore$ $\overline{MY} \parallel \overline{PB}$ and $MY = \frac{1}{2}PB$........(1) {midpt. thm.}

Likewise in $\triangle CBQ$, $\overline{MX} \parallel \overline{CQ}$ and $MX = \frac{1}{2}CQ$........(2)

But $PB = CQ$ $\therefore$ $MX = MY$ {comparing (1) and (2)}

$\therefore$ $\triangle MXY$ is isosceles.

Since $\overline{MX} \parallel \overline{CQ}$ and $\overline{MY} \parallel \overline{PB}$

where $\overline{CQ} \perp \overline{PB}$

then $\overline{MX} \perp \overline{MY}$

i.e., $\underline{\angle YMX = 90°}$.

4.6 We label the other vertices as shown,
and let $\angle ABC = 2\alpha$, $\angle ACB = 2\beta$.

$\therefore$ Exterior angle $A = 2\alpha + 2\beta$ {exterior angle of $\triangle ABC$}

$\therefore$ $\angle QAB = \alpha + \beta = \angle PAC$

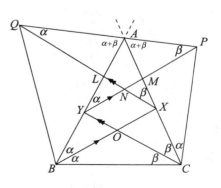

Now $\angle MXN = \angle XCO = \beta$ {corresponding $\angle$'s}

and $\angle LYN = \angle YBO = \alpha$ {corresponding $\angle$'s}

and $\angle APY + \alpha = \alpha + \beta$ {exterior angle of $\triangle$ theorem in $\triangle APY$}

$\therefore$ $\angle APY = \beta$

$\therefore$ $APCY$ is a cyclic quadrilateral

     {$\overline{AY}$ subtends equal angles of β at P and C}

$\therefore$ $\angle PCA = \angle PYA = \alpha$

Thus $\angle PCB = \alpha + 2\beta$........(1)

Also $\angle AQX = \alpha$ {exterior angle of triangle theorem in $\triangle AQX$}

$\therefore$ $\overline{AX}$ subtends equal angles of α at Q and B

$\therefore$ $AXBQ$ is a cyclic quadrilateral.

$\therefore$ $\angle BQX = \angle BAX = 180 - (2\alpha + 2\beta)$

$\therefore$ $\angle BQP = 180 - 2\alpha - 2\beta + \alpha$

$\therefore$ $\angle BQP = 180 - (\alpha + 2\beta)$........(2)

From (1) and (2), $\angle PCB + \angle BQP = 180^{o}$

$\therefore$ $BCPQ$ is a cyclic quadrilateral.

4.7 Let $\angle APB = \alpha$ and $\angle AQC = \beta$

$\triangle$'s APB and AQC are isosceles   {external point to circle theorem}

$\therefore$ $AP = BP$ and $AQ = QC$ {isosceles triangle theorem}

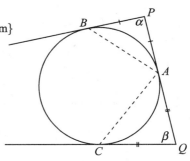

$\therefore$ $\angle BAP = \dfrac{180^{o} - \alpha}{2}$

Likewise $\angle CAQ = \dfrac{180^{o} - \beta}{2}$

$\therefore$ $\angle BAC = 180^{o} - \left(\dfrac{180^{o} - \alpha}{2}\right) - \left(\dfrac{180^{o} - \beta}{2}\right)$

$\qquad = 180^{o} - 90^{o} + \dfrac{\alpha}{2} - 90^{o} + \dfrac{\beta}{2}$

$\qquad = \dfrac{\alpha}{2} + \dfrac{\beta}{2}$

$\qquad = \underline{\dfrac{\alpha + \beta}{2}}$,   the average of the angles at P and Q.

4.8 **Proof:** Let M be the point of intersection of

$\overline{AC}$ and $\overline{BD}$, and let $\angle BMC = \theta$, $OM = a$,

radius be r.

Draw $\overline{OT} \perp \overline{BD}$

Now $YT = YM + MT$

$\qquad = (r - a)\cos\theta + a\cos\theta$

$\qquad = r\cos\theta$

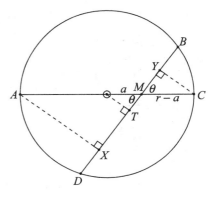

and in $\triangle AMX$, $\cos\theta = \dfrac{MX}{a + r}$

$\therefore$ $TX = MX - MT$

$\qquad = (a + r)\cos\theta - a\cos\theta$

$\qquad = r\cos\theta$.

Thus $YT = TX$

But T bisects chord $\overline{BD}$ {perpendicular from
                              centre bisects chord}

$\therefore$ $\underline{BY = DX}$

4.9 Let L, M be midpoints of sides $\overline{AD}$, $\overline{FG}$, resp.
The midpoint of $\overline{LM}$ is the centre, O, of the
cube, which is also the point of intersection
of the diagonals of the cube.

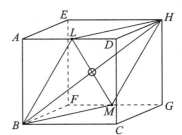

To prove: $\overline{BH} \perp \overline{LM}$

Consider the quadrilateral $LHMB$ (which
has diagonals $\overline{LM}$ and $\overline{BH}$).

If each side of the cube is $2x$ units,

then $LH = HM = MB = BL = \sqrt{5}\,x$ {Pythagoras}

$\therefore$ $LHMB$ is a rhombus.

$\therefore$ $\overline{LM} \perp \overline{BH}$ {diagonals of a rhombus are $\perp$}

Similarly $\overline{EC} \perp \overline{LM}$

Clearly $\overline{LM}$ is not perpendicular to $\overline{AG}$ and $\overline{DF}$.

Thus $\underline{\overline{LM}}$ is perpendicular to $\underline{\overline{BH}}$ and $\underline{\overline{EC}}$.

4.10 Let $\angle DST = \angle TSB = a,$
  $\angle BRT = \angle TRD = b,$ and $\angle ADC = c.$

$\therefore$ $\angle SBA = \angle CBR = c$ {exterior angle of cyclic quad. theorem}

Thus $\angle TPB = a + c$ {exterior angle of triangle theorem}
  $\angle TQB = b + c$
$\therefore$ $\angle STR = 360^{o} - (a+c) - (b+c) - (180^{o} - c)$ {in PBQT}
i.e. $\angle STR = 180^{o} - (a+b+c)\ldots\ldots(1)$

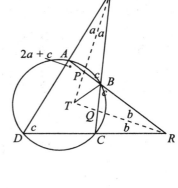

But $\angle DAR = 2a + c$ {exterior angle of Δ theorem}
Thus in $\Delta DAR,$
  $(2a+c) + c + 2b = 180^{o}$
$\therefore$ $2a + 2b + 2c = 180^{o}$
$\therefore$ $a + b + c = 90^{o}.$
$\therefore$ in (1), $\underline{\angle STR = 90^{o}},$ the required result.

4.11 Let the fixed base angles be of size $\alpha.$

Now $\sin \alpha = \dfrac{d_1}{AP}$ and $\sin \alpha = \dfrac{d_2}{PB}$

$\therefore$ $d_1 + d_2 = AP \sin \alpha + PB \sin \alpha$
  $= \sin \alpha (AP + PB)$
  $= \sin \alpha . AB$ where $\sin \alpha$ and AB are fixed.

Thus $\underline{d_1 + d_2}$ is constant for all positions of $P.$

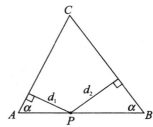

4.12 $\underline{AM : BC = 3 : 2}$
Let $\overline{BL}$ and $\overline{CK}$ be the medians from B and C respectively.
All 3 medians meet at $G,$ the centroid, where
$AG : GM = 2 : 1$ {centroid theorem}
Let $GM = a$
$\therefore$ $AG = 2a$
$\therefore$ $AM = 3a$
$\therefore$ $BC = 2a$
$\therefore$ $BM = MC = a$
Thus $B,$ G and C lie on a circle, centre $M,$ of radius $a.$
$\therefore$ $\angle BGC = 90^{o}$ {angle in a semi-circle theorem}
$\therefore$ $\overline{BG} \perp \overline{CG}$
$\therefore$ $\underline{\overline{BL} \perp \overline{CK}}$

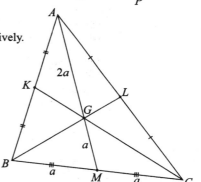

4.13 **a** Sides are $\sqrt{10}$ units
  and $\sqrt{10} = \sqrt{3^2 + 1^2}$
  i.e. $10 = 3^2 + 1^2$

b A square with area $4p + 3$ can be constructed on
the pegboard if there are integers a and b such that
$a^2 + b^2 = 4p + 3.$

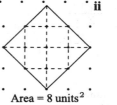

Area = 8 units^2

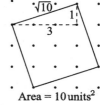

Area = 10 units^2

a	b	a^2	b^2	$a^2 + b^2$
$2n$	$2m$	$4n^2$	$4m^2$	$4(n^2 + m^2)$
$2n$	$2m+1$	$4n^2$	$4m^2 + 4m + 1$	$4(n^2 + m^2 + m) + 1$
$2n+1$	$2m$	$4n^2 + 4n + 1$	$4m^2$	$4(n^2 + m^2 + n) + 1$
$2n+1$	$2m+1$	$4n^2 + 4n + 1$	$4m^2 + 4m + 1$	$4(n^2 + m^2 + n + m) + 2$

Since $a,$ b are either odd or even, the above table shows the $\underline{\text{impossibility of}}$
$\underline{a^2 + b^2 = 4p + 3.}$

4.14 Join $\overline{AB}$ and $\overline{AC}$.

Now $\alpha_1 = \alpha_2$ and $\beta_1 = \beta_2$ {angle between tangent
and chord theorem}

Thus $\triangle$'s AYC, BZA are equiangular and $\therefore$ similar.
Likewise $\triangle$'s AXB, CZA are similar.

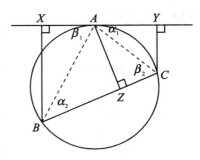

Thus $\dfrac{BX}{AX} = \dfrac{AZ}{CZ}$ and $\dfrac{CY}{AY} = \dfrac{AZ}{BZ}$

$\therefore$ $BX.CY = AX.\dfrac{AZ}{CZ}.AZ.\dfrac{AY}{BZ}$

i.e. $BX.CY = (AZ)^2 \left(\dfrac{AX}{CZ}.\dfrac{AY}{BZ}\right)$ ....(1)

But $\dfrac{AX}{AB} = \dfrac{CZ}{CA}$ and $\dfrac{AY}{AC} = \dfrac{BZ}{BA}$

$\therefore$ $\dfrac{AX}{CZ} = \dfrac{AB}{AC}$ and $\dfrac{AY}{BZ} = \dfrac{AC}{AB}$

$\therefore$ $\dfrac{AX}{CZ}.\dfrac{AY}{BZ} = \dfrac{AB}{AC}.\dfrac{AC}{AB} = 1$

Thus from (1) $BX.CY = (AZ)^2$

$\therefore$ $\underline{AZ = \sqrt{BX.CY}}$

4.15 **a** We mark equal distances because
lengths of tangents from an external
point are equal.

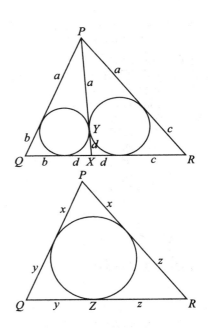

Now $(a+b) + (a+c) + (c+2d+b) = r+q+p$
$\therefore$ $2a + 2b + 2c + 2d = r+q+p$

Now $QX = b+d$
and as $2(a+c) + 2(b+d) = p+q+r$
$\therefore$ $2q + 2QX = p+q+r$

$\therefore$ $QX = \dfrac{p-q+r}{2}$

b Now $2x + 2y + 2z = p+q+r$
$\therefore$ $2y + 2(x+z) = p+q+r$
$\therefore$ $2y + 2q = p+q+r$

$QZ = \dfrac{p-q+r}{2} = QX$

i.e. $\underline{Z \text{ is at } X}$.

4.16 We wish to minimise PF.

But $PF = PN$ {definition of parabola}

$\therefore$ PF is a minimum when PN is a minimum
and this clearly occurs when P is at O.
i.e. $\underline{P \text{ is at the vertex}}$.

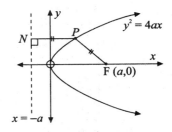

4.17 Let A be $\left(\dfrac{s^2}{4}, s\right)$, $s \neq 0$ and B be $\left(\dfrac{t^2}{4}, t\right)$, $t \neq 0$.

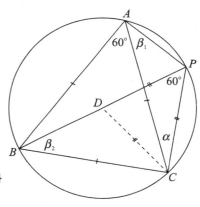

Now $\overline{OB} \perp \overline{OA}$. $\therefore$ $m_{OB}.m_{OA} = -1$

$$\therefore \quad \frac{s}{\frac{s^2}{4}} \cdot \frac{t}{\frac{t^2}{4}} = -1$$

$$\therefore \quad st = \frac{-s^2 t^2}{16}$$

$$\therefore \quad s^2 t^2 + 16st = 0$$
$$\therefore \quad st(st + 16) = 0$$
$$\therefore \quad st = -16 \dots\dots(1) \qquad \{\text{as} \;\; st \neq 0\}$$

Now $m_{AB} = \dfrac{t - s}{\frac{t^2}{4} - \frac{s^2}{4}} = \dfrac{4(t - s)}{(t + s)(t - s)} = \dfrac{4}{t + s}$ $\{\text{as} \;\; t \neq s\}$

$\therefore$ $\overleftrightarrow{AB}$ has equation $4x - [t + s]y = 4\left(\dfrac{s^2}{4}\right) - [t + s]s$

i.e. $4x - [t + s]y = -st = 16$ $\{\text{using } (1)\}$

which <u>passes through $(4, 0)$</u> regardless of the values of s and t.

4.18 Locate point D on $\overline{PB}$ such that $PD = PC$.
We must therefore prove that $AP = BD$.
[This will result in $BP = AP + CP$]

Proof: Join $\overline{DC}$.

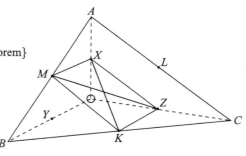

$\overline{BC}$ subtends equal angles at A and P.
$\therefore$ $\angle BPC = 60^{\varrho}$
Thus $\triangle DPC$ is isosceles with vertical angle 60^{ϱ}.
Hence $\triangle DPC$ is equilateral.
$\therefore$ $DP = PC = DC \dots\dots(a)$
If we let $\angle ACP = \alpha$
then $\angle ACD = 60 - \alpha$
$\therefore$ $\angle DCB = 60 - (60 - \alpha)$ $\{\triangle ABC$ is equilateral, given$\}$
$\therefore$ $\angle DCB = \alpha$
Thus, in $\triangle$'s APC and BDC,
(1) $\angle PCA = \angle DCB$ $\{$proved above$\}$
(2) $AC = BC$ $\{$given$\}$
(3) $PC = DC$ $\{$proved above at (a)$\}$
$\therefore$ $\triangle$'s APC and BDC are congruent. $\{$SAS$\}$
$\therefore$ $AP = BD$
$\therefore$ $BP = BD + DP$ and $\therefore$ $\underline{BP = AP + CP}$.

4.19 Join $\overline{XM}, \overline{MK}, \overline{KZ}, \overline{ZX}$
In $\triangle AOC$, X and Z are midpoints of $\overline{AO}$
and $\overline{OC}$ respectively.

$\therefore$ $\overline{XZ} \parallel \overline{AC}$ and $XZ = \frac{1}{2}AC\dots\dots(1)$ $\{$midpoint theorem$\}$
Similarly, in $\triangle ABC$,

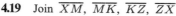

$\overline{MK} \parallel \overline{AC}$ and $MK = \frac{1}{2}AC\dots\dots(2)$

Thus $\overline{XZ} \parallel \overline{MK}$ and $XZ = MK$
$\therefore$ $XZKM$ is a parallelogram.

Hence the diagonals $\overline{MZ}$ and $\overline{KX}$ bisect each other.
It can similarly be shown that $\overline{LY}$ bisects $\overline{KX}$.
Hence $\overline{KX}, \overline{MZ},$ and $\overline{LY}$ are concurrent.

4.20 Let $\angle B = \angle C + 90^{\circ}$. P and Q are points as illustrated.
Let $\angle C = \alpha_1$. $\therefore$ $\angle PBA = \alpha_2$ {given}
and $\angle QAB = \alpha_3$ {alternate angles equal as $\overline{AQ} \parallel \overline{PB}$}
Thus $\alpha_1 = \alpha_3$.

$\therefore$ $\overline{AQ}$ is a tangent to the circumcircle of A, B, C

{converse to angle between a tangent and a chord thm.}

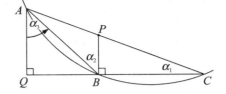

4.21   **a** Let S be the point of intersection of the
circumcircles of Δ's ACY, ABZ.
Now $\angle ASB = 120^{\circ}$ {$ZASB$ a cyclic quad.}
and $\angle ASC = 120^{\circ}$ {likewise}
$\therefore$ $\angle BSC = 120^{\circ}$ {sum of angles at a pt.}
$\therefore$ $BSCX$ is a cyclic quadrilateral.
$\therefore$ S lies on arc BC, i.e., on circumcircle of ΔBCX.

b Let L, M, K be centres of the circles shown.

$\overline{LM}$ is a perpendicular bisector of $\overline{AS}$.

$\overline{LK}$ is a perpendicular bisector of $\overline{BS}$.

$\overline{MK}$ is a perpendicular bisector of $\overline{CS}$.

$\therefore$ ΔLMK can be split into 3 cyclic
quadrilaterals {as shown}, and since
$\angle ASB = \angle ASC = \angle BSC = 120^{\circ}$,
each remaining angle at L, M, K is 60°.
{opposite angles of cyclic quad. suppl.}
$\therefore$ $\underline{\Delta KLM}$ is equilateral.

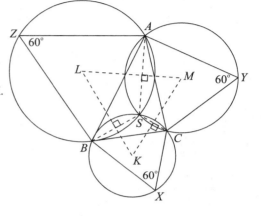

4.22 Join $\overline{PQ}$, $\overline{QR}$, and $\overline{RS}$, and let the
orthocentre be O. Let $\angle PBD = \alpha_1$.
Now $BDQP$ is a cyclic quadrilateral.

{$\overline{BD}$ subtends equal angles at P and Q}
$\therefore$ $\angle PQD = 180^{\circ} - \alpha$ {opposite angles of cyclic
quadrilateral are supp.}

Also $BDOF$ is a cyclic quadrilateral.
{$\angle BFO + \angle ODB = 90^{\circ} + 90^{\circ} = 180^{\circ}$}
$\therefore$ $\alpha_1 = \alpha_2$ {exterior angle of cyclic quad. thm.}

But $OQDR$ is a cyclic quadrilateral.
{$\angle ORD + \angle OQD = 90^{\circ} + 90^{\circ} = 180^{\circ}$}

$\therefore$ $\alpha_2 = \alpha_3$ {subtended by same chord $\overline{DR}$}

Thus $\angle PQR = (180 - \alpha) + \alpha = 180^{\circ}$

$\therefore$ $\underline{P, Q, R}$ are collinear.

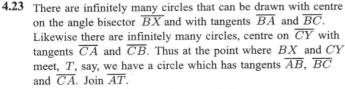

Similarly Q, R, S are collinear, and so $\underline{P, Q, R, S}$ are collinear.

4.23 There are infinitely many circles that can be drawn with centre
on the angle bisector $\overline{BX}$ and with tangents $\overline{BA}$ and $\overline{BC}$.
Likewise there are infinitely many circles, centre on $\overline{CY}$ with
tangents $\overline{CA}$ and $\overline{CB}$. Thus at the point where $\overline{BX}$ and $\overline{CY}$
meet, T, say, we have a circle which has tangents $\overline{AB}$, $\overline{BC}$
and $\overline{CA}$. Join $\overline{AT}$.

Now A is an external point to this circle.

$\therefore$ AT bisects $\angle BAC$ {external point to circle thm.}

Thus the 3 angle bisectors are concurrent.

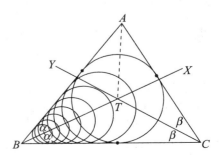

4.24 Let O be the origin and l lie on the x-axis.
V lies on the y-axis and V is $(0, k)$, k a constant.

Slope of $\overline{BV} = \dfrac{0 - k}{b - 0} = \dfrac{-k}{b}$

$\therefore$ slope of $AW = \dfrac{b}{k}$

$\therefore$ equation of $\overleftrightarrow{AW}$ is $bx - ky = -b^2$,

which cuts the y-axis at $M\left(0, \dfrac{b^2}{k}\right)$.

$\therefore$ C is $\left(b, \dfrac{b^2}{k}\right)$. Likewise D is $\left(-b, \dfrac{b^2}{k}\right)$

where b varies and k is a constant.

Thus C and D lie on $y = \dfrac{1}{k}x^2$ i.e., on a fixed parabola.

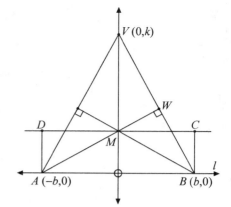

4.25 Let $\dfrac{1}{OA} + \dfrac{1}{OB} = k$, a constant for all positions of A and B.

Let A be $(a, 0)$ and B be $(0, b)$ of a rectangular coordinate system.

The equation of $\overleftrightarrow{AB}$ is $bx + ay = ab$ where $\dfrac{1}{a} + \dfrac{1}{b} = k$.

Now point $P\left(\dfrac{1}{k}, \dfrac{1}{k}\right)$ is a fixed point on the line $\overleftrightarrow{AB}$

for all values of a and b.

Check: $b\left(\dfrac{1}{k}\right) + a\left(\dfrac{1}{k}\right) = \dfrac{a + b}{k}$

$= \left[\dfrac{a + b}{\frac{1}{a} + \frac{1}{b}}\right]\cdot\dfrac{ab}{ab}$

$= \dfrac{(a + b)ab}{(b + a)}$

$= ab$

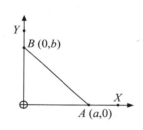

Thus for all positions of A and B, the line $\overleftrightarrow{AB}$ passes through a fixed point.

4.26 Let P be at A originally.

arc $PQ = (2r)\theta$

$\therefore$ arc $P_1 Q = 2\theta r$ also.

But arc $P_1 Q = r\phi$

Thus $2\theta r = \phi r$

$\therefore$ $\phi = 2\theta$

Thus P_1 and R coincide.
{angle at centre is double angle
at circumference theorem}

$\therefore$ P moves on a diameter.

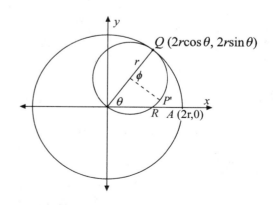

4.27 Join $\overline{EO}$ and $\overline{OD}$.

Let $\angle CEO = \alpha_1$, $\angle CDO = \beta_1$

$\triangle OXD$ is isosceles $\therefore$ $\beta_1 = \beta_2$

$\triangle AXC$ is isosceles $\therefore$ $\beta_2 = \beta_3$

and $\beta_3 = \beta_4$

{vertically opposite angles}

Likewise $\alpha_1 = \alpha_2 = \alpha_3 = \alpha_4$

Now $\angle OAC = 2\beta$ {exterior angle of $\triangle$ theorem}

Consequently $\angle OMC = \alpha + 2\beta$

{exterior angle of $\triangle AMC$}

$\therefore$ $\angle EOM = \alpha + 2\beta - \alpha = 2\beta$

{exterior angle of $\triangle OEM$}

Thus arc EX subtends 2β at the centre.

Hence $\angle EDX = \beta$

But $\angle ODX = \beta$

$\therefore$ O lies on ED $\therefore$ $\overline{ED}$ is a diameter.

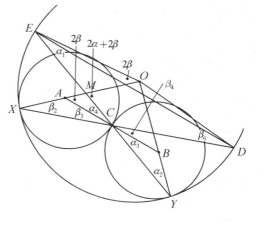

4.28 Join $\overline{CX}$, $\overline{CY}$, $\overline{CP}$, $\overline{CQ}$ and assume

$\overline{QX}$ and $\overline{PY}$ do not pass through C.

Now A, C and B are collinear. {property of touching circles}

Let $\angle PQC = \alpha$

$\therefore$ $\angle QCB = \alpha$ {$\triangle CBQ$ is isosceles}

$\therefore$ $\angle CBP = 2\alpha$ {exterior angle of $\triangle CBQ$}

$\therefore$ $\angle CAY = 2\alpha$ {alternate angles for parallels $\overline{XY}$ and $\overline{PQ}$}

$\therefore$ $\angle AXC = \alpha$ {interior angles of isosc. $\triangle XAC$}

Now $\angle AXC = \angle CQB$ and $\angle AXQ = \angle BQX$

$\therefore$ C lies on XQ.

Similarly $\angle XYC = \angle XYP$, $\therefore$ YP goes through C.

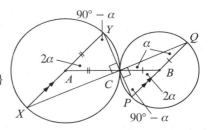

4.29 Since E is the midpoint of $\overline{AD}$, and $\overline{AD}$ subtends a right angle at C, $\overline{AD}$ is a diameter of a circle which passes through A, C and D, and E is its centre.

If $\angle CAD = \angle DAB = \alpha$, say, and CA is produced to F, PA is the exterior bisector of $\angle FAB$.

$\therefore$ $\angle FAP = \angle PAB = \beta$, say

Now at A, $2\alpha + 2\beta = 180$ $\therefore$ $\beta = 90 - \alpha$.

In $\triangle ACD$, $\angle D = 90 - \alpha$

In $\triangle CED$, $\angle C = 90 - \alpha$, since $\triangle$ in isosceles

$\therefore$ $\overline{BP}$ subtends equal angles at A and C.

$\therefore$ B, P, A and C are concyclic.

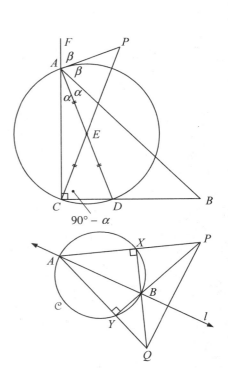

4.30 Let l meet $\mathcal{C}$ in A and B as shown. Draw $\overrightarrow{PA}$ and $\overrightarrow{PB}$ to meet the circle again in X and Y respectively. Let $\overline{XB}$ and $\overline{AY}$ produced meet in Q. Then $\overline{PQ}$ is perpendicular to l.

Proof: In $\triangle APQ$, $\overline{QX} \perp \overline{AP}$ and $\overline{PY} \perp \overline{AQ}$.

Thus B is the orthocentre of $\triangle APQ$.

Hence, $\overline{AB}$ produced (i.e., l) is perpendicular to $\overline{PQ}$.

4.31 Place the triangle on the Cartesian plane as illustrated.

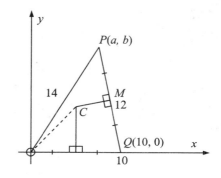

The centre of the circumcircle is located at the intersection of the perpendicular bisectors of the sides.

Now $OP = \sqrt{a^2 + b^2} = 14$

$\therefore\quad a^2 + b^2 = 196 \ldots\ldots(1)$

and $PQ = \sqrt{(a-10)^2 + b^2} = 12$

$\therefore\quad (a-10)^2 + b^2 = 144$

Thus $(a-10)^2 + 196 - a^2 = 144$

$\therefore\quad a^2 - 20a + 100 + 196 - a^2 = 144$

$\therefore\quad a = \frac{38}{5}$

Hence in (1) $b^2 = 196 - \left(\frac{38}{5}\right)^2 = \frac{3456}{25}$ and $\therefore\quad b = \frac{\sqrt{3456}}{5} = \frac{24\sqrt{6}}{5}$

M is therefore $\left(\frac{a+10}{2}, \frac{b}{2}\right)$ i.e. $\left(\frac{44}{5}, \frac{12\sqrt{6}}{5}\right)$ and slope of $\overleftrightarrow{PQ}$ is $\frac{b-0}{a-10} = \frac{\frac{24\sqrt{6}}{5}}{-2.4} = -2\sqrt{6}.$

$\therefore\quad \overleftrightarrow{CM}$ has slope $\frac{1}{2\sqrt{6}}$ and so the equation of $\overleftrightarrow{CM}$ is

$$x - 2\sqrt{6}y = \left(\frac{44}{5}\right) - 2\sqrt{6}\left(\frac{12\sqrt{6}}{5}\right)$$

i.e. $x - 2\sqrt{6}y = \frac{44}{5} - \frac{144}{5}$

i.e. $x - 2\sqrt{6}y = -20$

But $x_c = 5$ $\therefore\quad 5 - 2\sqrt{6}y_c = -20$

$\therefore\quad y_c = \frac{25}{2\sqrt{6}}$

$\therefore\quad r^2 = x_c^2 + y_c^2 = 25 + \frac{625}{24} = \frac{1225}{24}$

$\therefore\quad r = \frac{35}{2\sqrt{6}},$ i.e., the radius is $\frac{35}{2\sqrt{6}}$ units.

4.32 Let $AB = BC = a$ and place triangle ABC on the Cartesian plane as illustrated.

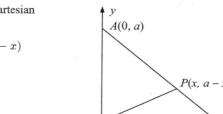

The equation of $\overline{AC}$ is $x + y = a$. Thus P is $(x, a-x)$

Now $(AP)^2 + (CP)^2 = (x-0)^2 + (a-x-a)^2$

$\qquad\qquad\qquad\qquad + (a-x)^2 + (0-a+x)^2$

$\qquad\qquad\qquad = x^2 + x^2 + (a-x)^2 + (x-a)^2$

$\qquad\qquad\qquad = 2x^2 + 2(a-x)^2$

$\qquad\qquad\qquad = 2[x^2 + (a-x)^2]$

$\qquad\qquad\qquad = \underline{2(BP)^2}$

4.33 When the knot comes to rest, the vector sum of the forces acting on the knot is zero. Since the weights on the string are equal, the triangle of forces is equilateral and the 3 strings will therefore meet at 120° angles to one another. If the largest angle of the triangle formed by the 3 holes is $\leqslant 120^o$, the knot will come to rest at the above defined point. However, if the largest angle formed by the 3 holes is $> 120^o$, the system is not stable and the knot will pass through the hole corresponding to the <u>obtuse angle</u>.

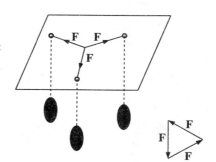

4.34 Let A, B, C and D have position vectors $\mathbf{a}$, $\mathbf{b}$, $\mathbf{c}$ and $\mathbf{d}$ relative to some origin O.

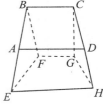

Then $\overrightarrow{AD} = \mathbf{d} - \mathbf{a}$, $\quad \overrightarrow{BC} = \mathbf{c} - \mathbf{b}$

Now $\quad \overrightarrow{AD} \cdot \overrightarrow{BC}$

$\quad = \quad (\mathbf{d} - \mathbf{a}) \cdot (\mathbf{c} - \mathbf{b})$

$\quad = \quad \underline{\mathbf{d} \cdot \mathbf{c} - \mathbf{a} \cdot \mathbf{c} - \mathbf{d} \cdot \mathbf{b} + \mathbf{a} \cdot \mathbf{b}}$

Also $\quad (AB)^2 + (CD)^2 - (AC)^2 - (BD)^2$

$\quad = \quad |\overrightarrow{AB}|^2 + |\overrightarrow{CD}|^2 - |\overrightarrow{AC}|^2 - |\overrightarrow{BD}|^2$

$\quad = \quad |\mathbf{b} - \mathbf{a}|^2 + |\mathbf{d} - \mathbf{c}|^2 - |\mathbf{c} - \mathbf{a}|^2 - |\mathbf{d} - \mathbf{b}|^2$

$\quad = \quad (\mathbf{b} - \mathbf{a}) \cdot (\mathbf{b} - \mathbf{a}) + (\mathbf{d} - \mathbf{c}) \cdot (\mathbf{d} - \mathbf{c}) - (\mathbf{c} - \mathbf{a}) \cdot (\mathbf{c} - \mathbf{a}) - (\mathbf{d} - \mathbf{b}) \cdot (\mathbf{d} - \mathbf{b})$

$\quad = \quad \mathbf{b} \cdot \mathbf{b} - 2\mathbf{a} \cdot \mathbf{b} + \mathbf{a} \cdot \mathbf{a} + \mathbf{d} \cdot \mathbf{d} - 2\mathbf{c} \cdot \mathbf{d} + \mathbf{c} \cdot \mathbf{c} - \mathbf{c} \cdot \mathbf{c} + 2\mathbf{a} \cdot \mathbf{c} - \mathbf{a} \cdot \mathbf{a} - \mathbf{d} \cdot \mathbf{d} + 2\mathbf{b} \cdot \mathbf{d} - \mathbf{b} \cdot \mathbf{b}$

$\quad = \quad \underline{-2(\mathbf{c} \cdot \mathbf{d} - \mathbf{a} \cdot \mathbf{c} - \mathbf{b} \cdot \mathbf{d} + \mathbf{a} \cdot \mathbf{b})}$

Thus $\quad \overrightarrow{AD} \perp \overrightarrow{BC} \quad \Longleftrightarrow \quad \overrightarrow{AD} \cdot \overrightarrow{BC} = 0$

$\qquad\qquad\qquad\qquad \Longleftrightarrow \quad \mathbf{d} \cdot \mathbf{c} - \mathbf{a} \cdot \mathbf{c} - \mathbf{d} \cdot \mathbf{b} + \mathbf{a} \cdot \mathbf{b} = 0$

$\qquad\qquad\qquad\qquad \Longleftrightarrow \quad (AB)^2 + (CD)^2 - (AC)^2 - (BD)^2 = 0$

$\qquad\qquad\qquad\qquad \Longleftrightarrow \quad \underline{(AB)^2 + (CD)^2 = (AC)^2 + (BD)^2}$

4.35 Since A, B, E and D are not coplanar, there is a unique sphere through these 4 points.

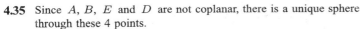

Now the intersection of the plane $ABFE$ and the sphere is a circle containing A, B, E and F since the quadrilateral is cyclic. Thus F is on the sphere.

Similarly, it follows that H, G and C lie on the sphere.

Thus all the vertices lie on the sphere.

4.36 $\overrightarrow{OB} = \overrightarrow{OA} + \overrightarrow{AB}$

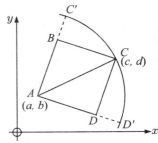

$\qquad = [a, b] + \tfrac{1}{\sqrt{2}} \overrightarrow{AC'}$

$\qquad = [a, b] + \tfrac{1}{\sqrt{2}} R_{45°} \overrightarrow{AC}$

$\qquad = [a, b] + \tfrac{1}{\sqrt{2}} R_{45°} [c - a, \ d - b]$

$\qquad = [a, b] + \tfrac{1}{\sqrt{2}} \left[\dfrac{(c - a) - (d - b)}{\sqrt{2}} , \ \dfrac{(c - a) + (d - b)}{\sqrt{2}} \right]$

$\left\{ R_\theta(x, y) = (x \cos\theta - y \sin\theta, \ x \sin\theta + y \cos\theta) = \left(\dfrac{x - y}{\sqrt{2}}, \dfrac{x + y}{\sqrt{2}} \right) \text{ for } \theta = 45° \right\}$

$\qquad = [a, b] + \left[\dfrac{c - a - d + b}{2}, \ \dfrac{c - a + d - b}{2} \right]$

$\qquad = \left[\dfrac{a + b + c - d}{2}, \ \dfrac{b + c + d - a}{2} \right]. \qquad \therefore \quad B \text{ is } \left(\dfrac{a + b + c - d}{2}, \dfrac{b + c + d - a}{2} \right).$

Likewise $\overrightarrow{OD} = \overrightarrow{OA} + \overrightarrow{AD}$

$\qquad\qquad = \overrightarrow{OA} + \tfrac{1}{\sqrt{2}} \overrightarrow{AD'}$

$\qquad\qquad = [a, b] + \tfrac{1}{\sqrt{2}} R_{-45°} \overrightarrow{AC}$

$\qquad\qquad \vdots$

$\qquad\qquad = \left[\dfrac{a + c + d - b}{2}, \ \dfrac{a + b + d - c}{2} \right]. \qquad \therefore \quad D \text{ is } \left(\dfrac{a + c + d - b}{2}, \dfrac{a + b + d - c}{2} \right)$

4.37 Let L, M be midpoints of $\overline{AB}$ and $\overline{CD}$.

Join $\overline{LM}$ and $\overline{BD}$, letting them meet at P.

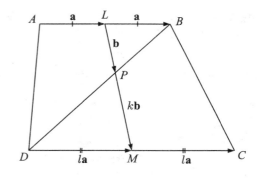

Let $\overrightarrow{AL} = \overrightarrow{LB} = \mathbf{a}$ and $\overrightarrow{LP} = \mathbf{b}$

Now $\overrightarrow{PM} = k\,\mathbf{b}$ and $\overrightarrow{DM} = \overrightarrow{MC} = l\,\mathbf{a}$
for some scalars k and l.

Now further, there exists a scalar m such that

$$\overrightarrow{BP} = m\overrightarrow{PD}$$
$$\therefore \quad -\mathbf{a} + \mathbf{b} = m(k\mathbf{b} - l\mathbf{a})$$
$$\therefore \quad -\mathbf{a} + \mathbf{b} = mk\mathbf{b} - ml\mathbf{a}$$
$$\therefore \quad (ml - 1)\mathbf{a} = (mk - 1)\mathbf{b}$$

which is absurd unless $ml - 1 = 0$ and $mk - 1 = 0$ {these vectors cannot be parallel}
Thus $ml = mk = 1$ and $\therefore$ $\underline{k = l}$.

Thus $\overrightarrow{AC} = \overrightarrow{AL} + \overrightarrow{LP} + \overrightarrow{PM} + \overrightarrow{MC}$

$$= \mathbf{a} + \mathbf{b} + k\mathbf{b} + l\mathbf{a}$$
$$= \mathbf{a}(1 + l) + \mathbf{b}(1 + l) \qquad \{\text{as } k = l\}$$
$$= (1 + l)(\mathbf{a} + \mathbf{b})$$
$$= (1 + l)\overrightarrow{AP}. \quad \text{Where} \quad l > 0 \quad \text{and} \quad \therefore \quad 1 + l \neq 0$$

$\therefore \quad \overrightarrow{AC} \parallel \overrightarrow{AP}$ {as one vector is a scalar multiple of the other.}

$\therefore \quad A,\ C,\ P$ are collinear.

Thus the diagonals and the <u>line joining</u> the centres of the parallel sides <u>meet at a common point.</u>

4.38 $\cos \alpha = \dfrac{x}{a}$ {in $\triangle PBT$}

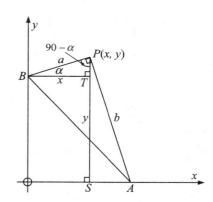

Also $\cos \alpha = \dfrac{y}{b}$ {in $\triangle PSA$}

$$\therefore \quad \frac{x}{a} = \frac{y}{b}$$

or $y = \dfrac{b}{a}x$

Since $OP^2 = x^2 + y^2$

$$= a^2 \cos^2 \alpha + b^2 \cos^2 \alpha$$
$$= \cos^2 \alpha.(a^2 + b^2)$$

Then $OP = \sqrt{a^2 + b^2}\ |\cos \alpha|$

$\therefore \quad OP \leqslant \sqrt{a^2 + b^2}$ {maximum value of $|\cos \alpha|$ is 1,
occurring when $\alpha = k\pi$, k in Z
P at (a, b) and $(-a, -b)$}

OR

$OAPB$ is a cyclic quadrilateral
        {$\angle BOA + \angle BPA = 180^{\circ}$}
Consequently, $\alpha_1 = \alpha_2$
        {angles in same segment theorem}
But α_1 is fixed (constant)
$\therefore \quad \alpha_2$ is constant
$\therefore \quad P$ lies on a line segment through O.

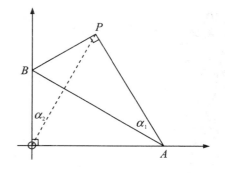

4.39 Construction

(1) Locate M, midpoint of $\overline{AB}$.

(2) Construct an isosceles triangle on $\overline{AB}$ with equal sides of length MT.

(3) Let the apex of the triangle be O; construct a circle, centre O, radius MT.

(4) Circle O touches "eye-level" at E.

$\therefore$ E is the required point.

Proof:

$\alpha_1 = \beta = \alpha_2$ {Equal chords subtend equal angles}

If E moves along "eye-level" and arrives at positions E_1 and E_2, it is clear that $\alpha_1 > \beta_1 \Rightarrow \beta \leqslant \alpha_1$, $\alpha_2 > \beta_2 \Rightarrow \beta \leqslant \alpha_2$ and $\beta_n = \alpha_n$ when E is the point of tangency of circle O and "eye-level". ....(1)

Suppose circle O cuts "eye-level" at E_1 and E_2, where $OE_1 = OE_2 = MT$.

But $\overline{OM} \parallel \overline{E_1T} \parallel \overline{E_2T}$, and $\therefore$ $E_1 = E_2 = E$.

Also $OMTE$ is a rectangle, and $\therefore$ $\overline{OE} \perp \overline{ET}$

$\therefore$ E is the point of tangency ....(2)

$\therefore$ From (1) and (2), the <u>construction provides</u> the required point E.

4.40 Let $\triangle DFG$ have area a units^2 and $\triangle FEC$ have area b units^2

$\therefore$ $\triangle GFC$ has area a units^2.

{triangles with the same base and height have equal areas}

Also $\triangle GBC$ has area $a + b$ units^2

$\therefore$ $\triangle DCF = 3a + b$ units^2

and $\triangle ABD = 3a + b$ units^2

But $ABCD$ has area $4b$ units^2 {$\triangle ADF$ is congruent to $\triangle ECF$}

$\therefore$ $3a + b = 2b$

$\therefore$ $b = 3a$ and hence, $\dfrac{\text{area } \triangle DFG}{\text{area } ABCD} = \dfrac{a}{4b} = \underline{\dfrac{1}{12}}$

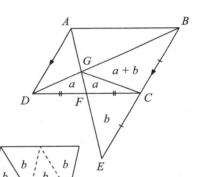

4.41 An Algebraic Argument:

$\triangle$'s BPQ, BAC are similar.

$\therefore$ $\dfrac{BM}{PQ} = \dfrac{BN}{AC}$

{corresponding line segments in the $\triangle$'s have lengths in proportion}

$\therefore$ $\dfrac{h - x}{x} = \dfrac{h}{b}$

$\therefore$ $hb - bx = hx$

$\therefore$ $hb = (h + b)x$

But $h > 0$, $b > 0$ $\Rightarrow$ $\dfrac{h + b}{2} \geqslant \sqrt{hb}$ {arithmetic-mean geometric-mean inequality}

$\therefore$ $\dfrac{hb}{2} = \left(\dfrac{h + b}{2}\right) x \geqslant \sqrt{hb}.x$

$\therefore$ $\dfrac{\sqrt{hb}}{2} \geqslant x$

$\therefore$ $\dfrac{hb}{4} \geqslant x^2$ {both sides were positive}

$$\therefore \quad \tfrac{1}{2}bh \geqslant 2x^2$$

$$\therefore \quad \tfrac{1}{2}[\text{area of } \triangle ABC] \geqslant \text{ area of square}$$

i.e.,　area of square $\leqslant \tfrac{1}{2}$[area of triangle]　with equality occurring $\iff$　$h = b$.

Thus the question is incorrect and should have read:

"Prove that the area of the square is less than or equal to a half the area of the triangle."

Geometric Argument:　(alternative solution)

Fold the triangle along lines $\overline{PS}$, $\overline{PQ}$ and $\overline{QR}$.
A' is the image of A, etc.
There are three cases.

Case (i)　　　　　　　Case (ii)　　　　　　Case (iii)

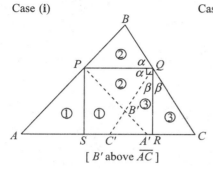

[B' above $\overline{AC}$]　　　[B' on $\overline{AC}$]　　　[B' below $\overline{AC}$]

In case **(ii)**,　area of square $= \tfrac{1}{2}$[area of triangle].

In cases **(i)** and **(iii)**, area ① + area ② + area ③ > area of square.

$\therefore$　area ① + area ② + area ③ + area of square > 2[area of square].

$\therefore$　area of $\triangle$ > 2[area of square].

$\therefore$　area of square $< \tfrac{1}{2}$[area of triangle].

Thus, combining results　**(i)**, **(ii)** and **(iii)**,　we have　area of square $\leqslant \tfrac{1}{2}$[area of triangle].

4.42　Consider the figure alongside.　Now　$\alpha_1 = \alpha_2$
{angle between a tangent and a chord theorem.}
Thus　$\triangle$'s XAT and XTB　are similar.
{$\alpha_1 = \alpha_2$　and $\angle X$ is common to both}

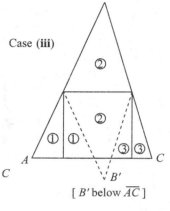

$$\therefore \quad \frac{XA}{XT} = \frac{XT}{XB}$$

$$\therefore \quad (XT)^2 = XA.XB$$

Thus in the figure given,　$(XY)^2 = XA.XB$
and similarly　$(XZ)^2 = XA.XB$

$$\therefore \quad (XY)^2 = (XZ)^2$$

$$\therefore \quad XY = XZ$$

4.43　Let $\overline{CD}$ have length h units.

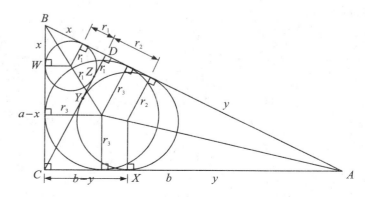

Then,　$h = CY + YD$

$\therefore$　$h = CX + YD$
{equal tangents theorem}

$\therefore$　$h = b - y + r_2$......(1)

Also　$h = CZ + ZD$

$\therefore$　$h = CW + ZD$

$\therefore$　$h = a - x + r_1$......(2)

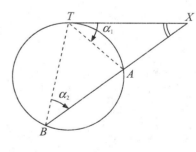

But along the hypotenuse

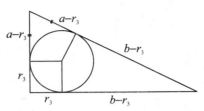

$$\therefore \quad (a - r_3) + (b - r_3) = x + y + r_1 + r_2$$

$$\therefore \quad a + b - 2r_3 = (a + r_1 - h) + (b + r_2 - h) + r_1 + r_2$$

$$\therefore \quad a + b - 2r_3 = a + b + 2r_1 + 2r_2 - 2h$$

$$\therefore \quad 2h = 2r_1 + 2r_2 + 2r_3$$

$$\therefore \quad h = \underline{r_1 + r_2 + r_3}$$

4.44 Triangles BZX, YZA are equiangular and $\therefore$ similar.

Thus $\dfrac{h_2}{h_1} = \dfrac{4a}{3a} = \dfrac{4}{3}.$

Hence $h_2 = \frac{4}{7}.12a = \dfrac{48a}{7}$

Likewise $h_3 = \frac{3}{5}.12a = \dfrac{36a}{5}$

$\therefore$ total shaded area

$$= 12a.6a - \left[\tfrac{1}{2}.3a.12a + \tfrac{1}{2}.4a.\dfrac{48a}{7} + \tfrac{1}{2}.2a.12a + \tfrac{1}{2}.3a.\dfrac{36a}{5} \right]$$

$$= a^2 \left[72 - 18 - \tfrac{96}{7} - 12 - \tfrac{54}{5} \right]$$

$$= a^2 . 17\tfrac{17}{35}$$

$\therefore$ fraction shaded $= \dfrac{a^2 . \frac{612}{35}}{72a^2} = \dfrac{17}{70}$

4.45 $\overrightarrow{AN} = \overrightarrow{AB} + \overrightarrow{BN}, \quad \overrightarrow{BP} = \overrightarrow{BC} + \overrightarrow{CP}, \quad \overrightarrow{CM} = \overrightarrow{CA} + \overrightarrow{AM}$

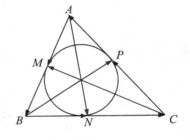

$$\therefore \quad \overrightarrow{AN} + \overrightarrow{BP} + \overrightarrow{CM}$$

$$= \overrightarrow{AB} + \overrightarrow{BC} + \overrightarrow{CA} + \overrightarrow{BN} + \overrightarrow{CP} + \overrightarrow{AM}$$

But $\overrightarrow{AB} + \overrightarrow{BC} + \overrightarrow{CA} = \mathbf{0}$ {triangle}

and $\overrightarrow{AN} + \overrightarrow{BP} + \overrightarrow{CM} = \mathbf{0}$ is given.

$$\therefore \quad \overrightarrow{BN} + \overrightarrow{CP} + \overrightarrow{AM} = \mathbf{0} \quad ....(1)$$

Let $|\overrightarrow{AB}| = c, \quad |\overrightarrow{BC}| = a, \quad |\overrightarrow{CA}| = b$ and $\dfrac{a+b+c}{2} = s,$

then $|\overrightarrow{BN}| = s - b, \quad |\overrightarrow{CP}| = s - c, \quad |\overrightarrow{AM}| = s - a ....(2)*$

Now (1) implies that one can draw a <u>triangle</u> XYZ such that

$$\overrightarrow{XY} = \overrightarrow{BN}, \quad \overrightarrow{YZ} = \overrightarrow{CP} \quad \text{and} \quad \overrightarrow{ZX} = \overrightarrow{AM}$$

As the sides of $\triangle XYZ$ would be parallel to the sides of

$\triangle ABC$ $(\overline{XY} \parallel \overline{BC}, \quad \overline{YZ} \parallel \overline{CA}, \quad \overline{ZX} \parallel \overline{AB})$ the angles of $\triangle XYZ$ will be equal to that of $\triangle ABC$.

$\therefore$ $\triangle XYZ$ is similar to $\triangle ABC$ and

$\therefore$ the sides of the two triangles will be proportional.

i.e. $s - b = ka, \quad s - c = kb, \quad s - a = kc ....(3)$

Now the perimeter of ΔXYZ is $(s-b)+(s-c)+(s-a)$
$$= 3s-(b+c+a) = 3s-2s = s$$
$$= \tfrac{1}{2}(a+b+c)$$

Using (3)
$\therefore \quad ka+kb+kc = \tfrac{1}{2}(a+b+c) \quad \therefore \quad k=\tfrac{1}{2}$

Hence, $\quad s-b=\tfrac{1}{2}a, \quad s-c=\tfrac{1}{2}b, \quad s-a=\tfrac{1}{2}c$

$\therefore \quad s = b+\tfrac{1}{2}a = c+\tfrac{1}{2}b = a+\tfrac{1}{2}c$

$\therefore \quad \tfrac{1}{2}a+\tfrac{1}{2}b = c \quad$ and $\quad \tfrac{1}{2}c+\tfrac{1}{2}b = a$

$\qquad a+b = 2c \qquad\qquad c+b = 2a \qquad \therefore \quad a=b=c$

i.e. $\quad \underline{\Delta ABC \ \text{is equilateral.}} \qquad$ **Note:** (2) can be proved easily if not common knowledge.

4.46 $\underline{P \text{ moves on a line segment with end points } (a,b) \text{ and } (-a,-b).}$

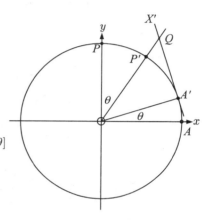

Let θ be the angle by which $\overline{OA}$ has turned anticlockwise.
$\therefore \quad A'$ is $(r\cos\theta, \ r\sin\theta)$

and the slope $\quad \overline{OA'} = \dfrac{r\sin\theta}{r\cos\theta} = \dfrac{\sin\theta}{\cos\theta}$

$\therefore \quad$ Slope of $\overleftrightarrow{A'X'} = \dfrac{-\cos\theta}{\sin\theta}$

$\therefore \quad$ Equation of $\overleftrightarrow{A'X'}$ is $\ [\cos\theta]x + [\sin\theta]y = r[\cos^2\theta + \sin^2\theta]$

$\qquad\qquad$ i.e. $\ [\cos\theta]x + [\sin\theta]y = r$ ....(1)

Now $\quad \angle AOP' = \dfrac{\pi}{2} - \theta$

$\therefore \quad$ slope of $\overline{OP'} = \tan\left(\dfrac{\pi}{2} - \theta\right) = \cot\theta = \dfrac{\cos\theta}{\sin\theta}$

$\therefore \quad$ Equation of $\overleftrightarrow{OP'}$ is $\ [\cos\theta]x - [\sin\theta]y = 0$ ....(2)

Now Q is the point where $\overleftrightarrow{OP'}$ and $\overleftrightarrow{A'X'}$ meet.

Solving (1) and (2) simultaneously we get $\quad x = \dfrac{r}{2\cos\theta}, \quad y = \dfrac{r}{2\sin\theta}$

and since $\quad \cos^2\theta + \sin^2\theta = 1, \quad$ then $\quad \left(\dfrac{r}{2x}\right)^2 + \left(\dfrac{r}{2y}\right)^2 = 1 \quad \therefore \quad \underline{\dfrac{1}{x^2} + \dfrac{1}{y^2} = \dfrac{4}{r^2}}$

<u>Sketch of locus</u>

Notice: The equation remains the same on replacing x by $-x$, $\ y$ by $-y$, $\ x$ by y, $\ y$ by $-x$, $\ x$ by $-y$.
Hence the graph is symmetrical about the axes and the lines $y = \pm x$.
It suffices therefore, to sketch the curve in quadrant 1 for $\ x \geqslant y$, and fill in the rest using symmetrical properties.

When $\quad x = y, \quad \dfrac{2}{x^2} = \dfrac{4}{r^2} \quad \therefore \quad x = \dfrac{r}{\sqrt{2}}$

i.e., the point $\quad \left(\dfrac{r}{\sqrt{2}}, \ \dfrac{r}{\sqrt{2}}\right)$

as $\quad x \to \infty, \quad \dfrac{1}{x^2} \to 0, \quad \therefore \quad \dfrac{1}{y^2} \to \dfrac{4}{r^2} \quad \therefore \quad y \to \dfrac{r}{2}, \quad$ and by symmetry , as $\quad y \to \infty, \quad x \to \dfrac{r}{2}$.

Thus the graph has asymptotes $\quad x = \pm\dfrac{r}{2}, \quad y = \pm\dfrac{r}{2}$.

4.47 **a** $OP.OP' = r^2$

Let P' be (X, Y) and P be (r, y)

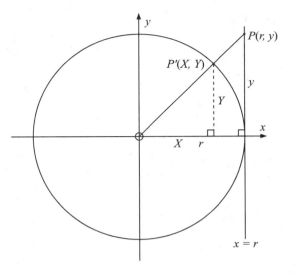

Now $\dfrac{Y}{X} = \dfrac{y}{r}$ {similar $\triangle$'s}

$\therefore\quad y = \dfrac{rY}{X}$

and $\sqrt{r^2 + y^2}.\sqrt{X^2 + Y^2} = r^2$

$\therefore\quad \sqrt{r^2 + \dfrac{Y^2 r^2}{X^2}}.\sqrt{X^2 + Y^2} = r^2$

$\therefore\quad \dfrac{r}{X}\sqrt{X^2 + Y^2}.\sqrt{X^2 + Y^2} = r^2$

$\therefore\quad X^2 + Y^2 = rX$

$\therefore\quad X^2 - rX + Y^2 = 0$

$\therefore\quad X^2 - rX + \left(\dfrac{r}{2}\right)^2 + Y^2 = \left(\dfrac{r}{2}\right)^2$

$\therefore\quad \left(X - \dfrac{r}{2}\right)^2 + Y^2 = \left(\dfrac{r}{2}\right)^2$

which is a circle, centre $\left(\dfrac{r}{2}, 0\right)$, radius $\dfrac{r}{2}$.

---

b For $n = 6$, the sketch is as shown.

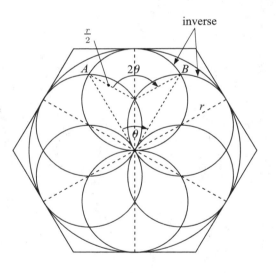

In general $\theta = \dfrac{2\pi}{n}$

Hence $2\theta = \dfrac{4\pi}{n}$ {angle at centre is double angle at circumference on same arc.}

$\therefore$ arc AB has length $\dfrac{2\theta}{2\pi}.2\pi\left(\dfrac{r}{2}\right)$

$= 2\theta.\dfrac{r}{2}$

$= \dfrac{4\pi}{n}.\dfrac{r}{2}$

$\therefore$ perimeter $= n.\dfrac{4\pi}{n}.\dfrac{r}{2}$

$= \underline{2\pi r}$ which is independent of n.

4.48 Let the radius be r and length l.

We insert 3-D coordinates as shown.

Let $P(X, Y, Z)$ be a point on the thread.

The projection of P on the yOz plane is $Q(0, r\cos\theta, r\sin\theta)$
$\{\theta$ as shown in figure.$\}$

Thus P is $(X, r\cos\theta, r\sin\theta)$, and N, the projection on to the xOy plane is $N(X, Y, 0)$ where $Y = r\cos\theta$.

Now suppose that the container is flattened out on to the xoy plane so that $\overline{EF}$ lies on the x-axis.

Then $B'C' = \frac{1}{2}(2\pi r) = \pi r$

Since the thread has minimum length, $\overline{A'C'}$ is a straight line and $P'T = QC = r\theta$.

$\triangle$'s $C'P'T'$ and $C'A'D'$ are similar.

$$\therefore \quad \frac{X}{r\theta} = \frac{l}{\pi r}$$

$$\therefore \quad \theta = \frac{\pi X}{l}$$

Since $Y = r\cos\theta$ then $Y = r\cos\left(\dfrac{\pi X}{l}\right)$

$\{r, l, \pi$ are constants$\}$

Thus the shadow is in the **shape of the cosine curve**.

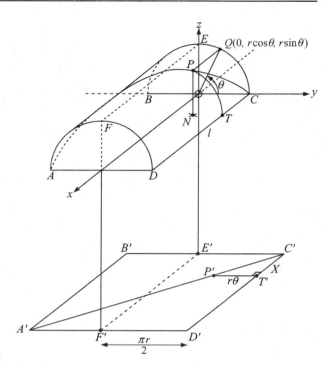

4.49 Draw $\overline{AX}$, $\overline{BY}$, $\overline{CZ}$ as shown, each concurrent at S.

Notation: $\triangle ABS$ means "the area of $\triangle ABS$".

Since areas of triangles with a common vertex and bases on the same line are in the same ratio as their bases,

we have $\quad \dfrac{\triangle ABX}{\triangle ABS} = \dfrac{AX}{AS} = \dfrac{\triangle ACX}{\triangle ACS}$

and since $\quad \triangle ABS = \triangle ACS$

$$\therefore \quad \triangle ABX = \triangle ACX \ldots\ldots(1)$$

but $\quad \dfrac{\triangle ABX}{\triangle ACX} = \dfrac{BX}{CX} \ldots\ldots(2)$

$$\therefore \quad BX = CX \qquad \{\text{comparing (1) and (2)}\}$$

$\therefore \quad \overline{AX}$ is a median of $\triangle ABC$.

Similarly $\overline{BY}$ and $\overline{CZ}$ are medians,

$\quad \therefore \quad$ <u>S is the centroid</u>.

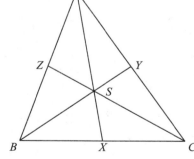

4.50 Let $ABCDEFGH$ be a cube with sides of length 1 unit.

Draw diagonals $\overline{AH}$, $\overline{BG}$ of faces shown.

Draw $\overline{A'H'}$ and $\overline{B'G'}$ parallel to these diagonals and equal in length.

Since $B'H' = A'G'$ {because of the symmetrical positioning of A', B', G' and H'} we deduce that $A'B'G'H'$ is a rectangle.

Allowing for the positions of A', B', G', H' to change along the given edges, the shape of the rectangle varies between two extreme positions.

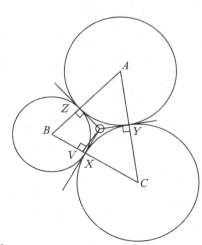

(1) $A'H' = AH = \sqrt{2}$ and $H'G' = HG = 1$
(2) $A'H' = EE = 0$ and $H'G' = EC = \sqrt{3}$.

This suggests that in some position the rectangle will be a square.

Let $G'C = x$ $\therefore$ $B'G' = \sqrt{2}x$

and $G'H' = \sqrt{(GG')^2 + (GH)^2 + (HH')^2}$ {3-D Pythagorean formula}

$$= \sqrt{(1-x)^2 + 1 + (1-x)^2}$$

Thus if $G'H' = B'G'$ then $\sqrt{2x^2 - 4x + 3} = \sqrt{2}x$

$$\therefore \quad 2x^2 - 4x + 3 = 2x^2$$

$$\therefore \quad x = \tfrac{3}{4}$$

Hence the side of the square is $\tfrac{3}{4}\sqrt{2}$ units, and $\tfrac{3}{4}\sqrt{2} > 1$.

Summary of Construction:

1. Find points A', B', G', H' on edges $\overline{AE}$, $\overline{BC}$, $\overline{CG}$, $\overline{EH}$ of the cube such that $EA' = EH' = CB' = CG' = \tfrac{3}{4}$ of the edge of the cube.

2. Drill a square hole normal to $A'B'G'H'$.

Thus a cube of edge greater than the edge of the given cube, but less than $\tfrac{3}{4}\sqrt{2}$ times the edge, can be passed through such a hole.

4.51 Let the common tangent at Y intersect the common tangent at Z at the point O.

Then $ZO = YO$........(1)

and $\overline{ZO} \perp \overline{AB}$, $\overline{YO} \perp \overline{AC}$.

Draw $\overline{OV} \perp \overline{BC}$,

then $BV + VC = BC$

But $BC = BX + XC = BZ + CY$

Hence $BV + VC = BZ + CY$........(2)

Also $(BV)^2 + (VO)^2 = (BO)^2 = (BZ)^2 + (ZO)^2$........(3)

and $(VC)^2 + (VO)^2 = (CO)^2 = (CY)^2 + (YO)^2$

i.e., $(VC)^2 + (VO)^2 = (CY)^2 + (ZO)^2$........(4) {from (1)}

Using (3) minus (4),

$$\therefore \quad (BV)^2 - (VC)^2 = (BZ)^2 - (CY)^2$$

$$\therefore \quad (BV + VC)(BV - VC) = (BZ + CY)(BZ - CY)$$

$$\therefore \quad BV - VC = BZ - CY........(5) \{\text{from (2)}\}$$

adding (2) and (5) $\therefore$ $2BV = 2BZ$

$\therefore$ $BV = BZ$

$\therefore$ $BV = BX$

$\therefore$ V and X are the same point.

$\therefore$ $\overline{OX} \perp \overline{BC}$

Now $(OX)^2 = (OB)^2 - (BX)^2$

$= (OB)^2 - (BZ)^2$

$= (OZ)^2$

$\therefore$ $\underline{OX = OZ = OY}$

Hence the circle through X, Y and Z touches $\overline{AB}$, $\overline{BC}$ and $\overline{CA}$.

i.e. is the <u>inscribed circle of $\triangle ABC$</u>.

4.52   **a**   As the earth and the moon appear equally large,
they subtend equal angles at P.

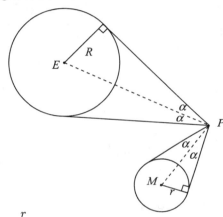

Thus $\sin \alpha = \dfrac{R}{PE} = \dfrac{r}{PM}$

$\therefore$ $\dfrac{PE}{PM} = \dfrac{R}{r}$ which is constant for all

such positions of P.

b   If $P(x, y, z)$, $E(A, B, C)$, $M(a, b, c)$

$r^2.(PE)^2 = R^2.(PM)^2$

$\therefore$ $r^2[(x - A)^2 + (y - B)^2 + (z - C)^2] = R^2[(x - a)^2 + (y - b)^2 + (z - c)^2]$

which on simplification has form

$x^2 + y^2 + z^2 + Kx + Ly + Mz + N = 0$,   for constants K, L, M, and N.

which is the equation of a sphere in 3-D coordinate geometry.

$\therefore$ $\underline{P \text{ lies on a sphere.}}$

5. ALGEBRA

5.1 Consider $x = 1 + \cfrac{1}{2 + \cfrac{1}{1 + \cfrac{1}{2 + \cfrac{1}{1 + \cfrac{1}{2 + 1}}}}}$ $\ddots$

$\therefore \quad x = 1 + \cfrac{1}{2 + \cfrac{1}{x}}$

$\therefore \quad x = 1 + \cfrac{1}{\left(\cfrac{2x+1}{x}\right)}$

$\therefore \quad x = 1 + \cfrac{x}{2x+1}$

$\therefore \quad x(2x+1) = 2x + 1 + x$

$\therefore \quad 2x^2 + x = 2x + 1 + x$

$\therefore \quad 2x^2 - 2x - 1 = 0$

$\therefore \quad x = \cfrac{2 \pm \sqrt{4 - 4.2.(-1)}}{4}$ {quadratic formula}

$\quad\quad = \cfrac{1 \pm \sqrt{3}}{2}$ on simplifying

$\quad\quad = \cfrac{1 + \sqrt{3}}{2}$ {as $x > 0$}

5.2 $x^3 + px^2 + qx + r = (x - a^2)(x - b^2)(x - [a^2 + b^2])$

$\quad\quad\quad\quad = (x^2 - [a^2 + b^2]x + a^2 b^2)(x - [a^2 + b^2])$

$\quad\quad\quad\quad = x^3 + x^2[-a^2 - b^2 - a^2 - b^2] + x[a^2 b^2 + (a^2 + b^2)^2] - a^2 b^2(a^2 + b^2)$

Thus $p = -2a^2 - 2b^2 \dots (1)$
$\left.\begin{array}{l} q = a^2 b^2 + (a^2 + b^2)^2 \dots (2) \\ r = -a^2 b^2(a^2 + b^2) \dots (3) \end{array}\right\}$ equating coefficients

$\therefore \quad a^2 + b^2 = -\cfrac{p}{2}$ from (1)

and consequently, $r = -a^2 b^2 \left(-\cfrac{p}{2}\right)$ and $a^2 b^2 = \cfrac{2r}{p}$

$\therefore$ in (2) $q = \cfrac{2r}{p} + \cfrac{p^4}{4}$

i.e., $\underline{4pq = 8r + p^5}$

5.3 If α is the common root, then

$$x^2 + ax + bc = (x - \alpha)(x - \beta_1) \quad \text{and} \quad x^2 + bx + ca = (x - \alpha)(x - \beta_2)$$

Equating coefficients $a = -\alpha - \beta_1$ and $bc = \alpha\beta_1$ and $b = -\alpha - \beta_2$ and $ca = \alpha\beta_2$

$\therefore$ $\beta_1 = -\alpha - a$ and $\beta_2 = -\alpha - b$

Also $bc + ca = \alpha\beta_1 + \alpha\beta_2$ and so $c(a + b) = \alpha(\beta_1 + \beta_2)$......(1)

Now since $\dfrac{bc}{ca} = \dfrac{\alpha\beta_1}{\alpha\beta_2}$ $\therefore$ $\dfrac{b}{a} = \dfrac{\beta_1}{\beta_2}$.   So, $\dfrac{b}{a} = \dfrac{-\alpha - a}{-\alpha - b}$.

$\therefore$ $-b\alpha - b^2 = -a\alpha - a^2$

$\therefore$ $a\alpha - b\alpha = b^2 - a^2$

$\therefore$ $\alpha(a - b) = (b - a)(b + a)$

Thus providing $a \neq b$, $a + b = -\alpha$......(2)

From (1) and (2) $\beta_1 + \beta_2 = -c$......(3)

Now $\beta_1\beta_2 = (-\alpha - a)(-\alpha - b)$

$$= \alpha^2 + a\alpha + b\alpha + ab$$
$$= \alpha^2 + \alpha(a + b) + ab$$
$$= \alpha^2 + \alpha(-\alpha) + ab$$
$$= \underline{ab}$$

Now β_1 and β_2 come from $x^2 - (\beta_1 + \beta_2)x + \beta_1\beta_2 = 0$ i.e., $\underline{x^2 + cx + ab = 0}$.

5.4 Try $f(x) = ax^n$

$\therefore$ $f(f(x)) = f(ax^n)$

$$= a(ax^n)^n$$
$$= a \times a^n x^{n^2}$$
$$= a^{n+1} . x^{n^2}$$

So we require $n^2 = 2$ $\therefore$ $n = \pm\sqrt{2}$

and $a^{n+1} = 4$

If $n = \sqrt{2}$, $a^{\sqrt{2}+1} = 4$

$$a = 4^{\frac{1}{\sqrt{2}+1}}$$

Thus $\underline{f(x) = 4^{\frac{1}{\sqrt{2}+1}} x^{\sqrt{2}}}$ would do.

5.5 $f(x, x) = x$..(a)

$f(x, y) = f(y, x)$..............................(b)

$(x + y)f(x, y) = yf(x, x + y)$............(c)

  a Letting $x = y = 2$ in (c) gives

$$4f(2, 2) = 2f(2, 4)$$
$$\therefore \quad 4 \times 2 = 2f(2, 4)$$
$$\therefore \quad \underline{f(2, 4) = 4}$$

  b Letting $x = 30$, $y = 10$ in (c) gives

$$10f(30, 40) = 40f(30, 10)$$
$$\therefore \quad f(30, 40) = 4f(10, 30) \qquad \text{\{using (b)\}}$$
$$= \tfrac{4}{20} . 20f(10, 10 + 20)$$
$$= \tfrac{1}{5} . 30f(10, 20) \qquad \text{\{using (c) again\}}$$

$$= 6f(10, 20)$$
$$= \tfrac{6}{10}.10f(10, 10 + 10)$$
$$= \tfrac{3}{5}.20f(10, 10) \qquad \{\text{using (c) again}\}$$
$$= 12.10 \qquad\qquad \{\text{using (a)}\}$$
$$= \underline{120}$$

5.6 Clearly $x = 2$ is a solution of $3^x + 4^x = 5^x$, and we show that it is the only solution, by graphical means.

Consider $y = \left(\tfrac{3}{5}\right)^x + \left(\tfrac{4}{5}\right)^x$.

y is the sum of two decreasing exponentials and is likewise decreasing.

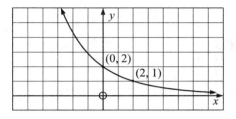

∴ $y = 1$ only at $x = 2$

i.e. $\left(\tfrac{3}{5}\right)^x + \left(\tfrac{4}{5}\right)^x = 1$ only at $x = 2$

∴ $3^x + 4^x = 5^x$ only at $\underline{x = 2}$.

5.7 $f(x) = ax^2 + bx + c$
$f(a) = c$
∴ $a^3 + ba + c = c$
∴ $a^3 + ba = 0$
∴ $a(a^2 + b) = 0$
∴ $b = -a^2$ $\{\text{as}\ a \neq 0\}$......(1)

$f(b) = b$
∴ $ab^2 + b^2 + c = b$......(2)

$f(c) = c$
$ac^2 + bc + c = c$
∴ $a^2c + bc = 0$
∴ $c(a^2 + b) = 0$......(3)

In (3), either $c = 0$ or $b = -ac$

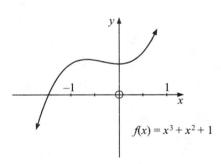

$f(x) = x^3 + x^2 + 1$

<u>Case $c = 0$</u>   ∴ $ab^2 + b^2 = b$ $\{\text{from (2)}\}$
∴ $ab^2 + b^2 - b = 0$
∴ $a^5 + a^4 + a^2 = 0$ $\{\text{using (1)}\}$
∴ $a^2(a^3 + a + 1) = 0$
∴ $a^3 + a^2 + 1 = 0$ $\{\text{as}\ a \neq 0\}$

which has an irrational solution between -1 and -2, which we shall call a_1.

Thus $f(x) = a_1 x^2 - a_1{}^2 x$ where a_1 is the one real solution of $a^3 + a^2 + 1 = 0$.

Case $c \neq 0$ From (3), $b = -ac$
∴ $-a^2 = -ac$
∴ $ac - a^2 = 0$
∴ $a(c - a) = 0$
∴ $c = a$ $\{\text{as}\ a \neq 0\}$

Thus in (2), $a(-a^2)^2 + (-a^2)^2 + a = -a^2$

i.e. $a^5 + a^4 + a^2 + a = 0$

∴ $a^4(a + 1) + a(a + 1) = 0$
∴ $a(a + 1)(a^3 + 1) = 0$

$$\therefore \quad a(a+1)(a+1)(a^2 - a + 1) = 0$$
$$\therefore \quad a(a+1)^2(a^2 - a + 1) = 0$$
$$\therefore \quad a = -1 \qquad \{a \neq 0 \quad \text{and} \quad a \text{ is real}\}$$

Thus $\quad a = -1, \quad b = -1, \quad c = -1$
$$\therefore \quad f(x) = -x^2 - x - 1$$
Thus either $\quad \underline{f(x) = -x^2 - x - 1}$

or $\quad \underline{f(x) = a_1 x^2 - a_1^2 x \quad \text{where} \quad a_1 \text{ is the real solution of} \quad a^3 + a^2 + 1 = 0.}$

5.8 Suppose Joan is 'ab' years old and John is 'cd'.
$$\therefore \quad \text{'}abcd\text{'} = 1000a + 100b + 10c + d = x^2 \qquad \{a \geqslant 1, \quad c \geqslant 1\}$$
Thus in 31 years time Joan is '$[a+3][b+1]$' and John is '$[c+3][d+1]$' years.
$$\therefore \quad \text{'}[a+3][b+1][c+3][d+1]\text{'}$$
$$= (a+3)1000 + (b+1)100 + (c+3)10 + d + 1$$
$$= 1000a + 100b + 10c + d + 3131$$
$$= x^2 + 3131$$
$$\therefore \quad x^2 + 3131 = y^2$$
$$\therefore \quad y^2 - x^2 = 3131 \quad \text{where} \quad 3131 = 31 \times 101 \quad \text{or} \quad 1 \times 3131$$
$$\therefore \quad (y+x)(y-x) = 101 \times 31 \quad \text{or} \quad 3131 \times 1$$
As $\quad y + x > y - x$, the possibilities are:

$y+x$	$y-x$	$2y$	y	x
101	31	132	66	35
3131	1	3132	1566	too large

$\therefore \quad \text{'}abcd\text{'} = 35^2 = 1225,$ i.e., Joan is $\underline{12}$ and John is $\underline{25}$.

5.9 If $\quad x = \sqrt[3]{a} + \sqrt[3]{b} \quad$ then
$$x^3 = (\sqrt[3]{a} + \sqrt[3]{b})^3$$
$$= (\sqrt[3]{a})^3 + 3(\sqrt[3]{a})^2(\sqrt[3]{b}) + 3(\sqrt[3]{a})(\sqrt[3]{b})^2 + (\sqrt[3]{b})^3$$
$$= a + 3a^{\frac{2}{3}}b^{\frac{1}{3}} + 3a^{\frac{1}{3}}b^{\frac{2}{3}} + b$$
$$= 3a^{\frac{1}{3}}b^{\frac{1}{3}}(a^{\frac{1}{3}} + b^{\frac{1}{3}}) + (a+b)$$

i.e. $\quad \underline{x^3 = 3(ab)^{\frac{1}{3}}x + (a+b).}$

Consider the graph of $\quad f(x) = x^3 - 6x - 6$
Now $\quad f'(x) = 3x^2 - 6$
$$= 3(x + \sqrt{2})(x - \sqrt{2})$$
and has sign diagram:

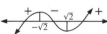

$\therefore \quad$ local max. at $\quad (-\sqrt{2}, -0.3432) \quad$ and
     local min. at $\quad (\sqrt{2}, -11.657)$
$\therefore \quad$ graph cuts x-axis exactly once,   i.e.,   one and only one real
root for $\quad x^3 - 6x - 6 = 0 \quad$ i.e. $\quad x^3 = 6x + 6$

For $\quad x^3 = 6x + 6, \qquad 3(ab)^{\frac{1}{3}} = 6 \quad$ and $\quad a + b = 6$
$\therefore \qquad ab = 8 \quad$ and $\quad a + b = 6$
$\therefore \qquad a = 4, \quad b = 2 \qquad$ and $\quad \therefore \quad \underline{\sqrt[3]{4} + \sqrt[3]{2}} \quad$ is the one and only real root.

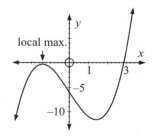

5.10 Let the lengths of the edges be a, b and c units.

$$4a + 4b + 4c = abc......(1)$$

Hence $\quad \dfrac{1}{ab} + \dfrac{1}{ac} + \dfrac{1}{bc} = \dfrac{1}{4}$

Without loss of generality we will assume $\quad a \leqslant b \leqslant c \quad$ so that $\dfrac{1}{ab}$ is the largest of the 3 fractions.

$\therefore \quad \dfrac{1}{ab} \geqslant \dfrac{1}{3}$ of $\dfrac{1}{4}$

i.e. $\quad ab \leqslant 12$

But $\quad \dfrac{1}{ab} < \dfrac{1}{4} \quad \therefore \quad ab > 4$

Consequently $\quad 5 \leqslant ab \leqslant 12$

Possibilities are:

a	1	1	1	1	1	1	1	1	2	2	2	2	3	3
b	5	6	7	8	9	10	11	12	3	4	5	6	3	4
c	24	14	X	9	8	X	X	X	10	6	X	4	X	X

and corresponding $c \longrightarrow$

reject as not an integer $\qquad$ reject as $\quad a \leqslant b \leqslant c$

$\therefore \quad \underline{(a, b, c) = (1, 5, 24), \ (1, 6, 14), \ (1, 8, 9), \ (2, 3, 10), \ (2, 4, 6)} \qquad$ i.e. 5 solutions in all.

5.11

$$a^2 = 3.2^b - 1$$

$\therefore \quad a^2 - 1 = 3.2^b$

$\therefore \quad (a+1)(a-1) = 3.2^b$

Thus 3.2^b is the product of 2 consecutive even integers, one of which contains the factor 3. The other factor is a power of 2.

Hence one of $\quad a+1$, $a-1 \quad$ has form 2^x, and the other $2^y.3$, where $\quad x \geqslant 0$, $y \geqslant 0$,

and $\quad |\, 2^x - 2^y.3 \,| = 2$

i.e. $\quad 2^x - 2^y.3 = \pm 2$

$\therefore \quad 3.2^y = 2^x \pm 2$

$\therefore \quad 3.2^{y-1} = 2^{x-1} \pm 1 \quad$ where RHS is not even.

$\therefore \quad 3.2^{y-1}$ is not even and this is possible only if $\quad y - 1 = 0 \qquad$ i.e. $\quad y = 1$.

Thus $\quad a+1 \quad$ or $\quad a - 1 = 6$

$\therefore \quad a = 5$ or 7

If $\quad a = 5, \quad 3.2^b = 24 \quad \therefore \quad 2^b = 8 \quad \therefore \quad b = 3$

If $\quad a = 7, \quad 3.2^b = 48 \quad \therefore \quad 2^b = 16 \quad \therefore \quad b = 4$

Thus $\quad \underline{a = 7, \ b = 4} \quad$ and $\quad \underline{a = 5, \ b = 3} \quad$ are the *only two solutions*.

5.12 Let $\quad X \quad = \sqrt{3 + \sqrt{5}} - \sqrt{3 - \sqrt{5}}$

$\therefore \quad X^2 = \left(\sqrt{3 + \sqrt{5}} - \sqrt{3 - \sqrt{5}} \right)^2$

$\qquad = 3 + \sqrt{5} - 2\sqrt{3 + \sqrt{5}}.\sqrt{3 - \sqrt{5}} + 3 - \sqrt{5} \quad \{(a-b)^2 = a^2 - 2ab + b^2\}$

$\qquad = 6 - 2\sqrt{(3 + \sqrt{5})(3 - \sqrt{5})}$

$\qquad = 6 - 2\sqrt{9 - 5}$

$\qquad = 6 - 2\sqrt{4}$

$\qquad = 2$

Thus $\quad X = \pm\sqrt{2}$. But X is clearly positive.

$\therefore \quad \underline{\sqrt{3 + \sqrt{5}} - \sqrt{3 - \sqrt{5}} = \sqrt{2}}$

5.13
$$8.9^x + 3.6^x - 81.4^x = 0$$
$$\therefore \quad 8.(3^x)^2 + 3.2^x.3^x - 81.(2^x)^2 = 0$$
$$\therefore \quad (8.3^x + 27.2^x)(3^x - 3.2^x) = 0$$
$$\therefore \quad 3^x - 3.2^x = 0 \qquad \{8.3^x + 27.2^x \text{ is always positive}\}$$
$$\therefore \quad 3^x = 3.2^x$$
$$\therefore \quad \left(\tfrac{3}{2}\right)^x = 3$$
$$\therefore \quad \log\left(\tfrac{3}{2}\right)^x = \log 3$$
$$\therefore \quad x\log\left(\tfrac{3}{2}\right) = \log 3$$
$$\therefore \quad x = \frac{\log 3}{\log 3 - \log 2} \qquad (\doteqdot 2.7095). \qquad \left\{\log\left(\frac{a}{b}\right) = \log a - \log b\right\}.$$

5.14 Let $\sqrt[3]{2+\sqrt{5}} = a$, and $\sqrt[3]{2-\sqrt{5}} = b$, say, and $X = a + b$

Now $(a+b)^3 = a^3 + 3a^2b + 3ab^2 + b^3$
$$\therefore \quad (a+b)^3 = a^3 + b^3 + 3ab(a+b)$$

Thus $X^3 = 2 + \sqrt{5} + 2 - \sqrt{5} + 3\sqrt[3]{(2+\sqrt{5})(2-\sqrt{5})}.X$

i.e. $X^3 = 4 + 3\sqrt[3]{-1}.X$

or $X^3 = 4 - 3X$
$$\therefore \quad X^3 + 3X - 4 = 0$$
$$\therefore \quad (X-1)(X^2 + X + 4) = 0$$
$$\therefore \quad X = 1 \quad \text{or} \quad \frac{-1 \pm \sqrt{-15}}{2}$$

Clearly X is real. $\therefore \quad \sqrt[3]{2+\sqrt{5}} + \sqrt[3]{2-\sqrt{5}} = \underline{1}$

5.15
If $\sqrt{8 - 4\sqrt{3}} = a + b\sqrt{3}$ where a and b are rational......(*)

then $8 - 4\sqrt{3} = (a + b\sqrt{3})^2$
$$\therefore \quad 8 - 4\sqrt{3} = a^2 + 2ab\sqrt{3} + 3b^2$$
$$\therefore \quad a^2 + 3b^2 = 8 \quad \text{and} \quad 2ab = -4$$
$$\therefore \quad a^2 + 3b^2 = 8 \quad \text{and} \quad ab = -2$$
$$\therefore \quad \left(\frac{-2}{b}\right)^2 + 3b^2 = 8$$
$$\therefore \quad \frac{4}{b^2} + 3b^2 = 8$$
$$\therefore \quad 3b^4 - 8b^2 + 4 = 0$$
$$\therefore \quad (3b^2 - 2)(b^2 - 2) = 0$$
$$\therefore \quad b^2 = \tfrac{2}{3} \quad \text{or} \quad 2$$
$$\therefore \quad b = \pm\tfrac{\sqrt{2}}{\sqrt{3}} \quad \text{or} \quad \pm\sqrt{2}, \quad \text{and} \quad a = \mp\sqrt{6} \quad \text{or} \quad \mp\sqrt{2}$$

all of which are irrational and contradictory to *.

However, using these values,

we get $\sqrt{8 - 4\sqrt{3}} = -\sqrt{6} + \sqrt{2}$ or $\sqrt{6} - \sqrt{2}$, of which $\sqrt{6} - \sqrt{2}$ is positive.
$$\therefore \quad \sqrt{8 - 4\sqrt{3}} = \underline{\sqrt{6} - \sqrt{2}}.$$

Check: $(\sqrt{6} - \sqrt{2})^2 = 6 - 2\sqrt{12} + 2 = 8 - 4\sqrt{3}.$

or alternatively

If $\sqrt{8-4\sqrt{3}} = \sqrt{a} - \sqrt{b}$ then $a > b$

and $8 - 4\sqrt{3} = (\sqrt{a} - \sqrt{b})^2$

$\therefore \quad 8 - 4\sqrt{3} = a - 2\sqrt{ab} + b$

$\therefore \quad 8 - 2\sqrt{12} = a + b - 2\sqrt{ab}$ and so $a + b = 8$ *and* $ab = 12$.

$\therefore \quad a = 6, \quad b = 2 \quad \{\text{as} \quad a > b\} \quad \therefore \quad \sqrt{8-4\sqrt{3}} = \sqrt{6} - \sqrt{2}.$

5.16

a $f(x) = [x] = \begin{cases} \vdots \\ -1 & \text{for } -1 \leqslant x < 0 \\ 0 & \text{for } 0 \leqslant x < 1 \\ 1 & \text{for } 1 \leqslant x < 2 \\ \vdots \end{cases}$

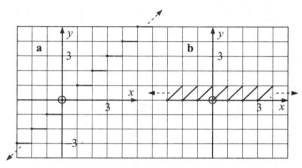

b $f(x) = x - [x] = \begin{cases} \vdots \\ x + 1 & \text{for } -1 \leqslant x < 0 \\ x & \text{for } 0 \leqslant x < 1 \\ x - 1 & \text{for } 1 \leqslant x < 2 \\ x - 2 & \text{for } 2 \leqslant x < 3 \\ \vdots \end{cases}$

5.17 Since $|x| + |y| = 3$ where $|x|$ and $|y|$ are non-negative integers, then $|x|$ and $|y|$ can be selected from $\{0, 1, 2, 3\}$

or

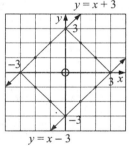

x	y	$|x-y|$	x	y	$|x-y|$
0	3	3	2	1	1
0	−3	3	2	−1	3
1	2	1	−2	1	3
1	−2	3	−2	−1	1
−1	2	3	3	0	3
−1	−2	1	−3	0	3

$(0,3), \ (0,-3), \ (1,-2), \ (-1,2), \ (2,-1), \ (-2,1), \ (3,0), \ (-3,0)$ are all solutions

5.18 $|x| + |x-1| = a$ ....(*)

If $x \geqslant 1$, then $x > 0$ and the equation is $\qquad x + x - 1 = a \quad \Rightarrow \quad x = \dfrac{a+1}{2}$

If $0 < x < 1$, then $x > 0$ but $x - 1 < 0 \quad \therefore \quad x - (x-1) = a \quad \Rightarrow \quad a = 1$

If $x \leqslant 0$ then $x - 1 < 0$, $\qquad\qquad \therefore \quad -x - (x-1) = a \quad \Rightarrow \quad x = \dfrac{1-a}{2}$

Thus: $\begin{cases} (1) & \text{if } x \geqslant 1, \quad x = \dfrac{a+1}{2} \text{ is a solution p.v. } a \geqslant 1. \quad \{\dfrac{a+1}{2} \geqslant 1 \quad \Rightarrow \quad a \geqslant 1\} \\ \\ (2) & \text{if } a = 1, \quad \text{any } x \text{ in } 0 < x < 1 \text{ will satisfy *.} \\ \\ (3) & \text{if } x \leqslant 0, \quad x = \dfrac{1-a}{2} \text{ is a solution p.v. } a \geqslant 1. \quad \{\dfrac{1-a}{2} \leqslant 0 \quad \Rightarrow \quad a \geqslant 1\} \end{cases}$

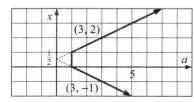

5.19 Let $PQ = x$ units

$\therefore \quad BR = (c - x)$ units

Now Δ's BPR and BCA are similar   {equiangular}

$\therefore \quad \dfrac{c - x}{PR} = \dfrac{c}{b}$

$\therefore \quad PR = \dfrac{b}{c}(c - x)$

$\therefore$ Area $PQAR = PQ.PR = x.\dfrac{b}{c}.(c - x) = -\dfrac{b}{c}x^2 + bx$

which is a quadratic in x which opens downwards $\bigwedge$ {as "A" < 0}

Thus maximum area is obtained when $x = -\dfrac{B}{2A} = \dfrac{-b}{\frac{-2b}{c}} = \dfrac{c}{2}$

Thus R is the midpoint of $\overline{AB}$ and hence P is the midpoint of $\overline{BC}$.

5.20 M_1 is (a_1, ma_1), M_2 is (a_2, ma_2),   etc.

Let $S = (P_1 M_1)^2 + (P_2 M_2)^2 + \ldots + (P_n, M_n)^2$

$\qquad = (b_1 - ma_1)^2 + (b_2 - ma_2)^2 + \ldots + (b_n - ma_n)^2$

$\qquad = m^2(a_1{}^2 + a_2{}^2 + a_3{}^2 + \ldots + a_n{}^2) - 2m(a_1 b_1 + a_2 b_2 + \ldots + a_n b_n) + (b_1{}^2 + b_2{}^2 + \ldots + b_n{}^2)^2$

which is a quadratic in m which opens upwards. $\bigvee$

Thus S is a minimum when $m = \dfrac{-B}{2A}$

$\qquad\qquad\qquad$ i.e. $m = \dfrac{a_1 b_1 + a_2 b_2 + \ldots + a_n b_n}{a_1{}^2 + a_2{}^2 + \ldots + a_n{}^2}$

5.21 $\qquad\qquad x = 16y \ldots\ldots(1)$

$\log_y x - \log_x y = \dfrac{8}{3} \ldots\ldots(2)$

From (2) $\dfrac{\log x}{\log y} - \dfrac{\log y}{\log x} = \dfrac{8}{3}$ $\left\{\log_a b = \dfrac{\log b}{\log a} \leftarrow$ base 10 logarithms$\right\}$

$\therefore \quad M - \dfrac{1}{M} - \dfrac{8}{3} = 0$ on letting $\dfrac{\log x}{\log y} = M$

$\therefore \quad 3M^2 - 8M - 3 = 0$

$\therefore \quad (3M + 1)(M - 3) = 0$

$\qquad\qquad \therefore \quad M = -\tfrac{1}{3}$ or 3

Thus $\dfrac{\log 16y}{\log y} = -\tfrac{1}{3}$ or 3

Hence $\qquad\qquad\qquad\qquad 3\log 16y = -\log y$ or $\qquad\qquad \log 16y = 3\log y$

$\qquad\qquad\qquad\qquad \therefore \quad (16y)^3 = y^{-1}$ or $\qquad\qquad\qquad 16y = y^3$

$\qquad\qquad\qquad\qquad \therefore \quad 4^6 y^4 = 1$ or $\qquad\qquad y(y^2 - 16) = 0$

$\qquad\qquad \therefore \quad (4^3 y^2 + 1)(4^3 y^2 - 1) = 0$ or $\quad y(y + 4)(y - 4) = 0$

$\qquad \therefore \quad (64y^2 + 1)(8y + 1)(8y - 1) = 0$ or $\qquad\qquad\qquad y = 0, \pm 4$

$\qquad\qquad \therefore \quad y = \pm\tfrac{1}{8}$ or $y = 0, \pm 4$

$\qquad\qquad\qquad\qquad \therefore \quad y = \tfrac{1}{8}$ or 4 {as $x > 0$ and $y > 0$}

Thus $x = 2, \quad y = \tfrac{1}{8}$ or $x = 64, \quad y = 4$.

5.22 Let the four roots be $\pm a,\ \pm 3a.$ {The form of the quartic indicates this suitable choice.}

$$\therefore\quad x^4 - (3m+2)x^2 + m^2\ = (x-a)(x+a)(x-3a)(x+3a)$$
$$= (x^2 - a^2)(x^2 - 9a^2)$$
$$= x^4 - 10a^2 x^2 + 9a^4$$

Thus, equating coefficients yields $3m + 2 = 10a^2$ ......(1)

$$m^2 = 9a^4 ......(2)$$

Hence
$$a^4 = \frac{m^2}{9} = \left(\frac{3m+2}{10}\right)^2$$
$$\therefore\quad 100m^2 = 9(9m^2 + 12m + 4)$$
$$\therefore\quad 19m^2 - 108m - 36 = 0$$
$$\therefore\quad (19m+6)(m-6) = 0$$
$$\therefore\quad m = \tfrac{-6}{19}\quad \text{or}\quad 6.$$

5.23 If $\dfrac{1}{\sqrt{3+2\sqrt2}} - \dfrac{1}{\sqrt{3-2\sqrt2}} = x,$

then $x^2 = \left(\dfrac{1}{\sqrt{3+2\sqrt2}} - \dfrac{1}{\sqrt{3-2\sqrt2}}\right)^2$

$$= \frac{1}{3+2\sqrt2} - 2.\frac{1}{\sqrt{3+2\sqrt2}}.\frac{1}{\sqrt{3-2\sqrt2}} + \frac{1}{3-2\sqrt2}$$

$$= \left(\frac{1}{3+2\sqrt2}\right).\left(\frac{3-2\sqrt2}{3-2\sqrt2}\right) - \frac{2}{\sqrt{(3+2\sqrt2)(3-2\sqrt2)}} + \left(\frac{1}{3-2\sqrt2}\right).\left(\frac{3+2\sqrt2}{3+2\sqrt2}\right)$$

$$= \frac{3-2\sqrt2}{9-8} - \frac{2}{\sqrt{9-8}} + \frac{3+2\sqrt2}{9-8}$$

$$= 3 - 2\sqrt2 - 2 + 3 + 2\sqrt2$$
$$= 4$$
                  and so $x = \pm 2.$

Now $3 + 2\sqrt2 > 3 - 2\sqrt2 > 0$

$$\therefore\quad \sqrt{3+2\sqrt2} > \sqrt{3-2\sqrt2}$$

$$\therefore\quad \frac{1}{\sqrt{3+2\sqrt2}} < \frac{1}{\sqrt{3-2\sqrt2}}$$

$$\therefore\quad \frac{1}{\sqrt{3+2\sqrt2}} - \frac{1}{\sqrt{3-2\sqrt2}} < 0 \quad \text{i.e.}\quad x < 0 \quad \text{and so}\quad \underline{x = -2.}$$

5.24 $\left(x+\dfrac{1}{x}\right)^2 = x^2 + 2 + \dfrac{1}{x^2} = x^2 + \dfrac{1}{x^2} + 2 = 7 + 2 = 9 \qquad \therefore\quad x + \dfrac{1}{x} = \pm 3$

Now $\left(\sqrt{x} + \dfrac{1}{\sqrt{x}}\right)^2 = x + 2 + \dfrac{1}{x} = x + \dfrac{1}{x} + 2 = 5 \quad \text{or}\quad -1$

$$\therefore\qquad \sqrt{x} + \frac{1}{\sqrt{x}} = \pm\sqrt{5}\quad \text{or}\quad \pm\sqrt{-1}$$

i.e. $\sqrt{x} + \dfrac{1}{\sqrt{x}} = \underline{\pm\sqrt{5}\quad \text{or}\quad \pm i}$

5.25
$$\left(x^{\frac{3}{2}} + \frac{1}{x^{\frac{3}{2}}}\right)^2 = x^3 + 2 + \frac{1}{x^3} \quad ......(1) \quad \{\text{Using } (a+b)^2 = a^2 + 2ab + b^2\}$$

Now
$$\left(x + \frac{1}{x}\right)^3 = \left(x^2 + 2 + \frac{1}{x^2}\right)\left(x + \frac{1}{x}\right)$$

$$= x^3 + 2x + \frac{1}{x} + x + \frac{2}{x} + \frac{1}{x^3}$$

$$= \left(x^3 + \frac{1}{x^3}\right) + 3\left(x + \frac{1}{x}\right)$$

Hence $3^3 = x^3 + \frac{1}{x^3} + 3(3)$ and so $x^3 + \frac{1}{x^3} = 18.$

Thus in (1) $\left(x^{\frac{3}{2}} + \frac{1}{x^{\frac{3}{2}}}\right)^2 = 20$ and consequently $x^{\frac{3}{2}} + \frac{1}{x^{\frac{3}{2}}} = \pm\sqrt{20}.$

However, $x^{\frac{3}{2}} = \sqrt{x^3}$ which is a positive quantity, $\therefore$ $x^{\frac{3}{2}} + \frac{1}{x^{\frac{3}{2}}} = \underline{\sqrt{20}}.$

5.26

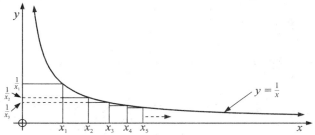

$$A = x_1^2 + (x_2 - x_1)^2 + (x_3 - x_2)^2 + (x_4 - x_3)^2 + ...$$
$$= x_1^2 + x_2^2 - 2x_1x_2 + x_1^2 + x_3^2 - 2x_2x_3 + x_2^2 + x_4^2 - 2x_3x_4 + x_3^2 + ...$$
$$= 2x_1^2 + 2x_2^2 + 2x_3^2 + ... - 2x_1x_2 - 2x_2x_3 - 2x_3x_4 - ......$$
$$= 2(x_1^2 - x_1x_2) + 2(x_2^2 - x_2x_3) + 2(x_3^2 - x_3x_4) + ...$$
$$= 2x_1^2 + 2(x_2^2 - x_1x_2) + 2(x_3^2 - x_2x_3) + 2(x_4^2 - x_3x_4) + ...$$

Now $x_2 - x_1 = \dfrac{1}{x_2}$ $\quad \therefore \quad x_2^2 - x_1x_2 = 1$

$\quad\quad x_3 - x_2 = \dfrac{1}{x_3}$ $\quad \therefore \quad x_3^2 - x_2x_3 = 1$

$\quad\quad \vdots$

etc. $\therefore$ $A = 2 + 2(1) + 2(1) + 2(1) + 2(1) + ...,$ which is <u>infinite</u>.

5.27 $f(a + b + ab) = f(a) + f(b) + f(ab)$

When $b = -1,$ $f(a - 1 - a) = f(a) + f(-1) + f(-a)$
$$f(-1) = f(a) + f(-1) + f(-a)$$
$$f(-a) = -f(a)......(1)$$

When $b = 0,$ $f(a + 0 + 0) = f(a) + f(0) + f(0)$
$$f(a) = f(a) + 2f(0)$$
$$f(0) = 0......(2)$$

Substituting $-b$ for $b,$ $f(a - b - ab) = f(a) + f(-b) + f(-ab)$
Using (1), $\quad\quad\quad\quad f(a - b - ab) = f(a) - f(b) - f(ab)$ and
$$f(a + b + ab) = f(a) + f(b) + f(ab)$$

Adding gives, $f(a - b - ab) + f(a + b + ab) = 2f(a)$

Substitute $\left.\begin{array}{l} x = a - b - ab \\ y = a + b + ab \end{array}\right\}$ $\therefore$ $2a = x + y$ and $a = \dfrac{x + y}{2}$.

i.e. $f(x) + f(y) = 2f\left(\dfrac{x + y}{2}\right)$ ......(3)

Substituting $2p$ for x, $2q$ for y $f(2p) + f(2q) = 2f(p + q)$

When $q = 0$, $f(2p) + f(0) = 2f(p)$

Using (2) $f(2p) = 2f(p)$......(4)

In particular, $f(x + y) = 2f\left(\dfrac{x + y}{2}\right)$

Using (3), $\underline{f(x + y) = f(x) + f(y)}.$

5.28   If $a + b\sqrt{2} + c\sqrt{3} + d\sqrt{6} = 0$

then $a + d\sqrt{6} = -b\sqrt{2} - c\sqrt{3}$

$\therefore$ $(a + d\sqrt{6})^2 = (-b\sqrt{2} - c\sqrt{3})^2$

$\therefore$ $a^2 + 2ad\sqrt{6} + 6d^2 = 2b^2 + 2bc\sqrt{6} + 3c^2$

$\therefore$ $a^2 + 6d^2 + 2ad\sqrt{6} = 2b^2 + 3c^2 + 2bc\sqrt{6}$

$\therefore$ $a^2 + 6d^2 = 2b^2 + 3c^2$ and $2ad = 2bc$ {since a, b, c, and d are rational.}

Since $ad = bc$,   then $\dfrac{a}{b} = \dfrac{c}{d} = t$,   say, where t is rational

$\therefore$ $a = bt$ and $c = dt$

Thus $b^2 t^2 + 6d^2 = 2b^2 + 3d^2 t^2$

$\therefore$ $b^2 t^2 + 6d^2 - 2b^2 - 3d^2 t^2 = 0$

$\therefore$ $t^2(b^2 - 3d^2) - 2(b^2 - 3d^2) = 0$

$\therefore$ $(b^2 - 3d^2)(t^2 - 2) = 0$

$\therefore$ $b^2 - 3d^2 = 0$ {as $t^2 - 2 = 0$ $\Rightarrow$ $t = \pm\sqrt{2}$ which is impossible as t is rational.}

$\therefore$ $b = \pm\sqrt{3}d$

$\therefore$ $b = d = 0$ since b and d are rational

Thus $a = c = 0$ also.

$\therefore$ $\underline{a = b = c = d = 0}$

5.29 $x^3 + qx = px^2 + r$ has roots p, q and r

$\therefore$ $x^3 - px^2 + qx - r = (x - p)(x - q)(x - r)$

$\therefore$ $x^3 - px^2 + qx - r = x^3 - [p + q + r]x^2 + [pq + qr + rp]x - [pqr]$

$\therefore$ $\left\{\begin{array}{l} p = p + q + r \\ pq + qr + rp = q......(1) \\ pqr = r \end{array}\right.$ {on equating coefficients}

Thus $q + r = 0$ and $r(pq - 1) = 0$ and so $pq = 1$ {as $r \neq 0$}

Thus $q = -r$ and $p = \dfrac{1}{q} = -\dfrac{1}{r}$

Hence in (1) $1 + (-r)r + r(-\dfrac{1}{r}) = -r$

$\therefore$ $1 - r^2 - 1 = -r$ {as $r \neq 0$}

$\therefore$ $r^2 = r$

$\therefore$ $r(r - 1) = 0$

$\therefore$ $r = 1$ as $r \neq 0$ $\therefore$ $\underline{p = -1,\ \ q = -1,\ \ r = 1}.$

5.30 **a**   If $x^3 + ax^2 + bx + c = 0$ has roots p, q, r

then $x^3 + ax^2 + bx + c = (x - p)(x - q)(x - r)$

$$= x^3 - [p + q + r]x^2 + [pq + qr + rp]x - pq$$

and equating coefficients yields $a = -[p + q + r]$, $b = pq + qr + rp$, $c = pqr$

b $(pq + qr + rp)^2 = p^2q^2 + q^2r^2 + r^2p^2 + 2pq^2r + 2p^2qr + 2pqr^2$

$\therefore$ $b^2 = p^2q^2 + q^2r^2 + r^2p^2 + 2pqr[q + p + r]$

$\therefore$ $b^2 = p^2q^2 + q^2r^2 + r^2p^2 + 2(-c)(-a)$

Thus $p^2q^2 + q^2r^2 + r^2p^2 = \underline{b^2 - 2ac}$

c   Since $p + q + r = 3\frac{1}{2}$

$$pq + qr + rp = -2\frac{1}{2}$$

$$pqr = -2, \quad \text{then } p, q, r \text{ are the roots of}$$

$$x^3 - \tfrac{7}{2}x^2 - \tfrac{5}{2}x + 2 = 0,$$

and $2x^3 - 7x^2 - 5x + 4 = 0$

$\therefore$ $(x + 1)(2x^2 - 9x + 4) = 0$

$\therefore$ $(x + 1)(x - 4)(2x - 1) = 0$ and so $x = -1, 4 \text{ or } \tfrac{1}{2}$

6 solutions:

p	-1	-1	$\frac{1}{2}$	$\frac{1}{2}$	4	4
q	4	$\frac{1}{2}$	-1	4	-1	$\frac{1}{2}$
r	$\frac{1}{2}$	4	4	-1	$\frac{1}{2}$	-1

5.31 Let BR be xm long.

$$\frac{BR}{QR} = \frac{PQ}{AP} \quad \{\Delta\text{'s } BRQ, QPA \text{ are similar}\}$$

$\therefore$ $\dfrac{x}{2} = \dfrac{2}{AP}$ and so $AP = \dfrac{4}{x}$.

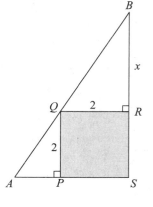

Now $AB = 3\sqrt{5}$

$\therefore$ $\sqrt{4 + x^2} + \sqrt{4 + \dfrac{16}{x^2}} = 3\sqrt{5}$ {Pythagoras}

Thus $\sqrt{4 + x^2} + \sqrt{\dfrac{4x^2 + 16}{x^2}} = 3\sqrt{5}$

$\therefore$ $\sqrt{4 + x^2} + \dfrac{2\sqrt{4 + x^2}}{x} = 3\sqrt{5}$

$\therefore$ $x\sqrt{4 + x^2} + 2\sqrt{4 + x^2} = 3\sqrt{5}x$

$\therefore$ $(x + 2)\sqrt{4 + x^2} = 3\sqrt{5}x$

$\therefore$ $(x + 2)^2(4 + x^2) = 45x^2$

which reduces to

$x^4 + 4x^3 - 37x^2 + 16x + 16 = 0$

$(x - 1)(x - 4)(x^2 + 9x + 4) = 0$

and $\therefore$ $x = 1, 4, \text{ or } \dfrac{-9 \pm \sqrt{65}}{2}$

1	1	4	-37	16	16
	0	1	5	-32	-16
4	1	5	-32	-16	0
	0	4	36	16	
	1	9	4	0	

i.e., $x = 1 \text{ or } 4$ {as the other two roots are negative.}

Thus there are two possible positions. The ladder will reach up the wall $\underline{3 \text{ m or } 6 \text{ m}}$.

5.32 $f(x) = (x - a - b)(x - a + b)(x + a - b)(x + a + b)$

$= (x - [a + b])(x + [a + b])(x - [a - b])(x + [a - b])$

$= (x^2 - [a + b]^2)(x^2 - [a - b]^2)$

$= x^4 + x^2(-a^2 - 2ab - b^2 - a^2 + 2ab - b^2) + [a + b]^2[a - b]^2$

$= x^4 - 2[a^2 + b^2]x^2 + [a^2 - b^2]^2$ which is a quadratic in x^2

which has minimum value $f\left(\dfrac{-B}{2A}\right)$ where $A = 1,\ B = -2[a^2 + b^2]$

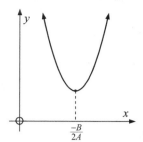

i.e.   minimum value is $f(a^2 + b^2)$

$= (a^2 + b^2)^2 - 2(a^2 + b^2)^2 + (a^2 - b^2)^2$

$= (a^2 - b^2)^2 - (a^2 + b^2)^2$

$= [a^2 - b^2 + a^2 + b^2][a^2 - b^2 - a^2 - b^2]$

$= \underline{-4a^2b^2}$

5.33

$$f(x) + 3f\left(\frac{1}{x}\right) = 2x \quad......(1)$$

Now replace x by $\dfrac{1}{x}$, $\therefore$ $f\left(\dfrac{1}{x}\right) + 3f(x) = \dfrac{2}{x} \quad.......(2)$

Substituting (2) into (1), $f(x) + 3\left[\dfrac{2}{x} - 3f(x)\right] = 2x$

$$\therefore \quad -8f(x) = 2x - \frac{6}{x}$$

$$\therefore \quad f(x) = \frac{3}{4x} - \frac{x}{4}$$

Consequently $f(-x) = \dfrac{3}{4(-x)} - \dfrac{(-x)}{4}$

$$= -\frac{3}{4x} + \frac{x}{4}$$

$$= -\left(\frac{3}{4x} - \frac{x}{4}\right)$$

$$= -f(x) \qquad \text{and} \quad \therefore \quad \underline{f(x) \quad \text{is an odd function}}$$

5.34 Let the A's represent the tail of the demonstration, and the B's its head. Let the policeman's speed be v m/min and that of the demonstration be V m/min. If the demonstration moves D m whilst the policeman moves d_1 m, then the demonstration moves $(700 - D)$ m   whilst the policeman moves d_2 m.

Thus on equating terms, $\dfrac{D}{V} = \dfrac{d_1}{v}$ $\{\text{time} = \dfrac{\text{dist.}}{\text{speed}}\}$

and $\dfrac{700 - D}{V} = \dfrac{d_2}{v}$

Thus $\dfrac{d_1}{D} = \dfrac{d_2}{700 - D}$ $\{\text{both} = \dfrac{v}{V}\}$

But $d_1 = 1400 + D$ and $d_2 = 700 + D$

$\therefore$ $\dfrac{1400 + D}{D} = \dfrac{700 + D}{700 - D}$

which simplifies to $D^2 + 700D - 490000 = 0$

which has solutions $D = \dfrac{700}{2}(-1 \pm \sqrt{5}) = \dfrac{700}{2}(\sqrt{5} - 1)$ as $D > 0$

But the total distance travelled by policeman is $d_1 + d_2 = 2100 + 2D = 1400 + 700\sqrt{5}$ m.

5.35   If α, β and δ are solutions of $x^3 + ax^2 + bx + c = 0$,

then $(x - \alpha)(x - \beta)(x - \delta) = x^3 + ax^2 + bx + c$

Thus $x^3 - [\alpha + \beta + \delta]x^2 + [\alpha\beta + \beta\delta + \alpha\delta]x - [\alpha\beta\delta] = x^3 + ax^2 + bx + c$

Equating coefficients
$$\alpha + \beta + \delta = -a$$
$$\alpha\beta + \beta\delta + \alpha\delta = b$$
$$\alpha\beta\delta = -c$$

Now $\delta = -a - (\alpha + \beta)$, $\quad \alpha\beta + \delta(\alpha + \beta) = b$, $\quad \delta = \dfrac{-c}{\alpha\beta}$

$\therefore \quad \alpha\beta + \left(\dfrac{-c}{\alpha\beta}\right)\left(-a + \dfrac{c}{\alpha\beta}\right) = b$ {substituting for δ in the middle equation}

$\therefore \quad \alpha\beta + \left(\dfrac{ac}{\alpha\beta} - \dfrac{c^2}{(\alpha\beta)^2}\right) = b$

$\therefore \quad (\alpha\beta)^3 - b(\alpha\beta)^2 + ac(\alpha\beta) - c^2 = 0$ on simplification.

i.e., $\underline{\alpha\beta}$ is a solution of $\underline{x^3 - bx^2 + acx - c^2 = 0}$

5.36
$$abc + 4(a + b + c) = 8 + 2(ab + bc + ca)$$
$$\therefore \quad abc - 2(ab + bc - ca) + 4(a + b + c) - 8 = 0$$
$$\therefore \quad abc - 2ab - 2bc - 2ca + 4a + 4b + 4c - 8 = 0$$
$$\therefore \quad (abc - 2ab) + (-2bc + 4b) + (-2ac + 4a) + (4c - 8) = 0$$
$$\therefore \quad ab(c - 2) - 2b(c - 2) - 2a(c - 2) + 4(c - 2) = 0$$
$$\therefore \quad (c - 2)[ab - 2b - 2a + 4] = 0$$
$$\therefore \quad (c - 2)(a - 2)(b - 2) = 0$$

$\therefore \quad \underline{a = 2, \quad b = 2 \quad \text{or} \quad c = 2}$
$\left\{\begin{array}{ll} a = 2, & b \text{ and } c \text{ any real numbers} \\ b = 2, & a \text{ and } c \text{ any real numbers} \\ c = 2, & a \text{ and } b \text{ any real numbers} \end{array}\right\}$

5.37
$$a^2 + b^2 + c^2 - ab - bc - ca = 0$$
$$\therefore \quad 2a^2 + 2b^2 + 2c^2 - 2ab - 2bc - 2ac = 0$$
$$\therefore \quad (a^2 - 2ab + b^2) + (b^2 - 2bc + c^2) + (c^2 - 2ca + a^2) = 0$$
$$\therefore \quad (a - b)^2 + (b - c)^2 + (c - a)^2 = 0$$

But all perfect squares are either zero or positive.

$\therefore \quad a - b = 0, \quad b - c = 0, \quad c - a = 0 \quad$ and so $\quad \underline{a = b = c}$

5.38
$$26 - 15\sqrt{3} = (a + b\sqrt{3})^3$$
$$\therefore \quad 26 - 15\sqrt{3} = a^3 + 3a^2(b\sqrt{3}) + 3a(b\sqrt{3})^2 + (b\sqrt{3})^3 \quad \text{\{Binomial Expansion\}}$$
$$= [a^3 + 9ab^2] + [3a^2b + 3b^3]\sqrt{3}$$

Thus since a and b are rational

$$a^3 + 9ab^2 = 26 \quad \text{and} \quad 3a^2b + 3b^3 = -15$$

i.e. $\quad a^3 + 9ab^2 = 26 \quad$ and $\quad a^2b + b^3 = -5$

thus $\quad \dfrac{a^3 + 9ab^2}{a^2b + b^3} = \dfrac{26}{-5}$ {Divine Inspiration!!}

$\therefore \quad \dfrac{\left(\frac{a}{b}\right)^3 + 9\left(\frac{a}{b}\right)}{\left(\frac{a}{b}\right)^2 + 1} = \dfrac{26}{-5}$ {Dividing each term on LHS by b^3}

$\therefore \quad \dfrac{t^3 + 9t}{t^2 + 1} = \dfrac{26}{-5}$ {Letting $t = \dfrac{a}{b}$}

which reduces to $5t^3 + 26t^2 + 45t + 26 = 0$

By inspection $t = -2$ is a solution and $\therefore$ $(t + 2)(5t^2 + 16t + 13) = 0$

$\therefore$ $t = -2$ as the quadratic has $\Delta = -4$ and therefore has no real solutions.

Thus $a = -2b$ and $\therefore$ $b(4b^2 + b^2) = -5$ i.e. $5b^3 = -5$

$\therefore$ $b = \underline{-1}$ and $a = \underline{2}$

5.39 $\dfrac{1}{1 + \sqrt{2} + 2\sqrt{3} - \sqrt{6}} = \dfrac{1}{(1 + \sqrt{2}) + \sqrt{3}(2 - \sqrt{2})} \cdot \dfrac{(1 + \sqrt{2}) - \sqrt{3}(2 - \sqrt{2})}{(1 + \sqrt{2}) - \sqrt{3}(2 - \sqrt{2})}$

$$= \dfrac{(1 + \sqrt{2}) - \sqrt{3}(2 - \sqrt{2})}{(1 + \sqrt{2})^2 - 3(2 - \sqrt{2})^2}$$

$$= \dfrac{1 + \sqrt{2} - 2\sqrt{3} + \sqrt{6}}{3 + 2\sqrt{2} - 3(6 - 4\sqrt{2})}$$

$$= \left(\dfrac{1 + \sqrt{2} - 2\sqrt{3} + \sqrt{6}}{-15 + 14\sqrt{2}}\right) \cdot \left(\dfrac{-15 - 14\sqrt{2}}{-15 - 14\sqrt{2}}\right)$$

$$= \dfrac{-15 - 15\sqrt{2} + 30\sqrt{3} - 15\sqrt{6} - 14\sqrt{2} - 28 + 28\sqrt{6} - 28\sqrt{3}}{225 - 392}$$

$$= \dfrac{-43 - 29\sqrt{2} + 2\sqrt{3} + 13\sqrt{6}}{-167}$$

$$= \tfrac{43}{167} + \tfrac{29}{167}\sqrt{2} - \tfrac{2}{167}\sqrt{3} - \tfrac{13}{167}\sqrt{6}$$

$\therefore$ $\underline{a = \tfrac{43}{167}, \quad b = \tfrac{29}{167}, \quad c = -\tfrac{2}{167}, \quad d = -\tfrac{13}{167}}$

5.40 $\quad 1 * a = (0 * 1) * a$ {using property (1)}

$\therefore$ $1 * a = a * 0 + 0 * a + 1 * a - 2a$ {using property (2)}

$\therefore$ $1 * a = a * 0 + a + 1 * a - 2a$

$\therefore$ $1 * a = a * 0 + 1 * a - a$

Thus $a * 0 = a$ for all integers a.   {subtract $1 * a$ from both sides}

Hence $a * b \quad = (a * b) * 0$

$\quad = 0 * ab + a * 0 + b * 0 - 0$

$\quad = \underline{ab + a + b}$

5.41 $x^2 = 3(xy - 3)....(*)$ $\therefore$ $x^4 = 9(x^2 y^2 - 6xy + 9)$

$\quad = 9(3(xy - 3)(1 - y) - 6xy + 9)$ $\{y^2 = 1 - y\}$

$\quad = 27(3y - xy - xy^2)$ {on simplifying}

$\quad = 27(3y - xy - x(1 - y))$ $\{y^2 = 1 - y, \quad$ again$\}$

$\quad = 27(3y - x)$

$\therefore$ $x^5 = 27(3xy - x^2)$ But if $x = 3$ in (*)

$\quad = 27(3xy - 3(xy - 3))$ $9 = 3(3y - 3)$ and $\therefore$ $y = 2$

$\quad = 27 \times 9$ So in $y^2 = 1 - y$, $4 = -1$

$\quad = 243$ a contradiction.

$\therefore$ $x = 3$ {as x is real} $\therefore$ no solutions exist.

5.42 $g(x, y) = 4x + y - 4$ is one of infinitely many possible functions.

Another is $g(x, y) = 5^{x-1} + y - 1$

Note: $g(x, y) = a(x - 1)(x - 2) + 4x + y - 4$ for a, any real number, gives us an infinite number of such functions.

5.43 The given example suggests that $p = 4r$.
We prove this conjecture.
If x is any real number,

$$
\begin{aligned}
f(x + 4r) &= f(r + [3r + x]) \\
&= f(r - [3r + x]) && \{\text{using (2)}\} \\
&= f(-2r - x) \\
&= f(-[x + 2r]) \\
&= -f(x + 2r) && \{\text{using (1)}\} \\
&= -f(r + [r + x[) \\
&= -f(r - [r + x]) && \{\text{using (2) again}\} \\
&= -f(-x) \\
&= f(x) && \text{for all } x.
\end{aligned}
$$

Thus $f(x)$ is periodic and $p = 4r$.

5.44 $APQR$ is a parallelogram.

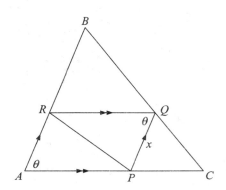

∴ $\angle PQR = \theta = \angle BAC$ where θ is a constant.
Let $PQ = x$ units
Now $\triangle PQC$ is similar to $\triangle ABC$ {equiangular}

∴ $\dfrac{x}{PC} = \dfrac{c}{b}$

∴ $PC = \dfrac{bx}{c}$

∴ $RQ = AP = b - \dfrac{bx}{c}$

Thus the area of $\triangle PQR$ is

$$
\begin{aligned}
A &= \tfrac{1}{2}.PQ.RQ \sin\theta \\
&= \tfrac{1}{2}.x.\left(b - \dfrac{bx}{c}\right)\sin\theta \\
&= \dfrac{b\sin\theta}{2c}[x(c - x)]
\end{aligned}
$$

where $\dfrac{b\sin\theta}{2c}$ is a constant.

Thus A is a maximum when $-x^2 + cx$ is a maximum

which occurs when $x = \dfrac{-B}{2A} = \dfrac{c}{2}$

Thus the area of $\triangle PQR$ is maximised when P is the midpoint of $\overline{AC}$.

5.45 **a** Letting $y = 0$, $f(x^2) = f(x^2) + f(0)$ ∴ $f(0) = 0$
   b Proof (by induction on n)
     i $f[(1.x)^2] = 1.f[x^2]$ is true ∴ $P(1)$ is true.

     ii Assume $P(k)$ is true, i.e. $f[(kx)^2] = kf[x^2]$ for k in Z^+.
        then $f[((k + 1)x)^2] = f[(kx + x)^2]$

$$
\begin{aligned}
&= f[(kx)^2] + f[x^2] && \{\text{given rule}\} \\
&= kf[x^2] + f[x^2] && \{\text{assumption}\} \\
&= (k + 1)f[x^2] && \text{as required.}
\end{aligned}
$$

     Thus $P(k + 1)$ is true whenever $P(k)$ is true and $P(1)$ is true.
     ∴ $P(n)$ is true for all n in Z^+.

5.46 **a** Since $[a] \leqslant a$ and $[b] \leqslant b$ then $m[a] + n[b] \leqslant ma + nb$

$\therefore \quad m[a] + n[b] \leqslant c.$

Since $m[a] + n[b]$ is an integer, and $[c]$ is the largest integer less than or equal to c

then $m[a] + n[b] \leqslant [c]$

b
$m\{a\} + n\{b\} - \{c\}$

$= m(a - [a]) + n(b - [b]) - (c - [c])$

$= ma + nb - c + [c] - m[a] - n[b]$

$= [c] - m[a] - n[b]$

$\geqslant 0 \quad$ from (1)

$\therefore \quad \underline{m\{a\} + n\{b\} - \{c\}} \quad$ is a non-negative integer.

5.47 **a** Suppose $b \neq 0$ and $a + b\sqrt{q} = 0.$

$$\therefore \quad \sqrt{q} = -\frac{a}{b} \quad \text{which is not possible}$$

as LHS is irrational and RHS is rational.

Thus the supposition is false. $\therefore \quad b = 0$ and consequently $a = 0$

i.e. $\underline{a = b = 0}$

b Suppose there exist rationals a and b such that

$$f(a + b\sqrt{p}) = \sqrt{q}$$

$\therefore \quad f(a) + f(b\sqrt{p}) = \sqrt{q} \qquad \{\text{property } (i)\}$

and $a + f(b).f(\sqrt{p}) = \sqrt{q} \qquad \{\text{properties } (ii) \text{ and } (iii)\}$

$\therefore \quad a + bf(\sqrt{p}) = \sqrt{q} \qquad \{\text{property } (iii)\}$

$\therefore \quad b^2 f(\sqrt{p}).f(\sqrt{p}) = (\sqrt{q} - a)^2$

$\therefore \quad b^2 f(p) = q - 2aq + a^2 \qquad \{\text{property } (ii)\}$

$\therefore \quad [b^2 p - q - a^2] + 2a\sqrt{q} = 0$

$\therefore \quad b^2 p - q - a^2 = 0 \quad \text{and} \quad 2a = 0$

$\therefore \quad a = 0 \quad \text{and} \quad b^2 p = q$

Hence $b^2 = 1$ as p and q are primes.

Consequently $p = q,$ contradicting the fact that p and q are given distinct.

The supposition is therefore <u>false</u>.

5.48 If $x = b^{\frac{1}{3}} + b^{\frac{2}{3}}$ is a root of a cubic then

$x^3 = [b^{\frac{1}{3}} + b^{\frac{2}{3}}]^3$

$= (b^{\frac{1}{3}})^3 + 3(b^{\frac{1}{3}})^2(b^{\frac{2}{3}}) + 3(b^{\frac{1}{3}})(b^{\frac{2}{3}})^2 + (b^{\frac{2}{3}})^3$

$= b + 3b^{\frac{4}{3}} + 3b^{\frac{5}{3}} + b^2$

$= 3b(b^{\frac{1}{3}} + b^{\frac{2}{3}}) + b^2 + b$

$= 3bx + [b^2 + b]$

$\therefore \quad b^{\frac{1}{3}} + b^{\frac{2}{3}}$ is a root of cubic $x^3 - 3bx - [b^2 + b] = 0,$ which has integral coefficients.

$b^{\frac{1}{3}} + b^{\frac{2}{3}}$	1	0	$-3b$	$-b^2 - b$
	0	$b^{\frac{1}{3}} + b^{\frac{2}{3}}$	$b^{\frac{2}{3}} + 2b + b^{\frac{4}{3}}$	$b + b^2$
	1	$b^{\frac{1}{3}} + b^{\frac{2}{3}}$	$b^{\frac{2}{3}} - b + b^{\frac{4}{3}}$	0

The other quadratic factor of the cubic is $x^2 + (b^{\frac{1}{3}} + b^{\frac{2}{3}})x + (b^{\frac{2}{3}} - b + b^{\frac{4}{3}})$

which has $\Delta = (b^{\frac{1}{3}} + b^{\frac{2}{3}})^2 - 4.1.(b^{\frac{2}{3}} - b + b^{\frac{4}{3}})$

$$= b^{\frac{2}{3}} + 2b + b^{\frac{4}{3}} - 4b^{\frac{2}{3}} + 4b - 4b^{\frac{4}{3}}$$

$$= -3b^{\frac{2}{3}} + 6b - 3b^{\frac{4}{3}}$$

$$= -3b^{\frac{2}{3}}(b^{\frac{2}{3}} - 2b^{\frac{1}{3}} + 1)$$

$$= -3b^{\frac{2}{3}}.(b^{\frac{1}{3}} - 1)^2$$

$$= -3\sqrt[3]{b^2}.(\sqrt[3]{b} - 1)^2$$

which is < 0 for all b except $b = 0$ or 1, which are perfect cubes and are $\therefore$ not to be considered.

Thus there are <u>no other real roots</u>.

5.49 **a** $x_1 + x_2 + x_3 = 0$ ......(1)

$x_2 + x_3 + x_4 = 0$ ......(2)

$x_3 + x_4 + x_5 = 0$ ......(3)

$\vdots \quad \vdots \quad \vdots \quad \vdots$

$x_{98} + x_{99} + x_{100} = 0$ ......(98)

$x_{99} + x_{100} + x_1 = 0$ ......(99)

$x_{100} + x_1 + x_2 = 0$ ......(100)

Comparing equations (1) and (2), $x_1 = x_4$.

Comparing equations (2) and (3), $x_2 = x_5$.

etc. $\therefore$ $x_3 = x_6$, $x_4 = x_7$, $x_5 = x_8$,

Thus $x_1 = \quad x_4 = \quad x_7 = \quad x_{10} = \quad .... = x_{97} = x_{100}$

$x_2 = \quad x_5 = \quad x_8 = \quad x_{11} = \quad .... = x_{98}$

$x_3 = \quad x_6 = \quad x_9 = \quad x_{12} = \quad .... = x_{99}$

Comparing (98) and (99) $\therefore$ $x_{98} = x_1$

(99) and (100) $\therefore$ $x_{99} = x_2$

(100) and (1) $\therefore$ $x_{100} = x_3$

Thus $x_1 = x_2 = x_3 = x_4 = x_5 = ... = x_{98} = x_{99} = x_{100}$.

In (1) $\therefore$ $3x_1 = 0$ $\Rightarrow$ $x_1 = 0$

$\therefore$ $x_1, x_2, x_3, x_4, ... , x_{100}$, <u>are all 0</u>.

b $x_1 + x_2 + x_3 = 0$

$x_2 + x_3 + x_4 = 0$

$x_3 + x_4 + x_5 = 0$

$\vdots \quad \vdots \quad \vdots \quad \vdots$

$x_{n-1} + x_n + x_1 = 0$

$x_n + x_1 + x_2 = 0$

As for part **a**

$\left.\begin{array}{l} x_1 = x_4 = x_7 = x_{10} = ... \\ x_2 = x_5 = x_8 = x_{11} = ... \\ x_3 = x_6 = x_9 = x_{12} = ... \end{array}\right\}$ ......(1)

and also

$\left.\begin{array}{l} x_{n-2} = x_1 \\ x_{n-1} = x_2 \\ x_n = x_3 \end{array}\right\}$ ......(2)

i <u>If n is not divisible by 3</u>, then from **a**, either $x_n = x_1$ and $x_{n-1} = x_3$

or $x_n = x_2$ and $x_{n-1} = x_1$

so that by (2) $x_1 = x_2 = x_3$

and hence <u>$x_1 = x_2 = x_3 = ... = x_n = 0$</u>.

ii If n is divisible by 3, the equations of (2) are included amongst the equations (1), and so the solution is not unique.

thus, $\quad x_1 = x_4 = x_7 = \ldots\ldots = x_{n-2} = a, \quad$ say,

$\quad\quad\quad x_2 = x_5 = x_8 = \ldots\ldots = x_{n-1} = b, \quad$ say

and $\quad x_3 = x_6 = x_9 = \ldots\ldots = x_n = -(a+b) \quad$ is a solution for any real a and b.

5.50   **a** $x^4 + 2x^3 - 2x - 4 = x^3(x+2) - 2(x+2)$

$$= (x+2)(x^3 - 2)$$

$$= (x+2)(x - 2^{\frac{1}{3}})(x^2 + 2^{\frac{1}{3}}x + 2^{\frac{2}{3}}) \quad \{a^3 - b^3 = (a-b)(a^2 + ab + b^2)\}$$

Thus, if $\quad x^4 + 2x^3 - 2x - 4 = 0$

$\therefore \quad (x+2)(x - 2^{\frac{1}{3}})(x^2 + 2^{\frac{1}{3}}x + 2^{\frac{2}{3}}) = 0$

$\therefore \quad \underline{x = -2 \text{ or } \sqrt[3]{2}} \quad$ the only real roots, as the remaining quadratic

has $\quad \Delta = (2^{\frac{1}{3}})^2 - 4(1)2^{\frac{2}{3}} \quad = 2^{\frac{2}{3}} - 4(2^{\frac{2}{3}}) \quad = -3(2^{\frac{2}{3}}) \quad$ which is negative.

b   In $\quad \triangle ADC, \quad \angle A = 120^o$

$\therefore \quad \angle D = \angle C = 30^o$

$\therefore \quad \angle DCB = 90^o$

$\therefore \quad \underline{DC = \sqrt{3}a} \quad\quad$ {Pythagoras in $\triangle DCB$}

Also $\quad \angle CBF = 90^o \quad\quad$ {alternate to $\angle DCB$}

$\therefore \quad \underline{BF = \sqrt{x^2 - a^2}} \quad$ {Pythagoras in $\triangle CBF$

Now $\quad \dfrac{EF}{EC} = \dfrac{BF}{DC} \quad\quad\quad$ {$\triangle$'s EFB, ECD are similar}

$\therefore \quad \dfrac{a}{a+x} = \dfrac{\sqrt{x^2 - a^2}}{\sqrt{3}a}$

$\therefore \quad \sqrt{3}a^2 = (a+x)\sqrt{x^2 - a^2}$

$\therefore \quad 3a^4 = (a^2 + 2ax + x^2)(x^2 - a^2)$

$\therefore \quad x^4 + 2ax^3 - 2a^3x - 4a^4 = 0 \quad\quad\quad$ {on reduction}

or $\quad \left(\dfrac{x}{a}\right)^4 + 2\left(\dfrac{x}{a}\right)^3 - 2\left(\dfrac{x}{a}\right) - 4 = 0 \quad\quad$ {on dividing each term by a^4}

or $\quad X^4 + 2X^3 - 2X - 4 = 0 \quad$ if we let $\quad X = \dfrac{x}{a}$.

but this equation by **a** has real roots $\quad X = -2 \quad$ or $\quad \sqrt[3]{2}$.

$\therefore \quad \dfrac{x}{a} = -2 \quad$ or $\quad \sqrt[3]{2} \quad$ and so $\quad \underline{x = a\sqrt[3]{2}} \quad$ {x and a are positive $\therefore \quad \dfrac{x}{a}$ is positive.}

5.51   **a** $(1+\sqrt{2})^1 = 1 + \sqrt{2} \quad\quad = a_1 + b_1\sqrt{2} \quad\quad \therefore \quad a_1 = 1, \quad b_1 = 1$

$(1+\sqrt{2})^2 = 3 + 2\sqrt{2} \quad\quad = a_2 + b_2\sqrt{2} \quad\quad \therefore \quad a_2 = 3, \quad b_2 = 2$

$(1+\sqrt{2})^3 = 7 + 5\sqrt{2} \quad\quad = a_3 + b_3\sqrt{2} \quad\quad \therefore \quad a_3 = 7, \quad b_3 = 5$

$(1+\sqrt{2})^3 = 17 + 12\sqrt{2} = a_4 + b_4\sqrt{2} \quad\quad \therefore \quad a_4 = 17, \quad b_4 = 12$

b $(1+\sqrt{2})^n = 1 + \binom{n}{1}\sqrt{2} + \binom{n}{2}(\sqrt{2})^2 + \binom{n}{3}(\sqrt{2})^3 + \ldots\ldots + (\sqrt{2})^n$

$$= a_n + b_n\sqrt{2}$$

$(1-\sqrt{2})^n = 1 + \binom{n}{1}(-\sqrt{2}) + \binom{n}{2}(-\sqrt{2})^2 + \binom{n}{3}(-\sqrt{2})^3 + \ldots\ldots + (-\sqrt{2})^n$

$$= 1 - \binom{n}{1}\sqrt{2} + \binom{n}{2}(\sqrt{2})^2 - \binom{n}{3}(\sqrt{2})^3 + \ldots\ldots$$

$$= a_n - b_n\sqrt{2}$$

$\therefore \quad |a_n - b_n\sqrt{2}| = |1 - \sqrt{2}|^n = |\sqrt{2} - 1|^n \qquad \{|a - b| = |b - a|\} \qquad \text{and} \quad \sqrt{2} - 1 < \tfrac{1}{2}$

$\therefore \quad |a_n - b_n\sqrt{2}| < (\tfrac{1}{2})^n \quad \text{for} \quad n = 1, 2, 3, \dots \quad \{\text{where } (\tfrac{1}{2})^n \text{ approaches 0 as } n \text{ gets larger}\}$

$\therefore \quad \underline{a_n} \quad \text{is the integer nearest to} \quad \underline{b_n\sqrt{2}}.$

c Consider $\quad N = (1 + \sqrt{2})^n + (1 - \sqrt{2})^n$

$$= a_n + b_n\sqrt{2} + a_n - b_n\sqrt{2} = 2a_n \quad \text{where } a_n \text{ is a positive integer.}$$

Thus N is a positive integer.

But $\quad (1 - \sqrt{2})^n \quad$ approaches zero, as n gets sufficiently large.

$\therefore \quad (1 + \sqrt{2})^n \quad$ approaches N, as n gets sufficiently large.

$\therefore \quad$ for large values of n, $\quad (1 + \sqrt{2})^n \quad$ is very close to <u>integral values</u>.

5.52 Let the third root be c.

$\therefore \quad x^3 - x + 1 = (x - a)(x - b)(x - c)$

$$= x^3 - [a + b + c]x^2 + [ab + bc + ca]x - abc.$$

Equating coefficients we get $\quad a + b + c = 0 \quad \dots\dots(1)$

$$ab + bc + ca = -1 \quad \dots\dots(2)$$

$$abc = -1 \quad \dots\dots(3)$$

Let $\quad r = ab \quad \therefore \quad$ from (3), $\qquad c = -\dfrac{1}{r}$

from (2), $\quad r + c(a + b) = -1$

$$a + b = \frac{-1 - r}{-\frac{1}{r}} = r^2 + r$$

Thus in (1) $\quad r^2 + r - \dfrac{1}{r} = 0 \quad$ and $\quad \therefore \quad r^3 + r^2 - 1 = 0.$

Thus $\quad r = \underline{ab} \quad$ is a root of $\quad x^3 + x^2 - 1 = 0.$

5.53 Let $\quad ax^2 + bx + c = (px + q)(\dfrac{a}{p}x + \dfrac{c}{q})$

and $\quad cx^2 + bx + a = (px + q)(\dfrac{c}{p}x + \dfrac{a}{q})$

Thus equating coefficients of x gives

$b = \dfrac{aq}{p} + \dfrac{cp}{q}\dots\dots(1) \quad$ and $\quad b = \dfrac{cq}{p} + \dfrac{ap}{q}\dots\dots(2)$

$\therefore \quad \dfrac{aq}{p} + \dfrac{cp}{q} = \dfrac{cq}{p} + \dfrac{ap}{q}$

$\therefore \quad aq^2 + cp^2 = cq^2 + ap^2$

$\therefore \quad p^2(c - a) = q^2(c - a)$

$\therefore \quad p^2 = q^2 \qquad\qquad \{a \neq c \Rightarrow a - c \neq 0\}$

$\therefore \quad p = \pm q$

If $\quad p = q, \quad$ in (1) $\quad b = a + c$

If $\quad p = -q, \quad$ in (1) $\quad b = -a - c$

$\therefore \quad a + b + c = 0 \quad$ or $\quad a - b + c = 0$

$\therefore \quad \underline{(a + b + c)(a - b + c) = 0}$

5.54 If there is one and only one solution of $\quad x^2 + ax + b = 0$

between 0 and 1, and $f(x) = x^2 + ax + b,$

then $f(0)$ and $f(1)$ have opposite signs.

$\therefore \quad \underline{b} \quad$ and $\quad \underline{1 + a + b} \quad$ have opposite signs......(1)

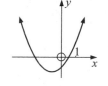
or
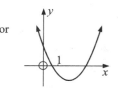

Consider $\dfrac{1}{x+2} + \dfrac{a}{x+1} + \dfrac{b}{x} = 0$

On simplification, this reduces to the quadratic $[1 + a + b]x^2 + [1 + 2a + 3b]x + 2b = 0$

where $\Delta = [1 + 2a + 3b]^2 - 4[1 + a + b].2b = [1 + 2a + 3b]^2 - 8b[1 + a + b]$

but from (1) $b[1 + a + b] < 0$ $\therefore$ $-8b[1 + a + b] > 0$ and hence $\Delta > 0$
$\therefore$ the equation has two real distinct roots, α, β, say.

Since $\alpha\beta = \dfrac{2b}{1 + a + b} < 0$ {as b, $1 + a + b$ are opposite in sign from (1) again}

we conclude that α, β are opposite in sign, so that one solution is positive and the other is negative, i.e. <u>one and only one positive solution.</u>

5.55 Let $x = [x] + h$ where $0 \leqslant h < 1$.

Then $2x = 2[x] + 2h$

$x + \tfrac{1}{2} = [x] + h + \tfrac{1}{2}$

$x - \tfrac{1}{2} = [x] + h - \tfrac{1}{2}$

<u>Consider two cases</u> (1) $0 \leqslant h < \tfrac{1}{2}$ $\therefore$ $\begin{cases} 0 \leqslant 2h < 1 \\ \tfrac{1}{2} \leqslant h + \tfrac{1}{2} < 1 \\ -\tfrac{1}{2} \leqslant h - \tfrac{1}{2} < 0 \end{cases}$

Thus $[2x] = 2[x]$

$[x + \tfrac{1}{2}] = [x]$

$[x - \tfrac{1}{2}] = [x] - 1$

Hence $[x + \tfrac{1}{2}] + [x - \tfrac{1}{2}] = 2[x] - 1.$

(2) $\tfrac{1}{2} \leqslant h < 1$ $\therefore$ $\begin{cases} 1 \leqslant 2h < 2 \\ 1 \leqslant h + \tfrac{1}{2} < 1\tfrac{1}{2} \\ 0 \leqslant h - \tfrac{1}{2} < \tfrac{1}{2} \end{cases}$

Thus $[2x] = 2[x] + 1$

$[x + \tfrac{1}{2}] = [x] + 1$

$[x - \tfrac{1}{2}] = [x]$

$\therefore$ $[x + \tfrac{1}{2}] + [x - \tfrac{1}{2}] = 2[x] + 1 = 2[x].$

Thus in each case, <u>two of the 3 expressions are equal</u> and the third is different from the others.

5.56 On the number line we mark x, $x + \dfrac{1}{n}$, $x + \dfrac{2}{n}$, ..., $x + \dfrac{n-1}{n}$

and we suppose there are k divisions less than $[x] + 1$ {as shown}

Now $x + \dfrac{k-1}{n} < [x] + 1 \leqslant x + \dfrac{k}{n}$

$\therefore$ $nx + k - 1 < n[x] + n \leqslant nx + k$

$\therefore$ $k - 1 - n[x] - n < -nx \leqslant k - n[x] - n$

$\therefore$ $n[x] - k + n \leqslant nx < n[x] - k + n + 1$

$\therefore$ $\underline{[nx] = n[x] + n - k}......(1)$

Thus $[x] + [x + \dfrac{1}{n}] + [x + \dfrac{2}{n}] + \text{........} + [x + \dfrac{n-1}{n}]$

$= \underbrace{[x] + [x] + \text{........} + [x]}_{k \text{ of these}} + \underbrace{[x] + 1 + [x] + 1 + [x] + 1 + \text{........} + [x] + 1}_{n - k \text{ of these}}$

$= k[x] + (n - k)([x] + 1)$

$$= k[x] + n[x] - k[x] + n - k$$
$$= n[x] + n - k$$
$$= [nx] \qquad \{\text{from (1)}\}$$

5.57 a Putting $x = 0$ in $f(x) \leqslant x$ gives $f(0) \leqslant 0$......(a)

Putting $x = y = 0$ in $f(x + y) \leqslant f(x) + f(x)$ gives
$$f(0) \leqslant f(0) + f(0)$$
$$\text{i.e.} \quad f(0) \leqslant 2f(0)$$
$$\therefore \quad 0 \leqslant f(0) \quad \text{or} \quad f(0) \geqslant 0......(b)$$
Thus from (a) and (b) $f(0) = 0$.

b Replace y by $-x$ in the second inequality
$$\therefore \quad f(x + (-x)) \leqslant f(x) + f(-x)$$
$$\therefore \quad f(0) \leqslant f(x) + f(-x)$$
$$\therefore \quad 0 \leqslant f(x) + f(-x)$$
$$\therefore \quad f(x) \geqslant -f(-x)$$
But $\quad f(-x) \leqslant -x \qquad \{\text{using the 1st inequality}\}$
$\therefore \quad -f(-x) \geqslant x$
Thus $\quad f(x) \geqslant -f(-x) \geqslant x$
i.e. $\quad f(x) \geqslant x \quad \text{and} \quad f(x) \leqslant x \qquad \therefore \quad \underline{f(x) = x \quad \text{for all } x.}$

5.58 Suppose that there do exist monic polynomials $g(x)$ and $h(x)$ of degree greater than or equal to 1 with integer coefficients such that $f(x) = g(x).h(x)$ for every real value of x.

Let $k(x) = g(x) + h(x)$ for every real value of x.
Now for every a_i, $f(a_i) = -1 \qquad \{i = 1, 2, 3, ..., n\}$
$$\therefore \quad g(a_i).h(a_i) = -1 \quad \text{for} \quad i = 1, 2, 3, ..., n.$$
But $g(a_i)$ and $h(a_i)$ are integers, so $g(a_i) = \pm 1$ and $h(a_i) = \mp 1$
Thus $g(a_i) = -h(a_i)$ for $i = 1, 2, 3, ..., n$.
Hence $k(a_i) = 0$ for $i = 1, 2, 3, ..., n$.
But the degree of $k(x)$ is less than n. $\quad \therefore \quad k(x) = 0$ for all x.
Hence $h(x) = -g(x)$ for all x.
Thus $f(x) = -[g(x)]^2$ for all x.
But $f(x)$ is monic and so is $g(x)$.
Hence by equating coefficients of x^n we get $1 = -1$, which is a <u>contradiction</u>.

5.59 Let $f(x)$ be a polynomial of degree n and suppose α is a zero of $f(x)$.
i.e. $f(\alpha) = 0$.
Then $\quad f(\alpha).f(\alpha + 1) = f(\alpha^2 + \alpha + 1) = f(\alpha(\alpha + 1) + 1) = 0 \quad ....(1)$
and $\quad f(\alpha - 1).f(\alpha) = f((\alpha - 1)\alpha + 1) = f(\alpha^2 - \alpha + 1) = 0 \quad ....(2)$
Thus if α is a zero of $f(x)$, then so are $\alpha^2 + \alpha + 1$ and $\alpha^2 - \alpha + 1$.

Now consider the following <u>two cases</u>:
a $\quad \alpha, \alpha^2 + \alpha + 1$ and $\alpha^2 - \alpha + 1$ are distinct.

By repeated use of (1) and (2) an infinite number of distinct zeros can be generated. Since $f(x)$ has at most n distinct roots, this is a contradiction.
b $\quad \alpha, \alpha^2 + \alpha + 1$ and $\alpha^2 - \alpha + 1$ are <u>not</u> distinct.

i If $\alpha = \alpha^2 + \alpha + 1 = \alpha^2 - \alpha + 1$.
This is obviously not possible as $\alpha^2 + \alpha + 1 = \alpha^2 - \alpha + 1 \Rightarrow \alpha = 0 \Rightarrow 0 = 1$.

ii If $\alpha = \alpha^2 + \alpha + 1$, then $\alpha^2 + 1 = 0 \Rightarrow \alpha = \pm i$
Thus $\alpha^2 - \alpha + 1 = -1 \mp i + 1 = \mp i$
$\pm i$ are therefore the only roots generated and since we are seeking polynomials with real coefficients $f(x) = k(x^2 + 1)^n$ where n is a positive integer, k is real and nonzero.

But $f(x).f(x+1) = f(x^2 + x + 1)$

$\therefore \quad k(x^2+1)^n.k([x+1]^2+1)^n = k([x^2+x+1]^2+1)^n$

and consequently $k^2 = k$ {equating leading coefficients}

$$\therefore \quad k = 1, \quad \text{since} \quad k \neq 0$$

$$\therefore \quad f(x) = (x^2+1)^n, \quad n \text{ a positive integer.}$$

iii If $\alpha = \alpha^2 - \alpha + 1$ then $\alpha^2 - 2\alpha + 1 = 0 \quad \Rightarrow \quad \alpha = 1$.
It follows that $\alpha^2 + \alpha + 1 = 3$ and an infinite number of roots 1, 3, 7, 13, ...
are generated, clearly a contradiction.

iv If $\alpha^2 + \alpha + 1 = \alpha^2 - \alpha + 1$ and $\therefore \quad \alpha = 0$ and $\therefore \quad \alpha^2 + \alpha + 1 = 1$.
Thus there are once again infinitely many roots, 0, 1, 3, 7, 13, ... generated and a
contradiction is achieved again.

The complete solution is $\underline{f(x) = (x^2+1)^n \quad \text{or} \quad 0,1}$ where n is a positive integer.

5.60 $$\frac{1}{x} + \frac{1}{a} + \frac{1}{b} = \frac{1}{x+a+b}$$

$$\therefore \quad \frac{ab+bx+ax}{abx} = \frac{1}{x+a+b}$$

$$\therefore \quad ([a+b]x+ab)(x+[a+b]) = abx$$

$$\therefore \quad [a+b]x^2 + [ab+[a+b]^2]x + ab[a+b] = abx$$

$$\therefore \quad [a+b]x^2 + [a+b]^2x + ab[a+b] = 0$$

$$\therefore \quad [a+b](x^2+[a+b]x+ab) = 0$$

$$\therefore \quad x^2+[a+b]x+ab = 0 \qquad \text{as} \quad a+b \neq 0$$

$$\therefore \quad (x+a)(x+b) = 0$$

$$\therefore \quad x = \underline{-a \quad \text{or} \quad -b}$$

5.61 $P(n)$ is "$1.2^{n-1} + 2.2^{n-2} + 3.2^{n-3} + \text{........} + (n-1).2 + n.1 = 2^{n+1} - 2 - n$
for all n in Z^+."

Proof: (by the Principle of Mathematical Induction)

i If $n = 1$,   LHS $= 1.2^0 = 1$
RHS $= 2^2 - 2 - 1 = 1$ $\therefore \quad \underline{P(1) \text{ is true.}}$

ii If $P(k)$ is true, then

$$1.2^{k-1} + 2.2^{k-2} + 3.2^{k-3} + \text{........} + (k-1).2 + k.1 = 2^{k+1} - 2 - k \text{ ....*}$$

{We need to show that

$$1.2^k + 2.2^{k-1} + 3.2^{k-2} + \text{........} + k.2 + (k+1).1 = 2^{k+2} - 2 - (k+1)\}$$

Now $1.2^k + 2.2^{k-1} + 3.2^{k-2} + \text{........} + k.2 + (k+1).1$

$= \quad (2^k + 2^{k-1} + 2^{k-2} + \text{........} + 2 + 1)$
$\quad + (2^{k-1} + 2.2^{k-2} + 3.2^{k-3} + \text{........} + (k-1).2 + k.1)$

$= \quad \dfrac{2^{k+1} - 1}{2 - 1} + 2^{k+1} - 2 - k \qquad \text{{from G.P. sum and from *}}$

$= \quad 2^{k+1} - 1 + 2^{k+1} - 2 - k$

$= \quad 2.2^{k+1} - 2 - k - 1$

$= \quad 2^{k+2} - 2 - (k+1)$

Thus $P(k+1)$ is true whenever $P(k)$ is true and $P(1)$ is true.
$\therefore \quad \underline{P(n) \text{ is true.}}$ {P. of M.I.}

6. PIGEON HOLE PRINCIPLE

6.1 **a** Divide the equilateral triangle T into 4 congruent equilateral triangles T_1, T_2, T_3, T_4 {as shown}. If 5 points are randomly chosen from T, then at least 2 must come from one of the smaller triangles, {P-H-P} and their maximum distance apart is 1 unit.
i.e.   at least 2 of them are within 1 unit of each other.

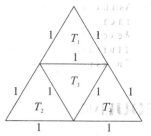

b If 17 points lie within T, at least 5 of them must lie within one of the smaller triangles, T_1, say, and since we have 5 points in T_1, then by (1) at least 2 points must be within $\frac{1}{2}$ a unit of each other.

c If $4^n + 1$ points lie in T_1, $(n \geqslant 1)$ and are chosen at random, then at least two of them are within $\underline{2^{1-n}}$ units of each other.

$$\begin{cases} n = 1, & 4^1 + 1 & : 1 = 2^0 \\ n = 2, & 4^2 + 1 & : \frac{1}{2} = 2^{-1} \\ n = 3, & 4^3 + 1 & : \frac{1}{4} = 2^{-2} \end{cases}$$

6.2 Fix the vertices A, B, C of the equilateral triangle.
The 4 vertices of the square K, L, M, N must be placed so that they lie on arcs $\overline{AB}, \overline{BC}$, or $\overline{CA}$.
Since 4 points are to be placed on 3 arcs, then at least 2 of the points lie on one arc.   {P-H-P}
Say, for example, K, L lie on arc AB.
Let P be the circumference of the circle.

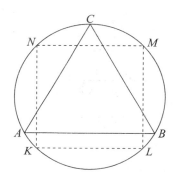

Then   arc $AB = \dfrac{P}{3}$,   and   arc $KL = \dfrac{P}{4}$.

Thus   arc $AK+$ arc $LB = \dfrac{P}{3} - \dfrac{P}{4} = \dfrac{P}{12}$.

Hence the smaller of the two arcs must have   length $\leqslant \frac{1}{2} \cdot \frac{P}{12} = \frac{P}{24}$,   the required result.

6.3 For each real number x there is a value of θ between $-\dfrac{\pi}{2}$ and $\dfrac{\pi}{2}$ such that $x = \tan \theta$.
Divide the straight angle into 6 equal angles.
From the 7 values of θ, we can always select two of them, θ_1 and θ_2, say $(\theta_1 > \theta_2)$ such that they lie in the same region.   {P-H-P}

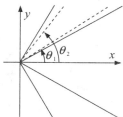

Thus $0 < \theta_1 - \theta_2 < 30^\varrho$.

Hence $\tan 0 < \tan(\theta_1 - \theta_2) < \tan 30^\varrho$

$$\therefore \quad 0 < \frac{\tan \theta_1 - \tan \theta_2}{1 + \tan \theta_1 \tan \theta_2} < \frac{1}{\sqrt{3}}$$

i.e.   we can always select two real numbers, x, y such that $0 < \dfrac{x - y}{1 + xy} < \frac{1}{\sqrt{3}}$.

6.4 The situation at any time during the season may be represented by a diagram as shown, where the vertices A, B, C, ..., J represent the teams, and joining 2 vertices represents the fact that these teams have, to date, played each other.

a Assume firstly that each team has played at least one match to date. Since each team has played each other team at most once, no more than 9 line segments can issue from any one vertex. Since there are 10 vertices, from each of which it is possible to draw 1, 2, 3, ..., 9 line segments, there must be at least 2 vertices from which an equal number of line segments is drawn.   {P-H-P}.

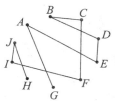

b Assume secondly that there are some isolated vertices, i.e., to date at least one team has not played a match.

We consider the non-isolated vertices and apply exactly the same reasoning to them as we did in **a**.

If there are n, say, non-isolated vertices, from each we can draw 1, 2, 3, ..., $n-1$ line segments. The result follows.

7. SEQUENCES, SERIES & PRODUCTS

7.1 **a** $\dfrac{1}{1+\sqrt{2}} + \dfrac{1}{\sqrt{2}+\sqrt{3}} + \dfrac{1}{\sqrt{3}+\sqrt{4}} + ... + \dfrac{1}{\sqrt{99}+\sqrt{100}}$

$= (\sqrt{2}-1) + (\sqrt{3}-\sqrt{2}) + (\sqrt{4}-\sqrt{3}) + ... + (\sqrt{100}-\sqrt{99})$

Each of these terms has form $\dfrac{1}{\sqrt{n}+\sqrt{n+1}} = \left(\dfrac{1}{\sqrt{n}+\sqrt{n+1}}\right)\left(\dfrac{\sqrt{n+1}-\sqrt{n}}{\sqrt{n+1}-\sqrt{n}}\right)$

$\left. = \dfrac{\sqrt{n+1}-\sqrt{n}}{n+1-n} = \sqrt{n+1}-\sqrt{n} \right\}$

$= -1 + \sqrt{100}$ {on cancelling, these two terms are the only ones remaining.}

$= -1 + 10$

$= \underline{9}$

b $\dfrac{1}{1+\sqrt{2}} + \dfrac{1}{\sqrt{2}+\sqrt{3}} + \dfrac{1}{\sqrt{3}+\sqrt{4}} + ... + \dfrac{1}{\sqrt{n-1}+\sqrt{n}} = \underline{\sqrt{n}-1}$ $(n \geqslant 2)$

$\dfrac{1}{\sqrt{a}+\sqrt{a+d}} + \dfrac{1}{\sqrt{a+d}+\sqrt{a+2d}} + \dfrac{1}{\sqrt{a+2d}+\sqrt{a+3d}} + ... + \dfrac{1}{\sqrt{a+(n-1)d}+\sqrt{a+nd}}$

$= \dfrac{\sqrt{a+nd}-\sqrt{a}}{d}$

7.2 If the overall square is 6 units by 6 units,

the sides of the small squares are 1, $\frac{4}{5}$, $\frac{3}{4}$ of $\frac{4}{5} = \frac{3}{5}$, $\frac{2}{3}$ of $\frac{3}{5} = \frac{2}{5}$, $\frac{1}{2}$ of $\frac{2}{5} = \frac{1}{5}$

i.e. $\frac{5}{5}$, $\frac{4}{5}$, $\frac{3}{5}$, $\frac{2}{5}$, $\frac{1}{5}$ respectively.

The total of the small squares

$= 20\left(\frac{5}{5}\right)^2 + 16\left(\frac{4}{5}\right)^2 + 12\left(\frac{3}{5}\right)^2 + 8\left(\frac{2}{5}\right)^2 + 4\left(\frac{1}{5}\right)^2$

$= \dfrac{4}{5^2}[5^3 + 4^3 + 3^3 + 2^3 + 1^3]$

But the total area is   36 square units $= 6^2$

$\therefore$ $6^2 = \dfrac{4}{5^2}[1^3 + 2^3 + 3^3 + 4^3 + 5^3]$ and so $1^3 + 2^3 + 3^3 + 4^3 + 5^3 = \dfrac{5^2 \times 6^2}{4}$

In general, $1^3 + 2^3 + 3^3 + 4^3 + ... + n^3 = \dfrac{n^2(n+1)^2}{4}$

7.3 $n^3 = [1^3 + 2^3 + 3^3 + ... + (n-1)^3 + n^3] - [1^3 + 2^3 + 3^3 + ... + (n-1)^3]$

$= \dfrac{n^2(n+1)^2}{4} - \dfrac{(n-1)^2 n^2}{4}$

$= \left(\dfrac{n(n+1)}{2}\right)^2 - \left(\dfrac{(n-1)n}{2}\right)^2$

where $n(n+1)$ and $(n-1)n$ are even {product of two consecutive integers is even}

Thus n^3 has been expressed as the difference of two perfect squares.

example: $1,000,000 = 100^3 = \left(\frac{100 \times 101}{2}\right)^2 - \left(\frac{99 \times 100}{2}\right)^2$

$$= 5050^2 - 4950^2.$$

7.4

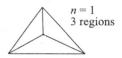

$n = 1$
3 regions

$n = 2$
5 regions

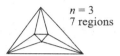

$n = 3$
7 regions

We guess: $\underline{R_n = 2n + 1}$ is the number of regions for n internal points.

Proof: (by induction on n)

   a The result is true for $n = 1$. (shown above)

   b Suppose $R_k = 2k + 1$ for k internal points.
For the triangle with $k + 1$ points, the addition of the last point replaces one triangle with 3 smaller triangles, thus causing a net increase of 2 triangles.

     Thus $\quad R_{k+1} = R_k + 2$
$$= 2k + 1 + 2$$
$$= 2k + 3$$
$$= 2(k + 1) + 1$$

     Thus, by induction, $\quad R_n = 2n + 1 \quad$ for all n in Z^+.

The <u>problem generalizes to 3 dimensions</u> by considering n points inside a tetrahedron.
The tetrahedron is then partitioned into smaller tetrahedrons, and the number of these is given by $\quad \underline{3n + 1}$.

7.5 $\dfrac{1}{x}, \dfrac{1}{y}, \dfrac{1}{z}$ in arithmetic progression means that $\quad \dfrac{1}{y} - \dfrac{1}{x} = \dfrac{1}{z} - \dfrac{1}{y}$

$$\therefore \quad \frac{2}{y} = \frac{z + x}{xz}$$

$$\therefore \quad 2xz = xy + yz ......(1)$$

Now $\quad (x - y + z)^2 = x^2 + y^2 + z^2 - 2xy - 2yz + 2xz$
$$= x^2 + 2xz + z^2 + y^2 - 2[xy + yz]$$
$$= x^2 - 2xz + z^2 + y^2$$
$$= (x - z)^2 + y^2$$

Thus $x - z$, y and $x - y + z$ are the <u>sides of a right-angled triangle.</u>
{converse of Pythagorean theorem} $\{x > y > z > 0, \quad x - z > 0, \quad y > 0, \quad x - y + z > 0\}$

7.6   Let $\quad P_n = (1 + 2)(1 + 2^2)(1 + 2^4)(1 + 2^8) \ldots \ldots (1 + 2^{2^n})$

$\therefore \quad P_0 = 1 + 2$

$\qquad P_1 = (1 + 2)(1 + 2^2) = 1 + 2 + 2^2 + 2^3$

$\qquad P_2 = (1 + 2)(1 + 2^2)(1 + 2^4) = (1 + 2 + 2^2 + 2^3)(1 + 2^4)$
$$= 1 + 2 + 2^2 + 2^3 + 2^4 + 2^5 + 2^6 + 2^7$$

$\qquad \vdots$

$\qquad P_n = 1 + 2 + 2^2 + 2^3 + 2^4 + \ldots \ldots + 2^{2^{n+1} - 1} \qquad$ {by induction}

Now $\quad 2P_n = 2 + 2^2 + 2^3 + 2^4 + 2^5 + \ldots \ldots + 2^{2^{n+1}}$

$\therefore \quad 2P_n + 1 = \underbrace{1 + 2 + 2^2 + 2^3 + 2^4 + \ldots \ldots + 2^{2^n}} + 2^{2^{n+1}}$

i.e. $\quad 2P_n + 1 = P_n + 2^{2^{n+1}} \qquad \therefore \quad P_n = 2^{2^{n+1}} - 1$

Thus $\quad (1 + 2)(1 + 2^2)(1 + 2^4) \ldots \ldots (1 + 2^{2^n}) = \underline{2^{2^{n+1}} - 1}$

or

$$P = (1+2)(1+2^2)(1+2^4)(1+2^8)........(1+2^{2^n})$$

$$\therefore \quad P(1-2) = (1-2)(1+2)(1+2^2)(1+2^{4)}........(1+2^{2^n})$$

$$= (1-2^2)(1+2^2)(1+2^4)........(1+2^{2^n})$$

$$= (1-2^4)(1+2^4)(1+2^8)........(1+2^{2^n})$$

$$= (1-2^8)(1+2^8)(1+2^{16})........(1+2^{2^n})$$

$$\vdots$$

$$= (1-2^{2^n})(1+2^{2^n})$$

$$= 1 - 2^{2^n+2^n}$$

$$\therefore \quad -P = 1 - 2^{2^{n+1}}$$

$$\therefore \quad \underline{P = 2^{2^{n+1}} - 1}$$

7.7 The nth term of the sequence is $\quad \underbrace{4444........4}_{n \text{ of these}} \underbrace{8888........8}_{n-1 \text{ of these}} 9$

$$= (4.10^{2n-1} + 4.10^{2n-2} + ... + 4.10^n) + (8.10^{n-1} + 8.10^{n-2} + ... + 8.10 + 8) + 1$$

$$= 4.10^n[1 + 10 + 10^2 + ... + 10^{n-1}] + 8[1 + 10 + 10^2 + ... + 10^{n-1}] + 1$$

$$= 4.10^n \left[\frac{10^n - 1}{10-1}\right] + 8\left[\frac{10^n - 1}{10-1}\right] + 1$$

$$= \tfrac{4}{9}.10^n[10^n - 1] + \tfrac{8}{9}[10^n - 1] + 1$$

$$= \tfrac{4}{9}.10^{2n} + \tfrac{4}{9}.10^n + \tfrac{1}{9}$$

$$= \underline{\left[\frac{2.10^n + 1}{3}\right]^2} \quad \text{and digital sum of } 2.10^n + 1 \text{ is 3}$$

$$\therefore \quad 3 \text{ is a factor of } 2.10^n + 1 \qquad \therefore \quad \frac{2.10^n + 1}{3} \text{ is an integer.}$$

or $\quad \dfrac{2.10^n + 1}{3} = \dfrac{2(1+9)^n + 1}{3} = \dfrac{2[1 + \binom{n}{1}9 + \binom{n}{2}9^2 + ... + \binom{n}{n}9^n] + 1}{3}$

$$= \frac{3 + 2\binom{n}{1}9 + 2\binom{n}{2}9^2 + ... + 2\binom{n}{n}9^n}{3}$$

$$= 1 + 2\binom{n}{1}3 + 2\binom{n}{2}3.9 + ... + 2\binom{n}{n}3.9^{n-1}, \quad \text{an integer.}$$

Thus all such terms are <u>perfect squares</u>.

7.8 If $\quad a_1 < a_2 < a_3 < a_4 < ....$ then $\quad a_n < a_{n+1} \quad$ for all n in Z^+.

Now $\quad b_{n+1} - b_n$

$$= \frac{a_1 + a_2 + a_3 + ... + a_{n+1}}{n+1} - \frac{a_1 + a_2 + a_3 + ... + a_n}{n}$$

$$= \frac{n(a_1 + a_2 + a_3 + ... + a_{n+1}) - (n+1)(a_1 + a_2 + a_3 + ... + a_n)}{n(n+1)}$$

$$= \frac{n(a_1 + a_2 + ... + a_n) + na_{n+1} - n(a_1 + a_2 + ... + a_n) - (a_1 + a_2 + ... + a_n)}{n(n+1)}$$

$$= \frac{(a_{n+1} - a_1) + (a_{n+1} - a_2) + ... + (a_{n+1} - a_n)}{n(n+1)}$$

$> 0 \quad$ for all n as $\quad a_{n+1} - a_1, \quad a_{n+1} - a_2, \quad$ etc. are all positive.

$\therefore \quad b_{n+1} > b_n \quad$ for all n in Z^+ and so the <u>sequence of b's is increasing</u> also.

7.9 $N = \underbrace{11111\ldots\ldots1}_{2n \text{ of these}} - \underbrace{22222\ldots\ldots2}_{n \text{ of these}}$

$= (10^{2n-1} + 10^{2n-2} + \ldots\ldots + 10^2 + 10^1 + 1) - (2.10^{n-1} + 2.10^{n-2} + \ldots\ldots + 2.10^2 + 2.10^1 + 2.)$

$= \left[\dfrac{10^{2n}-1}{10-1}\right] - 2\left[\dfrac{10^n-1}{10-1}\right]$ {sum of GP formula}

$= \dfrac{10^{2n} - 1 - 2.10^n + 2}{9}$

$= \dfrac{10^{2n} - 2.10^n + 1}{9}$

$= \underline{\left[\dfrac{10^n - 1}{3}\right]^2}$ where $10^n - 1$ consists of 9's and is $\therefore$ divisible by 3.

       and $\therefore \left[\dfrac{10^n-1}{3}\right]^2$ is (an integer)^2

or $\dfrac{10^n - 1}{3} = \dfrac{(1+9)^n - 1}{3} = \dfrac{1 + \binom{n}{1}9 + \binom{n}{2}9^2 + \ldots\ldots + 9^n - 1}{3}$

           $= \binom{n}{1}3 + \binom{n}{2}3.9 + \ldots\ldots + 3.9^{n-1}$ which is an integer.

$\therefore$ $\underline{N \text{ is a perfect square.}}$

7.10   **a**   The addition of the rth line to the set-up containing $(r-1)$ lines adds another r regions.

i.e. $R_r = R_{r-1} + r$ where $R_1 = 2$.

$\therefore$ $R_n = R_{n-1} + n$

       $= R_{n-2} + (n-1) + n$

       $= R_{n-3} + (n-2) + (n-1) + n$

       $\vdots$

       $= R_1 + 2 + 3 + \ldots\ldots + (n-1) + n$

       $= 1 + (1 + 2 + 3 + \ldots\ldots + n)$

       $= 1 + \dfrac{n(n+1)}{2}$

       $= \underline{\dfrac{n^2 + n + 2}{2}}$ [A formal inductive proof of this result uses the recurrence relationship $R_r = R_{r-1} + r$, where $R_1 = 2$.]

n = 1   n = 2   n = 3   n = 4

2   4   7   11

b

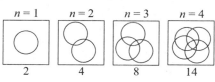

n = 1   n = 2   n = 3   n = 4

2   4   8   14

In a similar way to a we observe that $R_n = R_{n-1} + 2(n-1)$ where $R_1 = 2$, and likewise we deduce that $\underline{R_n = n^2 - n + 2}$.

7.11 $a_1 = 1$, $a_{n+1} = \frac{1}{2}\left(a_n + \dfrac{2}{a_n}\right)$, $n \geqslant 1$ $\therefore$ $a_n = \frac{1}{2}\left(a_{n-1} + \dfrac{2}{a_{n-1}}\right)$

   a   Proposition, $P(n)$: $\dfrac{a_n - \sqrt{2}}{a_n + \sqrt{2}} = \left(\dfrac{1 - \sqrt{2}}{1 + \sqrt{2}}\right)^{2^{n-1}}$ for all n in Z^+.

   Proof: (By Mathematical Induction)

     i   If $n = 1$, LHS $= \dfrac{a_1 - \sqrt{2}}{a_1 + \sqrt{2}} = \dfrac{1 - \sqrt{2}}{1 + \sqrt{2}}$,   RHS $= \left(\dfrac{1 - \sqrt{2}}{1 + \sqrt{2}}\right)^1 = \dfrac{1 - \sqrt{2}}{1 + \sqrt{2}}$, $\therefore$ $P(1)$ is true.

ii If $P(k)$ is true, then $\dfrac{a_k - \sqrt{2}}{a_k + \sqrt{2}} = \left(\dfrac{1 - \sqrt{2}}{1 + \sqrt{2}}\right)^{2^{k-1}}$.

$$\therefore \quad \frac{a_{k+1} - \sqrt{2}}{a_{k+1} + \sqrt{2}} = \frac{\frac{1}{2}\left(a_k + \dfrac{2}{a_k}\right) - \sqrt{2}}{\left(\frac{1}{2}a_k + \dfrac{2}{a_k}\right) + \sqrt{2}}$$

$$= \frac{a_k + \dfrac{2}{a_k} - 2\sqrt{2}}{a_k + \dfrac{2}{a_k} + 2\sqrt{2}}$$

$$= \frac{a_k{}^2 - 2\sqrt{2}a_k + 2}{a_k{}^2 + 2\sqrt{2}a_k + 2}$$

$$= \left(\frac{a_k - \sqrt{2}}{a_k + \sqrt{2}}\right)^2$$

$$= \left(\frac{1 - \sqrt{2}}{1 + \sqrt{2}}\right)^{2^{k-1}\cdot 2}$$

$$= \left(\frac{1 - \sqrt{2}}{1 + \sqrt{2}}\right)^{2^{k}}$$

Thus $P(k+1)$ is true whenever $P(k)$ is true. $\therefore$ $P(n)$ is true.

b Now $-1 - \sqrt{2} < 1 - \sqrt{2} < 1 + \sqrt{2}$

$$\therefore \quad -1 < \frac{1 - \sqrt{2}}{1 + \sqrt{2}} < 1$$

Thus $\left(\dfrac{1 - \sqrt{2}}{1 + \sqrt{2}}\right)^{2^{n-1}}$ approaches 0 as n gets very large

{for $|r| < 1$, r^n approaches 0 as n gets very large}

$\therefore$ $\dfrac{a_n - \sqrt{2}}{a_n + \sqrt{2}}$ approaches 0.

$\therefore$ $a_n - \sqrt{2}$ approaches 0.

$\therefore$ for n sufficiently large, a_n is very close to $\sqrt{2}$.

$$\begin{bmatrix}
\text{Note:} \quad a_1 = 1 \\
a_2 = \frac{1}{2}(1 + \frac{2}{1}) \quad = \frac{3}{2} \quad = 1 \cdot 5 \\
a_3 = \frac{1}{2}(\frac{3}{2} + \frac{4}{3}) \quad = \frac{17}{12} \; \doteqdot 1 \cdot 4167 \\
a_4 = \frac{1}{2}(\frac{17}{12} + \frac{24}{17}) = \frac{577}{408} \doteqdot 1 \cdot 4142157 \\
\text{etc. give successively better approximations to} \quad \sqrt{2} \doteqdot 1 \cdot 414213562 \ldots\ldots
\end{bmatrix}$$

7.12

$n = 1$	$n = 2$	$n = 3$	$n = 4$
$P_1 = 4$	$P_2 = 6$	$P_3 = 8$	$P_4 = 10$

We guess $P_n = 2(n + 1)$

It seems that when the number of points is increased by 1, the number of triangles increases by 2. This is clear as there are <u>two</u> possible cases.

An additional point may either fall

a   within an existing triangle,

∴   one triangle is replaced by 3,   i.e.,   an additional 2.

or

b   on a side of two existing triangles,

∴   two triangles are replaced by 4,   i.e.,   an additional 2.

Thus the truth of P_n follows by induction.

7.13 Let the number of trees in the plantation at the end of winter in year $n+1$ be

$$x_{n+1} = \tfrac{9}{10}x_n + 100$$

$$\therefore \quad x_{n+2} = \tfrac{9}{10}x_{n+1} + 100 \qquad \{\text{replacing } n \text{ by } n+1\}$$

$$= \tfrac{9}{10}\left(\tfrac{9}{10}x_n + 100\right) + 100$$

$$= \left(\tfrac{9}{10}\right)^2 x_n + 100\left(1 + \tfrac{9}{10}\right)$$

$$x_{n+3} = \tfrac{9}{10}x_{n+2} + 100$$

$$= \tfrac{9}{10}\left[\left(\tfrac{9}{10}\right)^2 x_n + 100\left(1 + \tfrac{9}{10}\right)\right] + 100$$

$$= \left(\tfrac{9}{10}\right)^3 x_n + 100\left(1 + \tfrac{9}{10} + \left(\tfrac{9}{10}\right)^2\right)$$

$$\vdots$$

$$x_{n+k} = \left(\tfrac{9}{10}\right)^k x_n + 100\left(1 + \tfrac{9}{10} + \left(\tfrac{9}{10}\right)^2 + \ldots\ldots + \left(\tfrac{9}{10}\right)^{k-1}\right) \quad \{\text{by induction}\}$$

i.e. $x_{n+k} = \left(\tfrac{9}{10}\right)^k x_n + 100 \left[\dfrac{1 - \left(\tfrac{9}{10}\right)^k}{1 - \tfrac{9}{10}}\right]$

or $\underline{x_{n+k} = \left(\tfrac{9}{10}\right)^k x_n + 1000\left[1 - \left(\tfrac{9}{10}\right)^k\right]}$

<u>when $n = 1970$ and $k = 10$</u>

$$x_{1980} = \left(\tfrac{9}{10}\right)^{10} x_{1970} + 1000\left[1 - \left(\tfrac{9}{10}\right)^{10}\right]$$

$$\therefore \quad 1200 \doteqdot 0 \cdot 34868\, x_{1970} + 651 \cdot 32$$

$$\therefore \quad 0 \cdot 34868 x_{1970} \doteqdot 548 \cdot 68$$

$$\therefore \quad x_{1970} \doteqdot 1573 \cdot 6$$

i.e.   <u>approximately 1574 trees in 1970.</u>

<u>As k increases</u>   (into the 21st century)

$$x_{1980+k} = \left(\tfrac{9}{10}\right)^k x_{1980} + 1000\left[1 - \left(\tfrac{9}{10}\right)^k\right]$$

$\left(\tfrac{9}{10}\right)^k$ gets closer to 0.

∴ x_{1980+k} gets closer to 1000 trees.

i.e.   eventually the number of trees
at the end of winter is <u>stable at 1000.</u>

7.14 $t_{AB_1} = 2$ secs

$t_{B_1B_2} = 2\left(\tfrac{9}{10}.2\right)$ secs $= 4\left(\tfrac{9}{10}\right)$ secs

$t_{B_2B_3} = 2\left(\tfrac{9}{10} \cdot \tfrac{9}{10}.2\right) = 4.\left(\tfrac{9}{10}\right)^2$ secs

$t_{B_3B_4} = 4\left(\tfrac{9}{10}\right)^3$ secs, etc.

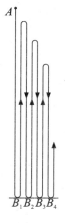

$\therefore$ total time

$$= 2 + 4\left(\tfrac{9}{10}\right) + 4\left(\tfrac{9}{10}\right)^2 + 4\left(\tfrac{9}{10}\right)^3 + \ldots\ldots$$

$$= 2 + 4\left(\tfrac{9}{10}\right)\left[1 + \tfrac{9}{10} + \left(\tfrac{9}{10}\right)^2 + \ldots\ldots\right] \quad \text{an infinite G.P. with} \quad a = 1, \ r = \tfrac{9}{10}.$$

$$= 2 + 4\left(\tfrac{9}{10}\right)\left(\cfrac{1}{1 - \tfrac{9}{10}}\right)$$

$$= 2 + 4\left(\tfrac{9}{10}\right)10$$

$$= 2 + 36$$

$$= \underline{38 \text{ seconds}}$$

7.15 Let the A.P. be $a_1, a_2, a_3, a_4, \ldots\ldots$

and the G.P. be $g_1, g_2, g_3, g_4, \ldots\ldots$

We are given that $a_1 = g_1$ and $a_2 = g_2$ and have to prove that $a_n \leqslant g_n$ for all $n \geqslant 3$.

Let $a_2 - a_1 = d$,   the common difference

and $\dfrac{g_2}{g_1} = r$,   the common ratio.

$\therefore \qquad r = \dfrac{a_2}{a_1} = \dfrac{a_1 + d}{a_1} = 1 + \dfrac{d}{a_1}$

Thus $g_n - a_n = g_1 . r^{n-1} - [a_1 + (n-1)d]$

$$= a_1\left[1 + \dfrac{d}{a_1}\right]^{n-1} - a_1 - (n-1)d$$

$$= a_1\left[1 + \binom{n-1}{1}\dfrac{d}{a_1} + \binom{n-1}{2}\dfrac{d^2}{a_1^2} + \ldots\ldots\right] - a_1 - (n-1)d$$

$$\geqslant a_1\left[1 + \binom{n-1}{1}\dfrac{d}{a_1}\right] - a_1 - (n-1)d$$

{as all other terms left out are positive, $n \geqslant 3$}

$\therefore \quad g_n - a_n \geqslant a_1 + (n-1)d - a_1 - (n-1)d$

$\therefore \quad g_n - a_n \geqslant 0 \quad$ for all $n \geqslant 3$

$\qquad \therefore \quad g_n \geqslant a_n \quad$ for all $n \geqslant 3$.

7.16   **a**   At the end of the 1st quarter I owe $\$20\,000 + 3\%$ of $\$20\,000 - R$,

where R is my quarterly repayment, $\theta_1 = (1.03).20\,000 - R \ldots\ldots(1)$

At the end of the 2nd quarter I owe $\theta_2 = \theta_1 + 3\%$ of $\theta_1 - R$

$\therefore \quad \theta_2 = (1.03)\theta_1 - R \ldots\ldots(2)$

Likewise $\theta_3 = (1.03)\theta_2 - R$

etc.

$$\vdots$$

$$\theta_n = (1.03)\theta_{n-1} - R \qquad \text{\{by induction\}}$$

and we want $\theta_{40} = 0$

$\therefore \quad R = 1.03\,\theta_{39}$

$$= 1.03[(1.03)\theta_{38} - R]$$

$$= (1.03)^2\theta_{38} - R(1.03)$$

$$= (1.03)^2[(1.03)\theta_{37} - R] - R(1.03)$$

$$= (1.03)^3\theta_{37} - R[1.03 + (1.03)^2]$$

$$\vdots \quad \text{etc.}$$

$$= (1.03)^{40}\theta_0 - R[1.03 + (1.03)^2 + \ldots\ldots + (1.03)^{39}]$$

$$\therefore \quad R[1 + 1.03 + (1.03)^2 + \text{........} + (1.03)^{39}] = (1.03)^{40}.\theta_0$$

$$\therefore \quad R = \frac{(1.03)^{40}.\theta_0}{1 + (1.03) + (1.03)^2 + \text{........} + (1.03)^{39}}$$

$$\therefore \quad R = \frac{(1.03)^{40}.\theta_0}{\dfrac{(1.03)^{40} - 1}{1.03 - 1}} = \frac{(1.03)^{40}.\theta_0.(0.03)}{(1.03)^{40} - 1} \qquad \text{where} \quad \theta_0 = 20,000.$$

$$\therefore \quad R = \frac{3.262038 \times 20000 \times 0.03}{2.262038}$$

$$= \$865.25$$

b For $\theta_0 = \$P$, repayments R, for n years at $r\%$ p.a., for m repayments per year

$$R = \frac{\left(1 + \dfrac{r}{100m}\right)^{mn} \times P \times \left(\dfrac{r}{100m}\right)}{\left(1 + \dfrac{r}{100m}\right)^{mn} - 1}$$

7.17 **a** Each side ———————— becomes ⟍⟋⟍⟋ i.e,. 3 parts become 4.

$$\therefore \quad P_2 = \tfrac{4}{3}P_1$$

$$P_3 = \tfrac{4}{3}P_2 = \left(\tfrac{4}{3}\right)^2 P_1$$

$$P_4 = \tfrac{4}{3}P_3 = \left(\tfrac{4}{3}\right)^3 P_1$$

$$\vdots$$

$$\underline{P_n = \left(\tfrac{4}{3}\right)^{n-1} P_1} \qquad \{\text{by induction}\}$$

b Also each new triangle has area $\tfrac{1}{9}$ of the previous sized triangle.

$$\therefore \qquad A_2 - A_1 = 3.\frac{A_1}{9}$$

and $\qquad A_3 - A_2 = 4.3.\dfrac{A_1}{9^2}$ $\qquad \{\text{after the first case we are adding 4 triangles}\}$

$$A_4 - A_3 = 4^2.3.\frac{A_1}{9^3}$$

$$\vdots$$

$$A_n - A_{n-1} = 4^{n-2}.3.\frac{A_1}{9^{n-1}} \qquad \{\text{by induction}\}$$

adding them we get

$$A_n - A_1 = \frac{3A_1}{9}\left[1 + \tfrac{4}{9} + \left(\tfrac{4}{9}\right)^2 + \text{........} + \left(\tfrac{4}{9}\right)^{n-2}\right]$$

i.e. $\quad A_n = A_1 + \dfrac{A_1}{3}\left[1 + \tfrac{4}{9} + \left(\tfrac{4}{9}\right)^2 + \text{........} + \left(\tfrac{4}{9}\right)^{n-2}\right]$

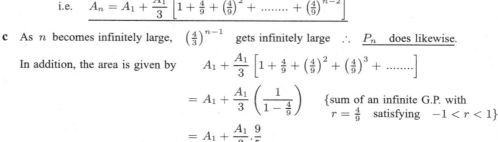

c As n becomes infinitely large, $\left(\tfrac{4}{3}\right)^{n-1}$ gets infinitely large $\therefore$ $\underline{P_n}$ does likewise.

In addition, the area is given by $\quad A_1 + \dfrac{A_1}{3}\left[1 + \tfrac{4}{9} + \left(\tfrac{4}{9}\right)^2 + \left(\tfrac{4}{9}\right)^3 + \text{........}\right]$

$$= A_1 + \frac{A_1}{3}\left(\frac{1}{1 - \tfrac{4}{9}}\right) \qquad \{\text{sum of an infinite G.P. with } r = \tfrac{4}{9} \text{ satisfying } -1 < r < 1\}$$

$$= A_1 + \frac{A_1}{3}.\frac{9}{5}$$

$$= A_1 + \frac{3A_1}{5}$$

$$= \frac{8A_1}{5}$$

∴ the curve contains a <u>finite area</u>.   (160% of the original area of C_1.)

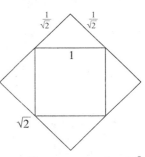

Area of large square = 2 units^2

For the <u>second example</u>,

notice that in C_3 8 square holes appear and in successive curves the inner region contains many more holes each of less area than in the previous case.
As n gets very large, so does P_n,
but A_n gets closer to $\underline{2A_1}$, no surprise as:
What happens to the <u>holes</u>?

7.18 **a** $S_4 = \frac{1}{1} + \frac{1}{2} + \frac{1}{3} + \frac{1}{4} + \frac{1}{1.2} + \frac{1}{1.3} + \frac{1}{1.4} + \frac{1}{2.3} + \frac{1}{2.4} + \frac{1}{3.4} + \frac{1}{1.2.3} + \frac{1}{1.2.4} + \frac{1}{1.3.4} + \frac{1}{2.3.4} + \frac{1}{1.2.3.4}$

$= \left(\frac{1}{1} + \frac{1}{2} + \frac{1}{3} + \frac{1}{1.2} + \frac{1}{2.3} + \frac{1}{1.3} + \frac{1}{1.2.3}\right) + \frac{1}{4} + \left(\frac{1}{1.4} + \frac{1}{2.4} + \frac{1}{3.4} + \frac{1}{1.2.4} + \frac{1}{1.3.4} + \frac{1}{2.3.4} + \frac{1}{1.2.3.4}\right)$

$= S_3 + \frac{1}{4} + \frac{1}{4}\left(\frac{1}{1} + \frac{1}{2} + \frac{1}{3} + \frac{1}{1.2} + \frac{1}{1.3} + \frac{1}{2.3} + \frac{1}{1.2.3}\right)$

$= S_3 + \frac{1}{4} + \frac{1}{4}S_3$

$= 3 + \frac{1}{4} + \frac{1}{4}.3$

$= \underline{4}$

b Proof, by the Principle of Mathematical Induction
P_n is "$S_n = n$ for all n in Z^+."

i If $n = 1$, $S_1 = 1$ is true   {given}
∴ $P(1)$ is true.

ii If $P(k)$ is true, then $S_k = k$.
But $S_{k+1} = S_k + \dfrac{1}{k+1} + \dfrac{1}{k+1}S_k$ {as illustrated in case S_4}

$= k + \dfrac{1}{k+1} + \dfrac{k}{k+1}$

$= k + \dfrac{1+k}{k+1}$

$= k + 1$

Thus $P(k+1)$ is true whenever $P(k)$ is true and as $P(1)$ is true
∴ $\underline{P(n)}$ is true   {P. of M.I.}

7.19 **a** **Proof**: (by Induction)

i If $n = 1$, $a_1 = r^0 a + s\left(\dfrac{1 - r^0}{1 - r}\right)$

∴ $a_1 = a$ which is true. ∴ $P(1)$ is true.

ii If $P(k)$ is true, then

$$a_k = r^{k-1}.a + s\left(\frac{1 - r^{k-1}}{1 - r}\right)$$

∴ $a_{k+1} = ra_k + s$

$$= r\left[r^{k-1}.a + s\left(\frac{1 - r^{k-1}}{1 - r}\right)\right] + s$$

$$= r^k a + s \left[r\left(\frac{1 - r^{k-1}}{1 - r} \right) + 1 \right]$$

$$= r^k a + s \left[\frac{r - r^k + 1 - r}{1 - r} \right]$$

$$= r^k a + s \left[\frac{1 - r^k}{1 - r} \right]$$

Thus $P(k+1)$ is true whenever $P(k)$ is true. $\therefore$ $P(n)$ is true.

b Let the $\triangle ABC$ have sides a units long

In $\triangle P_1 P_2 C$, $\sin 30^\circ = \dfrac{x_2}{a - x_1} = \dfrac{1}{2}$

$\therefore$ $x_2 = -\frac{1}{2} x_1 + \frac{1}{2} a$

Likewise in $\triangle P_2 P_3 A$,

$x_3 = -\frac{1}{2} x_2 + \frac{1}{2} a$

In general, $x_{n+1} = -\frac{1}{2} x_n + \frac{1}{2} a$ {by induction}

$\therefore$ By **a**, $x_n = \left(-\frac{1}{2} \right)^{n-1} x_1 + \frac{1}{2} a \left(\dfrac{1 - \left(-\frac{1}{2} \right)^{n-1}}{1 - \left(-\frac{1}{2} \right)} \right)$

$\qquad = \left(-\frac{1}{2} \right)^{n-1} x_1 + \dfrac{a}{3} \left(1 - \left(-\frac{1}{2} \right)^{n-1} \right)$

and as n gets infinitely large, $\left(-\frac{1}{2} \right)^{n-1}$ approaches 0.

$\therefore$ x_n approaches $\dfrac{a}{3}$,

a position where $\triangle P_n P_{n+1} P_{n+2}$ is equilateral.

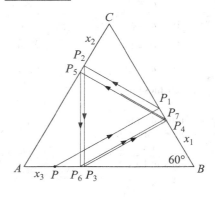

c <u>Notation:</u> Let the measure of $\angle A_n$ be a_n.

Now $a_{n+1} = \theta_1 + \phi_1$

$\qquad = \theta_2 + \phi_2$ {angles subtended by same arc}

$\qquad = \frac{1}{2} b_n + \frac{1}{2} c_n$

$\qquad = \frac{1}{2}(b_n + c_n)$

$\qquad = \frac{1}{2}(180^\circ - a_n)$

$\qquad = -\frac{1}{2} a_n + 90^\circ$

$\therefore$ From **a**

$a_n = \left(-\frac{1}{2} \right)^{n-1} a_1 + 90^\circ \left(\dfrac{1 - \left(-\frac{1}{2} \right)^{n-1}}{\frac{3}{2}} \right)$

$\qquad = \left(-\frac{1}{2} \right)^{n-1} a_1 + 60^\circ \left(1 - \left(-\frac{1}{2} \right)^{n-1} \right)$

where $\left(-\frac{1}{2} \right)^{n-1}$ approaches 0 as n gets very large.

$\therefore$ a_n approaches 60° as n gets large.

Likewise $b_n \to 60^\circ$ and $c_n \to 60^\circ$

i.e. the triangle $A_n B_n C_n$ is tending to become more and more <u>equilateral</u>.

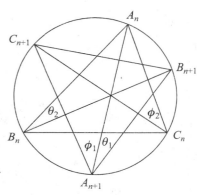

8. DIFFERENT BASES

8.1 If $215_a = 341_b$, then clearly $a \geqslant 6$ and $b \geqslant 5$.

Now $2.a^2 + 1.a + 5 = 3.b^2 + 4.b + 1$

i.e. $2a^2 + a + 5 = 3b^2 + 4b + 1$ where a and b are positive integers,
and $6 \leqslant a \leqslant 10$ and $5 \leqslant b \leqslant 10$.

If $a = 6$, $3b^2 + 4b - 82 = 0$ and thus $b = \frac{1}{6}(-4 \pm \sqrt{1000})$

If $a = 7$, $3b^2 + 4b - 109 = 0$ and thus $b = \frac{1}{6}(-4 \pm \sqrt{1324})$

If $a = 8$, $3b^2 + 4b - 140 = 0$ and thus $b = \frac{1}{6}(-4 \pm \sqrt{1696})$

If $a = 9$, $3b^2 + 4b - 175 = 0$ and thus $b = \frac{-25}{3}$ or 7

If $a = 10$, $3b^2 + 4b - 214 = 0$ and thus $b = \frac{1}{6}(-4 \pm \sqrt{2584})$

Of these possible solutions, only $\underline{a = 9}$ and $\underline{b = 7}$ is acceptable.

8.2 In the decimal system, (base 10), the fractions which terminate have denominators of the form $2^m.5^n$ where m, n are non-negative integers.
i.e.   they terminate if the denominator has no prime divisors other than 2 or 5.
Thus in base 6, fractions terminate if their denominators have no prime divisors other than 2 or 3.

a $\frac{1}{8} = \frac{1}{2^3}$ $\therefore$ $\frac{1}{8}$ will terminate in base 6.

$\frac{1}{8} = \frac{0}{6} + \frac{4}{6^2} + \frac{3}{6^3}$

$= \underline{(0 \cdot 043)_6}$

b $0 \cdot \bar{a} = 0 \cdot aaaa \ldots\ldots$

$= \frac{a}{6} + \frac{a}{6^2} + \frac{a}{6^3} + \frac{a}{6^4} + \ldots\ldots$

$= \frac{a}{6}\left(1 + \frac{1}{6} + \frac{1}{6^2} + \frac{1}{6^3} + \ldots\ldots\right)$

$= \frac{a}{6} \cdot \left(\dfrac{1}{1 - \frac{1}{6}}\right)$

$= \frac{a}{6} \cdot \dfrac{1}{\frac{5}{6}}$

$= \dfrac{a}{5}$

"$0 \cdot \overline{ab}$"

$= \dfrac{\text{"}ab\text{"}}{6^2} + \dfrac{\text{"}ab\text{"}}{6^4} + \dfrac{\text{"}ab\text{"}}{6^6} + \ldots\ldots$

$= \dfrac{\text{"}ab\text{"}}{36}\left(1 + \frac{1}{6^2} + \frac{1}{6^4} + \ldots\ldots\right)$

$= \dfrac{\text{"}ab\text{"}}{36} \cdot \left(\dfrac{1}{1 - \frac{1}{36}}\right)$

$= \dfrac{\text{"}ab\text{"}}{36 - 1}$

$= \dfrac{\text{"}ab\text{"}}{35}$

c   Thus $\frac{1}{5} = (0.\bar{1})_6$ and $\frac{1}{7} = (0.\overline{05})_6$.

8.3 **a** We must show that $a^{n+4} - a^n$ is divisible by 10   (i.e.   by 5 and 2).

Now $a^{n+4} - a^n = a^n(a^4 - 1)$

$= a^n(a^2 + 1)(a + 1)(a - 1)$

$= a^n(a^2 - 4 + 5)(a + 1)(a - 1)$

$= a^n(a^2 - 4)(a + 1)(a - 1) + 5a^n(a + 1)(a - 1)$

$= a^{n-1}(a - 2)(a - 1)a(a + 1)(a + 2) + 5a^n(a + 1)(a - 1)$

the first term contains the product of 5 consecutive integers, one of which must be divisible by 5.
$\therefore$ $\underline{a^{n+4} - a^n}$ is divisible by 5.

$(a - 1)a(a + 1)$ is a common factor of both terms in $a^{n+4} - a^n$ expansion.
i.e.,   the product of 3 consecutive integers, one of which is even
$\therefore$ $\underline{a^{n+4} - a^n}$ is divisible by 2.

b Clearly the same expression is divisible by 2×3 since it has as factors the three consecutive integers $a - 1$, a, and $a + 1$.

Thus a^n and a^{n+4} end in the same digit in a number system in base 6.

8.4 **a** Since each number ends in a 2, it is even and $\therefore$ divisible by 2.

For each number, the sum of the digits is 3 which is divisible by 3, and hence each number is divisible by 3.

Combining, each number is divisible by 6.

b $(12)_n = n + 2$ If $(12)_n$ is divisible by 6, then $n + 2 = 6a$, say where a is in Z^+.

$(102)_n = n^2 + 2$ $\therefore$ $n = 6a - 2$

$(1002)_n = n^3 + 2$

$\vdots$

etc.   Now $n^{i+1} = n.n^i + 2$

$= n(n^i + 2) - 2n + 2$

$= n(n^i + 2) - (2n - 2)$

$= n(n^i + 2) - (12a - 6)$ {as $n = 6a - 2$}

Thus if $n^i + 2$ is divisible by 6, then so is $n^{i+1} + 2$

Thus if $n = 6a - 2$, each number is divisible by 6

$n = 4, 10, 16, 22, 28, \ldots\ldots$ etc.

8.5 $(abc)_{10} = 100a + 10b + c$,   where c is odd

$= 99a + 9b + (a + b + c)$

$\therefore$ $(abc)_{10}$ is divisible by 9 $\therefore$ $a + b + c$ is divisible by 9......(*)

Furthermore $(abc)_9 = 81a + 9b + c$

$= 80a + 10b + (a - b + c)$

$\therefore$ $(abc)_9$ is divisible by 10 $\therefore$ $a - b + c$ is divisible by 10.

Since a, b, c can take only values between 0 and 8, then either

(1) $a - b + c = 0$

or   (2) $a - b + c = 10$

In case (1) $a + b + c = 9k$ {from (*)}

Thus $b = 9t$ where t is in Z.

and as $0 \leqslant b \leqslant 8$, clearly $b = 0$ $\therefore$ $a + c = 0$ $\therefore$ $a = c = 0$.

But c is odd $\therefore$ this case is not acceptable.

In case (2) $a + c = b + 10$

$\therefore$ $a + b + c = 2b + 10 = 9k$ {from *}

$\therefore$ $2(b + 5) = 9k$

$\therefore$ $b + 5 = 9t$ {and $k = 2t$}

$\therefore$ $b = 9t - 5$ {where $0 \leqslant b \leqslant 8$}

$\therefore$ $b = 4$ {when $t = 1$}

$\therefore$ $a + c = 14$ where c is odd

$\therefore$ $a = 7$, $c = 7$ as $0 \leqslant a \leqslant 8$, $0 \leqslant c \leqslant 8$

The required solution is $a = 7$, $b = 4$, $c = 7$.   i.e., number $= 747_{10} = 1020_9$

8.6 **a** Let the binary form for x be $(b_n b_{n-1} b_{n-2} \ldots\ldots b_3 b_2 b_1 b_0)_2$

i.e. $x = 2^n b_n + 2^{n-1} b_{n-1} + 2^{n-2} b_{n-2} + \ldots\ldots + 2^3 b_3 + 2^2 b_2 + 2 b_1 + b_0$

where the b_i values are either 0 or 1.

Let a be the difference between the number of 1's in odd numbered places and the number of 1's in even numbered places in this expression.

Then $a = (b_1 + b_3 + b_5 + \ldots\ldots) - (b_0 + b_2 + b_4 + \ldots\ldots)$,   since the $b_i = 0$ or 1.

$\therefore$ $x + a = (b_0 + 2b_1 + 4b_2 + 8b_3 + 16b_4 + \ldots\ldots + 2^n b_n)$

$$+(-b_0 + b_1 - b_2 + b_3 - b_4 + b_5 - \ldots\ldots - (-1)^n b_n)$$

$$= 3b_1 + 3b_2 + 9b_3 + 15b_4 + \ldots\ldots + [2^n - (-1)^n]b_n$$

and it is easily seen (by induction) that $2^n - (-1)^n$ is divisible by 3 for $n = 1, 2, 3, 4, \ldots\ldots$
Hence $x + a$ is divisible by 3.

$\therefore$ $a = (x + a) - x$ is divisible by 3   {as $(x + a), x,$ are divisible by 3}

b   Similarly if a is divisible by 3, then $x = (x + a) - a$ is also divisible by 3.

9. COUNTING

9.1   A triangle is formed by selecting 3 points and joining them with straight line segments.

This can be done in $C_3^9 = \dfrac{9.8.7}{3.2.1} = 84$ ways.

Thus there are <u>84</u> different triangles possible.

9.2

				1						
			1	1	1					
		1	2	3	2	1				
	1	3	6	7	6	3	1			
1	4	10	16	19	16	10	4	1		

$1 = 3^0$ Each number in the triangle makes a contribution
$3 = 3^1$ to 3 numbers in the next row, and if $S_r =$ sum of
$9 = 3^2$ numbers in r^{th} row, then $S_{r+1} = 3.S_r$.
$27 = 3^3$ From the triangle results, we propose that
$81 = 3^4$ $\underline{S_n = 3^{n-1}}$ for all n in Z^+.

Proof: (by Induction on n)

(1) $S_1 = 3^0 = 1$ $\therefore$ $P(1)$ is true.

(2)   If $P(k)$ is true,   i.e. $S_k = 3^{k-1}$,   then $S_{k+1} = 3S_k = 3.3^{k-1} = 3^k$

Thus $P(k+1)$ is true whenever $P(k)$ is true.

$\therefore$ $\underline{P(n)}$ is true.

9.3   Denote the wives by A, B, C and $D,$ and their respective husbands a, b, c and $d.$
First we seat the wives.
The first wife has a choice of 8 seats but this does not lead to different seating arrangements as once the couples are seated we may move this wife to any other setting simply by rotating the table and leaving the seating unchanged.
Once the first wife is seated there are $3.2.1 = 6$ possibilities for the other 3 wives.
Thus the 4 wives may be seated in 6 different ways.
For each arrangement of wives there are only 2 possibilities for the husbands, as shown.

Hence there are $6.2 = \underline{12}$ different ways of seating the couples.

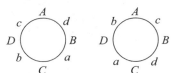

9.4   **a** $r\binom{n}{r} = r.\dfrac{n!}{r!(n-r)!}$

$$= \dfrac{n!}{(r-1)!(n-r)!}$$

$$= \dfrac{n.(n-1)!}{(r-1)!(n-r)!}$$

$$= \underline{n\binom{n-1}{r-1}}$$

b Consider $(1+x)^n = 1 + \binom{n}{1}x + \binom{n}{2}x^2 + \binom{n}{3}x^3 + \text{........} + \binom{n}{n}x^n$ {binomial expansion}

Let $x = 1$ and note that $\binom{n}{0} = 1$.

$$\therefore \quad 2^n = \binom{n}{0} + \binom{n}{1} + \binom{n}{2} + \binom{n}{3} + \text{........} + \binom{n}{n}$$

c In **b**, replace n by $n-1$.

$$\begin{cases} \qquad 2^{n-1} = \binom{n-1}{0} + \binom{n-1}{1} + \binom{n-1}{2} + \text{........} + \binom{n-1}{n-1} \\[2mm] \therefore \quad n.2^{n-1} = 1.\binom{n}{1} + 2\binom{n}{2} + 3\binom{n}{3} + \text{........} + n\binom{n}{n} \qquad \text{\{from a\}} \\[2mm] \therefore \quad \binom{n}{1} + 2\binom{n}{2} + 3\binom{n}{3} + \text{........} + n\binom{n}{n} = n.2^{n-1} \end{cases}$$

9.5 The numbers required here have an odd number of digits, $2r+1$, say.
Once the first $r+1$ digits are chosen, the number is fixed due to the nature of the numbers required.
There are $\binom{9}{r+1}$ ways of choosing the first $r+1$ digits. $\{\, r = 1, 2, 3, \text{........}, 8\}$
Thus the required number is $\binom{9}{2} + \binom{9}{3} + \binom{9}{4} + \text{........} + \binom{9}{9}$

$$= \left[\binom{9}{0} + \binom{9}{1} + \binom{9}{2} + \text{........} + \binom{9}{9}\right] - \left[\binom{9}{0} + \binom{9}{1}\right]$$
$$= 2^9 - [1 + 9]$$
$$= 512 - 10$$
$$= \underline{502}$$

9.6 Each rectangle is determined by a pair of opposite
sides. The number of ways of choosing pairs of
opposite sides is $\binom{m+2}{2}$ and $\binom{n+2}{2}$ respectively.
Thus the total number of rectangles is

$$\binom{m+2}{2}\binom{n+2}{2}$$
$$= \frac{(m+2)(m+1)}{2.1} . \frac{(n+2)(n+1)}{2.1}$$
$$= \frac{(m+2)(m+1)(n+2)(n+1)}{4}.$$

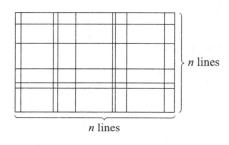

n lines

n lines

9.7 There are P^{10}_{7} possible seating arrangements for the 7 people who want to sit on side 1.
Likewise there are P^{10}_{6} possible seating arrangements for those
people who desire to sit on side 2.
The remaining 7 people can sit in 7! different ways.
Thus the total number of seating arrangements is $P^{10}_{7}.P^{10}_{6}.7!$

S_1 7 + 3

S_2 6 + 4

Generalization: If there are $2n$ people, p wish to sit on one side and q on the other,
then the total number of different seating arrangements is $\underline{P^{n}_{p}.P^{n}_{q}.(2n - p - q)!}$

9.8   **a**   Total numbers existing $= 6! = \underline{720}$

   b   Total numbers divisible by 3 is $6! = \underline{720}$,   since for a number to be divisible by 3, the sum of its
digits must be divisible by 3.
Sum of digits $= 6 + 5 + 4 + 3 + 2 + 1 = 21 = 7 \times 3$,   and the digits, and thus the sum of the digits,
are the same for all the numbers.

   c   Total number divisible by 9 is $\underline{0}$, since for a number to be divisible by 9, the sum of its digits must be
divisible exactly by 9.   Sum of its digits $= 21$,   which cannot be divided exactly by 9. The digits of
all the numbers are the same, hence the sum of the digits of each number is 21.

   d   For a number to be divisible by 11, the sum of the even-positioned digits must differ by 0 or 11 from
the sum of the odd-positioned digits.

i sum of the digits differing by 0

This is not possible as there are 3 pairs of numbers, i.e., if 6 and 1 were even positioned digits, then 2 and 5 would be odd positioned digits to make the sum of even positioned digits $= 7 =$ sum of odd positioned digits. However, the remaining two digits are not equal, hence the total sum of even positioned digits $\neq$ sum of the odd positioned digits.

ii sum of digits differing by 11

This is not possible since the maximum difference between the sum of the odd positioned and even positioned digits is 9, i.e., when even (or odd) positioned digits are 6, 5, 4, (sum is 15) and odd (or even) positioned digits are 1, 2, 3 (sum is 6), then difference $= 15 - 6 = 9$.

Hence <u>none</u> of the numbers is divisible by 11.

9.9 If the rook initially moves in a vertical direction each path can be described as $v_1 h_1 v_2 h_2 v_3 h_3 v_4$ where $v_1 + v_2 + v_3 + v_4 = 7$ and $h_1 + h_2 + h_3 = 7$.

The number of ways the vertical motion can be split up is $\binom{6}{3}$, since the first 3 moves can move to any of 6 rows, but the last move is predetermined and the number of ways the horizontal motion can be split is $\binom{6}{2}$.

$\therefore$ If the first move is vertical, the total number of ways is $\binom{6}{3}\binom{6}{2}$.

Hence the total number of ways is $2\binom{6}{3}\binom{6}{2} = 2.20.15$
$$= \underline{600}.$$

9.10 **a** Order: $A, B, \begin{cases} C \\ D \end{cases}$

We distinguish between 2 cases:

i C and D on different days.
In the order $ABCD$ there are $\binom{14}{4}$ choices for the days of the tests and for the order $ABDC$ there are likewise $\binom{14}{4}$ choices.

ii C and D on the same day.
The number of possibilities is $\binom{14}{3}$.

$\therefore$ Total number of possibilities is $\binom{14}{4} + \binom{14}{4} + \binom{14}{3} = 2\binom{14}{4} + \binom{14}{3} = \underline{2,366}$.

b An alternative method of solving **a** :
If test B is on day r, then $2 \leqslant r \leqslant 13$, there are $r - 1$ choices for A and $(14 - r)^2$ choices for C and D.
Hence total number of choices is $\underline{1.12^2 + 2.11^2 + 3.10^2 + \text{........} + 12.1^2 = 2,366}$

Using the same reasoning for n days, (i.e. generalizing), we have

$$1.(n-2)^2 + 2.(n-3)^2 + 3.(n-4)^2 + \text{........} + (n-2).1^2$$
$$= 2\binom{n}{4} + \binom{n}{3}$$
$$= \frac{2.n.(n-1)(n-2)(n-3)}{4.3.2.1} + \frac{n(n-1)(n-2)}{3.2.1}.\frac{4}{4}$$
$$= \frac{n(n-1)(n-2)[2n-6+4]}{4.3.2.1}$$
$$= \frac{n(n-1)^2(n-2)}{12}.$$

9.11 **a** $\binom{n}{r}$ is the number of ways of selecting r objects from a set of n objects.

$\therefore$ $\binom{n}{r}$ must be a <u>positive integer</u>.

b Since $\binom{n}{r} = \binom{n}{n-r}$, it is sufficient to consider $r \leqslant \dfrac{n}{2}$ only.

Now $\binom{n}{r} = \dfrac{n(n-1)(n-2)\ldots\ldots(n-r+1)}{r(r-1)(r-2)\ldots\ldots 1} = \dfrac{n}{1}\cdot\dfrac{n-1}{2}\cdot\dfrac{n-2}{3}\cdot\ldots\ldots\cdot\dfrac{n-r+1}{r}\ldots\ldots(*)$

Since $\quad r \leqslant \dfrac{n}{2} \quad$ then $\quad n \geqslant 2r$

$\therefore \quad n - r \geqslant r$

$\therefore \quad n - r + 1 > r$

$\therefore \quad \dfrac{n-r+1}{r} > 1 \quad$ where $\quad r = 2, 3, 4, \ldots\ldots \quad$ {given}

Thus $\quad \dfrac{n-1}{2} > 1, \quad \dfrac{n-2}{3} > 1, \quad \dfrac{n-3}{4} > 1, \ldots\ldots, \quad \dfrac{n-r+1}{r} > 1.$

$\therefore \quad \binom{n}{r} > n \qquad$ {in $*$}

But $\binom{n}{r}$ can only have prime factors which are less than n.

Hence $\binom{n}{r}$ <u>cannot itself be prime for $\quad 1 < r < n - 1$.</u>

c If $\quad \underline{n = 2^m - 1,}$

$\binom{n}{r} = \binom{2^m - 1}{r} = \dfrac{2^m - 1}{1}\cdot\dfrac{2^m - 2}{2}\cdot\dfrac{2^m - 3}{3}\cdot\dfrac{2^m - 4}{4}\cdot\ldots\ldots\cdot\dfrac{2^m - r}{r}$

The numerator of each factor in odd positions is odd (e.g., $2^m - 1$, $2^m - 3$, etc)

And $\dfrac{2^m - 2}{2} = \dfrac{2^m - 1}{1} \quad$ is odd,

Also $\dfrac{2^m - 4}{4} = 2^{m-2} - 1,$

and $\dfrac{2^m - 6}{6} = \dfrac{2^{m-1} - 3}{3} \quad$ where numerator is odd, etc.

$\therefore \quad$ after cancelling the numerator is odd and so is the denominator.

Since $\binom{n}{r}$ is integral, for $n = 2^m - 1$ it is odd.

Now every second integer is divisible by 2 and every fourth integer is divisible by 4, etc.

Thus $\dfrac{2^m - 2}{2}, \dfrac{2^m - 4}{4}, \dfrac{2^m - 6}{6}, \dfrac{2^m - 8}{8} \quad$ all have the same power of 2 in numerator and denominator and these powers of 2 will all cancel one another.

$\{n \geqslant r \quad \Rightarrow \quad 2^m \geqslant r \quad \Rightarrow \quad 2^m - r \geqslant 0 \quad \Rightarrow \quad 2^m - r + 1 > 0$

$\therefore \quad$ the numerator is always a positive integer$\}$.

Thus $\binom{n}{r}$ has no factors of 2 and is $\therefore$ <u>odd.</u>

d <u>For $\quad n = 2^m$</u>

$\binom{n}{r} = \dfrac{2^m}{r}\cdot\dfrac{2^m - 1}{1}\cdot\dfrac{2^m - 2}{2}\cdot\dfrac{2^m - 3}{3}\cdot\ldots\ldots\cdot\dfrac{2^m - r + 1}{r - 1}$

where $\dfrac{2^m - 2}{2}, \dfrac{2^m - 4}{4}$, etc. all cancel to produce integers, thus removing all powers of 2

in numerator and denominator, except for $\dfrac{2^m}{r}$.

We are left with a comparison of 2^m and r where $\quad r < 2^m$.

It is certain that the highest power of 2 in r is less than 2^m.

$\therefore \quad \dfrac{2^m}{r} = 2^s \cdot k \quad$ where s is at least 1.

$\therefore \quad \binom{n}{r}$ has at least one factor of 2 in the numerator more than it has in the denominator.

$\therefore \quad \binom{n}{r}$ is <u>even.</u>

9.12 **a** $\binom{n}{r} + \binom{n}{r+1} = \dfrac{n!}{r!(n-r)!} + \dfrac{n!}{(r+1)!(n-r-1)!}$

$$= \dfrac{(n+1)!}{(r+1)!(n-r)!} \left[\dfrac{r+1}{n+1} + \dfrac{n-r}{n+1} \right]$$

$$= \binom{n+1}{r+1} \left[\dfrac{n+1}{n+1} \right]$$

$$= \underline{\binom{n+1}{r+1}} \qquad \text{as} \quad n \neq 1.$$

b $\binom{n}{r} - \binom{n}{r-1} + \binom{n}{r-2} - \binom{n}{r-3} + \ldots\ldots + (-1)^r \binom{n}{0}$

$= \left[\binom{n-1}{r-1} + \binom{n-1}{r} \right] - \left[\binom{n-1}{r-2} + \binom{n-1}{r-1} \right] + \left[\binom{n-1}{r-3} + \binom{n-1}{r-2} \right]$

$\quad - \left[\binom{n-1}{r-4} + \binom{n-1}{r-3} \right] + \ldots\ldots + (-1)^{r-2} \cdot \left[\binom{n-1}{1} + \binom{n-1}{2} \right]$

$\quad + (-1)^{r-1} \cdot \left[\binom{n-1}{0} + \binom{n-1}{1} \right] + (-1)^r \cdot \binom{n-1}{0}$ {using **a**}

$= \underline{\binom{n-1}{r}}$ {all other terms cancel}

c Proposition $P(n)$ is: $\binom{r}{r} + \binom{r+1}{r} + \binom{r+2}{r} + \ldots\ldots + \binom{r+n}{r} = \binom{r+n+1}{r+1}$ for all n in Z^+.
  Proof: (by induction on n)

    i If $n = 0$, LHS $= \binom{r}{r} = 1$

                     RHS $= \binom{r+1}{r+1} = 1$ $\therefore$ $P(0)$ is true.

    ii If $P(k)$ is true, then
               $\binom{r}{r} + \binom{r+1}{r} + \binom{r+2}{r} + \ldots\ldots + \binom{r+k}{r} = \binom{r+k+1}{r+1}$

      Thus $\binom{r}{r} + \binom{r+1}{r} + \ldots\ldots + \binom{r+k}{r} + \binom{r+k+1}{r}$

      $= \binom{r+k+1}{r+1} + \binom{r+k+1}{r}$

      $= \binom{r+k+2}{r+1}$ {using (1)}

    $= \binom{r+[k+1]+1}{r+1}$

      Thus $P(k+1)$ is true whenever $P(k)$ is true.
    $\therefore$ $\underline{P(n)}$ is true for all $n \geqslant 0$.

9.13 Given: (1) there are originally 32 blacks and 30 whites or vice versa.
             (2) On each move, one piece changes colour and one of each colour is removed.
             (3) At the end, there are two counters.
From (1) and (3), 60 counters are removed during play.
From (2), they are removed 2 at a time, so there are 30 moves.
During each move, the difference between the number of blacks and the number of whites changes by 2. This is because the two removed do not affect it, whilst the number of one goes up one, while the number of the other goes down one.
If there were x blacks and y whites before, then afterwards there are $(x-2)$ and y respectively or x and $(y-2)$ respectively, so the new difference is $(x-y) \pm 2$.
    Therefore every pair of moves affects the difference by a multiple of 4.
    Therefore after every pair moves, the difference is $4a + 2$.
As there are two counters at the end, the difference must be ± 2, because there are 15×2 moves.
    Therefore the <u>two</u> final counters are the <u>same colour</u>.

9.14 **a** We select the captain first. This can be done in 11 ways.
      There are 21 remaining members and 10 are required in the team, and these can be selected in $\binom{21}{10}$ ways.
      Thus the total number of choices is $11\binom{21}{10} = \underline{3,879,876}$.

b   This identity can be proved by considering the general solution of **a**, taking n instead of 11.

The number of choices is therefore $n.\binom{2n-1}{n-1}$,   the RHS of the identity.

We get the LHS by counting the choices in a different way.
Suppose we select i members from A and $n - i$ from team B.
There are i ways of choosing the captain from A.

Thus we have $i\binom{n}{i}\binom{n}{n-i}$ selections where $i = 1,\ 2,\ 3,\ 4,\ \ldots\ldots, n$

$$= i\binom{n}{i}^2 \qquad \text{as} \quad \binom{n}{i} = \binom{n}{n-i} \qquad \text{\{Pascal's Rule\}}$$

Thus the total number of selections is $1\binom{n}{1}^2 + 2\binom{n}{2}^2 + 3\binom{n}{3}^2 + \ \ldots\ldots\ +n\binom{n}{n}^2$

$$\therefore \quad \underline{1\binom{n}{1}^2 + 2\binom{n}{2}^2 + 3\binom{n}{3}^2 + \ \ldots\ldots\ +n\binom{n}{n}^2 = n\binom{2n-1}{n-1}}.$$

9.15 Tickets are numbered $1,\ 2,\ 3,\ 4,\ \ldots\ldots, n$.

We construct a model which gives a combinational interpretation.
Let the numbers be placed on a moving belt which may be stopped at random.
At each stopping place <u>one</u> number is engaged and this will be the number called.
Furthermore, assume that after each stop the belt slips so that the immediately subsequent number cannot be engaged. Thus consecutive numbers cannot be called.
This means that for calling r numbers, the total number of stops is $n - (r - 1)$,   since the stops after the first $r - 1$ halts are eliminated.

This makes the number of choices for stops $\binom{n-r+1}{r}$.

9.16 $\binom{2}{2}\binom{4}{2} \ \ldots\ldots\ \binom{2n-2}{2}\binom{2n}{2} = \dfrac{2!}{2!0!}\cdot\dfrac{4!}{2!2!}\cdot\dfrac{6!}{2!4!}\cdot\dfrac{8!}{2!6!}\cdot \ \ldots\ldots\ \dfrac{(2n-2)!}{2!(2n-4)!}\cdot\dfrac{(2n)!}{2!(2n-2)!}$

$$= \frac{(2n)!}{2^n}$$

$$= \frac{2n(2n-1)(2n-2)(2n-3)(2n-4)\ldots\ldots 4.3.2.1}{2^n}$$

$$= \frac{2^n.n(n-1)(n-2)\ldots\ldots 2.1.(2n-1)(2n-3)\ldots\ldots 5.3.1}{2^n}$$

$$= n!(2n-1)(2n-3)\ldots\ldots 5.3.1.$$

Combinational Interpretation.
Suppose we are allocating n tennis courts to $2n$ players taking part in a tournament. Each form of the above identity represents a way of organising the tournament.

a   Select a pair for court 1. This can be done in $\binom{2n}{2}$ ways.

Select a pair for court 2. This can be done in $\binom{2n-2}{2}$ ways, and continuing in this

manner, the total number of allocations is $\binom{2n}{2}\binom{2n-2}{2}\binom{2n-4}{2}\ldots\ldots\binom{2}{2}$.

b   First of all, pair off the players. Pick out any player; his opponent can be chosen in $(2n - 1)$ ways.
Pick any one of the remaining players, and choose his opponent. This can be done in $(2n - 3)$ ways.
Thus the total number of pairings is $(2n - 1)(2n - 3)\ldots\ldots .3.1$,   and the total number of ways of allocating the n pairs to n courts is $n!$.
Hence the total number of allocations is $n!(2n - 1)(2n - 3)\ldots\ldots 5.3.1$.

c   The courts may be chosen by simply lining up the players, letting the first 2 go to court 1, the second two to court 2 and so on.
The players can be lined up in $(2n)!$ ways.
However, in this way we obtain 2^n times the number of allocations, since once the players are chosen for a certain court, the allocation does not distinguish between the order of the opponents.

Hence $(2n)! = 2^n \times (\text{total allocations}) \qquad \therefore \quad \text{total allocations} = \dfrac{(2n)!}{2^n}$.

9.17 Suppose the 5 people are identified by the numbers 1, 2, 3, 4, 5. P_{12} means   "1 phones 2".
8 telephone calls is the minimum necessary.
After $P_{12}, P_{23}, P_{34}, P_{45}, P_{51}, P_{52}, P_{53}, P_{54}$,   everyone knows everything.
In general, for n persons, $2n - 2$ telephone calls is the minimum number necessary.
We shall show that

> (1) $2n - 2$ calls are sufficient, and
> (2) $2n - 2$ calls are necessary for everyone to know everything.

<u>To show</u>   (1): $\underbrace{P_{12}, P_{23}, P_{34}, \ldots\ldots, P_{n-1/n},}_{n - 1 \text{ of these}}$ $\underbrace{P_{n1}, P_{n2}, P_{n3}, \ldots\ldots, P_{n/n-1}}_{n - 1 \text{ of these}}$ are $2n - 2$
calls <u>sufficient</u> for everyone to know everything.

<u>To show</u>   (2):   If A is the first person to know everything, $n - 1$ calls have had to be made
already, since each of $n - 1$ people have already divulged their
information somehow to A.
Since the $n - 1$ persons other than A do not yet know everything, A can
phone each of them so that they will now know everything.
This makes $n - 1 + n - 1 = 2n - 2$ necessary phone calls.

9.18

5 on one line:	4
4 on one line, 1 on another:	$4 \times 3 = 12$
3 on one line, 2 on another:	$4 \times 3 = 12$
3 on one line, 1 on another, 1 on another:	$4 \times 3 = 12$
2 on one line, 2 on another, 1 on another:	$4 \times 3 \times 2 = 24$
2 on one line, 1 each on other 3 lines:	4
	$\overline{68}$

10. IRRATIONALS

10.1 The solution of $2^x = 3$ is irrational.

Suppose the solution is rational. Then there exist positive integers p and q such that $2^{\frac{p}{q}} = 3$
$$\therefore \quad 2^p = 3^q$$

which is absurd as 2^p is even and 3^q is odd.
$\therefore$ our suppostion is false. $\therefore$ the <u>solution is irrational</u>.

10.2   **a** Suppose $\log_{10} 2$ is rational.

Therefore positive integers p and q exist such that $\log_{10} 2 = \dfrac{p}{q}$. $\therefore \quad 2 = 10^{\frac{p}{q}}$
$$\therefore \quad 2^q = 10^p$$

Now since $p \geqslant 1$,   5 must be a factor of 10^p, and hence must be a factor of 2^q, which is absurd.
$\therefore$ our supposition is false.   Thus $\log_{10} 2$ is irrational.

b Suppose $\log_{\frac{1}{2}} 12$ is rational.

then $\log_{\frac{1}{2}} 12 = \dfrac{p}{q}$ where p, q are coprime integers, $q \neq 0$......(1)

$\therefore \qquad 12 = \left(\tfrac{1}{2}\right)^{\frac{p}{q}} = 2^{-\frac{p}{q}}$

$\therefore \qquad 12^q = 2^{-p}$ {raise both sides to the power q}

$\therefore \qquad 2^{2q}3^q = 2^{-p}$

$\therefore \qquad 3^q = 2^{-p-2q}$

$\therefore \qquad 2^{\frac{-p-2q}{q}} = 3$ where $\dfrac{-p - 2q}{q}$ is rational and this contradicts **10.1**

$\therefore \quad \log_{\frac{1}{2}} 12$ is irrational.

10.3 Suppose $\log_{10}(2^a 5^b)$ is rational.

$\therefore$ $\log_{10} 2^a 5^b = \dfrac{p}{q}$ where p, q are integers, $q \neq 0$

$\therefore$ $2^a 5^b = 10^{\frac{p}{q}}$

$\therefore$ $2^{aq} 5^{bq} = 2^p 5^p$

$\therefore$ $aq = p$ and $bq = p$ {unique factorization theorem}

$\therefore$ $aq = bq$

$\therefore$ $q(a - b) = 0$

$\therefore$ $q = 0$ or $a = b$,   both of which are impossible

                $\{q \neq 0$ for $\dfrac{p}{q}$ to be rational; $a \neq b$,   given$\}$

$\therefore$ $\underline{\log(2^a 5^b)}$ is irrational.

10.4   **a**   Any integer x can be expressed in exactly one of the forms $3n, \; 3n + 1, \; 3n - 1,$ $\{n \varepsilon Z\}$

$\therefore$ $x^2 = 9n^2, \quad 9n^2 + 6n + 1$ or $9n^2 - 6n + 1$

Thus for x^2 to be divisible by 3, $x = 3n$.

$\therefore$ $\underline{x \text{ is divisible by 3.}}$

b   Assume $\sqrt{3}$ is rational.

Then $\sqrt{3} = \dfrac{p}{q}$ where p, q are positive integers which are coprime.

Now $3 = \dfrac{p^2}{q^2}$

$\therefore$ $p^2 = 3q^2$

$\therefore$ p^2 is divisible by 3.

$\therefore$ $\underline{p \text{ is divisible by 3}}$......(1)

We therefore let $p = 3k$ for some integer k.

Hence $p^2 = 9k^2$

Thus $9k^2 = 3q^2$

$\therefore$ $q^2 = 3k^2$

$\therefore$ q^2 is divisible by 3.

$\therefore$ $\underline{q \text{ is divisible by 3.}}$ (2)

$\therefore$ p and q have a common factor of 3, contradicting the fact that p and q are coprime.

$\therefore$ our assumption is false.

i.e. $\underline{\sqrt{3} \text{ is irrational.}}$

c   Suppose $a + b\sqrt{3} = c + d\sqrt{3}$ where $b \neq d$.

Then $a - c = \sqrt{3}(d - b)$

$\therefore$ $\sqrt{3} = \dfrac{a - c}{d - b}$ where $d - b \neq 0$,   and a, b, c, d are integers.

$\therefore$ $\sqrt{3}$ is rational, a contradiction.

$\therefore$ our supposition is false.

Hence $\underline{b = d}$,   and clearly $\underline{a = c}$,   follows also.

10.5 Suppose that $\sqrt{2}, \sqrt{3}, \sqrt{5}$ can be terms of a single A.P.

Then $\sqrt{2} = a$,   say, $\sqrt{3} = a + kd$ and $\sqrt{5} = a + ld$, $\{k$ and l are non-zero integers$\}$.

$\therefore$ $\sqrt{3} = \sqrt{2} + kd$ and $\sqrt{5} = \sqrt{2} + ld$

$\therefore$ $kd = \sqrt{3} - \sqrt{2}$ and $ld = \sqrt{5} - \sqrt{2}$

$$\therefore \quad \frac{\sqrt{3} - \sqrt{2}}{k} = \frac{\sqrt{5} - \sqrt{2}}{l} \quad (= d)$$

$$\therefore \quad l\sqrt{3} - l\sqrt{2} = k\sqrt{5} - k\sqrt{2}$$

$$\therefore \quad (k - l)\sqrt{2} = k\sqrt{5} - l\sqrt{3}$$

$$\therefore \quad (k - l)^2 . 2 = 5k^2 + 3l^2 - 2kl\sqrt{15} \qquad \{\text{squaring both sides}\}$$

$$\therefore \qquad \sqrt{15} = \frac{5k^2 + 3l^2 - 2(k - l)^2}{2kl} \qquad \text{where} \quad kl \neq 0$$

i.e. $\qquad \sqrt{15} = \dfrac{3k^2 + l^2 + 4kl}{2kl} \qquad\qquad$ where $\quad kl \neq 0$

which is a contradiction as $\sqrt{15}$ is irrational and the RHS is clearly rational.
Thus our supposition is false,

and $\quad \underline{\sqrt{2}, \ \sqrt{3}, \ \sqrt{5} \quad \text{cannot be terms of a single A.P.}}$

10.6   **a**   Let $\qquad \sqrt{5} - \sqrt{2} = x$

$$\therefore \qquad 5 - 2\sqrt{10} + 2 = x^2$$

$$\therefore \qquad\qquad 7 - x^2 = 2\sqrt{10}$$

$$\therefore \quad 49 - 14x^2 + x^4 = 40$$

$$x^4 - 14x^2 + 9 = 0$$

Thus $\quad \sqrt{5} - \sqrt{2} \quad$ is a root of $\quad x^4 - 14x^2 + 9 = 0.$

But by the 'theorem on rational roots', the only possible rational roots are $\pm 1, \ \pm 3, \ \pm 9,$
and $\quad \sqrt{5} - \sqrt{2} \quad$ is not equal to any of these (6) values.

$$\therefore \quad \sqrt{5} - \sqrt{2} \quad \text{is not a rational root.}$$

$$\therefore \quad \underline{\sqrt{5} - \sqrt{2} \quad \text{is irrational.}}$$

b   Suppose $\quad \log 5 \quad$ is rational.

i.e., $\qquad \log_{10} 5 = \dfrac{p}{q} \quad$ where $\quad p, \ q \quad$ are integers, $q \neq 0, \quad p < q \ \ldots\ldots(*)$

$$\therefore \qquad\qquad 10^{\frac{p}{q}} = 5$$

$$\therefore \qquad \left(10^{\frac{p}{q}}\right)^q = 5^q$$

$$\therefore \qquad\qquad 10^p = 5^q$$

$$\therefore \qquad\quad 2^p . 5^p = 5^q$$

$$\therefore \qquad\qquad 2^p = 5^{q-p}$$

which is not possible $\quad \{\text{even} = \text{odd}\}$
unless $\quad p = 0 \quad$ and $\quad q - p = 0, \quad$ i.e., $\quad q = 0, \quad$ which contradicts $(*)$

$\therefore \quad$ supposition is false.

$\therefore \quad \underline{\log 5 \quad \text{is irrational.}}$

10.7   **a** $\dfrac{r}{s} \quad$ satisfies $\quad ax^2 + bx + c = 0$

$$\therefore \quad a\left(\frac{r}{s}\right)^2 + b\left(\frac{r}{s}\right) + c = 0$$

$$\therefore \quad ar^2 + brs + cs^2 = 0$$

$$\therefore \quad ar^2 = -s(br + cs)\ldots\ldots\text{(a)} \quad \text{and} \quad cs^2 = -r(ar + bs)\ldots\ldots\text{(b)}$$

Since r and s are coprime, from (a) we deduce $\underline{s \text{ is a factor of } a}$
and from (b), $\underline{r \text{ is a factor of } c}.$

b $x = \sqrt{p}$ is a root of $x^2 - p = 0$

Suppose $\sqrt{p}$ is a rational root, then there exist positive integers r and s such that

$$\sqrt{p} = \frac{r}{s}, \quad \text{where} \quad \left\{ \begin{array}{l} s \text{ is a factor of } 1 \text{ and} \\ r \text{ is a factor of } -p \end{array} \right. \quad \{\text{from } \mathbf{a}\}$$

$\therefore \quad s = 1 \quad$ and $\quad r = 1$ or p

$\therefore \quad \dfrac{r}{s} = 1$ or p

$\therefore \quad \sqrt{p} = 1$ or p

$\therefore \qquad p = 1 \qquad \{\text{as } p > 0\}$

which is false, as p is prime.

Our suppostion is false, and hence $\sqrt{p}$ is irrational.

10.8 Suppose $\qquad \tan^2(5^\circ) \quad$ is rational

$\therefore \qquad 1 + \tan^2(5^\circ) \quad$ is rational

$\therefore \qquad \sec^2(5^\circ) \quad$ is rational $\qquad \{1 + \tan^2\theta = \sec^2\theta\}$

$\therefore \qquad \dfrac{1}{\cos^2(5^\circ)} \quad$ is rational

$\therefore \qquad \cos^2(5^\circ) \quad$ is rational

$\therefore \qquad \frac{1}{2} + \frac{1}{2}\cos(10^\circ) \quad$ is rational $\qquad \{\cos^2\theta = \frac{1}{2} + \frac{1}{2}\cos 2\theta\}$

$\therefore \qquad \cos 10^\circ \quad$ is rational

$\therefore \qquad 4\cos^3(10^\circ) - 3\cos(10^\circ) \quad$ is rational

$\therefore \qquad \cos(30^\circ) \quad$ is rational $\quad \{\cos 3\theta = 4\cos^3\theta - 3\cos\theta\}$

$\qquad$ which is false as $\cos 30^\circ = \frac{\sqrt{3}}{2}$, which is irrational

$\therefore \quad \tan^2(5^\circ) \quad$ is irrational

and $\quad \therefore \quad \underline{\tan(5^\circ) \quad \text{is irrational}}$.

$[x \text{ rational} \Rightarrow x^2 \text{ rational} \quad \therefore \quad x^2 \text{ irrational} \Rightarrow x \text{ irrational}]$

10.9

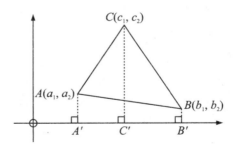

a Area $\triangle ABC$

$= \text{area trapezium } AA'C'C + \text{area trapezium } CC'B'B - \text{area trapezium } AA'B'B$

$= \left(\dfrac{a_2 + c_2}{2}\right)(c_1 - a_1) + \left(\dfrac{c_2 + b_2}{2}\right)(b_1 - c_1) - \left(\dfrac{a_2 + b_2}{2}\right)(b_1 - a_1)$

which is <u>rational</u> as $a_1,\ a_2,\ b_1,\ b_2,\ c_1,\ c_2,$ are integers.

b Suppose that $\triangle ABC$ is equilateral, with sides of length x.

Its area is $\quad \therefore \quad \dfrac{x}{2} \cdot \dfrac{\sqrt{3}x}{2} = \dfrac{\sqrt{3}x^2}{4}$

where $\quad x^2 = (b_1 - a_1)^2 + (b_2 - a_2)^2 \qquad \{\text{distance between 2 points formula}\}$

$\therefore \quad x^2$ is rational. $\qquad \{\text{in fact } x^2 \text{ is an integer}\}$

$\therefore$ area $\triangle ABC = \dfrac{\sqrt{3}x^2}{4}$ is irrational, as $\sqrt{3}$ is irrational.

which contadicts **a**. $\therefore$ our supposition is false, i.e., $\underline{\triangle ABC \quad \text{cannot be equilateral}}$

10.10 Suppose that $\sqrt{2}$ is rational i.e. $\sqrt{2} = \dfrac{p}{q}$ where p, q are positive integers with no common factors.
In the given triangle let $AC = p$ and $AB = q$.

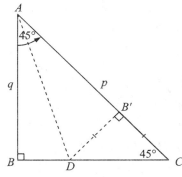

Now $\sin 45^{\circ} = \dfrac{1}{\sqrt{2}} = \dfrac{q}{p}$

$\therefore$ $\dfrac{p}{q} = \sqrt{2}$ and $p > q$

Now $AB' = q$ $\therefore$ $B'C = p - q$
$\therefore$ $BD = p - q$ also
and $\therefore$ $DC = q - (p - q) = 2q - p$

Thus, in $\triangle DB'C$, $\cos 45^{\circ} = \dfrac{1}{\sqrt{2}} = \dfrac{p - q}{2q - p}$

$\therefore$ $\dfrac{2q - p}{p - q} = \sqrt{2}$

It is also true that $p - q$ and $2q - p$ are coprime.   {as p and q are}
Thus we have another rational expression for $\sqrt{2}$ in lowest terms where both numerator and denominator are smaller than the original ones.
We can continue this process indefinitely to generate an infinite sequence of rational expressions for $\sqrt{2}$ (in lowest terms) where each member has a smaller positive integer denominator than the previous one.
Thus $\sqrt{2}$ is irrational.

[This proof is an example of a proof using **"Fermat's Principle of infinite descent"**.]

10.11 Let $\sqrt[3]{9} = \dfrac{p}{q}$ where p and q are integers, $q \neq 0$.

$\therefore$ $9 = \dfrac{p^3}{q^3}$

$\therefore$ $p^3 = q^3(2^3 + 1^3) = (2q)^3 + q^3$

which is impossible   {Fermat's last theorem, proved at last by Andrew Wiles, 1995}

Thus $\sqrt[3]{9}$ is irrational.

11. DIOPHANTINE EQUATIONS

11.1 $V =$ area of end $\times$ length $= \pi r^2 h$
total surface area $=$ area of circular end $+$ area of curved surface

$\therefore$ $A = \pi r^2 + (2\pi r).h$

i.e. $A = \pi r^2 + 2\pi r h$

If numerical values are the same, then

$\pi r^2 h = \pi r^2 + 2\pi r h$

$\therefore$ $rh = r + 2h$

$\therefore$ $rh - 2h = r$

$\therefore$ $h(r - 2) = r$

$\therefore$ $h = \dfrac{r}{r - 2} = \dfrac{r - 2 + 2}{r - 2} = 1 + \dfrac{2}{r - 2}$

i.e., $h = 1 + \dfrac{2}{r - 2}$

no top

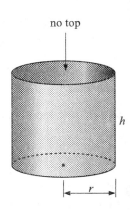

Thus for h to be a positive whole number, $r - 2 = 1$ or 2

$$\therefore \quad r = 3 \text{ or } 4.$$

$r = 3$ is the case given

$\therefore \quad r = 4$ is the only and only one other case.

11.2   If $\sqrt{x} - \sqrt{11} = \sqrt{y}$

then $(\sqrt{x} - \sqrt{11})^2 = y$

$\therefore \quad x - 2\sqrt{11x} + 11 = y$

$\therefore \quad x + 11 - y = 2\sqrt{11x}$

Thus $11x$ must be a perfect square.

Hence $x = 11n^2$ for integer n, and when this is so,

$$x + 11 - y = 22n$$

$\therefore \quad 11n^2 + 11 - y = 22n$

$\therefore \quad y = 11n^2 - 22n + 11$

$\therefore \quad y = 11(n - 1)^2$

Thus, as $n \geqslant 1$ can take infinitely many values,

there are <u>infinitely many solutions</u> of the form $x = 11n^2$, $y = 11(n-1)^2$

Now $\dfrac{x}{y} = \dfrac{n^2}{(n-1)^2} = \left(\dfrac{n}{n-1}\right)^2 = \left(1 + \dfrac{1}{n-1}\right)^2 \leqslant 4.$

{clearly a maximum value when $n = 2$}

$\therefore \quad \dfrac{x}{y}$ is a <u>maximum of 4</u> when $n = 2$,   i.e. $x = 44$, $y = 11$.

11.3 $m = 100a + 10b + c$

and $2m = 100c + 10b + a$

$\therefore \quad m = 99c - 99a = 99(c - a)$

Thus m is a multiple of 99.

But $m = 99a + (a + 10b + c)......(1)$

$\therefore \quad a + 10b + c$ is divisible by 99

as $0 < a + 10b + c < 108$,   then $a + 10b + c = 99$

$\therefore \quad b = 9$ {if $b = 8$, $a + c = 19$ which is impossible.

$b = 7$, $a + c = 29$ etc.}

and $a + c = 9$

Thus $m = 99a + 99 = 99(a + 1)$ {from (1)}

But $m = 99(c - a) = 99(9 - 2a)$

$\therefore \quad a + 1 = 9 - 2a$

$\therefore \quad 3a = 8$

$\therefore \quad a = \frac{8}{3}$ which is a contradicion as a is an integer.

$\therefore$ There are <u>no such integers with this property.</u>

11.4 Let x denote the number of students donating a full set of coins   i.e. $50 + 20 + 10 + 5 + 2 + 1$
$= 88$ cents   and y denote the number of students donating only the 'silver' coins   i.e.,   85 cents.

$\therefore \quad 88x + 85y = 2000$,   where x, y are integers.

Thus $88x = 5(400 - 17y)$

$\therefore \quad x = 5t$ and $400 - 17y = 88t$ for t a positive integer.

Also $17y = 8(50 - 11t)$

$\therefore \quad y = 8u$ and $50 - 11t = 17u$

and the only positive solution for $17u + 11t = 50$ is   <u>$u = 1$, $t = 3$</u>

Hence $y = 8$ and $x = 15$

$\therefore \quad x + y = 23$ <u>students are contributors.</u>

11.5
$$x^3 - 1 = 2^y$$
$$\therefore \quad (x-1)(x^2+x+1) = 2^y$$
$$\therefore \quad x-1 = 2^a \quad ....(1) \quad \text{and} \quad x^2+x+1 = 2^{y-a}, \quad 0 < a < y \quad ....(2)$$
$$\{\text{If} \quad a = 0, \quad x = 2, \quad 7 = 2^y \text{ is not possible}\}$$
$$x = 2^a + 1 \quad \{\text{from (1)}\}$$
$$\text{Thus} \quad (2^a+1)^2 + 2^a + 1 + 1 = 2^{y-a} \quad \{\text{from (2)}\}$$
$$\therefore \quad 2^{2a} + 2.2^a + 1 + 2^a + 2 = 2^{y-a}$$
$$\therefore \quad 2^{2a} + 2^{a+1} + 2^a + 3 = 2^{y-a}$$

which is false as LHS is odd
RHS is even.

$\therefore$ no integer solutions exist.

11.6 Any integer a can be written in the form $8k+b$ where k and b are integers $0 \leqslant b \leqslant 7$.
Thus $a^2 = (8k)^2$ or $(8k+1)^2$ or $(8k+2)^2$ or .... or $(8k+7)^2$
$\therefore \quad a^2 = 64k^2, \quad 64k^2+16k+1, \quad 64k^2+32k+4, \quad 64k^2+48k+9,$
$64k^2 + 64k + 16, \quad 64k^2 + 80k + 25, \quad 64k^2 + 96k + 36,$
or $64k^2 + 112k + 49$
$\therefore$ on division by 8, a^2 leaves a remainder of 0, 1, or 4

$\therefore \quad a^2 + b^2$ leaves a remainder of
0, 1, 2, 4, or 5 when divided by 8.

		a	
	0	1	4
0	0	1	4
b 1	1	2	5
4	4	5	0

Now $\dfrac{a^2+b^2}{8} = c + \dfrac{d}{8}$ where $d \neq 6$
$\therefore \quad a^2 + b^2 = 8c + d$ has no integer
solutions for a, b and c when $d = 6$.

11.7 Since $x^2 - 2y^2 = (x+\sqrt{2}y)(x-\sqrt{2}y)$, we find two such factors with a product of -1,
and $1+\sqrt{2}, 1-\sqrt{2}$ will do.
Now $(1+\sqrt{2})^n = 1 + \binom{n}{1}\sqrt{2} + \binom{n}{2}(\sqrt{2})^2 + \binom{n}{3}(\sqrt{2})^3 + ... + (\sqrt{2})^n = a_n + b_n\sqrt{2}.$
and $(1-\sqrt{2})^n = 1 - \binom{n}{1}\sqrt{2} + \binom{n}{2}(\sqrt{2})^2 - \binom{n}{3}(\sqrt{2})^3 + ... + (-\sqrt{2})^n = a_n - b_n\sqrt{2}.$
Thus $(a_n + b_n\sqrt{2})(a_n - b_n\sqrt{2}) = (1+\sqrt{2})^n(1-\sqrt{2})^n = (-1)^n$
$\therefore \quad a_n^2 - 2b_n^2 = -1$ provided n is odd.
Hence $x = a_n, y = b_n$ are integer solutions of $x^2 - 2y^2 = -1$, provided n is odd.
$(1+\sqrt{2})^1 = 1 + 1\sqrt{2} \quad \Rightarrow \quad x = 1, y = 1$
$(1+\sqrt{2})^3 = 7 + 5\sqrt{2} \quad \Rightarrow \quad x = 7, y = 5$
$(1+\sqrt{2})^5 = 41 + 29\sqrt{2} \quad \Rightarrow \quad x = 41, y = 29$
$(1+\sqrt{2})^7 = 239 + 169\sqrt{2} \quad \Rightarrow \quad x = 239, y = 169$
Since there are infinitely many odd numbers, there are infinitely many solutions, four of which are listed above.

12. DIVISIBILITY

12.1 Let $T = n^3 + 11n = n(n^2+11)$
a If n is even, T is even.
If n is odd, n^2 is odd and n^2+11 is even. $\} \Rightarrow$ T is even.

b n can have exactly one of the forms $3a$, $3a + 1$, $3a + 2$,   for a in Z.

If $n = 3a$, T is divisible by 3.

If $n = 3a + 1$, $n^2 + 11 = 9a^2 + 6a + 12$ is divisible by 3.

If $n = 3a + 2$, $n^2 + 11 = 9a^2 + 12a + 15$ is divisible by 3 $\Rightarrow$ $\underline{T \text{ is divisible by 3.}}$

∴ $\underline{T \text{ is divisible by }\ 2.3 = 6.}$

12.2 Since p and q are odd,

$$p^2 - q^2 = (2a + 1)^2 - (2b + 1)^2, \quad \text{say, for}\quad a, b \ \text{ in } Z.$$
∴ $p^2 - q^2 = (2a + 1 + 2b + 1)(2a + 1 - 2b - 1)$

∴ $p^2 - q^2 = (2a + 2b + 2)(2a - 2b)$

∴ $p^2 - q^2 = 4(a - b)(a + b + 1)$

If a and b are both odd or both even, then $a - b$ is even.

If one of a, b is odd and the other even, then $a + b + 1$ is even.

Thus in all possible cases, one of $(a - b)$, $(a + b + 1)$ is even.

∴ $\underline{p^2 - q^2 \text{ is divisible by 8.}}$

12.3 **a** We want possible integers x^3 such that $x^3 = 7k + 5$ where k is also an integer.

Using modular arithmetic, either x leaves a remainder of   0, 1, 2, 3, 4, 5, or 6   when divided by 7, which is written as $x \equiv 0, 1, 2, 3, 4, 5, 6 \pmod 7$

∴ $x^3 \equiv 0, 1, 1, 6, 1, 6, 6 \pmod 7$

[e.g. If $x = 5$ then $x^3 = 5^3$,   i.e. $x^3 = 125$,   i.e. $x^3 \equiv 6$,

as when 125 is divided by 7, the remainder is 6]

∴ $x^3 \equiv 0, 1, \text{ or } 6 \pmod 7$

Thus since $x^3 \not\equiv 5 \pmod 7$,   there are <u>no</u> perfect cubes which when divided by 7 leave a remainder of 5.

b We want integers x^3 such that $x^3 = 12k + 9$, k an integer.

Since $x^3 = 3(4k + 3)$ where $4k + 3$ is an integer

then x^3 is divisible by 3 $\Rightarrow$ x is divisible by 3.

∴ $x \equiv 0, 3, 6 \text{ or } 9 \pmod 2$

∴ $x^3 \equiv 0, 3, 0 \text{ or } 9 \pmod{12}$

Thus since $x^3 \equiv 9 \pmod{12}$ is a solution, then there are <u>infinitely many</u> perfect cubes which leave a remainder of 9 when divided by 12.

[$x^3 = (12n + 9)^3$, n an integer, gives us the form of all possible perfect cubes.]

12.4 **a**   "abc" $= 100a + 10b + c$

$= (98a + 7b) + (2a + 3b + c)$

$= 7(14a + b) + (2a + 3b + c)$

∴   "abc" is divisible by 7 $\Longleftrightarrow$ $\underline{2a + 3b + c \text{ is divisible by 7.}}$

b $n = 100a + 10b + c$

$= 100(7 - b - c) + (10b + c)$

$= 700 - 90b - 99c$

$= 700 - 91b - 98c + b - c$

$= 7(100 - 13b - 14c) + (b - c)$

Thus n is divisible by 7 $\Longleftrightarrow$ $b - c$ is divisible by 7

$\Longleftrightarrow$ $b - c = 7n$ (n in Z)

$\Longleftrightarrow$ $b = c$ or $c \pm 7$ {the latter two cases being impossible as $a + b + c = 7$}

$\Longleftrightarrow$ $\underline{b = c}$

12.5 $N = n^6 - n^2 = n^2(n^4 - 1) = n^2(n^2 + 1)(n^2 - 1)$ or $n^2(n^2 + 1)(n - 1)(n + 1)$

   a $n - 1, n$ and $n + 1$ are 3 consecutive integers and hence one of them is divisible by 3

$\therefore$ $n^6 - n^2$ is divisible by 3......(1)

   b   If n is even, n^2 is divisible by 4.

If n is odd, $n^2 - 1 = (2a + 1)^2 - 1 = 4a^2 + 4a$ is divisible by 4.

$\therefore$ $n^6 - n^2$ is divisible by 4......(2)

   c   It is true that $n = 5b, 5b + 1, 5b + 2, 5b + 3,$ or $5b + 4$ where b is in Z.

If $n = 5b$, $n^2 = 25b^2$

$n = 5b + 1$, $n - 1 = 5b$

$n = 5b + 2$, $n^2 + 1 = 25b^2 + 20b + 5$

$n = 5b + 3$, $n^2 + 1 = 25b^2 + 30b + 10$

$n = 5b + 4$, $n + 1 = 5b + 5$

Thus in every possible case, one of the factors of $n^6 - n^2$ is divisible by 5,

$\therefore$ $n^6 - n^2$ is divisible by 5......(3)

Thus $n^6 - n^2$ is divisible by $3.4.5. = 60$.

12.6   **a**   If p is a prime not less than 5, then p is odd.   {2 is the only even prime}

$\therefore$ $p^2 - 1 = (2a + 1)^2 - 1$ {a is in Z.}

$= 4a^2 + 4a$

$= 4a(a + 1)$

which is divisible by 8 as $a(a + 1)$ is even   {the product of 2 consecutive

integers is even.}

   b   It is true that exactly one of $p - 1, p, p + 1$ is divisible by 3.

But p is prime and $\geqslant 5$ $\therefore$ p can't be divisible by 3.

Thus one of $p - 1, p + 1$ is divisible by 3

$\therefore$ $(p - 1)(p + 1)$ is divisible by 3

$\therefore$ $p^2 - 1$ is divisible by 3

$\therefore$ $p^2 - 1$ is divisible by $8.3 = 24$.

12.7   **a**   Let the 5 digit number be $a.10^4 + b.10^3 + c.10^2 + d.10 + e$

Now $a.10^4 + b.10^3 + c.10^2 + d.10 + e$

$= (9999a + 999b + 99c + 9d) + (a + b + c + d + e)$

$= 3(3333a + 333b + 33c + 3d) + (a + b + c + d + e)$

Thus the number is divisible by 3 $\iff$ $a + b + c + d + e$ is divisible by 3.

   b   "2^n followed by 2^{n+1} digits" has form $2^n.10^a + 2^{n+1}$ for $a \geqslant 1$

$= 2^n(10^a + 2)$

where $10^a + 2 = 12, 102, 1002, 10002,$ etc. Each is divisible by 3 since the sum of their digits is always 3   {Test for divisibility by 3}

"2^{n+1} followed by 2^n digits" has form $2^{n+1}.10^b + 2^n$ for $b \geqslant 1$

$= 2^n(2.10^b + 1)$

where $2.10^b + 1 = 21, 201, 2001, 20001, \ldots$ and these are also divisible by 3.

Thus all such numbers are divisible by 3.

12.8 If n is not divisible by 7 then $n = 7a + x$ where $x = 1, 2, 3, 4, 5$ or 6.

$\therefore \quad n^3 = (7a + x)^3 = (7a)^3 + 3(7a)^2 x + 3(7a)x^2 + x^3$

Thus $n^3 = 7A + x^3$ where A is an integer.

If
$$
\begin{array}{llll}
x = 1, & n^3 = 7A + 1 & \therefore \quad n^3 - 1 = 7A \\
x = 2, & n^3 = 7A + 8 & \therefore \quad n^3 - 1 = 7A + 7 & = 7(A + 1) \\
x = 3, & n^3 = 7A + 27 & \therefore \quad n^3 + 1 = 7A + 28 & = 7(A + 4) \\
x = 4, & n^3 = 7A + 64 & \therefore \quad n^3 - 1 = 7A + 63 & = 7(A + 9) \\
x = 5, & n^3 = 7A + 125 & \therefore \quad n^3 + 1 = 7A + 126 & = 7(A + 18) \\
x = 6, & n^3 = 7A + 216 & \therefore \quad n^3 + 1 = 7A + 217 & = 7(A + 31)
\end{array}
$$

Thus $\underline{n^3 + 1 \text{ or } n^3 - 1 \text{ is divisible by } 7}$

12.9 $2^{35} + 3^{35}$ is divisible by $2 + 3 = \underline{5}$.

$2^{35} + 3^{35} = (2^5)^7 + (3^5)^7$ is divisible by $2^5 + 3^5 = 275 = 5^2 . 11$

$\therefore$ is divisible by $\underline{11}$ also

$2^{35} + 3^{35} = (2^7)^5 + (3^7)^5$ is divisible by $2^7 + 3^7 = 128 + 2187 = 2315 = 5 . 463$

$\therefore$ is divisible by $\underline{463}$ also.

Challenge: How many prime divisors of $2^{105} + 3^{105}$ can you find?

12.10

$$\frac{x}{y} = 1 - \tfrac{1}{2} + \tfrac{1}{3} - \tfrac{1}{4} + \dots + \tfrac{1}{1321} - \tfrac{1}{1322} + \tfrac{1}{1323}$$

$\therefore \frac{x}{y} = \left(1 + \tfrac{1}{2} + \tfrac{1}{3} + \tfrac{1}{4} + \tfrac{1}{5} + \dots + \tfrac{1}{1321} + \tfrac{1}{1322} + \tfrac{1}{1323}\right) - 2\left(\tfrac{1}{2} + \tfrac{1}{4} + \tfrac{1}{6} + \dots + \tfrac{1}{1322}\right)$

$\therefore \frac{x}{y} = \left(1 + \tfrac{1}{2} + \tfrac{1}{3} + \tfrac{1}{4} + \tfrac{1}{5} + \dots + \tfrac{1}{1321} + \tfrac{1}{1322} + \tfrac{1}{1323}\right) - \left(1 + \tfrac{1}{2} + \tfrac{1}{3} + \dots + \tfrac{1}{661}\right)$

$\therefore \frac{x}{y} = \tfrac{1}{662} + \tfrac{1}{663} + \tfrac{1}{664} + \dots + \tfrac{1}{1323}$ $\{1323 - 661 = 662 \text{ of these}\}$

$\therefore \frac{x}{y} = \left(\tfrac{1}{622} + \tfrac{1}{1323}\right) + \left(\tfrac{1}{663} + \tfrac{1}{1322}\right) + \dots + \left(\tfrac{1}{992} + \tfrac{1}{993}\right)$

$\therefore \frac{x}{y} = \tfrac{1985}{662.1323} + \tfrac{1985}{663.1322} + \dots + \tfrac{1985}{992.993}$

$= 1985 \left(\tfrac{1}{662.1323} + \tfrac{1}{663.1322} + \dots + \tfrac{1}{992.993}\right)$

$= 1985 . \dfrac{p}{q}$ where p and q are integers with no common factors

and where q has no factor common with 1985.

$\therefore \quad \underline{x \text{ is divisible by } 1985.}$

12.11 Any positive integer x can be expressed in the form $5a, 5a \pm 1, 5a \pm 2$, where a is an integer.

Hence $x^4 = (5a)^4 = 5(125a^4)$

or $(5a \pm 1)^4 = (5a)^4 \pm 4 . (5a)^3 + 6(5a)^2 \pm 4 . (5a) + 1$

or $(5a \pm 2)^4 = (5a)^4 \pm 4 . (5a)^3 . 2 + 6 . (5a)^2 . 2^2 \pm 4 . (5a) . 2^3 + 16$

$\therefore \quad x^4$ has form $5b$ or $5b + 1$

Suppose x is not divisible by 5 $\therefore \quad x^4 = 5b + 1$ for some integer b.

Thus $5b + 1 + y^4 = 5z + 1$

$\therefore \quad y^4 = 5(z - b)$ where $z - b$ is an integer.

$\therefore \quad y^4$ is divisible by 5

$\therefore \quad y$ is divisible by 5 $\{$as 5 is a prime$\}$

Similarly if y is not divisible by 5, x is divisible by 5.

Thus $\underline{x \text{ or } y \text{ is divisible by } 5.}$

12.12 **a** Let $a + b = 7p$ and $a^2 + b^2 = 7q$ where p, q are in Z.

Now $a^2 + b^2 = (a + b)^2 - 2ab$

$\therefore \qquad 7q = (7p)^2 - 2ab$

$\therefore \qquad 2ab = 49p^2 - 7q = 7(7p^2 - q)$

$\therefore$ at least one of a, b is divisible by 7   {Unique factorization theorem}

$\therefore$ both a, b are divisible by 7.   {as $a + b = 7p$}

b As in the argument of **a** we deduce that

$$2ab = 49(49p - q)$$

$\therefore \quad ab$ is a factor of 49

However, the rest of the argument fails as 49 is not a prime.

[e.g., $a = 7$, $b = 42$ $\therefore$ $a + b = 49$ and $a^2 + b^2 = 49.37$]

12.13 Let the divisors of N be $d_1, d_2, d_3, \ldots, d_n$ $(d_1 < d_2 < d_3 < \ldots < d_n)$

$\therefore \quad d_1 d_n = N$

$\qquad d_2 d_{n-1} = N$

$\qquad d_3 d_{n-2} = N$, etc.

$\therefore \quad \dfrac{1}{d_1} = \dfrac{d_n}{N}$,

$\qquad \dfrac{1}{d_2} = \dfrac{d_{n-1}}{N}$, etc.

Now $\dfrac{1}{d_1} + \dfrac{1}{d_2} + \dfrac{1}{d_3} + \ldots + \dfrac{1}{d_n}$

$= \dfrac{d_n}{N} + \dfrac{d_{n-1}}{N} + \dfrac{d_{n-2}}{N} + \ldots + \dfrac{d_1}{N}$

$= \dfrac{d_n + d_{n-1} + d_{n-2} + \ldots + d_1}{N}$

$= \dfrac{5N}{N}$ {given that $d_1 + d_2 + d_3 + \ldots + d_n = 5N$}

$= 5$

12.14 $11^{10} - 1 = (1 + 10)^{10} - 1$

$\qquad = 1 + \binom{10}{1}10 + \binom{10}{2}10^2 + \binom{10}{3}10^3 + \ldots + \binom{10}{10}10^{10} - 1$

$\qquad = 10^2 + \binom{10}{2}10^2 + \binom{10}{3}10^3 + \ldots + \binom{10}{10}10^{10}$

$\qquad = 10^2 \left[1 + \binom{10}{2} + 10\binom{10}{3} + \ldots + 10^8\binom{10}{10}\right]$

where $\left[1 + \binom{10}{2} + \ldots + 10^8\binom{10}{10}\right]$ is an integer.

$\therefore 11^{10} - 1$ is divisible by 100.

Generalization: $(1 + a)^a - 1$ is divisible by a^2 for any positive integer a.

12.15 $60 = 3.4.5$, so we must show that the product is divisible by 3, 4 and 5.

a Each of a, b, c is of the form $3k$ or $3k \pm 1$

Hence a^2, b^2, c^2 have form $9k^2$ or $9k^2 \pm 6k + 1$

i.e. a^2, b^2, c^2 fall into 2 classes (1) $3m$

$\qquad\qquad\qquad\qquad\qquad\qquad$ (2) $3m + 1$, where m is an integer

and at least two of a^2, b^2, c^2 must fall into the same class.

Without loss of generality, suppose a^2 and b^2 are in the same class.

$$\therefore \quad a^2 - b^2 = (3m_1) - (3m_2) \quad \text{or} \quad (3m_1 + 1) - (3m_2 + 1)$$
$$= 3(m_1 - m_2) \quad \text{\{in both cases\}}$$

$\therefore$ At least one of the differences is divisible by 3.

b Each of a, b, c is of the form $2k$ or $2k + 1$ \{even or odd\}

$\therefore \quad a^2, b^2, c^2$ have form $4k^2$ or $4k^2 + 4k + 1$.

Thus a^2, b^2, c^2 fall into two classes   (1) $4m$
(2) $4m + 1$ \{m in Z\}

and using a similar argument to **a**, the given product is divisible by 4.

c Since none of a, b, c is divisible by 5, each has form $5k \pm 1$ or $5k \pm 2$

The squares of a, b and c are then of the form $25k^2 \pm 10k + 1$ or $25k^2 \pm 20k + 4$

$\therefore \quad a^2, b^2, c^2$ fall into two classes   (1) $5m + 1$
(2) $5m + 4$

and once again using a similar argument to **a**, the given product is divisible by 5.

$$\left[\begin{array}{l} (5m_1 + 1) - (5m_2 + 1) = 5(m_1 - m_2) \\ (5m_1 + 4) - (5m_2 + 4) = 5(m_1 - m_2) \quad \text{also.} \end{array} \right]$$

12.16 **a** Observe that $3^{2m} - 1 = (3^m + 1)(3^m - 1)$ and $3^m + 1$ and $3^m - 1$ are even.

Since $3^m + 1$ and $3^m - 1$ differ by 2, they are two consecutive even numbers.

Thus one of $3^m + 1$, $3^m - 1$ is divisible by a single power of 2 only.
\{because it must be of the form $2.(\text{odd number})$\}

If $3^{2m} - 1$ is divisible by 2^r

then $3^{2m} - 1 = 2^r . A$ where A is odd

$\therefore \quad 2^r . A = (3^m + 1)(3^m - 1)$

and since one of $3^m + 1$, $3^m - 1$ is divisible by a single power of 2, then the other one must be divisible by 2^{r-1}.

i.e.   one of $3^m + 1$, $3^m - 1$ is divisible by 2^{r-1}.

b For $k = 1,$ $3^1 - 1 = 2$ is divisible by 2^1
$k = 2,$ $3^2 - 1 = 8$ is divisible by 2^2
$k = 4,$ $3^4 - 1 = 80$ is divisible by $2^4 = 16$

For the remaining cases we divide our argument into 2 classes depending on whether k is even or odd.

If k is even, let $k = 2a$ and suppose that 2^k divides into $3^k - 1$.

i.e. 2^{2a} divides into $3^{2a} - 1$.

Now by **a**, 2^{2a-1} divides into either $3^a + 1$ or $3^a - 1$,   which

is absurd, as $2^{2a-1} = \frac{1}{2}.(4^a) > 3^a + 1$ and $3^a - 1$ as $a \geqslant 3$.

If k is odd,   then $k \geqslant 3$

and $3^k - 1 = (3 - 1)(3^{k-1} + 3^{k-2} + \dots + 3^2 + 3 + 1)$
$\{x^n - 1 = (x - 1)(x^{n-1} + x^{n-2} + \dots + x^2 + x + 1)\}$
$= 2.(\text{the sum of } k \text{ odd numbers})$
$= 2.(\text{an odd number})$

$\therefore \quad 3^k - 1$ is divisible by 2, and no higher power of 2

i.e. $3^k - 1$ cannot be divisible by 2^k for $k \geqslant 3$.

Thus except for $k = 1, 2, 4,$ $3^k - 1$ is not divisible by 2^k for any other k in Z^+.

12.17 **a** a must have form $3m + 1$ or $3m + 2$,
and likewise d must have form $3n + 1$ or $3n + 2$ $\{m, n$ in $Z\}$

a	d	$a + d$	$a + 2d$
$3m + 1$	$3n + 1$	$3m + 3n + 2$	$3m + 6n + 3$
$3m + 1$	$3n + 2$	$3m + 3n + 3$	$3m + 6n + 5$
$3m + 2$	$3n + 1$	$3m + 3n + 3$	$3m + 6n + 4$
$3m + 2$	$3n + 2$	$3m + 3n + 4$	$3m + 6n + 6$

It is clear that in all possible cases, <u>one of $a + d$ or $a + 2d$ is divisible by 3</u>.

b Suppose that none of $a + d, a + 2d, a + 3d, \ldots\ldots, a + (p - 1)d$ is divisible by p.

$\therefore$ none of $a, a + d, a + 2d, a + 3d, \ldots\ldots, a + (p - 1)d$ is divisible by p......(1)

But $a = pm + \alpha$ where $1 \leqslant \alpha \leqslant p - 1$, α in Z

and $d = pn + \beta$ where $1 \leqslant \beta \leqslant p - 1$, β in Z.

$$\therefore \quad a + d = p(m + n) + (\alpha + \beta)$$
$$a + 2d = p(m + 2n) + (\alpha + 2\beta)$$
$$a + 3d = p(m + 3n) + (\alpha + 3\beta)$$
$$\vdots$$
$$a + (p - 1)d = p(m + (p - 1)n) + (\alpha + (p - 1)\beta).$$

Now when $a, a + d, a + 2d, \ldots\ldots, a + (p - 1)d$ are divided by p, the remainders are the same as when $\alpha, \alpha + \beta, \alpha + 2\beta, \ldots\ldots, \alpha + (p - 1)\beta$ are divided by p, and there are p of these remainders which can take values of $1, 2, 3, 4, \ldots\ldots, p - 1$.

Thus <u>two</u> of these remainders are equal, say those when $a + kd$ and $a + ld$ are divided by p.

Thus $[a + kd] - [a + ld]$ is dividible by p.

$\therefore$ $d(k - l)$ is divisible by p.

$\therefore$ d is divisible by p as $k - l < p$ $\{k, l$ are in $\{1, 2, 3, \ldots\ldots, p - 1\}\}$
contrary to that which was given.

Hence our supposition is false.

$\therefore$ <u>one of $a, a + d, a + 2d, a + 3d, \ldots\ldots, a + (p - 1)d$ is divisible by p.</u>

12.18 **a** $(a + b)^2 = a^2 + 2ab + b^2$

$\therefore$ $2ab = (a + b)^2 - (a^2 + b^2)$ where $a + b$ and $a^2 + b^2$ are divisible by p.

$\therefore$ $2ab$ is divisible by p.

$\therefore$ p divides at least one of a and b.

If p divides a then p divides b as $b = (a + b) - a$

If p divides b then p divides a as $a = (a + b) - b$

$\therefore$ p divides a and b.

b $(a + b + c)^3 = ([a + b] + c)^3$

$$= [a + b]^3 + 3[a + b]^2 c + 3[a + b]c^2 + c^3$$
$$= a^3 + b^3 + c^3 + 3a^2 b + 3ab^2 + 3a^2 c + 3ac^2 + 3bc^2 + 3b^2 c + 6abc$$
$$= a^3 + b^3 + c^3 + 3(ab + bc + ca)(a + b + c) - 3abc$$

$\therefore$ $(a + b + c)^3 - (a^3 + b^3 + c^3) = 3(ab + bc + ca)(a + b + c) - 3abc$

where $a + b + c$ and $a^3 + b^3 + c^3$ are divisible by p.

$\therefore$ p divides $3abc$.

$\therefore$ p divides at least one of a, b and c. $\{$since $p > 3$, given$\}$

If p divides a, then p divides $b + c = (a + b + c) - a$

and p divides $b^2 + c^2 = (a^2 + b^2 + c^2) - a^2$

$\therefore$ p divides both b and c. $\{$from **a**$\}$

A similar argument follows if p divides b or c.

$\therefore$ p divides each of a, b and c.

12.19   **a**   Consider $\binom{p}{r}$ where $r = 1, 2, 3, 4, \ldots\ldots, p-1$.

Now $\binom{p}{r} = \dfrac{p.(p-1).(p-2).\ldots\ldots.(p-r+1)}{r.(r-1).(r-2).\ldots\ldots.1}$ is an integer. Therefore all factors in

the denominator divide into the factors of the numerator, but none of them divide into p as p is prime and $r < p$.

$\therefore$ $r(r-1)(r-2)\ldots\ldots3.2.1$ divides into $(p-1)(p-2)(p-3)\ldots\ldots(p-r+1)$

Thus $\binom{p}{r}$ is divisible by p for $r = 1, 2, 3, 4, \ldots\ldots, p-1$.

b   **Proof**   (by induction on r)

The proposition $P(r)$ is $\binom{p-1}{r} - (-1)^r$ is divisible by p

for $r = 0, 1, 2, 3, \ldots\ldots, p-1$.

i $\binom{p-1}{0} - (-1)^0 = 1 - 1 = 0$ is divisible by p $\therefore$ $P(0)$ is true.

ii   If $P(k)$ is true then $\binom{p-1}{k} - (-1)^k = ap$,   where a is a positive integer.

Now $\binom{p-1}{k} + \binom{p-1}{k+1} = \binom{p}{k+1}$ where $\binom{p}{k+1}$ is divisible by p for

$k = 0, 1, 2, \ldots\ldots, p-2$ {proved in a}

$\therefore$ $ap + (-1)^k + \binom{p-1}{k+1} = bp$ where a, b are integers.

$\therefore$ $\binom{p-1}{k+1} + (-1)^k = p(b-a)$

$\therefore$ $\binom{p-1}{k+1} - (-1)^{k+1} = p(b-a)$ where $b-a$ is an integer.

$\therefore$ $P(k+1)$ is true whenever $P(k)$ is true.
$\therefore$ $P(r)$ is true for all $r = 0, 1, 2, 3, \ldots\ldots, p-1$.

12.20   Let $E_n = \dfrac{(mn)!}{(m!)^n}$.   Our proposition is $P(n) : E_n$ is an integer.

Proof: (By induction on n)

i $E_1 = \dfrac{m!}{m!} = 1$ $\therefore$ $P(1)$ is true.

ii   If $P(k)$ is true   i.e. $E_k = \dfrac{(mk)!}{(m!)^k}$ is an integer,

then $E_{k+1} = \dfrac{(m[k+1])!}{(m!)^{k+1}} = \dfrac{(km+m)!}{m!(km)!} \cdot \dfrac{(km)!}{(m!)^k}$

Thus $E_{k+1} = \binom{km+m}{m} . E_k$ where both members of this product are integers.

$\left\{ \binom{km+m}{m} \text{ is a 'combination' and is } \therefore \text{ an integer.} \right\}$

Therefore $P(k+1)$ is true whenever $P(k)$ is true.
$\therefore$ $P(n)$ is true for all n in Z^+.

13. NUMBER THEORY

13.1 Suppose $\dfrac{n}{p}$ is not prime.

Then $\dfrac{n}{p}$ has at least two prime factors a, b say where $a \leqslant b$ and these must be factors of n.

Thus $pab \leqslant n$ ....(1)

But p is the smallest prime factor of n. $\therefore$ $p \leqslant a \leqslant b$

Hence $p^3 \leqslant pab$

and $\therefore$ by (1) $p^3 \leqslant n$

$\Rightarrow \quad p \leqslant \sqrt[3]{n}$, which contradicts the given $p > \sqrt[3]{n}$

Thus our supposition is false $\Rightarrow \dfrac{n}{p}$ is also a prime.

13.2 We need to show that $(x-1)^2 + x^2 + (x+1)^2 = y^3$

i.e. $3x^2 + 2 = y^3$ does not have integer solutions.

Now $3x^2 + 3 = y^3 + 1$

$\therefore \quad 3(x^2 + 1) = (y+1)(y^2 - y + 1)$ ....(1)

$\therefore$ 3 is a factor of $y + 1$ or $y^2 - y + 1$

Case 1:   If $y + 1 = 3n$ where n is an integer

then $y = 3n - 1$ and (1) becomes

$3(x^2 + 1) = 3n(9n^2 - 6n + 1 - 3n + 1 + 1)$

$\therefore \quad x^2 + 1 = n(9n^2 - 9n + 3)$

i.e. $x^2 + 1 = 3n(3n^2 - 3n + 1)$

i.e. $x^2 + 1$ is a multiple of 3, ...(*)

But in $(\bmod\,3)$, $x \equiv 0, 1$ or 2

$\therefore \quad x^2 + 1 \equiv 1$ or 2

$\therefore \quad x^2 + 1$ cannot be a multiple of 3, a contradition to (*)

Case 2:   If $y^2 - y + 1 = 3m$ where m is an integer

then $y^2 - y = 3m - 1$

But $y^2 - y = y(y - 1)$ is even {product of consecutive integers one of which is even}

$\therefore$ m is odd.

Let $m = 2a + 1$

$\therefore$ $y^2 - y = 3(2a + 1) - 1 = 6a + 2$

Thus $y^2 - y \equiv 2 \pmod 6$

But in $\bmod\,6$, $y \equiv 0, 1, 2, 3, 4$ or 5

and $y^2 - y \equiv 0, 0, 2, 0, 0$ or 2

Hence $y \equiv 2$ or 5

$\therefore \quad y = 6b + 2$ or $6b + 5$

Thus in (1) $3(x^2 + 1) = (6b + 3)(36b^2 + 24b + 4 - 6b - 2 + 1)$

$\therefore \quad 3(x^2 + 1) = 3(2b + 1)(36b^2 + 18b + 3)$

$\therefore \quad x^2 + 1 = 3(2b + 1)(12b^2 + 6b + 1)$

i.e. $x^2 + 1$ is a multiple of 3, once again a contradiction.

or $3(x^2 + 1) = (6b + 6)(36b^2 + 60b + 25 - 6b - 5 + 1)$

$3(x^2 + 1) = 6(b + 1)(36b^2 + 54b + 21)$

$\therefore \quad x^2 + 1 = 6(b + 1)(12b^2 + 18b + 7)$

i.e. $x^2 + 1$ is a multiple of 3, again a contradiction.

13.3 If the two numbers are m and n then there must be another way to factor the product mn into two distinct numbers >1, otherwise Pam would have known the numbers at the start. [For instance, we could not have $m = 3$ and $n = 9$, but we could have $m = 3$, $n = 6$ since $3 \times 6 = 2 \times 9$.]

The fact that Pam can determine the numbers after Sam's first statement tells us that of all the ways of factoring the product into two distinct factors greater than 1 (and there are at least 2 such ways) only one of them yields two factors which have a total < 25. [We know for instance that the product is not 18 since $3 + 6 < 25$ and $2 + 9 < 25$. The product could be $75 = 5 \times 15 = 3 \times 25$ since there are two factorizations, but only one where the total is less than 25.]

Let us say that a number is "good" if it can be factored in at least 2 ways into different integers (> 1), but just one such factorization has sum of factors < 25. [Thus 75 is good but 18 and 27 are not.]

After Pam's second statement, what information does Sam have? He knows the sum and he knows that the product is good. [If the sum were 20, for instance, he would know that 5 and 15 is possible, since their product is good. The numbers can't be 3 and 17 or 6 and 14 since their products are not good. However $9 \times 11 = 99$ is also good, so Sam would not know whether 5 and 15 or 9 and 11 were the numbers.]

The fact that Sam does know at the end tells us that what ever the sum is, there is only one way to break it up into two numbers >1 whose product is good.

Trial and error shows us that 15 is the only sum since 5×10 is good and no other product of numbers adding to 15 is good.   <u>The numbers are 5 and 10.</u>

13.4 $\underbrace{11111111........111}_{121} = \underbrace{(11111111111)}_{11 \text{ of them}}.[1 + 10^{11} + 10^{22} + ... + 10^{110}]$

a product of 2 integers and $\therefore$ <u>is not prime.</u>

13.5 A prime number, by definition, is an integer greater than 1 having no positive factors other than 1 and itself Now any integer n can be expressed in exactly one of the forms $3a, 3a + 1, 3a + 2$, where a is an integer. Thus each of our triples can be written in one of the forms:

(1) $3a, 3a + 2, 3a + 4$ or (2) $3a + 1, 3a + 3, 3a + 5$ or (3) $3a + 2, 3a + 4, 3a + 6.$

If $a < 1$, each triplet contains at least one integer $\leqslant 1$ and $\therefore$ no primes.

If $a = 0$, $3a, 3a + 1$, and $3a + 4$ are certainly not primes.

If $a \geqslant 1$, we get the triplet 3, 5, 7, from (1) if $a = 1$, but in every other case for
$a \geqslant 1$, one member in each triple is divisible by 3.

$\{3a$ in (1), $3a + 3$ in (2), $3a + 6$ in (3)$\}$

13.6 $m^4 + 4n^4 = m^4 + 4m^2n^2 + 4n^4 - 4m^2n^2$
$= (m^2 + 2n^2)^2 - (2mn)^2$
$= (m^2 + 2n^2 + 2mn)(m^2 + 2n^2 - 2mn)$
$= ([m + n]^2 + n^2)([m - n]^2 + n^2)$

and since $m \geqslant 2$, $n \geqslant 2$ both of these factors are > 1. $\therefore$ <u>$m^4 + 4n^4$ is composite.</u>

13.7 a

1	$13 = 6 + 7$	$25 = 12 + 13$
2	$14 = 2 + 3 + 4 + 5$	$26 = 5 + 6 + 7 + 8$
$3 = 1 + 2$	$15 = 7 + 8$	$27 = 13 + 14$
4	16	$28 = 1 + 2 + 3 + 4 + 5 + 6 + 7$
$5 = 2 + 3$	$17 = 8 + 9$	$29 = 14 + 15$
$6 = 1 + 2 + 3$	$18 = 5 + 6 + 7$	$30 = 9 + 10 + 11$
$7 = 3 + 4$	$19 = 9 + 10$	$31 = 15 + 16$
8	$20 = 2 + 3 + 4 + 5 + 6$	32
$9 = 4 + 5$	$21 = 10 + 11$	
$10 = 1 + 2 + 3 + 4$	$22 = 4 + 5 + 6 + 7$	
$11 = 5 + 6$	$23 = 11 + 12$	
$12 = 3 + 4 + 5$	$24 = 7 + 8 + 9$	

The numbers from 1 to 30 that cannot be written in this way are <u>1, 2, 4, 8, 16</u>

b Assuming that this pattern continues, all integers which are powers of 2 cannot be written in this way.

$$2^0 = 1 \qquad 2^5 = 32 \qquad 2^{10} = 1024$$
$$2^1 = 2 \qquad 2^6 = 64 \qquad 2^{11} = 2048$$
$$2^2 = 4 \qquad 2^7 = 128$$
$$2^3 = 8 \qquad 2^8 = 256$$
$$2^4 = 16 \qquad 2^9 = 512$$

Thus only   1024   can not be written this way.

c We conjecture that "no power of two can be written as the sum of consecutive positive integers."

Proof: Suppose $2^n = x + (x+1) + (x+2) + \ldots\ldots + (x+k)$
where x, k in Z^+ and $k \geqslant 1$.

$$\therefore \quad 2^n = \frac{k+1}{2}(x + x + k) \qquad \{\text{Sum of A.P.} \quad a = x$$
$$l = x + k$$
$$\therefore \quad 2^n = \frac{(k+1)(2x+k)}{2} \qquad\qquad\qquad n = k + 1$$
$$\text{is} \quad \frac{n}{2}(a+l)\}$$
$$\therefore \quad 2^{n+1} = (k+1)(2x+k)$$

$\Rightarrow$ both $(k+1)$ and $(2x+k)$ are powers of 2. ....(1)
$\{k + 1 \geqslant 2 \quad 2x + k \geqslant 3\}$

Now if k is even, $k + 1$ is odd, a contradiction to (1)
  if k is odd, $2x + k$ is odd, once more a contradiction to (1)
Thus the supposition is false.

$\therefore$ No power of 2 can be written in this way.

13.8 When $x = 0$, $ax^2 + bx + c = c$ is an integer   ....(1)
   $x = 1$, $a + b + c$ is an integer   ....(2)
   $x = 2$, $4a + 2b + c$ is an integer   ....(3)

Thus c is an integer   {from (1)}
and $\therefore$ $a + b$ is an integer   {from (2)}   ....(4)
Thus as $4a + 2b + c$ is an integer
  then $2a + 2(a + b) + c$ is an integer
   $\Rightarrow$ $2a$ is an integer   {from (4), (1)}
   $\Rightarrow$ $a = p$ or $p + \frac{1}{2}$ where p is an integer

Case 1.   (For $a = p$,   an integer.)
   $\therefore$ b is an integer   (from (4)}
   and c is an integer
   $\therefore$ $ax^2 + bx + c$ is an integer whenever x is an integer.

Case 2.   (For $a = p + \frac{1}{2}$, p an integer.)
   $ax^2 + bx + c$
   $= (p + \frac{1}{2})x^2 + (k - p - \frac{1}{2})x + c$ {If $a + b = k$, k in Z,
   then $b = k - a = k - p - \frac{1}{2}\}$
   $= px^2 + (k - p)x + \frac{1}{2}x^2 - \frac{1}{2}x + c$
   $= px^2 + (k - p)x + \frac{1}{2}x(x - 1) + c$
   where $\frac{1}{2}x(x - 1)$ is an integer since one of $x, x - 1$ is even.
   $\therefore$ $ax^2 + bx + c$ is an integer in this case also.

13.9 **a**

$10^2 = 100$	$15^2 = 225$	$20^2 = 400$	$25^2 = 625$	$30^2 = 900$
$11^2 = \boxed{121}$	$16^2 = 256$	$21^2 = 441$	$26^2 = \boxed{676}$	$31^2 = 961$
$12^2 = 144$	$17^2 = 289$	$22^2 = \boxed{484}$	$27^2 = 729$	$32^2 = 1024$
$13^2 = 169$	$18^2 = 324$	$23^2 = 529$	$28^2 = 784$	
$14^2 = 196$	$19^2 = 361$	$24^2 = 576$	$29^2 = 841$	

Thus there are 3 perfect squares,   121,   484   and   676   of the form   "*aba*".

b   "$abab$" $= 1000a + 100b + 10a + b$
$\qquad\qquad = 1010a + 101b$
$\qquad\qquad = 101(10a + b)$ where 101 is a prime and $10a + b \leqslant 99$.
$\qquad \therefore$ "$abab$" cannot be a perfect square.

13.10   Notice that $n(n + 1)(n + 2) > n^3$ (1)

Also notice that $(n + 1)^2 = n^2 + 2n + 1$
$\qquad\qquad \therefore \quad (n + 1)^2 > n^2 + 2n$
$\qquad\qquad$ i.e. $(n + 1)^2 > n(n + 2)$
$\qquad\qquad \therefore \quad (n + 1)^3 > n(n + 1)(n + 2)$ (2)

From (1) and (2) $n^3 < n(n + 1)(n + 2) < (n + 1)^3$
i.e., $n(n + 1)(n + 2)$ always lies between two consecutive perfect cubes.
Note: Can you prove that $n(n + 1)(n + 2)$ cannot be   *(i)*   a perfect square,
$\qquad\qquad\qquad\qquad\qquad\qquad\qquad\qquad\qquad\qquad\quad$ *(ii)*   a perfect power?

13.11   If $a^3 + a = b^2$ where a and b are integers then $a(a^2 + 1) = b^2$ .... (*)
Now consider a and $a^2 + 1$ having a common factor t where $t \geqslant 2$.
Now $a = tk$ and $a^2 + 1 = tl$ where k and l are positive integers.
$\qquad \therefore \quad t^2 k^2 + 1 = tl$
$\qquad\quad$ i.e. $t(l - tk^2) = 1$
$\therefore \quad t = 1$ and $l - tk^2 = 1$ {as both t and $l - tk^2$ are integers}
$\therefore \quad a$ and $a^2 + 1$ are coprime.
$\quad \therefore$ both a *and* $a^2 + 1$ are perfect squares {from $*$}
But $a^2 + 1$ cannot be a perfect square as a^2 is a perfect square, and the only consecutive perfect squares are 0 and 1, where $a = 0$ which is not permissible.
$\qquad \therefore \quad a^3 + a = b^2$ has no positive integer solutions.

13.12 If $p = 1 + 2 + 2^2 + 2^3 + \ \text{........} \ + 2^n$ is prime, then the sum of the proper divisors
of $2^n p = 1 + 2 + 2^2 + 2^3 + \ \text{........} \ + 2^n + p + 2p + 2^2 p + 2^3 p + \ \text{........} \ + 2^{n-1} p.$
$\qquad = (1 + 2 + 2^2 + 2^3 + \ \text{........} \ + 2^n) + p(1 + 2 + 2^2 + 2^3 + \ \text{........} \ + 2^{n-1})$

$\qquad = p + p(2^n - 1) \qquad \{ 1 + 2 + 2^2 + \ \text{........} \ + 2^{n-1} = \dfrac{1(1 - 2^n)}{1 - 2} = 2^n - 1, \quad \text{sum of GS}\}$

$\qquad = p + p2^n - p$
$\qquad = p2^n$
$\therefore \quad p2^n$ is a perfect number.

13.13 $18{,}000 = 2^4 . 3^2 . 5^3$

The divisors of $18{,}000$ are numbers of the form $2^a 3^b 5^c$ where $\quad \begin{cases} a = 0,\ 1,\ 2,\ 3,\ 4 \\ b = 0,\ 1,\ 2 \\ c = 0,\ 1,\ 2,\ 3 \end{cases}$

Thus the number of divisors of $18{,}000$ is $5.3.4 = \underline{60}$ {5 possible selections for a, 3 for b, 4 for c}
When $(1 + 2 + 2^2 + 2^3 + 2^4)(1 + 3 + 3^2)(1 + 5 + 5^2 + 5^3)$ is expanded out, we will get all 60
terms of the form $2^a 3^b 5^c$ which are the divisors of $18{,}000$ as a sum.
$\quad$ i.e., $2^0 3^0 5^0 + 2^1 3^0 5^0 + 2^0 3^1 5^0 + 2^0 3^0 5^1 + 2^1 3^0 5^1 + \ \text{........} \ + 2^4 . 3^2 . 5^3$
$\qquad$ Hence the sum of the divisors $= 31.13.156 = \underline{62{,}868}.$

13.14   **a**   Since n is composite, let $n = ab$ where a, b are primes.

$$\therefore \quad 2^n - 1 = 2^{ab} - 1 \qquad a \geqslant 2, \quad b \geqslant 2$$
$$= (2^a)^b - 1$$
$$= (2^a - 1)((2^a)^{b-1} + (2^a)^{b-2} + \text{........} + (2^a)^2 + (2^a) + 1)$$

{Using $x^n - 1 = (x - 1)(x^{n-1} + x^{n-2} + x^{n-3} + \text{........} + x^2 + x + 1)$} where both factors are $\geqslant 3$

$\therefore \quad \underline{2^n - 1 \quad \text{is composite.}}$

b   From **a** n composite $\Rightarrow$ $2^n - 1$ is composite

$\therefore$ if $2^n - 1$ is not composite $\Rightarrow$ n is not composite

i.e. $\underline{2^n - 1 \quad \text{prime} \quad \Rightarrow \quad n \quad \text{is prime.}}$

{if $A \Rightarrow B$ then   not $B \Rightarrow$ not A is logically correct}

13.15   If two integers a and b $(a > b)$ have HCF h, then there are integers k and l such that $a = kh$ and $b = lh$ where $k > l$,   and k, l are coprime.

The LCM of a and b is $\dfrac{ab}{h}$ {[LCM].[HCF] $= ab$}

$$= klh$$

Thus $klh = (kh - lh)^2$ and $\therefore$ $kl = h(k - l)^2 \text{..........(1)}$

$\therefore$ $k - l$ is a factor of kl

But k, l are coprime means that $\begin{cases} k - l \quad \text{and } k \text{ are coprime and} \\ k - l \quad \text{and } l \text{ are coprime} \end{cases}$

and $\therefore$ $k - l$ and kl are coprime.

Thus $k - l = 1$ {since it is a factor of kl and coprime to kl, $\therefore$ only ± 1 factors}

$\therefore$ $h = kl$ {from (1)}

$\therefore$ $h = l(l + 1)$ i.e.,$\underline{\text{the HCF is the product of consecutive integers.}}$

13.16   7. $7^4 = 2401$ and $7^8 \equiv 4801$ (mod 10000)   i.e. 7^8 ends in   4801.

$\therefore$ 7^{12} ends in   7201

7^{16} ends in   9601

7^{20} ends in   2001

7^{40} ends in   4001 $7^{1000} = (7^{100})^{10}$

7^{80} ends in   8001 $\equiv (0001)^{10}$

7^{100} ends in   0001 $\equiv 0001$ $\therefore$ last 4 digits are $\underline{0001}$.

13.17 $1225 = 35^2$

$112225 = 335^2$

$11122225 = 3335^2$

We guess: $\underbrace{11111........1}_{n} \cdot \underbrace{22222........2}_{n+1} \cdot 5 = \underbrace{(3333........35)^2}_{n}$ and $\therefore$ $\sqrt{M} = \underbrace{3333........3}_{n} 5$

n of these 3's

Notice: $N = 5 + 2(10 + 10^2 + 10^3 + \text{........} + 10^{n+1}) + (10^{n+2} + 10^{n+3} + \text{........} + 10^{2n+1})$

$= 5 + 20(1 + 10 + 10^2 + \text{........} + 10^n) + 10^{n+2}(1 + 10 + \text{........} + 10^{n-1})$

$= 5 + 20\left(\dfrac{10^{n+1} + 1}{10 - 1}\right) + 10^{n+2}\left(\dfrac{10^{n-1} - 1}{10 - 1}\right)$

$= \dfrac{45 + 20 \cdot 10^{n+1} - 20 + 10^{2n+2} - 10^{n+2}}{9}$

$= \dfrac{10^{2n+2} + 10 \cdot 10^{n+1} + 25}{9}$

$= \underline{\left(\dfrac{10^{n+1} + 5}{3}\right)^2}$ where $10^{n+1} + 5$ has digital sum of 6 and is $\therefore$ divisible by 3

$\therefore$ $\left(\dfrac{10^{n+1} + 5}{3}\right) = (\text{integer})^2.$

or $\dfrac{10^{n+1}+5}{3} = \frac{1}{3}[(1+9)^{n+1}+5]$

$= \frac{1}{3}\left[1 + \binom{n+1}{1}9 + \binom{n+2}{2}9^2 + \ \ldots\ldots\ + 9^{n+1} + 5\right]$

$= \frac{1}{3}\left[6 + \binom{n+1}{1}9 + \binom{n+2}{2}9^2 + \ \ldots\ldots\ + 9^{n+1}\right]$ an integer as $\binom{n+1}{r}$'s are integers.

etc.

13.18   **a** $x^2 - 2x + 3 = x^2 - 2x + 1 + 2$
$= (x-1)^2 + 2$
> 0 as $(x-1)^2 \geqslant 0$,   for all x.

b $x^4 - 2x^3 + 3x^2 - 4x + 5$
$= x^2(x^2 - 2x + 1) + 2x^2 - 4x + 5$
$= x^2(x-1)^2 + 2(x^2 - 2x + 1) + 3$
$= x^2(x-1)^2 + 2(x-1)^2 + 3$
> 0 for all x.

c $x^6 - 2x^5 + 3x^4 - 4x^3 + 5x^2 - 6x + 7$
$= x^4(x^2 - 2x + 1) + 2x^4 - 4x^3 + 5x^2 - 6x + 7$
$= x^4(x-1)^2 + 2x^2(x^2 - 2x + 1) + 3x^2 - 6x + 7$
$= x^4(x-1)^2 + 2x^2(x-1)^2 + 3(x^2 - 2x + 1) + 4$
$= x^4(x-1)^2 + 2x^2(x-1)^2 + 3(x-1)^2 + 4$
> 0 for all x.

d $x^8 - 2x^7 + 3x^6 - 4x^5 + 5x^4 - 6x^3 + 7x^2 - 8x + 9$
$= x^6(x^2 - 2x + 1) + 2x^6 - 4x^5 + 5x^4 - 6x^3 + 7x^2 - 8x + 9$
$= x^6(x-1)^2 + 2x^4(x^2 - 2x + 1) + 3x^4 - 6x^3 + 7x^2 - 8x + 9$
$= x^6(x-1)^2 + 2x^4(x-1)^2 + 3x^2(x^2 - 2x + 1) + 4x^2 - 8x + 9$
$= x^6(x-1)^2 + 2x^4(x-1)^2 + 3x^2(x-1)^2 + 4(x-1)^2 + 5$
> 0 for all x.

13.19   **a**   For a, b coprime, suppose p is a prime which is a factor of ab.
then p divides exactly one of a and b.
say p divides a, but p does not divide b.
$\therefore$ p does not divide $a + b$
Thus no prime factor of ab divides $a + b$
$\Rightarrow$ ab and $a + b$ are coprime.

b   Let the two integers be A and B with   HCF. $= h$
$\therefore$ $A = ha$ and $B = hb$ where a, b are coprime.
Now $A + B = h(a + b) = 216\ldots\ldots..(1)$

But their   LCM $= \dfrac{AB}{\text{HCF}} = 480$ {[LCM][HCF] $= AB$}

$\Rightarrow$ $abh^2 = 480h$
$\Rightarrow$ $abh = 480\ldots\ldots..(2)$
But in (1) and (2), $a + b$ and ab have no common factors
Thus $h =$ HCF of 216 and 480
$=$ HCF of $2^3 3^3$ and $2^5.3.5$
$= 2^3.3$
$= 24$

$\therefore$ $a + b = 9$ {from (1)}
and $ab = 20$ {from (2)}
$\therefore$ $a = 4$, $b = 5$ {on solving simultaneously, assuming $a \leqslant b$}
Hence $A = 96$, $B = 120$.

13.20 We will assume that the numbers x, y, z satisfy the given conditions and $x + y + z = 96$.

Now $x + y$ is divisible by z $\Rightarrow$ 96 is divisible by z.

Likewise 96 is divisible by x and y.

$\therefore$ x, y, z are members of the set $\{96, 48, 32, 24, 16, 12, 8, 6, 4, 3, 2, 1\}$

Suppose $x < y < z$

Since $x + y$ is divisible by z, then

$$x + y \geqslant z$$
$$\Rightarrow \quad 96 - z \geqslant z$$
$$\Rightarrow \quad z \leqslant 48$$

But if $z < 48$ then $z \leqslant 32$, $y \leqslant 24$, $x \leqslant 16$.

$\Rightarrow$ $x + y + z \leqslant 72$, a contradictiton to the fact: $x + y + z = 96$

Thus $z = 48$.

Hence if $z = 48$ then $y \leqslant 32$. But if $y < 32$, then $y \leqslant 24$ and $x \leqslant 16$.

$\therefore$ $x + y + z \leqslant 88$, once again a contradiction.

Thus $y = 32$

and hence $x = 96 - 48 - 32 = 16$, i.e., $x = 16$.

Thus $\underline{x = 16, \quad y = 32, \quad z = 48}$ is the only possible solution, if in fact it is a solution.
Simple calculations indicate that this is the one and ony solution.

13.21 Suppose n is odd $\therefore$ $2^n + 1$

$$= 2^{2a+1} + 1, \quad a \text{ in } Z$$
$$= 2.4^a + 1$$
$$= 2.(1 + 3)^a + 1$$
$$= 2.(1 + \binom{a}{1}3 + \binom{a}{2}3^2 + \ldots\ldots + \binom{a}{a}3^a) + 1$$
$$= 3 + 2\binom{a}{1}.3 + 2\binom{a}{2}.3^2 + \ldots\ldots + 2\binom{a}{a}3^a$$

which is divisible by 3 for all a.

$\therefore$ $2^n + 1$ is composite.

i.e. n odd $\Rightarrow$ $2^n + 1$ is composite.

thus $2^n + 1$ not composite $\Rightarrow$ n not odd

$2^n + 1$ prime $\Rightarrow$ n is even.

Suppose $n = 2b$ where b is odd

then $2^{2b} + 1 = 4^b + 1$

$$= (5 - 1)^b + 1$$
$$= 5^b + \binom{b}{1}5^{b-1}(-1) + \binom{b}{2}5^{b-2}(-1)^2 + \ldots\ldots + \binom{b}{b-1}5.(-1)^{b-1} + (-1)^b + 1$$

which is divisble by 5, a contradiction as $2^n + 1$ is prime.

Thus $2^n + 1$ is prime $\Rightarrow$ n cannot have an odd factor > 1

$\Rightarrow$ $\underline{n \text{ must be a power of } 2.}$

13.22 The roots of $x^2 + 2ax + 2b = 0$ are $x = \dfrac{-2a \pm \sqrt{4a^2 - 4.1.2b}}{2} = -a \pm \sqrt{a^2 - 2b}$,

and these roots are rational $\Leftrightarrow$ $a^2 - 2b$ is a perfect square.

Let us suppose then that $a^2 - 2b = k^2$, k in Z

then $a^2 - k^2 = 2b$

$\therefore$ $(a + k)(a - k) = 2b$

$\therefore$ at least one of $(a + k)$, $(a - k)$ is even..........(1)

If a is even, k is odd (or vice versa), condition (1) is violated.

If a is even, k is even
or a is odd, k is odd $\Big\}$ both $a + k$ and $a - k$ are even

$\Rightarrow$ $2b = 4l$, l in Z and $\therefore$ $b = 2l$,

which contadicts the condition that b is odd.

Hence $a^2 - 2b$ cannot be a perfect square. $\underline{\text{Thus the roots are irrational.}}$

13.23 There are 4 situations to consider:

(1) $\dfrac{10n + a}{10n + b} = \dfrac{a}{b}$ (2) $\dfrac{10n + a}{10b + n} = \dfrac{a}{b}$ (3) $\dfrac{10a + n}{10b + n} = \dfrac{a}{b}$ (4) $\dfrac{10a + n}{10n + b} = \dfrac{a}{b}$

where a, b and n are positive integers less than 10, and $a < b$.

Case (1) If $\dfrac{10n + a}{10n + b} = \dfrac{a}{b}$, then $10bn + ab = 10an + ab$

$\Rightarrow \quad 10bn = 10an$

$\Rightarrow \qquad a = b$, which is not permissable. $\{as \ \ a < b\}$

Case (2) If $\dfrac{10n + a}{10b + n} = \dfrac{a}{b}$, then $10bn + ab = 10ab + an$

$\Rightarrow \quad 10bn = 9ab + an < 9ab + bn$ $\{as \ \ a < b\}$

$\Rightarrow \quad 9bn < 9ab$

$\Rightarrow \qquad n < a$

$\Rightarrow \qquad n \leqslant a - 1$

Thus $na = 10bn - 9ab \leqslant 10b(a - 1) - 9ab$

$\Rightarrow \quad na \leqslant ab - 10b$

$\Rightarrow \quad na \leqslant b(a - 10)$ where $a - 10$ is negative.

$\Rightarrow \quad na$ is negative, a contradiction.

Case (3) If $\dfrac{10a + n}{10b + n} = \dfrac{a}{b}$, then $10ab + bn = 10ab + an$

$\Rightarrow \quad a = b$, which is not permissable as $a < b$.

Case (4) If $\dfrac{10a + n}{10n + b} = \dfrac{a}{b}$, then $10ab + bn = 10an + ab$

$\Rightarrow \quad 10an = 9ab + bn = b(9a + n)$

$\Rightarrow \quad 10an > 9ab + an$ $\qquad \{a < b\}$

$\Rightarrow \quad 9an > 9ab$

$\Rightarrow \qquad n > b$

We now construct a table of values of $a\left[= \dfrac{bn}{10n - 9b}\right]$ for various values of b and n, under the restriction $n > b$.

n \ b	1	2	3	4	5	6	7	8
1	*	*	*	*	*	*	*	*
2	$\frac{2}{11}$	*	*	*	*	*	*	*
3	$\frac{3}{21}$	$\frac{6}{12}$	*	*	*	*	*	*
4	$\frac{4}{31}$	$\frac{8}{22}$	$\frac{12}{13}$	*	*	*	*	*
5	$\frac{5}{41}$	$\frac{10}{32}$	$\frac{15}{23}$	$\frac{20}{14}$	*	*	*	*
6	$\frac{6}{51}$	$\frac{12}{42}$	$\frac{18}{33}$	$\boxed{\frac{24}{24}}$	$\boxed{\frac{30}{15}}$	*	*	*
7	$\frac{7}{61}$	$\frac{14}{52}$	$\frac{21}{43}$	$\frac{28}{34}$	$\frac{35}{25}$	$\frac{42}{16}$	*	*
8	$\frac{8}{71}$	$\frac{16}{62}$	$\frac{24}{53}$	$\frac{32}{44}$	$\frac{40}{35}$	$\frac{48}{26}$	$\frac{56}{17}$	*
9	$\frac{9}{81}$	$\frac{18}{72}$	$\frac{27}{63}$	$\frac{36}{54}$	$\boxed{\frac{45}{45}}$	$\frac{54}{36}$	$\frac{63}{27}$	$\boxed{\frac{72}{18}}$

The 4 ringed answers are the only integer values of a that exist.

Thus $a = 1,$ $b = 4,$ $n = 6$ i.e. $\frac{1\cancel{6}}{\cancel{6}4} = \frac{1}{4}$ ✓

$a = 2,$ $b = 5,$ $n = 6$

$a = 1,$ $b = 5,$ $n = 9$ $\frac{2\cancel{6}}{\cancel{6}5} = \frac{2}{5}$ ✓

$a = 4,$ $b = 8,$ $n = 9$ $\frac{1\cancel{9}}{\cancel{9}5} = \frac{1}{5}$ ✓

$\frac{4\cancel{9}}{\cancel{9}8} = \frac{4}{8}$

We do not allow the last solution as cancellation does not reduce the fraction to lowest terms.

13.24   Suppose $x^2 + x + 11 = a^2$ where a is an integer.

$\therefore$ $x^2 + x = a^2 - 11$

$\therefore$ $4x^2 + 4x = 4a^2 - 44$

$\therefore$ $4x^2 + 4x + 1 = 4a^2 - 43$

$\therefore$ $4a^2 - (2x + 1)^2 = 43$

$\therefore$ $(2a + 2x + 1)(2a - 2x - 1) = 43$

Since 43 is prime, then

$2a + 2x + 1$	$2a - 2x - 1$	$4a$	a	x
1	43	44	11	-11
43	1	44	11	10
-1	-43	-44	-11	10
-43	-1	-44	-11	-11

Thus there are 2 and only two integers x such that $x^2 + x + 11$ is a perfect square.
These are $x = 10,$ $x = -11$.

13.25

$$
\begin{array}{cccccc}
 & & 4 & a & b \\
 & \times & & 3 & c \\
\hline
 & 3 & 6 & d & e \\
f & g & 7 & i & \\
\hline
j & k & 3 & l & m \\
\end{array}
$$

c must be 8 or 9

If $c = 8$ "ab"   is   51, 52, 53, ..., 61, 62. $\Big\}$ ....(1)

If $c = 9$ "ab"   is   00, 01, 02, ..., 10, 11.

Now
$$
\begin{array}{ccc}
4 & a & b \\
\times & & 3 \\
\hline
\cdot \quad \cdot & 7 & \cdot \\
\end{array}
$$

$\therefore$ "ab"   is   24, 25, 26
or   57, 58, 59 $\Big\}$ ....(2)
or   90, 91, 92, or 93.

From (1) and (2) $c = 8$,   and   "ab" = "57", "58", or "59"

On trialling each of these:
$$
\begin{array}{ccccc}
 & & 4 & 5 & 7 \\
 & \times & & 3 & 8 \\
\hline
 & 3 & 6 & 5 & 6 \\
1 & 3 & 7 & 1 & \\
\hline
1 & 7 & 3 & 6 & 6 \\
\end{array}
$$

So $a = 5,$ $b = 7,$ $c = 8,$ $d = 5,$ $e = 6,$ $f = 1,$ $g = 3,$ $i = 1,$ $j = 1,$ $k = 7,$ $l = m = 6.$

13.26 $2^{2^{2^{(2^2)}}} = 2^{2^{(2^4)}} = 2^{2^{16}} = 2^{65536} = (10^{0.30103})^{65536}$ $\{2 = 10^{\log 2} = 10^{0.30103}\}$

$= 10^{19728 \cdot 302}$

$\doteq \underline{10^{0.302}} \times 10^{19728}$

real between 1 and 10

$\therefore$ $2^{2^{2^2}}$ has $\underline{19729}$ digits $\left[\begin{array}{ll} 200 = 2 \times 10^2 & \text{has 3 digits} \\ 20000 = 2 \times 10^4 & \text{has 5 digits} \end{array}\right]$

13.27 $ab = cd \quad \Rightarrow \quad \dfrac{a}{c} = \dfrac{d}{b}$

Let $\dfrac{a}{c} = \dfrac{d}{b} = \dfrac{p}{q}$ where p, q have no common factors i.e. are coprime.

Thus there exist positive integers s and t such that
$$a = ps \qquad b = qt$$
$$c = qs \qquad d = pt$$

Hence $\quad a^2 + b^2 + c^2 + d^2$
$$= p^2 s^2 + q^2 t^2 + q^2 s^2 + p^2 t^2$$
$$= p^2(s^2 + t^2) + q^2(s^2 + t^2)$$
$$= \underline{(s^2 + t^2)(p^2 + q^2)}$$

where neither $\;s^2 + t^2\;$ nor $\;p^2 + q^2\;$ is 1.

$\therefore \quad a^2 + b^2 + c^2 + d^2\quad$ cannot be prime.

Note: The condition is still true with $\;a^2 + b^2 + c^2 + d^2\;$ replaced by $a^k + b^k + c^k + d^k\;$ for any integer $\;k \geqslant 2$.

13.28   Suppose the sum of two odd integers can be a perfect power.

i.e. $(2a + 1)^2 + (2b + 1)^2 = m^n\quad$ where $\quad a, b, m$ and n are integers with $\quad n \geqslant 2$.

$\therefore \quad 4a^2 + 4a + 1 + 4b^2 + 4b + 1 = m^n$

i.e. $4a^2 + 4a + 4b^2 + 4b + 2 = m^n$

$\therefore \quad$ since L.H.S. is even, m must be even,

and letting $\;m = 2c, \;$ say, where c is an integer

$4a^2 + 4a + 4b^2 + 4b + 2 = (2c)^n = 2^n c^n$

$\Rightarrow \quad 2a^2 + 2a + 2b^2 + 2b + 1 = 2^{n-1}.c^n \quad$ where $\quad n - 1 \geqslant 1$

which is a contradiction as the LHS. is odd and the RHS. is even.

Thus the supposition is false.

Therefore the sum of two odd integers cannot be a perfect power.

13.29 $(x + y)^2 = x^2 + y^2 + 2xy \quad$ and $\quad (x - y)^2 = x^2 + y^2 - 2xy$

$\therefore \quad (x + y)^2 = 4xy + (x - y)^2 \quad$ and hence $\quad (x + y)^2 \geqslant 4xy \quad$ with equality when $\quad x = y$.

Thus $\quad (2 - z)^2 \geqslant 4[2 - z(x + y)]$

$\therefore \quad 4 - 4z + z^2 \geqslant 8 - 4z(2 - z)$

which simplifies to $\quad 3z^2 - 4z + 4 \leqslant 0$

i.e. $\quad z^2 - \tfrac{4}{3}z + \tfrac{4}{3} \leqslant 0$

and on completing the square $\quad (z - \tfrac{2}{3})^2 + \tfrac{8}{9} \leqslant 0 \quad$ which is impossible.

13.30   **Experimentation:**   Pascal's Triangle.

If $\;n = 2^k\;$ then $\;\dbinom{n-1}{r} = \dbinom{2^k - 1}{r} = \dfrac{(2^k - 1)(2^k - 2)(2^k - 3)\ldots\ldots(2^k - a)\ldots\ldots(2^k - r)}{1 \;.\; 2 \;.\; 3 \;\ldots\ldots\; a \;\ldots\ldots\; r}$

Now a can be factorized as $a = 2^q.b$ where $0 \leqslant q < k$ and b is odd.

Since $\dfrac{2^k - a}{2^q} = \dfrac{2^k - 2^q b}{2^q} = 2^{k-q} - b$ then $\dfrac{2^k - a}{2^q}$ is odd.

Thus $\dbinom{n-1}{r}$ is the product of only odd factors and is therefore <u>odd</u>.

For $-1 \leqslant r \leqslant n-1$, $\dbinom{n}{r} = \dbinom{n-1}{r-1} + \dbinom{n-1}{r}$ {Pascal's Identity}

$\therefore$ $\dbinom{n}{r}$ is the sum of two odds {previous part}

i.e. $\dbinom{n}{r}$ is <u>even</u>.

13.31 Let us assume that it can. i.e. $2^n - 1 = a^k$ where $a \geqslant 2$, $k \geqslant 2$.

We notice that $2^n - 1$ is odd $\Rightarrow$ a^k is odd $\Rightarrow$ a is odd.

Now $2^n = a^k + 1$

(a) If k is even, $a^k = (a^k - 1) + 1$

$\qquad = (a^{2t} - 1) + 1$

$\qquad = (a^t + 1)(a^t - 1) + 1$

and since a is odd, a^t is odd. $\therefore$ $a^t + 1$ and $a^t - 1$ are even

$\therefore$ $a^k = 4M + 1$, M in Z^+ $\therefore$ $a^t + 1$ and $a^t - 1$ are even

$\Rightarrow$ $2^n = 4M + 2 = 2(2M + 1)$ $\therefore$ $2^{n-1} = 2M + 1$

which is a contradiction as the L.H.S. is even and R.H.S. is odd.

(b) If k is odd, $\therefore$ $a^t + 1$ and $a^t - 1$ are even

$a^k + 1 = (a + 1)(a^{k-1} - a^{k-2} + a^{k-3} - a^{k-4} + \ldots\ldots - a + 1)$ {check this}

$\therefore$ $2^n = (a + 1)\left(\left[a^{k-1} - a^{k-2}\right] + \left[a^{k-3} - a^{k-4}\right] + \ldots\ldots + \left[a^2 - a\right] + 1 \right)$

where the second factor is odd, as each term in square brackets is even.

Once again we have a contradiction.

13.32 We observe: $\quad 2^2 = 1 + 3 \qquad\qquad 3^2 = 1 + 3 + 5$

$\qquad\qquad\qquad 2^3 = 3 + 5 \qquad\qquad 3^3 = 7 + 9 + 11$

$\qquad\qquad\qquad 2^4 = 7 + 9 \qquad\qquad 3^4 = 25 + 27 + 29$

$\qquad\qquad\qquad 2^5 = 15 + 17 \qquad\quad 3^5 = 79 + 81 + 83$

If n is even,

$\quad n^k = (n^{k-1} - [n-1]) + (n^{k-1} - [n-3]) + \ldots\ldots + (n^{k-1} - 3) + (n^{k-1} - 1)$

$\qquad\quad + (n^{k-1} + 1) + (n^{k-1} + 3) + \ldots\ldots + (n^{k-1} + [n-3]) + (n^{k-1} + [n-1])$

If n is odd,

$\quad n^k = (n^{k-1} - [n-1]) + (n^{k-1} - [n-3]) + \ldots\ldots + (n^{k-1} - 2) + n^{k-1}$

$\qquad\quad + (n^{k-1} + 2) + (n^{k-1} + 4) + \ldots\ldots + (n^{k-1} + [n-3]) + (n^{k-1} + [n-1])$

13.33 With problems like this one, consider small powers of the base number.

$\qquad$ e.g. $7^1 = 7$, $\quad 7^2 = 49$, $\quad 7^3 = 343$, $\quad 7^4 = 2401$, etc.

Using the binomial expansion,

$7^{1000} = (2400 + 1)^{250}$

$\quad = 2400^{250} + \dbinom{250}{1} 2400^{249} + \ldots\ldots + \dbinom{250}{247} 2400^3 + \dbinom{250}{248} 2400^2 + \dbinom{250}{249} 2400 + 1$

All of these terms end in at least 6 zeros,

since the binomial coefficients $\dbinom{250}{r}$ are integers.

$\therefore$ 7^{1000} ends in whatever the last 3 terms added end in.

These are $\quad \frac{250 \cdot 249}{2 \cdot 1} \cdot 2400^2 + 250 \cdot 2400 + 1$

$\quad = 179280000000 + 600000 + 1$

$\quad = 179280600001$

Thus $\quad \underline{600001}$ are the last 6 digits.

13.34 If $\ x^p + y^p = z^p \ $ for positive integers $\ x, y$ and $z \ $ (z a prime), then without loss of generality,

$$x \leqslant y \leqslant z$$

Now $\quad x + y \leqslant z + z = 2z$

i.e., $\quad \underline{x + y \leqslant 2z} \qquad (1)$

Also $\quad (x+y)^p = x^p + \binom{p}{1}x^{p-1}y + \binom{p}{2}x^{p-2}y^2 + \cdots\cdots + \binom{p}{p-1}xy^{p-1} + y^p$

$\qquad\qquad\qquad\qquad\qquad\qquad\qquad$ {Binomial expansion}

$\therefore \quad (x+y)^p > x^p + y^p \quad$ as omitted RHS terms are all positive.

$\therefore \quad (x+y)^p > z^p \quad$ {as $\ x^p + y^p = z^p$}

$\therefore \quad \underline{x + y > z} \qquad (2)$

From (1) and (2) $\quad \underline{z < x + y \leqslant 2z} \qquad (3)$

Now $\quad x^p + y^p = (x+y)(x^{p-1} - x^{p-2}y + x^{p-3}y^2 - \cdots\cdots - xy^{p-2} + y^{p-1}) \quad$ {p is odd}

$\therefore \quad x + y$ is a factor of z^p

and as z is prime $\ x + y = 1, z, z^2, z^3, \ldots\ldots, z^p \ $ which contradicts (3)

Thus z is $\underline{\text{not prime}}$.

13.35 $\qquad n_1 < n_2 < n_3 < \cdots\cdots < n_{15}$

$\qquad\qquad n_r \cdot n_s = n_{rs} \quad$ where $\ r \neq s \ $ and $\ rs \leqslant 15$

(1) $\qquad {n_2}^2 \cdot n_3 = n_2(n_2 \cdot n_3) = n_2 \cdot n_6 = n_{12} = n_4 \cdot n_3$

$\Rightarrow \quad {n_2}^2 = n_4 > n_3$

$\therefore \quad \underline{n_3 < {n_2}^2}$

(2) $\qquad$ If $\quad n_2 = 2 \quad$ then $\quad n_4 = 4$

$\therefore \quad n_3 = 3 \quad$ {as $\ n_2 < n_3 < n_4 \ $ and $\ n_3$ is an integer}

Thus $\quad n_6 = n_2 \cdot n_3 = 6$

$\Rightarrow \quad n_5 = 5 \quad$ {as $\ n_4 < n_5 < n_6$}

$\therefore \quad n_{15} = n_3 \cdot n_5 = 3 \cdot 5 = \underline{15}$

13.36

4th	3rd	2nd	1st
M	A	K	E
+ S	A	F	E
P	L	A	N	S

It is certain that $\ \underline{P = 1}, \ $ since we cannot carry more than 1. On examining $\underline{\text{column 3}}$, we may have

$\qquad A + A = A \quad$ or $\quad 10 + A$

or $\quad A + A + 1 = A \quad$ or $\quad 10 + A$

Solving these yields $\quad A = 0, 10, -1 \ $ or $\ 9$

Thus $\quad \underline{A = 9}$

Thus the 4th column is now $\quad M + S + 1 = 10 + L$

or $\quad M + S = 9 + L \ldots\ldots(1)$

In columns 1 and 2, $\quad \begin{cases} 2E = S \\ K + F = 10 + N \end{cases}$ or $\begin{cases} 10 + S \\ K + F + 1 = 10 + N \quad \ldots\ldots(2) \\ \text{i.e.,} \quad K + F = 9 + N \end{cases}$

from which it is clear that S is even

$\therefore \quad S = 2, 4, 6$ or 8.

Case 1: $\quad S = 2 \quad \therefore \quad M - L = 7 \ $ which is impossible as $\ $ Max. $M = 8$, Min. $L = 2$

$\qquad\qquad\qquad\qquad\qquad\qquad\qquad \Rightarrow \quad M - L \leqslant 6$.

Case 2: $S = 4$ $\therefore$ $M - L = 5$ $\therefore$ $M = 8$, $L = 3$ _____ (a)

or $M = 7$, $L = 2$ _____ (b)

but we reject (b) as $S = 4 \Rightarrow E = 2$ or 7

We display the possibilities

P	A	S	M	L	E	K, F, N	$(K + F) - N = 9$ or 10
1	9	4	8	3	2	5, 6, 7	NO
1	9	4	8	3	7	2, 5, 6	9 when $N = 2$

Thus $PLANS \equiv 13924$ is a solution.

Case 3:   If $S = 6$, $M - L = 3$

$\therefore$ $M = 8$, $L = 5$ and $E = 3$, $K + F - N = 10$

$M = 7$, $L = 4$ or 8, $K + F - N = 9$

$M = 5$, $L = 2$

Possibilites are

P	A	S	M	L	E	K, F, N	$(K + F) - N = 9$ or 10
1	9	6	8	5	3	2, 4, 7	NO (when $E = 3$, $K + F - N = 10$)
1	9	6	7	4	{3	2, 5, 8	NO
					{8	2, 3, 5	NO
1	9	6	5	2	{3	4, 7, 8	NO
					{8	3, 4, 7	NO

Case 4:   If $S = 8$, $M - L = 1$ $\therefore$ $M = 7$, $L = 6$ ____ (a)   and $E = 4$ (can't be 9)

$M = 6$, $L = 5$ ____ (b)

$M = 5$, $L = 4$ ____ (c) $K + F - N = 10$

$M = 4$, $L = 3$ ____ (d)

$M = 3$, $L = 2$ ____ (e) $\therefore$ reject (c) and (d).

Possibilities are:

P	A	S	M	L	E	K, F, N	$K + F - N = 10$
1	9	8	7	6	4	2, 3, 5	NO
1	9	8	6	5	4	2, 3, 7	NO
1	9	8	3	2	4	5, 6, 7	NO

Therefore $PLANS \equiv 13924$ is a unique solution.

14. PROBABILITY

14.1   **a**   There are $C_2^n = \dfrac{n(n - 1)}{2}$ ways of choosing 2 numbers from the set $S = \{1, 2, 3, 4, \ldots\ldots, n\}$.

Since n is a multiple of 4, there are $\dfrac{n}{4}$ pairs where one number is four times the other.

$\therefore$ P [one number is four times the other] $= \dfrac{\frac{n}{4}}{\frac{n(n-1)}{2}} = \dfrac{1}{2(n - 1)}$.

b   If $n = 12$, $S = \{1, 2, 3, 4, \ldots\ldots, 12\}$ Total

multiples of 1 are   :   2, 3, 4, 5, 6, 7, 8, 9, 10, 11, 12   11

multiples of 2 are   :   4, 6, 8, 10, 12   5

multiples of 3 are   :   6, 9, 12   3

multiples of 4 are   :   8, 12   2

multiples of 5 are   :   10   1

multiples of 6 are   :   12 $\underline{1}$

                                                                  23

$\therefore$ P [one is a multiple of the other, $n = 12$] $= \dfrac{23}{C_2^{12}} = \dfrac{23}{66}$

14.2 P [randomly selected row has at least 8 seedlings]

$= P[(8S, 2S')$ or $(9S, 1S')$ or $(10S, 0S')]$

$= \binom{10}{2}\left(\frac{1}{2}\right)^8\left(\frac{1}{2}\right)^2 + \binom{10}{1}\left(\frac{1}{2}\right)^9\left(\frac{1}{2}\right)^1 + \left(\frac{1}{2}\right)^{10}$ {Binomial probabilities}

$= \frac{45+10+1}{2^{10}}$

$= \frac{7}{128}$ on simplification

$\therefore$ P [randomly chosen row has less then 8 seedlings] $= 1 - \frac{7}{128} = \frac{121}{128}$

and P [all rows have less than 8 seedlings] $= \left(\frac{121}{128}\right)^{10}$

$\therefore$ P [row with max. germination contains at least 8 seedlings]

$= P$ [at least one row has 8 or more seedlings]

$= 1 - \left(\frac{121}{128}\right)^{10}$

$\doteqdot \underline{0\cdot430}$ (to 3 s.f.)

14.3 A is the event of a family having at most one boy.

B is the event of a family having every child of the same sex.

$\therefore$ $P[A] = P[n$ girls or $(n-1)$ girls and 1 boy]

$= \left(\frac{1}{2}\right)^n + \binom{n}{1}\left(\frac{1}{2}\right)^{n-1}\frac{1}{2}$ {binomial probabilities}

$= \left(\frac{1}{2}\right)^n(1+n)$

$P[B] = P[n$ boys or n girls]

$= \left(\frac{1}{2}\right)^n + \left(\frac{1}{2}\right)^n$

$= 2\left(\frac{1}{2}\right)^n$

Now A and B independent $\therefore$ $P[A \cap B] = P[A].P[B]$

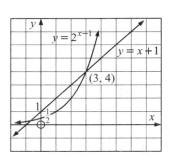

$\therefore$ $P[n$ girls$] = \left(\frac{1}{2}\right)^n(1+n).2.\left(\frac{1}{2}\right)^n$

$\therefore$ $\left(\frac{1}{2}\right)^n = 2.\left(\frac{1}{2}\right)^n(1+n).\left(\frac{1}{2}\right)^n$

$\therefore$ $2^{n-1} = n+1$

From the graph, $y = n+1$ meets $y = 2^{n-1}$ at one point, where $n = 3$, when n is a positive integer.

$\therefore$ $\underline{n = 3}$ is the only possible solution.

14.4   Let $P[A$ hits$] = 2p$,   and $P[B$ hits$] = p$.

$\therefore$ P [target is hit] $= P$ [at least one of them hits it]

$= P[A.B$ or $A.B'$ or $A'.B]$

$= 2p.p + 2p(1-p) + (1-2p).p$

$= -2p^2 + 3p$

$\therefore$ $-2p^2 + 3p = \frac{1}{2}$

$\therefore$ $4p^2 - 6p + 1 = 0$

$\therefore$ $p = \dfrac{6 \pm \sqrt{20}}{8}$ {using the quadratic formula}

$\therefore$ $2p = \dfrac{6 \pm 2\sqrt{5}}{4}$

$P[A$ hits$] = \dfrac{3 - \sqrt{5}}{2} \doteqdot \underline{0\cdot382}$ {the solution $\dfrac{3 + \sqrt{5}}{2} > 1$ and so is meaningless}

14.5 We would assume that $a \neq 1$, $b \neq 1$ i.e., we would assume that the typist would know that coefficients of 1 are not included.

    a and b can be any of the digits 2, 3, 4, 5, ..., 9

    c can be any of the digits 1, 2, 3, 4, ..., 9

    $\therefore$ total number of guesses $= 8 \cdot 8 \cdot 9 = \underline{576}$

and for a guess to yield real roots

    $\Rightarrow \quad b^2 - 4ac \geqslant 0$

    i.e., $\quad b^2 \geqslant 4ac$

    i.e., $\quad \dfrac{b^2}{4} \geqslant ac$

For $b = 2, \quad ac \leqslant 1$

       $b = 3, \quad ac \leqslant 2\frac{1}{4}$

       $b = 4, \quad ac \leqslant 4$

       $\vdots$

       $b = 9, \quad ac \leqslant 20\frac{1}{4}$

		\multicolumn{8}{c}{a values}	
	max. ac	2	3	4	5	6	7	8	9	Totals
2	1	0	0	0	0	0	0	0	0	0
3	$2\frac{1}{4}$	1	0	0	0	0	0	0	0	1
4	4	2	1	1	0	0	0	0	0	4
5	$6\frac{1}{4}$	3	2	1	1	1	0	0	0	8
6	9	4	3	2	1	1	1	1	1	14
7	$12\frac{1}{4}$	6	4	3	2	2	1	1	1	20
8	16	8	5	4	3	2	2	2	1	27
9	$20\frac{1}{4}$	9	6	5	4	3	2	2	2	33
										107

(b values in left column)

    3   values of c when $a = 5$ and $ac \leqslant 16$

The total number of possible values of c is 107   (for $a, b \; \varepsilon \{2, 3, ..., 9\}$)

    $\therefore \quad P\,[\text{real roots}] = \frac{107}{576}$

14.6 Let X arrive after x hours. $(0 \leqslant x \leqslant 1)$ after 1 p.m.,

and Y arrive after y hours. $(0 \leqslant y \leqslant 1)$

They will meet provided that $\;-\frac{1}{2} \leqslant x - y \leqslant \frac{1}{2}$.

{i.e. the difference between their arrival times is not more than $\frac{1}{2}$ hour.}

The region $\{(x, y) : -\frac{1}{2} \leqslant x - y \leqslant \frac{1}{2}\}$ is shaded, and comparing areas

    $P\,[\text{they meet}] = \dfrac{\text{shaded area}}{\text{area of square}} = \dfrac{1 - \frac{1}{4}}{1} = \dfrac{3}{4}$

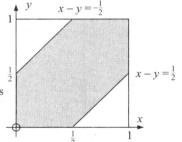

14.7 $P\,[\text{product is not a multiple of 6}]$

$= P\,[M_2{}' \cap M_3{}']$ {$M_3{}'$ is the event of "product is not a multiple of 3."}

$= P\,[M_2{}'] + P\,[M_3{}'] - P\,[M_2{}' \cup M_3{}']$

$= \left(\frac{1}{2}\right)^n + \left(\frac{2}{3}\right)^n - \left(\frac{1}{3}\right)$

> In every set of six consecutive integers,
>
> $\frac{1}{2}$ of them are not divisible by 2: form $6n + 1$, $6n + 3$, $6n + 5$
>
> $\frac{2}{3}$ of them are not divisible by 3: form $6n + 1$, $6n + 2$, $6n + 4$, $6n + 5$
>
> $\frac{1}{3}$ of them are not divisble by 2 or 3: form $6n + 1$, $6n + 5$

$\therefore \quad P\,[\text{product is a multiple of 6}] = 1 - \left[\left(\frac{1}{2}\right)^n + \left(\frac{2}{3}\right)^n - \left(\frac{1}{3}\right)^n\right] = \underline{1 - \left(\frac{1}{2}\right)^n - \left(\frac{2}{3}\right)^n + \left(\frac{1}{3}\right)^n}$

14.8 $P\,[\text{red from original bag}] = \dfrac{2r}{a+b+2r}.$

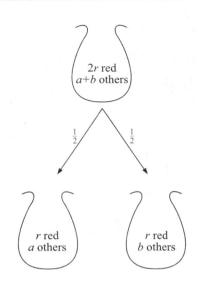

2r red
a+b others

$\frac{1}{2}$ $\frac{1}{2}$

r red
a others

r red
b others

$P\,[\text{red from (1) or red from (2) }] = \frac{1}{2}\cdot\dfrac{r}{a+r} + \frac{1}{2}\cdot\dfrac{r}{r+b}$

and we wish to show $\dfrac{r}{2(a+r)} + \dfrac{r}{2(b+r)} \geqslant \dfrac{2r}{a+b+2r}$ ......(*)

Proof: (By contradiction).   Assume the opposite   i.e.,

$$\dfrac{r}{2(a+r)} + \dfrac{r}{2(b+r)} < \dfrac{2r}{a+b+2r}$$

$$\therefore \quad \dfrac{r(b+r)+r(a+r)}{2(a+r)(b+r)} < \dfrac{2r}{a+b+2r}$$

$$\therefore \quad \dfrac{r(a+b+2r)}{2(a+r)(b+r)} < \dfrac{2r}{a+b+2r}$$

$$\therefore \quad (a+b+2r)^2 < 4(a+r)(b+r)$$

{each denominator is positive}

$$\therefore \quad a^2 + b^2 + 4r^2 + 2ab + 4ar + 4br < 4ab + 4br + 4ar + 4r^2$$

$$\therefore \quad a^2 - 2ab + b^2 < 0$$

$$\therefore \quad (a-b)^2 < 0 \quad \text{a contradiction.}$$

Hence (*) is true.   {equality occurring when $a = b$}

14.9 $P\,[\text{not picking a pair}]$

$= P\,[2r \text{ all different shoes from } 2n]$

$= \dfrac{2n}{2n}\cdot\dfrac{2n-2}{2n-1}\cdot\dfrac{2n-4}{2n-2}\cdot\dfrac{2n-6}{2n-3}\,\ldots\ldots\ldots\,\dfrac{2n-(4r-2)}{2n-(2r-1)}$

↑   ↑   ↑   ↑   ↑
1st   2nd   3rd   4th $(2r)$th

{**Explanation:**   For the 1st choice we want any of the $2n$ shoes.
For the 2nd choice we have $(2n-1)$ to choose from,
and we want $2n-2$ of them (not the first, and not to choose its partner, etc.).}

$= 2^r\cdot\dfrac{n(n-1)(n-2)(n-3)\ldots\ldots(n-2r+1)}{2n(2n-1)(2n-2)(2n-3)\ldots\ldots(2n-2r+1)}\cdot\dfrac{(2n-2r)\,!}{(2n-2r)\,!}\cdot\dfrac{(n-2r)\,!}{(n-2r)\,!}$

$= \dfrac{2^r\cdot n!\cdot(2n-2r)!}{(2n)!\cdot(n-2r)!}$

14.10 Tickets are $1, 2, 3, 4, \ldots\ldots, 2n$.

a   Let the 3 drawn numbers be x, y, z where $x < y < z$.
The possible range of values of x is $1, 2, 3, 4, \ldots\ldots, n-1$.

$$\left\{\begin{array}{l} \text{If}\ \ x = n-1,\ \ \text{then}\ \ y \geqslant n \Rightarrow\ \ z \geqslant 2n-1\ \ \therefore\ \ z = 2n-1\ \ \text{or}\ \ z = 2n.\\ \text{but if}\ \ x \geqslant n,\ \ \text{then}\ \ y \geqslant n+1 \Rightarrow 2n+1\ \ \text{which is impossible.} \end{array}\right\}$$

If $x = 1,$ y can be $2, 3, 4, 5, \ldots\ldots, 2n-1$ i.e. $2n-2$ choices for y
    $x = 2,$ y can be $3, 4, 5, 6, \ldots\ldots, 2n-2$ i.e. $2n-4$ choices for y

$\vdots$ $\vdots$

$x = n-1,$ y can be $n, n+1$ i.e. 2 choices for y

$$\therefore \quad P\left[x + y = z\right] = \frac{2 + 4 + 6 + 8 + \dots\dots + (2n - 4) + (2n - 2)}{C_3^{2n}}$$

$\{C_3^{2n} = $ total number of unrestricted ways of choosing 3 numbers from a set of $2n\}$

$$= \frac{\dfrac{n-1}{2}(2 + 2n - 2)}{\dfrac{2n(2n-1)(2n-2)}{3 \cdot 2 \cdot 1}} \qquad \diagdown \; \begin{array}{l} \text{sum of A.P. with} \quad a = 2, \\ l = 2n - 2, \quad \text{“}n\text{”} = n - 1 \end{array}$$

$$= \frac{n-1}{2}(2n)\frac{6}{2n(2n-1)(2n-2)}$$

$$= \frac{3}{2(2n-1)}$$

b P [sum of first two $=$ third] $= \frac{1}{3}P\left[x + y = z, \quad \text{in any order}\right]$

$$= \frac{1}{2(2n-1)}$$

14.11   Tickets: 1, 2, 3, 4, $\dots\dots$, $2^n = N$,   where $n > 1$, n in Z^+.

   a   For a win it is necessary to have a smaller number s such that $1 \leqslant s \leqslant \dfrac{N}{2}$.

   There are $\dfrac{N}{2}$ such numbers and hence $\dfrac{N}{2}$ possible pairs.

$$\therefore \quad P\left[\text{win}\right] = \frac{\dfrac{N}{2}}{C_2^N} \qquad \{C_2^N = \text{total unrestricted number of ways}\}$$

$$= \frac{N}{2} \cdot \frac{2}{N(N-1)}$$

$$= \frac{1}{N-1}$$

$$= \frac{1}{2^n - 1}$$

   b   For a refund we must draw number pairs $(s, 2^k \cdot s)$ where $2 \leqslant k \leqslant n$,   and $2^k \cdot s \leqslant N$

   Thus $s \leqslant \dfrac{N}{2^k}$ i.e. $s \leqslant 2^{n-k}$

$$\text{There are} \quad \overset{\overset{\displaystyle k=n}{\downarrow}}{2^0} + \overset{\overset{\displaystyle k=n-1}{\downarrow}}{2^1} + 2^2 + \dots\dots + \overset{\overset{\displaystyle k=2}{\downarrow}}{2^{n-2}} \quad \text{of these}$$

$$= \frac{2^{n-1} - 1}{2 - 1} \qquad \{\text{sum of a G.S. with} \quad a = 1, \quad r = 2, \quad \text{“}n\text{”} = n - 1\}$$

$$= 2^{n-1} - 1$$

$$= \frac{2^n - 2}{2}$$

$$\therefore \quad P\left[\text{refund}\right] = \frac{\dfrac{2^n - 2}{2}}{C_2^N}$$

$$= \frac{2^n - 2}{2} \cdot \frac{2}{2^n(2^n - 1)}$$

$$= \frac{2^n - 2}{2^n(2^n - 1)}$$

15. GEOMETRICAL CONSTRUCTIONS

15.1 Let the given angles be β and δ.

Let $\overline{AD}$ be the bisector of angle BAC having length d units.

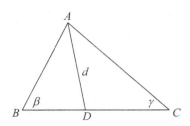

We note that $\angle BAD = \angle CAD = \dfrac{180^\circ - \beta - \delta}{2}$

$$= 90^\circ - \left(\tfrac{\beta+\delta}{2}\right)$$

Thus $\angle ADB = 180^\circ - \beta - \left[90^\circ - \left(\tfrac{\beta+\delta}{2}\right)\right]$

$$= 90^\circ - \beta + \left(\tfrac{\beta+\delta}{2}\right)$$

$$= 90^\circ + \left(\tfrac{\delta-\beta}{2}\right)$$

likewise $\angle ADC = 90^\circ + \left(\tfrac{\beta-\delta}{2}\right)$

Hence the **construction**:

(1) draw $\overline{AD}$ of length d units,

(2) construct $\triangle ACD$ on base AD such that
$$\angle CAD = 90^\circ - \left(\tfrac{\beta+\delta}{2}\right) \quad \text{and} \quad \angle ADC = 90^\circ + \left(\tfrac{\beta-\delta}{2}\right),$$

(3) likewise construct $\triangle ABD$ on base AD such that
$$\angle BAD = 90^\circ - \left(\tfrac{\beta+\delta}{2}\right) \quad \text{and} \quad \angle ADB = 90^\circ + \left(\tfrac{\delta-\beta}{2}\right),$$

(4) $\triangle ABC$ is the required triangle.

15.2 Let the circle be C.

Construction:

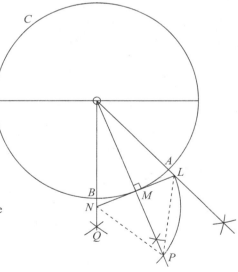

(a) Divide C into 8 equal arcs by:
    (1) finding the centre, O.
    (2) drawing a diameter through O.
    (3) successively bisecting the arcs obtained.

(b) Take one of the arcs, AB say, and construct a circle touching arc AB and touching rays $\overrightarrow{OA}, \overrightarrow{OB}$, as follows.
    (1) Find M, the midpoint of arc AB.
    (2) Draw a line perpendicular to $\overline{OM}$ at M, (and is therefore a tangent to C) cutting $\overrightarrow{OA}$ in L and $\overrightarrow{OB}$ in N.
    (3) Bisect angle LNQ and locate P where this line meets ray $\overrightarrow{OM}$.
    (4) With centre P, radius PM draw the circle.
    (P is equidistant from $\overrightarrow{OA}, \overrightarrow{OB}$ and $\overline{LN}$)

(c) Locate the other circles.

15.3 **Construction:**

(1) Inscribe a circle touching $\overline{AB}, \overline{BC}$ and passing through P.

(2) draw the tangent at P cutting $\overline{AB}$ at X, $\overline{BC}$ at Y.

Then: BXY is the required triangle of least perimeter.

Proof: If L is the perimeter, then

$$L = BX + XY + YB$$
$$= BX + (XP + PY) + YB$$
$$= BX + XM + YN + YB$$

{tangent from an external point theorem}

$$= BM + BN$$
$$= 2(BM)$$

Now draw any other line $X'PY'$ through P,

and draw a second circle touching $\overline{AB}$, $\overline{BC}$ and $\overline{X'Y'}$. Since P is outside circle 2, circle 2 has a greater diameter than circle 1.

$\therefore$ new perimeter $L' > L$ {as $BM' > BM$}
$\therefore$ L is the least perimeter.

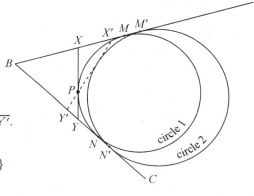

15.4   Construction:

(1)   Locate any point P on l and construct a line m' parallel to m, through P.

(2)   Draw a perpendicular between m' and m, and assume it is of length a.

(3)   Construct l' parallel to l, and a distnace a units from it.   {as shown}.

(4)   Locate X, the point of intersection of l' and m'. X is equidistant from l and m.

(5)   Locate Y, another point, by retracing steps (1) to (4) above.

(6)   The required bisector is the line $\overleftrightarrow{XY}$.

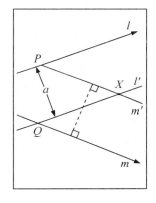

15.5   Construction:

(1)   Draw a circle, centre B, radius AB, to meet l in C and D.

(2)   Locate R, the midpoint of $\overline{AC}$.

(3)   Draw BM through R, cutting l at M. Then $\angle AMB = \angle BMC$. This is because $\overline{BR}$ is the perpendicular bisector of $\overline{AC}$ and we can easily establish the congruence of $\triangle$'s AMR, CMR.   {S.A.S.}

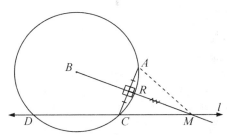

The construction is <u>not</u> always possible. It is possible only if the distance from B to l is less than AB.

15.6   Construction:

(1)   Locate A', B', the images of A, B under a reflection in l.

(2)   Locate A'', B'', by translating $|MN|$ units parallel to l.   {as shown}

Join $\overline{AB''}$ and $\overline{A''B}$ to find the positions of M and N on l.

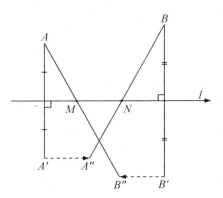

15.7   Construction:

(1)   Draw small square $WXYZ$ with Y not on $\overline{BC}$.
(2)   Produce $\overline{AY}$ to meet $\overline{BC}$ at R.
(3)   Draw $\overline{RS} \perp \overline{AC}$, $\overline{RQ} \parallel \overline{AC}$, $\overline{QP} \perp \overline{AC}$
       $PQRS$ is the required square.
       {a cunning use of enlargement}

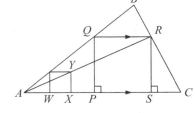

15.8   Let P' be the mirror image of P with respect to $\overline{AB}$,
and Q' be the mirror image of Q with respect to $\overline{AC}$.

Construction: Join $\overline{P'Q'}$. $\overline{P'Q'}$ meets $\overline{AB}$ in S and $\overline{AC}$ in T.
             Path $PSTQ$ is as short as possible.

Proof: The length of $PSTQ$ = length of $P'STQ'$
            and for X any point on $\overline{AB}$, Y any point on $\overline{AC}$,
            length of $P'STQ' \leqslant$ length of $P'XYQ'$
            {a constant, as P', Q' are fixed.}

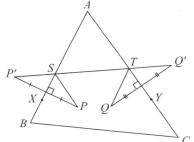

15.9   Construction:

(1)   Join $\overline{C_1 C_2}$, the line segment joining the centres.
(2)   Join $\overline{AX}$, where X is the midpoint of $\overline{C_1 C_2}$.
(3)   Draw $\overline{MAN} \perp \overline{AX}$ cutting the circles in M and N.
       The line $\overleftrightarrow{MN}$ satisfies the requirements that $MA = AN$.

Proof: Draw $\overline{C_1 R}$, $\overline{C_2 S} \perp \overline{MN}$
            Then $MR = RA$ and $AS = SN$.
            However $C_1 X = XC_2$
            and $\therefore$ $RA = AS$ {similarity}
            $\therefore$ $MR = RA = AS = SN$
            $\Rightarrow$ $MA = AN$.

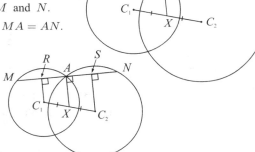

15.10 Construction:

(1)   On $\overline{DC}$ mark R such that $RD = BP$.
(2)   Find the midpoint O of $\overline{PR}$.
(3)   With centre O, radius OP draw a circle to cut $\overline{BC}$
       at Q and $\overline{AD}$ at S.
(4) $PQRS$ is the required rectangle.

Proof: $\angle PQR = \angle PSR = 90^{\varrho}$ {angles in semicircle}
            Also SQ is a diameter   {symmetry of figure}
            $\Rightarrow$ $\angle SPQ = \angle SRQ = 90^{\varrho}$
            Thus $PQRS$ is a rectangle.

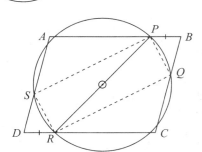

15.11 Steps:

(1)   Construct a 2×1 rectangle as shown with $\overline{A'B'}$
       on $\overline{XY}$, $A'B' = 2$ units, $A'D' = 1$ unit.
(2)   Draw XCC' as shown. From C draw $\overline{CB} \perp \overline{XY}$
       and $\overline{CD} \parallel \overline{YX}$ meeting $\overline{XZ}$ in D.
       Draw $\overline{DA} \parallel \overline{CB}$.
(3) $ABCD$ is the required rectangle.
       {it is an enlargement of $A'B'C'D'$, (centre X).}

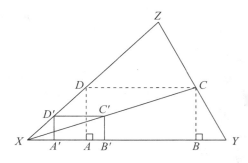

15.12 Let the required triangle be ABC, and we are given, say, AB, $\angle ABC$ and $BC + CA$.

Construction: let $l_1 = AB$, $l_2 = BC + CA$, and $\angle ABC = \theta$.

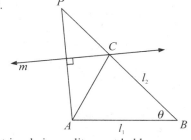

(1) Draw $\overline{AB}$ and at B construct $\angle ABC = \theta$.
(2) Draw $\overline{BP}$ of length l_2.
(3) Join $\overline{AP}$.
(4) Perpendicularly bisect $\overline{AP}$ with line m.
     C is located at the intersection of m and $\overline{PB}$.
     It is clear that $AC = CP$.
$$\therefore \quad AC + BC = CP + BC = PB = l_2$$

This construction is valid for any θ provided that $l_2 > l_1$, since the triangle inequality must hold.

15.13 $PX + PY + PZ$
$= P'X' + P'P + PZ$ {under rotations, lengths are preserved}
Thus $PX + PY + PZ$ is minimised when $X'P'PZ$ is a straight line.

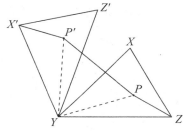

Thus our method is:
(1) Construct an equilateral $\triangle XYA$ on side $\overline{XY}$.
     Join $\overline{AZ}$.
(2) Construct an equilateral $\triangle XZB$ on $\overline{XZ}$. Join $\overline{BY}$.
(3) P is the point of intersection of $\overline{AZ}$ and $\overline{BY}$.

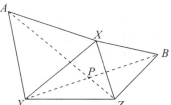

15.14 Construction:

(1) Draw any line n through P meeting l at A and m at B.
(2) Draw n' parallel to n cutting l at C, m at D.
(3) Join AD.
(4) From P draw $\overline{PR} \parallel m$, cutting $\overline{AD}$ at R, and $\overline{RS} \parallel l$, cutting $\overline{CD}$ at S.
     The required line is $\overleftrightarrow{PS}$.

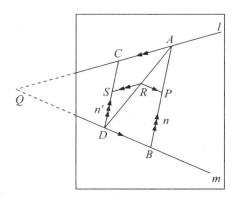

Proof: When any 3 concurrent lines are cut by two parallel lines such as $\overline{AB}$, $\overline{CD}$, we get pairs of similar $\triangle$'s with sides in proportion.

Thus $\dfrac{AP}{PB} = \dfrac{CS}{SD}$

and this ratio is correctly obtained

by our construction, as $\dfrac{AP}{PB} = \dfrac{AR}{RD} = \dfrac{CS}{SD}$.

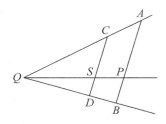

15.15 Given $\angle DAB = \theta$, say, and $AC + DB = l$, say.

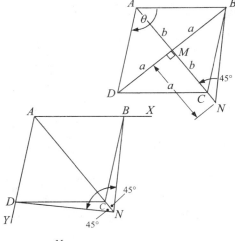

Construction:

(1) Produce $\overline{AB}$ to X and $\overline{AD}$ to Y.

(2) Bisect $\angle DAB$.

(3) $l = 2a + 2b$ $\therefore$ $a + b = \dfrac{l}{2}$ is calculated.

Locate N on the angle bisector such that

$$AN = \frac{l}{2}.$$

(4) Construct angles of 45° at N on $\overline{AN}$ and B, D are points of intersection with $\overline{AX}$ and $\overline{AY}$ respectively.

(5) Draw $\overline{BC} \parallel \overline{AY}$ cutting $\overline{AN}$ at C.

(6) Join $\overline{CD}$.

15.16 Construction:

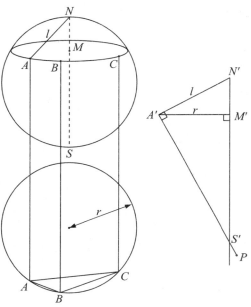

(1) With centre N on the surface of the sphere draw a circle on the surface. Let the distance from N to each point on this surface be l.

(2) Mark out 3 points A, B, C on this circle and use your "compass" to determine the distances AB, BC and CA.

(3) On your sheet of paper construct $\triangle ABC$ and construct the circumcircle of $\triangle ABC$. Let the circumcircle have radius r.
    (clearly $r < l$.)

(4) Construct on the piece of paper a right-angled triangle $N'M'A'$ with side $A'M' = r$ and $A'N' = l$.
    {This triangle is a true replica of $\triangle NMA$ inside the solid sphere.}

(5) Produce $\overleftrightarrow{N'M'}$. Construct $\angle N'A'P$ of 90°. $\overleftrightarrow{N'M'}$ and $\overleftrightarrow{A'P}$ meet at S'.

(6) $N'S' = NS$, the diameter of the sphere.

15.17 Construction:

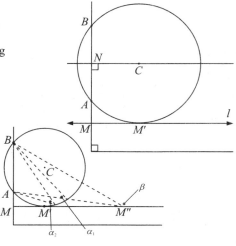

(1) Perpendicularly bisect $\overline{AB}$ at N.

(2) With radius MN, draw an arc of a circle, centre B, to cut the perpendicular bisector at C.

(3) With centre C and radius MN draw a circle passing through A, B and touching l at M'. M' is such that $\angle AM'B$ is as large as possible.

Proof:

Locate M'', where M'' lies on l but is outside the circle.

It is clear that for all positions of M''

$$\alpha_1 \geqslant \beta$$

Thus $\alpha_2 \geqslant \beta$ {as $\alpha_1 = \alpha_2$, subtended by the same arc AB}

i.e. $\beta \leqslant \alpha_2$ where β is variable and α_2 is fixed.

$\therefore$ The greatest possible value of β is α_2.

$\Rightarrow$ $\angle AM'B$ is as large as possible.

16. INEQUALITIES

16.1 To prove: $\dfrac{ax + by}{2} \leqslant \dfrac{a+b}{2} \cdot \dfrac{x+y}{2}$ for $a \geqslant b, \quad x \leqslant y$

Proof: $\dfrac{a+b}{2} \cdot \dfrac{x+y}{2} - \dfrac{ax+by}{2}$

$$= \dfrac{ax + bx + ay + by}{4} - \dfrac{2ax + 2by}{4}$$

$$= \dfrac{bx + ay - ax - by}{4}$$

$$= \dfrac{(a-b)(y-x)}{4}$$

$$\geqslant 0 \quad as \quad a - b \geqslant 0 \quad \text{and} \quad y - x \geqslant 0.$$

Thus $\dfrac{ax+by}{2} \leqslant \dfrac{a+b}{2} \cdot \dfrac{x+y}{2}$

16.2 $\dfrac{a}{b} < \dfrac{c}{d}$ for a, b, c, d positive $\Rightarrow \quad ad < bc$ or $bc - ad > 0 \ldots\ldots (1)$

Now $\dfrac{a+c}{b+d} - \dfrac{a}{b} = \dfrac{b(a+c) - a(b+d)}{(b+d) \cdot b}$

$$= \dfrac{bc - ad}{(b+d)b}$$

$$> 0 \quad \text{from (1) as} \quad b + d > 0, \quad b > 0.$$

Also $\dfrac{c}{d} - \dfrac{a+c}{b+d} = \dfrac{(b+d)c - d(a+c)}{d(b+d)}$

$$= \dfrac{bc - ad}{d(b+d)}$$

$$> 0 \quad \text{from (1), also.}$$

Thus $\dfrac{a+c}{b+d} > \dfrac{a}{b}$ and $\dfrac{c}{d} > \dfrac{a+c}{b+d}$

$$\Rightarrow \quad \dfrac{a}{b} < \dfrac{a+c}{b+d} < \dfrac{c}{d}$$

16.3 $\dfrac{a^3 + b^3}{2} - \left(\dfrac{a+b}{2}\right)^3$

$$= \dfrac{a^3 + b^3}{2} - \dfrac{a^3 + 3a^2 b + 3ab^2 + b^3}{8}$$

$$= \dfrac{4a^3 + 4b^3 - a^3 - 3a^2 b - 3ab^2 - b^3}{8}$$

$$= \dfrac{3a^3 + 3b^3 - 3a^2 b - 3ab^2}{8}$$

$$= \tfrac{3}{8}[a^3 + b^3 - a^2 b - ab^2]$$

$$= \tfrac{3}{8}[a^2(a - b) - b^2(a - b)]$$

$$= \tfrac{3}{8}(a^2 - b^2)(a - b)$$

$$= \tfrac{3}{8}(a - b)^2(a + b) \geqslant 0, \quad \text{as} \quad (a-b)^2 \geqslant 0 \quad \text{and} \quad a + b > 0.$$

Thus $\dfrac{a^3 + b^3}{2} \geqslant \left(\dfrac{a+b}{2}\right)^3$

16.4 **a** Since $(\sqrt{x} - \sqrt{y})^2 \geqslant 0$, for $x > 0$, $y > 0$
$\{x > 0, \quad y > 0 \text{ ensure that } \sqrt{x}, \sqrt{y} \text{ have meaning.}\}$
$\therefore \quad x - 2\sqrt{xy} + y \geqslant 0 \quad \text{for} \quad x > 0, \quad y > 0.$
$\therefore \quad x + y \geqslant 2\sqrt{xy}$
$\therefore \quad \dfrac{x + y}{2} \geqslant \sqrt{xy}$

b Thus for positive x and y, $x + y \geqslant 2\sqrt{xy}$
$\therefore \quad a + b \geqslant 2\sqrt{ab}, \quad b + c \geqslant 2\sqrt{bc}, \quad c + a \geqslant 2\sqrt{ca}$
hence $(a + b)(b + c)(c + a) \geqslant 2\sqrt{ab} \cdot 2\sqrt{bc} \cdot 2\sqrt{ca}$
i.e., $\underline{(a + b)(b + c)(c + a) \geqslant 8abc}.$

16.5 Now $a + b > c$, $b + c > a$, and $c + a > b$. {Triangle inequality}
$\therefore \quad a + b - c > 0, \quad b + c - a > 0, \quad c + a - b > 0$
and $(a + b - c)(b + c - a)(c + a - b) > 0.$
Thus $(ab + b^2 - bc + ac + bc - c^2 - a^2 - ab + ac)(c + a - b) > 0$
i.e., $(b^2 - c^2 - a^2 + 2ac)(c + a - b) > 0$
Thus $b^2c - c^3 - a^2c + 2ac^2 + ab^2 - ac^2 - a^3 + 2a^2c - b^3 + bc^2 + a^2b - 2abc > 0$
i.e., $-a^3 - b^3 - c^3 + [a^2b + ab^2 + b^2c + a^2c + ac^2] - 2abc > 0 \dots\dots(1)$

Now $a(b - c)^2 + b(c - a)^2 + c(a - b)^2 + 4abc$
$= a(b^2 - 2bc + c^2) + b(c^2 - 2ac + a^2) + c(a^2 - 2ab + b^2) + 4abc$
$= ab^2 - 2abc + ac^2 + bc^2 - 2abc + a^2b + a^2c - 2abc + b^2c + 4abc$
$= [ab^2 + a^2b + ac^2 + a^2c + bc^2 + b^2c] - 2abc$
$> \underline{a^3 + b^3 + c^3} \qquad \text{\{from (1)\}}$

16.6 Let $AD = BC = x$ cm.
Since Δ's RAD and CBT are right-angled isosceles,
then $RA = BT = x$, also.
But $RT = 10\sqrt{2}$ cm {Pythagoras in ΔRST}
$\therefore \quad AB = 10\sqrt{2} - 2x$ cm.
Thus area $ABCD$, $A = x(10\sqrt{2} - 2x) = -2x^2 + 10\sqrt{2}\,x$,
a quadratic in x.
Thus $A = -2(x^2 - 5\sqrt{2}\,x)$

$\therefore \quad A = -2\left(x^2 - 5\sqrt{2}\,x + \left(\tfrac{5\sqrt{2}}{2}\right)^2\right) + 2 \cdot \left(\tfrac{5\sqrt{2}}{2}\right)^2 \qquad \text{\{completing the square\}}$

$\therefore \quad A = -2\left(x - \tfrac{5\sqrt{2}}{2}\right)^2 + 25$

$\therefore \quad A \leqslant 25$ with equality occurring when $x = \tfrac{5\sqrt{2}}{2}$ $\left\{-2\left(x - \tfrac{5\sqrt{2}}{2}\right)^2 \text{ is always } \leqslant 0\right\}$

$\therefore$ maximum area is 25 cm^2 occurring when $\underline{A \text{ is } \tfrac{5\sqrt{2}}{2} \text{ cm from } R.}$

16.7 Consider $(1 + a)(1 + b)(1 + c) - (1 + s)$
$= (1 + a + b + ab)(1 + c) - 1 - s$
$= 1 + a + b + ab + c + ac + bc + abc - 1 - a - b - c$
$= ab + ac + bc + abc$
$> 0 \quad \text{as} \quad a, b, c \quad \text{are} > 0$
Thus $(1 + a)(1 + b)(1 + c) > 1 + s \qquad \text{or} \quad 1 + s < (1 + a)(1 + b)(1 + c) \dots\dots (1)$

Now consider $\quad (1+a)(1+b)(1+c)(1-s)$

$$= (1+a+b+c+ab+bc+ac+abc)(1-a-b-c)$$
$$= 1+a+b+c+ab+bc+ac+abc$$
$$-a-a^2-ab-ac-a^2b-abc-a^2c-a^2bc$$
$$-b-ab-b^2-bc-ab^2-b^2c-abc-ab^2c$$
$$-c-ac-bc-c^2-abc-bc^2-ac^2-abc^2$$
$$= 1-a^2-ac-a^2b \dots \dots \text{ etc.}$$
$$= 1- \text{ (a collection of positive terms)}$$

$\therefore \quad (1+a)(1+b)(1+c)(1-s) < 1$

and since $\quad 1-s > 0 \quad$ then $\quad (1+a)(1+b)(1+c) < \dfrac{1}{1-s} \dots \dots (2)$

Combining (1) and (2) gives the required result.

16.8 Suppose $\quad \dfrac{a}{b}+\dfrac{b}{c}+\dfrac{c}{a} > \frac{1}{2}\left(a^2+b^2+c^2+\dfrac{1}{a^2}+\dfrac{1}{b^2}+\dfrac{1}{c^2}\right)$

$\therefore \quad \dfrac{2a}{b}+\dfrac{2b}{c}+\dfrac{2c}{a} > a^2+b^2+c^2+\dfrac{1}{a^2}+\dfrac{1}{b^2}+\dfrac{1}{c^2}$

$\therefore \quad 0 > \left(a^2-\dfrac{2a}{b}+\dfrac{1}{b^2}\right)+\left(b^2-\dfrac{2b}{c}+\dfrac{1}{c^2}\right)+\left(c^2-\dfrac{2c}{a}+\dfrac{1}{a^2}\right)$

$\therefore \quad \left(a-\dfrac{1}{b}\right)^2+\left(b-\dfrac{1}{c}\right)^2+\left(c-\dfrac{1}{a}\right)^2 < 0,$

which is false as each perfect square is $\geqslant 0$.

$\therefore \quad$ supposition is false, and its opposite,

$$\underline{\dfrac{a}{b}+\dfrac{b}{c}+\dfrac{c}{a} \leqslant \frac{1}{2}\left(a^2+b^2+c^2+\dfrac{1}{a^2}+\dfrac{1}{b^2}+\dfrac{1}{c^2}\right)} \quad \text{is true.}$$

Equality occurs when $\quad a-\dfrac{1}{b}=b-\dfrac{1}{c}=c-\dfrac{1}{a}=0.$

i.e., $\quad ab=bc=ca=1.$

i.e., $\quad \underline{a=b=c=1}.$

16.9 $\quad \dfrac{x^4-1}{4}-\dfrac{x^3-1}{3}=\dfrac{3(x^4-1)-4(x^3-1)}{12}$

$$= \dfrac{3(x^2+1)(x+1)(x-1)-4(x-1)(x^2+x+1)}{12}$$

$$= \dfrac{(x-1)}{12}\left[3(x^3+x^2+x+1)-4(x^2+x+1)\right]$$

$$= \dfrac{(x-1)}{12}\left[3x^3-x^2-x-1\right]$$

$$= \dfrac{(x-1)}{12}(x-1)(3x^2+2x+1)$$

$$= \dfrac{(x-1)^2}{12}\cdot(3x^2+2x+1) \quad \text{where the quadratic has } \text{``}a\text{''} > 0$$
$$\text{and} \quad \Delta = b^2-4ac = -8 < 0$$

$\therefore \quad$ the quadratic is positive for all x.

and since $\quad (x-1)^2 \geqslant 0 \quad$ for all x,

then $\quad \dfrac{x^4-1}{4}-\dfrac{x^3-1}{3} \geqslant 0 \quad$ for all x

i.e., $\quad \underline{\dfrac{x^3-1}{3} \leqslant \dfrac{x^4-1}{4}} \quad$ for all x.

16.10   Using $\dfrac{x+y}{2} \geqslant \sqrt{xy}$ for positives x and y

then $(x+y)^2 \geqslant 4xy$
Now if $x = a+c$ and $y = b+d$
we have $s = a+b+c+d = x+y$

$\therefore \quad s^2 \geqslant 4(a+c)(b+d)$

i.e., $\quad s^2 \geqslant 4(ab+bc+cd+da)$ where da is positive.

$\therefore \quad s^2 > 4(ab+bc+cd)$

i.e., $\quad (ab+bc+cd) < \dfrac{s^2}{4}.$

16.11   We have $w_1 + w_2 + w_3 + \ldots\ldots + w_n = 1$

Now we suppose that none of the w_k is heavier than $\dfrac{1}{2^k}$ kg,   i.e. $w_k \leqslant \dfrac{1}{2^k}$

Then $w_1 + w_2 + w_3 + \ldots\ldots + w_n \leqslant \frac{1}{2} + \frac{1}{4} + \frac{1}{8} + \ldots\ldots + \dfrac{1}{2^k}$

i.e. $\leqslant \dfrac{\frac{1}{2}\left(1 - \left(\frac{1}{2}\right)^n\right)}{1 - \frac{1}{2}}$ {sum of Geom Sequence formula with $\quad a = \frac{1}{2}, \quad r = \frac{1}{2}, \quad$ "n" $= n$}

i.e. $\leqslant 1 - \left(\frac{1}{2}\right)^n$

$< 1,$ which is a contradiction, and

$\therefore \quad$ the supposition is false.

16.12   In each round $a+b+c$ points are awarded, and since the players earned 39 points in all,

then the number of rounds was $\dfrac{39}{a+b+c}.$

Since there was more than one round, $\dfrac{39}{a+b+c} \geqslant 2$ i.e., $\quad a+b+c \leqslant 19\frac{1}{2} \ldots\ldots$ (1)

and as $a > b > c,$ where a, b and c are unequal positive integers,
then $a+b+c \geqslant 6 \ldots\ldots$ (2).

Thus $a+b+c = 13$ {$a+b+c$ must be a factor of 39}
and there were 3 rounds.

Since Bill won the second and he got at least c points in the other two rounds, his total score
is at least $a+2c$ i.e. $10 \geqslant a+2c$

$\therefore \quad a \leqslant 10 - 2c \ldots\ldots$ (3)

The best that Anne could have done was $2a+b$ i.e. $2a+b \geqslant 20$

$\Rightarrow \quad 2a+b \geqslant a+b+c+7$
{as $a+b+c = 13$}
$\Rightarrow \quad a \geqslant c+7 \ldots\ldots$ (4)

Since $c \geqslant 1,$ from (3) $a \leqslant 8$ and from (4) $a \geqslant 8.$ Thus $\underline{a = 8},$

but since $a \geqslant c+7,$ $c \leqslant a-7$ i.e., $c \leqslant 1$ $\therefore$ $\underline{c = 1}$ and $\underline{b = 4}.$

Hence,

	Anne	Bill	Claire
1st round	8	1	4
2nd round	4	(8)	1
3rd round	8	1	4
Total	20	10	9

As Bill scored 8 for round 2, he must score 1 in each of the other two rounds. Claire could not have won any round. $\therefore$ Anne won 1st and 3rd. Hence we can complete the table.

Thus Anne won the first round and Claire scored 4 points in the 3rd round.

16.13   Consider $N = 3(x^2 + y^2 + z^2) - 2(xy + yz + zx) - 3$
$$= 3x^2 + 3y^2 + 3z^2 - 2xy - 2yz - 2zx - 3$$
$$= x^2 + y^2 + z^2 + [2x^2 + 2y^2 + 2z^2 - 2xy - 2yz - 2zx] - 3$$
$$= x^2 + y^2 + z^2 + (x - y)^2 + (y - z)^2 + (z - x)^2 - 3$$

Consider these cases:

(a)   None of x, y, z is zero.

In this case $x^2 + y^2 + z^2 \geqslant 3$ and $(x - y)^2 + (y - z)^2 + (z - x)^2 \geqslant 0$.
{equality obtained when $x = y = z = \pm 1$}

and $\therefore$ $N \geqslant 3 + 0 - 3$
i.e. $N \geqslant 0 ...... (1)$

(b)   One of x, y, z is 0.

In this case $x^2 + y^2 + z^2 \geqslant 2$ and $(x - y)^2 + (y - z)^2 + (z - x)^2 \geqslant 2$.
{when x, say, is 0, $y = z = \pm 1$}

$\therefore$ $N \geqslant 2 + 2 - 3$
i.e. $N \geqslant 1 ...... (2)$

(c)   Two of $x, y,$ and z are 0.

In this case $x^2 + y^2 + z^2 \geqslant 1$ and $(x - y)^2 + (y - z)^2 + (z - x)^2 \geqslant 2$
{when say, $x = y = 0,$ $z = \pm 1$}

$\therefore$ $N \geqslant 1 + 2 - 3$
i.e. $N \geqslant 0 ...... (3)$

Thus overall, $N \geqslant 0,$ hence $\underline{3(x^2 + y^2 + z^2) - 2(xy + yz + zx) \geqslant 3}.$

16.14   **a** $f(x) = (ax - d)^2 + (cx - b)^2$
$$= a^2 x^2 - 2adx + d^2 + c^2 x^2 - 2bcx + b^2$$
$$= [a^2 + c^2]x^2 - 2[ad + bc]x + [d^2 + b^2],$$
a quadratic function in x which is never negative.

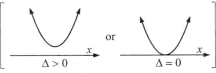

or

$\Delta > 0$ $\Delta = 0$

Thus $\Delta = B^2 - 4AC \leqslant 0$
$\therefore$ $4[ad + bc]^2 - 4[a^2 + c^2][d^2 + b^2] \leqslant 0$
$\therefore$ $[ad + bc]^2 \leqslant [a^2 + c^2][d^2 + b^2]$
$\therefore$ $\sqrt{[ad + bc]^2} \leqslant \sqrt{a^2 + c^2} . \sqrt{d^2 + b^2}$
$\therefore$ $|ad + bc| \leqslant \sqrt{a^2 + c^2} . \sqrt{d^2 + b^2}$ {$\sqrt{x^2} = |x|$}

b   **i**   It is sufficient to prove: area $\triangle AXD =$ area $\triangle CXB$.

Now $\dfrac{AC}{AX} = \dfrac{BD}{BX}$ {$\triangle$'s CAX, DBX are similar}

$\therefore$ $AX . BD = BX . AC$
$\therefore$ $\frac{1}{2}AX . BD = \frac{1}{2}BX . AC$
$\therefore$ area $\triangle AXD =$ area $\triangle CXB$
$= $ Area $\triangle OAD +$ Area $\triangle OBC$
$= $ Area $\triangle OAD +$ (Area $\triangle OCX +$ Area $\triangle CXB$)
$= $ Area $\triangle OAD +$ Area $\triangle OCX +$ Area $\triangle AXB$
$= $ Area $\triangle OCD$.

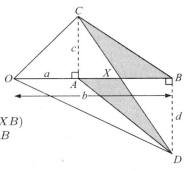

ii   Let $\angle COD = \theta$.

Now $OC = \sqrt{a^2 + c^2}$ and $OD = \sqrt{b^2 + d^2}$ {Pythagoras}

$\therefore$ area $\triangle OCD = \frac{1}{2}\sqrt{a^2 + c^2} . \sqrt{b^2 + d^2} \sin \theta$

$\therefore$ area $\triangle OCD \leqslant \frac{1}{2}\sqrt{a^2 + c^2} \cdot \sqrt{b^2 + d^2}$ ...... (1)

$\{\sin\theta$ has maximum value 1, when $\theta = 90^\circ\}$

Now   Area $\triangle OCD =$ Area $\triangle AOD +$ Area $\triangle OBC$

i.e.,   Area $\triangle OCD = \frac{1}{2}ad + \frac{1}{2}bc$ ...... (2)

Thus $\frac{1}{2}ad + \frac{1}{2}bc \leqslant \frac{1}{2}\sqrt{a^2 + c^2} \cdot \sqrt{b^2 + d^2}$ {from (1) and (2)}

$\Rightarrow$ $ad + bc \leqslant \sqrt{a^2 + b^2} \cdot \sqrt{b^2 + d^2}$

16.15

n	$(n+1)^n$	n^{n+1}
1	2	1
2	9	8
3	64	81
4	625	1024
5	$\vdots$	$\vdots$

It appears from the table of values that

$(n+1)^n > n^{n+1}$ for $n = 1$ and 2   only.

i.e.,   <u>for $n \geqslant 3$, $(n+1)^n < n^{n+1}$</u>;   proposition $P(n)$

Proof: (By Induction on n)

(1)   From the table the statement is true for $n = 3$.

(2)   If the statement is true for $n = k$,

then $(k+1)^k < k^{k+1}$ i.e. $\dfrac{(k+1)^k}{k^{k+1}} < 1$

Hence $\dfrac{(k+2)^{k+1}}{(k+1)^{k+2}} < \dfrac{(k+2)^{k+1}}{(k+1)^{k+2}} \cdot \dfrac{k^{k+1}}{(k+1)^k}$ $\left\{ \text{as} \quad \dfrac{k^{k+1}}{(k+1)^k} > 1 \right\}$

$\therefore$ $\dfrac{(k+2)^{k+1}}{(k+1)^{k+2}} < \dfrac{(k^2 + 2k)^{k+1}}{(k+1)^{2k+2}}$

$\therefore$ $\dfrac{(k+2)^{k+1}}{(k+1)^{k+2}} < \left(\dfrac{k^2 + 2k}{k^2 + 2k + 1} \right)^{k+1}$

$\therefore$ $\dfrac{(k+2)^{k+1}}{(k+1)^{k+2}} < 1$ $\left\{ \text{as} \quad \dfrac{k^2 + 2k}{k^2 + 2k + 1} < 1, \quad k \text{ in } Z^+ \right\}$

Thus $P(k+1)$ is true whenever $P(k)$ is true. $\Rightarrow$ <u>$P(n)$ is true for all $n \geqslant 3$.</u>

16.16   For two positives a and b, $\left(\sqrt{\dfrac{a}{b}} - \sqrt{\dfrac{b}{a}} \right)^2 \geqslant 0$

$\therefore$ $\dfrac{a}{b} - 2\sqrt{\dfrac{a}{b}} \cdot \sqrt{\dfrac{b}{a}} + \dfrac{b}{a} \geqslant 0$

$\therefore$ $\dfrac{a}{b} + \dfrac{b}{a} \geqslant 2\sqrt{\dfrac{a}{b} \cdot \dfrac{b}{a}} = 2$ ...... (1)

Now consider $(x + y + z)\left(\dfrac{1}{x} + \dfrac{1}{y} + \dfrac{1}{z} \right)$

$= 1 + \dfrac{y}{x} + \dfrac{z}{x} + \dfrac{x}{y} + 1 + \dfrac{z}{y} + \dfrac{x}{z} + \dfrac{y}{z} + 1$

$= 3 + \left(\dfrac{y}{x} + \dfrac{x}{y} \right) + \left(\dfrac{x}{z} + \dfrac{z}{x} \right) + \left(\dfrac{y}{z} + \dfrac{z}{y} \right)$

$\geqslant 3 + 2 + 2 + 2$ {using (1)}

i.e. $(x + y + z)\left(\dfrac{1}{x} + \dfrac{1}{y} + \dfrac{1}{z} \right) \geqslant 9$

But $x + y + z = 1$, $\therefore$ <u>$\dfrac{1}{x} + \dfrac{1}{y} + \dfrac{1}{z} \geqslant 9$.</u>

16.17 Use $\dfrac{x+y}{2} \geqslant \sqrt{xy}$ for all positives x and y {the arith-geom means inequality}

If $x = \dfrac{a+b}{2}$ and $y = \dfrac{c+d}{2}$ (i.e. $x > 0, \quad y > 0$)

then $\dfrac{\dfrac{a+b}{2} + \dfrac{c+d}{2}}{2} \geqslant \sqrt{\dfrac{a+b}{2}} \cdot \sqrt{\dfrac{c+d}{2}}$

$\therefore \quad \dfrac{a+b+c+d}{4} \geqslant \sqrt{\dfrac{ac+bc+ad+bd}{4}}$

$\therefore \quad \dfrac{(a+b+c+d)^2}{16} \geqslant \dfrac{ac+bc+ad+bd}{4}$

$\therefore \quad 4(ac+bc+ad+bd) \leqslant (a+b+c+d)^2.$

16.18 $0 < a \leqslant b \leqslant c \leqslant d \leqslant e$ and $a+b+c+d+e = abcde$

Observe that $a+b+c+d+e \leqslant 5e$

$\therefore \quad abcde \leqslant 5e$

$\therefore \quad abcd \leqslant 5$

$\therefore$ only possibilities are:

a	b	c	d	
1	1	1	1	(1)
1	1	1	2	(2)
1	1	1	3	(3)
1	1	1	4	(4)
1	1	1	5	(5)
1	1	2	2	(6)

Case (1) $4 + e = e \quad \Rightarrow \quad 4 = 0$ which is absurd $\therefore$ reject.

Case (2) $5 + e = 2e \quad \Rightarrow \quad e = 5 \quad \checkmark$

Case (3) $6 + e = 3e \quad \Rightarrow \quad e = 3 \quad \checkmark$

Case (4) $7 + e = 4e \quad \Rightarrow \quad e = \frac{7}{3}$ reject as e is an integer.

Case (5) $8 + e = 5e \quad \Rightarrow \quad e = 2$ reject as $e \geqslant d.$

Case (6) $6 + e = 4e \quad \Rightarrow \quad e = 2 \quad \checkmark$

$\therefore$ solutions: $\underline{(1,\,1,\,1,\,2,\,5)\,; \quad (1,\,1,\,1,\,3,\,3)\,; \quad (1,\,1,\,2,\,2,\,2).}$

16.19 This inequality can be established by various means including

(1) Mathematical Induction

(2) The arithmetic-geometric mean inequality for n positives.

However, we must use the inequality $\dfrac{x+y}{2} \geqslant \sqrt{xy},$ for $x > 0, \quad y > 0.$

Proof   When $\underline{n \text{ is even}},$ $n! = [1 \cdot n] \cdot [2 \cdot (n-1)] \cdot [3(n-2)] \cdot \dots\dots \left[\dfrac{n}{2} \left(\dfrac{n}{2} + 1 \right) \right]$

but $\sqrt{xy} \leqslant \dfrac{x+y}{2} \quad \Rightarrow \quad xy \leqslant \left(\dfrac{x+y}{2} \right)^2, \quad x > 0, \quad y > 0.$

$\therefore \quad n! \leqslant \underbrace{\left(\dfrac{n+1}{2} \right)^2 \cdot \left(\dfrac{n+1}{2} \right)^2 \dots\dots \left(\dfrac{n+1}{2} \right)^2}_{\frac{n}{2} \text{ of these}}$

$\therefore \quad n! \leqslant \left(\dfrac{n+1}{2} \right)^{2 \cdot \frac{n}{2}}$

$\therefore \quad \underline{n! \leqslant \left(\dfrac{n+1}{2} \right)^n}$

When n is odd,

$$n! = [1 \cdot n] \cdot [2(n-1)] \cdot 3[(n-2)] \cdots \cdots \left[\left(\frac{n-1}{2}\right)\left(\frac{n+3}{2}\right)\right] \cdot \left(\frac{n+1}{2}\right)$$

$$\therefore \quad n! \leqslant \left(\frac{n+1}{2}\right)^2 \cdot \left(\frac{n+1}{2}\right)^2 \cdot \left(\frac{n+1}{2}\right)^2 \cdots \cdots \underbrace{\left(\frac{n+1}{2}\right)^2} \cdot \left(\frac{n+1}{2}\right)$$

$$\frac{n-1}{2} \text{ of these}$$

$$\therefore \quad n! \leqslant \left(\frac{n+1}{2}\right)^{2 \cdot \frac{n-1}{2}} \cdot \left(\frac{n+1}{2}\right)$$

$$\therefore \quad \underline{n! \leqslant \left(\frac{n+1}{2}\right)^n}.$$

16.20 $\quad 2^{\frac{1}{2}n(n-1)} = 2^{1+2+3+4+\cdots\cdots+(n-1)} \qquad \left\{1+2+3+4+\cdots\cdots+n = \frac{n(n+1)}{2}\right\}$

$$= 2^1 \cdot 2^2 \cdot 2^3 \cdot 2^4 \cdots\cdots 2^{n-1}$$

But $\quad 2^{n-1} > n \quad$ for all n in Z^+

$\{$as $\quad 2^{n-1} = (1+1)^{n-1} = \binom{n-1}{0} + \binom{n-1}{1} + \binom{n-1}{2} + \cdots\cdots + \binom{n-1}{n-1}$

where each combination is positive.$\}$

$$\therefore \quad 2^{n-1} > \binom{n-1}{0} + \binom{n-1}{1} = 1 + n - 1 = n$$

$$\therefore \quad 2^{\frac{1}{2}n(n-1)} > 1 \cdot 2 \cdot 3 \cdot 4 \cdots\cdots n$$

i.e. $\quad 2^{\frac{1}{2}n(n-1)} > n!$

16.21 Suppose both of $\quad x_1{}^2 + b_1 x + c_1 = 0, \quad x_2{}^2 + b_2 x + c_2 = 0 \quad$ have unreal roots.

$\Rightarrow \quad b_1{}^2 - 4c_1 < 0 \quad$ and $\quad b_2{}^2 - 4c_2 < 0$

$\Rightarrow \quad b_1{}^2 < 4c_1 \quad$ and $\quad b_2{}^2 < 4c_2$

$\Rightarrow \quad 2(c_1 + c_2) > \dfrac{b_1{}^2}{2} + \dfrac{b_2{}^2}{2}$

$\Rightarrow \quad b_1 b_2 > \dfrac{b_1{}^2}{2} + \dfrac{b_2{}^2}{2}$

$\Rightarrow \quad 2b_1 b_2 > b_1{}^2 + b_2{}^2 \qquad \{$and $\therefore \quad b_1{}^2 - 2b_1 b_2 + b_2{}^2 < 0\}$

$\Rightarrow \quad (b_1 - b_2)^2 < 0 \quad$ which is false.

$\therefore \quad$ the supposition is false.

and $\therefore \quad$ at least one of the equations has two real roots.

16.22 $\qquad (a+b+c)^2 = a^2 + b^2 + c^2 + 2(ab + bc + ca)$

$\therefore \quad 2(ab + bc + ca) = (a+b+c)^2 - (a^2 + b^2 + c^2)$

$\therefore \quad 2(ab + bc + ca) = (a+b+c)^2 - 1$

$\therefore \quad ab + bc + ca = -\frac{1}{2} + \dfrac{(a+b+c)^2}{2}$

$\therefore \quad ab + bc + ca \geqslant -\frac{1}{2} \cdots\cdots (1) \qquad$ as $\quad \dfrac{(a+b+c)^2}{2} \geqslant 0 \quad$ for all $\quad a, b, c.$

Now $\quad (a-b)^2 + (b-c)^2 + (c-a)^2 \geqslant 0 \quad$ for all $\quad a, b, c.$

$\therefore \quad a^2 - 2ab + b^2 + b^2 - 2bc + c^2 + c^2 - 2ca + a^2 \geqslant 0$

$\therefore \quad 2(a^2 + b^2 + c^2) \geqslant 2(ab + bc + ca)$

$\therefore \quad ab + bc + ca \leqslant a^2 + b^2 + c^2$

$\therefore \quad ab + bc + ca \leqslant 1 \ldots\ldots (2)$

Combining (1) and (2) we get $-\frac{1}{2} \leqslant ab + bc + ca \leqslant 1.$

16.23 Proposition: "for $n \geqslant 2$, $a_1 a_2 a_3 \ldots\ldots a_n > a_1 + a_2 + a_3 + \ldots\ldots + a_n + 1 - n$".

Proof: (By the Principal of Mathematical Induction)

(1)   If $\underline{n = 2}$,   If $a_1 > 1$ and $a_2 > 1$

then $a_1 - 1 > 0$ and $a_2 - 1 > 0$

$\therefore \quad (a_1 - 1)(a_2 - 1) > 0$

$\therefore \quad a_1 a_2 - a_2 - a_1 + 1 > 0$

$\therefore \quad a_1 a_2 > a_1 + a_2 - 1$

i.e., $a_1 a_2 > a_1 + a_2 + 1 - 2$ and so $\therefore \quad P(2)$ is true.

(2)   If $P(k)$ is true, then

$$a_1 a_2 a_3 \ldots\ldots a_k > a_1 + a_2 + a_3 + \ldots\ldots + a_k + 1 - k \ldots\ldots(*) P(2)$$

Thus $a_1 a_2 a_3 \ldots\ldots a_k \cdot a_{k+1}$

$> (a_1 a_2 a_3 \ldots\ldots a_k) + a_{k+1} + 1 - 2$ {using case $n = 2$}

i.e., $> a_1 + a_2 + a_3 + \ldots\ldots + a_k + 1 - k + a_{k+1} + 1 - 2$ {using $*$}

i.e., $> a_1 + a_2 + a_3 + \ldots\ldots + a_k + a_{k+1} - k$

i.e., $> a_1 + a_2 + a_3 + \ldots\ldots + a_k + a_{k+1} + 1 - (k + 1)$

Thus $P(k + 1)$ is true whenever $P(k)$ is true, and as $P(2)$ is true.

$\therefore \quad \underline{P(n) \text{ is true.}}$ {P. of M.I.}

16.24   Letting $b + c = x$, $c + a = y$, $a + b = z$,

$x + y = a + b + 2c = z + 2c$

$\therefore \quad c = \dfrac{x + y - z}{2}$,   likewise $a = \dfrac{y + z - x}{2}$, $b = \dfrac{z + x - y}{2}$.

Thus, $\dfrac{a}{b + c} + \dfrac{b}{c + a} + \dfrac{c}{a + b}$

$= \dfrac{y + z - x}{2x} + \dfrac{z + x - y}{2y} + \dfrac{x + y - z}{2z}$

$= \frac{1}{2}\left(\dfrac{y}{x} + \dfrac{z}{x} - 1 + \dfrac{z}{y} + \dfrac{x}{y} - 1 + \dfrac{x}{z} + \dfrac{y}{z} - 1 \right)$

$\geqslant \frac{1}{2}(2 - 1 + 2 - 1 + 2 - 1) \geqslant \frac{3}{2}$ $\left\{ \dfrac{a}{b} + \dfrac{b}{a} \geqslant 2 \text{ for all } a > 0, \ b > 0 \right\}$

16.25 Now $\dfrac{a^2 + b^2}{2c} + \dfrac{b^2 + c^2}{2a} + \dfrac{c^2 + a^2}{2b}$

$\geqslant \dfrac{2ab}{2c} + \dfrac{2bc}{2a} + \dfrac{2ac}{2b}$ $\{(x - y)^2 \geqslant 0 \quad \Rightarrow \quad x^2 + y^2 \geqslant 2xy\}$

i.e. $\geqslant \dfrac{ab}{c} + \dfrac{bc}{a} + \dfrac{ac}{b}$

i.e. $\geqslant \dfrac{a^2 b^2 + b^2 c^2 + a^2 c^2}{abc}$

But $a^2(b - c)^2 + b^2(c - a)^2 + c^2(a - b)^2 \geqslant 0$

$\therefore \quad a^2(b^2 - 2bc + c^2) + b^2(c^2 - 2ca + a^2) + c^2(a^2 - 2ab + b^2) \geqslant 0$

$$\therefore \quad 2a^2b^2 + 2b^2c^2 + 2c^2a^2 \geqslant 2a^2bc + 2ab^2c + 2abc^2$$

$$\therefore \quad a^2b^2 + b^2c^2 + c^2a^2 \geqslant abc(a + b + c)$$

$$\therefore \quad \frac{a^2b^2 + b^2c^2 + c^2a^2}{abc} \geqslant a + b + c \quad ....(2)$$

Hence $\quad \dfrac{a^2 + b^2}{2c} + \dfrac{b^2 + c^2}{2a} + \dfrac{c^2 + a^2}{2b} \geqslant a + b + c. \quad$ {using (1) and (2)}

16.26 Since $\quad (x - y)^2 + (y - z)^2 + (z - x)^2 + x^2 + y^2 + z^2 \geqslant 0,$

then $\quad x^2 - 2xy + y^2 + y^2 - 2yz + z^2 + z^2 - 2zx + x^2 + x^2 + y^2 + z^2 \geqslant 0$

$$\therefore \quad 3x^2 + 3y^2 + 3z^2 \geqslant 2xy + 2yz + 2zx$$

$$\therefore \quad \underline{x^2 + y^2 + z^2 \geqslant \tfrac{2}{3}(xy + yz + zx)}$$

16.27 **a** Using $\quad \dfrac{x + y}{2} \geqslant \sqrt{xy} \quad$ for $\quad x \geqslant 0, \quad y \geqslant 0$

where $\quad xy = 1, \quad \Rightarrow \quad \underline{x + y \geqslant 2}$

b as $\quad k > 0, \quad \sqrt{k}$ exists and $\quad xy = k \quad$ then $\quad \dfrac{x}{\sqrt{k}} \cdot \dfrac{y}{\sqrt{k}} = 1$

$$\therefore \quad \frac{x}{\sqrt{k}} + \frac{y}{\sqrt{k}} \geqslant 2 \quad \text{\{using result of (1)\}}$$

$$\therefore \quad \frac{x + y}{\sqrt{k}} \geqslant 2$$

$$\therefore \quad x + y \geqslant 2\sqrt{k}$$

c $\quad f(s) - 3 = s^2 + \dfrac{2}{s} - 3$

$$= \frac{s^3 - 3s + 2}{s}$$

$$= \frac{(s + 2)(s^2 - 2s + 1)}{s}$$

$$= \frac{(s + 2)(s - 1)^2}{s}$$

-2	1	0	-3	2
	0	-2	4	-2
	1	-2	1	0

d $\qquad g(t) = t + \dfrac{2}{\sqrt{t}}$

$$\therefore \quad g(t) - 3 = \frac{(\sqrt{t} + 2)(\sqrt{t} - 1)^2}{\sqrt{t}} \quad \text{\{using result (3) with} \quad t = s^2\}$$

and as $\sqrt{t}$ is positive, each factor is positive or zero in the case of $(\sqrt{t} - 1)^2$.

$\therefore \quad g(t) - 3 \geqslant 0 \quad$ for all $\quad t > 0.$

$\therefore \quad g(t) \geqslant 3 \quad$ for all $\quad t > 0,$ equality occurring when $\quad t = 1.$

e If $\quad x, y, z$ are positive and $\quad xyz = 1,$

then by (2), as $\quad xy = \dfrac{1}{z},$ this means that $\quad x + y \geqslant 2\sqrt{\dfrac{1}{z}}$

i.e. $\quad x + y \geqslant \dfrac{2}{\sqrt{z}}$

thus $\quad x + y + z \geqslant \quad z + \dfrac{2}{\sqrt{z}} \geqslant 3 \quad$ {from (4)}

$$\therefore \quad xyz = 1 \quad \Rightarrow \quad x + y + z \geqslant \quad 3$$

{**Note:** equality occurs when $\quad z = 1 \quad$ and $\quad \therefore \quad x = y = z = 1$}

f   for positives x, y, z,   let $G = \sqrt[3]{xyz}$.

Now $xyz = G^3$

$\therefore \quad \dfrac{x}{G} \cdot \dfrac{y}{G} \cdot \dfrac{z}{G} = 1$

$\therefore \quad \dfrac{x}{G} + \dfrac{y}{G} + \dfrac{z}{G} \geqslant 3 \qquad$ {by (5)}

$\therefore \quad \dfrac{x+y+z}{3} \geqslant G$

$\therefore \quad \dfrac{x+y+z}{3} \geqslant \sqrt[3]{xyz}$ with equality occurs when $\dfrac{x}{G} = \dfrac{y}{G} = \dfrac{z}{G} = 1$,   i.e. $x = y = z$

16.28   **a** $(a-b)^2 + (b-c)^2 + (c-a)^2$ is never negative

i.e. $(a-b)^2 + (b-c)^2 + (c-a)^2 \geqslant 0$ for all a, b, c

$\Rightarrow \quad a^2 - 2ab + b^2 + b^2 - 2bc + c^2 + c^2 - 2ac + a^2 \geqslant 0$

$\Rightarrow \quad 2a^2 + 2b^2 + 2c^2 \geqslant 2ab + 2bc + 2ca$

$\Rightarrow \quad \underline{a^2 + b^2 + c^2 \geqslant ab + bc + ca}$

b $(a+b+c)(a^2+b^2+c^2-ab-bc-ca)$

$= a^3 + ab^2 + ac^2 - a^2b - abc - ca^2 + ba^2 + b^3 + bc^2 - ab^2 - b^2c - abc + ca^2 + cb^2 + c^3$
$\quad -abc - bc^2 - c^2a$

$= \underline{a^3 + b^3 + c^3 + 3abc}.$

c   Thus $a^3 + b^3 + c^3 - 3abc = (a+b+c)(a^2+b^2+c^2-ab-bc-ca)$

$\therefore \quad a^3 + b^3 + c^3 - 3abc \geqslant 0$ for all positive a, b, c {from (1)}

$\therefore \quad a^3 + b^3 + c^3 \geqslant 3abc$ for all positives a, b, c

and if we let $a^3 = x$, $b^3 = y$, $c^3 = z$,

we obtain $x + y + z \geqslant 3\sqrt[3]{x} \cdot \sqrt[3]{y} \cdot \sqrt[3]{z}$ for all positives x, y, z

i.e. $\dfrac{x+y+z}{3} \geqslant \sqrt[3]{xyz}$ for all positives x, y and z.

[**Note:**   Equality occurs when $(a-b)^2 = (b-c)^2 = (c-a)^2 = 0$ i.e.   when $x = y = z$.]

d   Let x, y, z be the sides of the box.
$V = xyz$ and $A = 2xy + 2yz + 2zx$ are expressions
for volume and total surface area, A being constant.

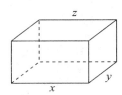

Now x, y and z positive $\Rightarrow$ $2xy, 2yz$, and $2zx$ are positive

Thus $\dfrac{2xy + 2yz + 2zx}{3} \geqslant \sqrt[3]{2xy \cdot 2yz \cdot 2zx}$ {using (3)}

Hence $\dfrac{A}{3} \geqslant (8V^2)^{\frac{1}{3}}$

$\therefore \quad 8V^2 \leqslant \dfrac{A^3}{27}$

$\therefore \quad V \leqslant \sqrt{\dfrac{A^3}{216}}$

where $\sqrt{\dfrac{A^3}{216}}$ is an obtainable constant (as A is fixed)

obtainable when $2xy = 2yz = 2zx$,   i.e.,   when $x = y = z$.
{Equality occurs when the 3 positives used in the inequality are equal.}

$\therefore \quad \underline{\text{maximum volume}}$ is $\sqrt{\dfrac{A^3}{216}}$ when the box is <u>a cube</u>.

16.29   For positives a, b, c and d,

$$\frac{a+b+c+d}{4} = \frac{\left(\frac{a+b}{2}\right) + \left(\frac{c+d}{2}\right)}{2} \geqslant \sqrt{\left(\frac{a+b}{2}\right) \cdot \left(\frac{c+d}{2}\right)} \qquad \left\{\text{using} \quad \frac{x+y}{2} \geqslant \sqrt{xy}\right\}$$

$$\therefore \quad \frac{a+b+c+d}{4} \geqslant \sqrt{\sqrt{ab} \cdot \sqrt{cd}} \qquad \left\{\text{using} \quad \frac{x+y}{2} \geqslant \sqrt{xy} \quad \text{twice more.}\right\}$$

Thus $\dfrac{a+b+c+d}{4} \geqslant \sqrt{\sqrt{abcd}}$

i.e., $\underline{\dfrac{a+b+c+d}{4} \geqslant \sqrt[4]{abcd}}$

with equality occurring when $\dfrac{a+b}{2} = \dfrac{c+d}{2}$, $a = b$ and $c = d$ i.e., when $\underline{a = b = c = d}$.

16.30 . $x \leqslant x+y+z \leqslant y \leqslant xyz \leqslant z$

Hence $z \geqslant y \geqslant x$......(1) $y + x \geqslant 0$......(2) $x + z \leqslant 0$......(3)

Since x, y and z are all non-zero, it follows from (2) and (3) that x, y and z are neither all positive or all negative.

By (1) z is the greatest and x is the smallest.

$\therefore \quad z > 0$ and $x < 0$

But $xyz \leqslant z \Rightarrow xy \leqslant 1$......(4)   {dividing both sides by the positive, z}

To find the sign of y, <u>assume y is positive</u>

Now $xyz \geqslant y$ where $y > 0$

$\Rightarrow \quad xz \geqslant 1$,   which is absurd as we have shown $z > 0$ and $x < 0$, $\therefore \quad xz < 0$.

Hence $\underline{y < 0}$ and $\therefore \quad xy > 0$

Thus from (4) $0 < xy \leqslant 1$ where x and y are negative integers

$\Rightarrow \quad \underline{x = y = -1}$.

and in (3) $-1 + z \leqslant 0$

$\Rightarrow \quad z \leqslant 1$ where z is a positive integer. $\therefore \quad \underline{z = 1}$

Thus $\underline{x = -1, \quad y = -1, \quad z = 1}$ is the only solution.

16.31 $m = $ smallest of $\{\,|\,a-b\,|, \quad |\,b-c\,|, \quad |\,c-a\,|\,\}$

Without loss of generality we assume $a \leqslant b \leqslant c$,   and $m = |\,a-b\,|$

e.g.   ⟵————————⟶
  $\quad a \quad\quad b \quad\quad c$

It is clear that for $|\,a-b\,| = m$, $|\,b-c\,| \geqslant m$,   and $\therefore \quad |\,a-c\,| \geqslant 2m$

$\therefore \quad |\,a-b\,|^2 + |\,b-c\,|^2 + |\,a-c\,|^2 \quad \geqslant m^2 + m^2 + 4m^2$

$\therefore \quad (a-b)^2 + (b-c)^2 + (a-c)^2 \quad \geqslant 6m^2$......(*)

a $3(a^2 + b^2 + c^2) - [(a-b)^2 + (b-c)^2 + (c-a)^2]$

$= 3a^2 + 3b^3 + 3c^2 - a^2 + 2ab - b^2 - b^2 + 2bc - c^2 - c^2 + 2ac - a^2$

$= a^2 + b^2 + c^2 + 2ab + 2bc + 2ca$

$= (a+b+c)^2$

$\geqslant 0$ for all a, b, c.

$3(a^2 + b^2 + c^2) \geqslant (a-b)^2 + (b-c)^2 + (c-a)^2$......(**)

b   combining ∗ and ∗∗

we get $3(a^2 + b^2 + c^2) \geqslant (a-b)^2 + (b-c)^2 + (c-a)^2 \geqslant 6m^2$

$\Rightarrow \quad \frac{1}{2}(a^2 + b^2 + c^2) \geqslant m^2$

or $m^2 \leqslant \frac{1}{2}(a^2 + b^2 + c^2)$

16.32 $f\left(\dfrac{x_1+x_2}{2}\right) < \frac{1}{2}[f(x_1)+f(x_2)]$ for $x_1 \neq x_2$......(*)

a $f\left(\dfrac{s_1+s_2+s_3+s_4}{4}\right) = f\left(\dfrac{\left(\dfrac{s_1+s_2}{2}\right)+\left(\dfrac{s_3+s_4}{2}\right)}{2}\right)$

$$< \frac{1}{2}\left[f\left(\dfrac{s_1+s_2}{2}\right)+f\left(\dfrac{s_3+s_4}{2}\right)\right]\qquad \text{\{from *\}}$$

$$< \frac{1}{2}\left[\frac{1}{2}\{f(s_1)+f(s_2)\}+\frac{1}{2}\{f(s_3)+f(s_4)\}\right]$$

i.e. $< \frac{1}{4}[f(s_1)+f(s_2)+f(s_3)+f(s_4)]$

for $\dfrac{s_1+s_2}{2} \neq \dfrac{s_3+s_4}{2}$, $s_1 \neq s_2$, $s_3 \neq s_4$,   i.e.,   for s_1, s_2, s_3, s_4 not all equal.

b   In (1), let $s_1 = a$, $s_2 = b$, $s_3 = c$, $s_4 = \dfrac{a+b+c}{3}$

$$\therefore \quad f\left(\dfrac{a+b+c+\dfrac{a+b+c}{3}}{4}\right) < \frac{1}{4}\left[f(a)+f(b)+f(c)+f\left(\dfrac{a+b+c}{3}\right)\right]$$

$$\therefore \quad f\left(\dfrac{3a+3b+3c+a+b+c}{12}\right) < \frac{1}{4}\left[f(a)+f(b)+f(c)+f\left(\dfrac{a+b+c}{3}\right)\right]$$

$$\therefore \quad 4f\left(\dfrac{a+b+c}{3}\right) < f(a)+f(b)+f(c)+f\left(\dfrac{a+b+c}{3}\right)$$

$$\therefore \quad 3f\left(\dfrac{a+b+c}{3}\right) < f(a)+f(b)+f(c)$$

$$\therefore \quad f\left(\dfrac{a+b+c}{3}\right) < \frac{1}{3}[f(a)+f(b)+f(c)] \quad \text{for}\quad a, b, c \quad \text{not all equal.}$$

16.33   **a**   For $A(a, 0), B(b, 0), C(c, 0)$,   then $\dfrac{b}{a} = \dfrac{c}{b}$ or $b^2 = ac$.

A' is $\left(a, \dfrac{1}{a}\right)$, B' is $\left(b, \dfrac{1}{b}\right)$, C' is $\left(c, \dfrac{1}{c}\right)$

$$\therefore \quad \text{Midpoint of } \overline{A'C'} \text{ is } M\left(\dfrac{a+c}{2}, \dfrac{\dfrac{1}{a}+\dfrac{1}{c}}{2}\right) = M\left(\dfrac{a+c}{2}, \dfrac{a+c}{2ac}\right)$$

Now $\overrightarrow{OB'} = \left[b, \dfrac{1}{b}\right]$ and $\overrightarrow{OM} = \left[\dfrac{a+c}{2}, \dfrac{a+c}{2ac}\right]$

$$= b\left[1, \dfrac{1}{b^2}\right] \qquad\qquad = \dfrac{a+c}{2}\left[1, \dfrac{1}{ac}\right]$$

$$= \dfrac{a+c}{2}\left[1, \dfrac{1}{b^2}\right]$$

Thus $\overrightarrow{OB'}$ and $\overrightarrow{OM}$ are parallel $\therefore$ OB' produced bisects the chord $\overline{A'C'}$.

b   Area $\triangle A'X'C'$

$= $ Area $AA'C'C - $ Area $AA'X'X - $ Area $XX'C'C$ {for X' on curve $A'C'$}

$$= \left(\dfrac{\dfrac{1}{a}+\dfrac{1}{c}}{2}\right)(c-a) - \left(\dfrac{\dfrac{1}{a}+\dfrac{1}{x}}{2}\right)(x-a) - \left(\dfrac{\dfrac{1}{x}+\dfrac{1}{c}}{2}\right)(c-x) \quad \text{for } X'\left(x, \dfrac{1}{x}\right)$$

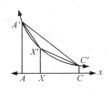

$$= \frac{1}{2}\left[\dfrac{c}{a}+1-1-\dfrac{a}{c}-\dfrac{x}{a}-1+1+\dfrac{a}{x}-\dfrac{c}{x}-1+1+\dfrac{x}{c}\right]$$

$$= \tfrac{1}{2}\left[\left(\frac{c}{a} - \frac{a}{c}\right) + x\left(\frac{1}{c} - \frac{1}{a}\right) + \frac{1}{x}(a - c)\right]$$

$$= \tfrac{1}{2}\left[\frac{c}{a} - \frac{a}{c} - (c - a)\left\{\frac{x}{ac} + \frac{1}{x}\right\}\right]$$

Now $\dfrac{\frac{x}{ac} + \frac{1}{x}}{2} \geqslant \sqrt{\dfrac{x}{ac}\cdot\dfrac{1}{x}}$ {Arithmetic-geometric means inequality}

$$\therefore -\left(\frac{x}{ac} + \frac{1}{x}\right) \leqslant -2\sqrt{\frac{1}{ac}}$$

with equality when $\dfrac{x}{ac} = \dfrac{1}{x}$ which maximises $-\left(\dfrac{x}{ac} + \dfrac{1}{x}\right)$ and $\therefore$ maximises the area.

Thus area is maximised when $\dfrac{x}{ac} = \dfrac{1}{x}$ i.e. $x^2 = ac = b^2$ $\therefore$ $x = b$

Thus $\triangle A'X'C'$ has maximum area when X is at B, and X' at B'.

c   Draw a line through B' parallel to $A'C'$.
If $b^2 = ac$,   then B' is the point on the curve $A'C'$ which is furthest from $\overline{A'C'}$.
So the line cuts the curve $A'C'$ once only, and is thus a tangent.

17. GEOMETRIC INEQUALITIES

17.1   The altitudes of a triangle are concurrent at the orthocentre O.
Since the triangle is acute-angled, O lies within $\triangle ABC$.
Now $OA + OB > c$, $OB + OC > a$,   and $OC + OA > b$
$\therefore$ $2[OA + OB + OC] > a + b + c$ {adding the above}

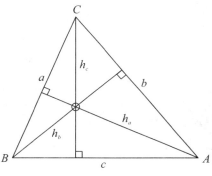

But $h_a > OA$, $h_b > OB$ and $h_c > OC$

$\therefore$ $h_a + h_b + h_c > OA + OB + OC > \dfrac{a + b + c}{2}$

$\therefore$ $\tfrac{1}{2} < \dfrac{h_a + h_b + h_c}{a + b + c}$ ...... (1)

Also $h_a < b$ and $h_a < c$
{In a right-angled $\triangle$, the 'legs' are less than the hypotenuse in length}

Likewise $h_b < a$ and $h_b < c$, $h_c < a$ and $h_c < b$
Thus $2h_a + 2h_b + 2h_c < 2a + 2b + 2c$

$\therefore$ $\dfrac{h_a + h_b + h_c}{a + b + c} < 1$ ...... (2)

and combining (1) and (2) gives the required result.

17.2   a   In $\triangle PQR$
$$p^2 = q^2 + r^2 - 2qr\cos P \qquad \text{\{Cosine Rule\}}$$
If P is acute, $\cos P > 0$, $\therefore$ $2qr\cos P > 0$
$\therefore$ $p^2 < q^2 + r^2$
If P is obtuse, $\cos P < 0$ $\therefore$ $p^2 > q^2 + r^2$
$p < p_1$ where $p_1{}^2 = q^2 + r^2$ $\therefore$ $p^2 < q^2 + r^2$ etc.

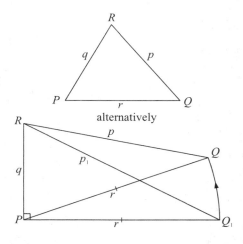

alternatively

b Label the figure $PQRS$ and draw diagonal $\overline{PR}$ and let $PR = x$.

Now $\theta + \phi = 180^{\circ}$ {$PQRS$ is a cyclic quadrilateral}

Hence either $\theta \geqslant 90^{\circ}$ and $\phi \leqslant 90^{\circ}$ ...... (1)

or $\theta \leqslant 90^{\circ}$ and $\phi \geqslant 90^{\circ}$ ...... (2)

For $\theta > 90^{\circ}$ and $\phi < 90^{\circ}$

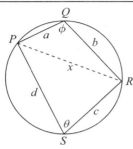

$x^2 > c^2 + d^2$ and $x^2 < a^2 + b^2$

Hence $a^2 + b^2 > x^2 > c^2 + d^2$

contradicting $a^2 + b^2 = c^2 + d^2$

Likewise, for $\theta < 90^{\circ}$ and $\phi > 90^{\circ}$

we get $a^2 + b^2 < c^2 + d^2$, a contradiction.

The only remaining possibility is $\theta = \phi = 90^{\circ}$.

Thus the angle between a and b is 90°,

and likewise the angle between c and d.

17.3 a $a \leqslant 1$ and $b \geqslant 1$

$\therefore$ $1 - a \geqslant 0$ and $b - 1 \geqslant 0$

$\therefore$ $(1 - a)(b - 1) \geqslant 0$

$\therefore$ $b - ab - 1 + a \geqslant 0$

$\therefore$ $a + b - ab \geqslant 1$

$\therefore$ $S - P \geqslant 1$

b Thus if $P = 1$, then $S \geqslant 2$, equality occurring when $a = b = 1$.

c Area $= \frac{1}{2}xy = k$, a constant

and $z^2 = x^2 + y^2$ {Pythagoras}

Now $x^2 y^2 = 4k^2$

$\therefore$ $\dfrac{x^2}{2k} \cdot \dfrac{y^2}{2k} = 1$

$\therefore$ $\dfrac{x^2}{2k} + \dfrac{y^2}{2k} \geqslant 2$ {from (2)} with equality when $\dfrac{x^2}{2k} = \dfrac{y^2}{2k}$, i.e., $x = y$.

$\therefore$ $x^2 + y^2 \geqslant 4k$

$\therefore$ $z^2 \geqslant 4k$

$\therefore$ $z \geqslant 2\sqrt{k}$

Minimum hypotenuse is $2\sqrt{k}$ occurring when $x = y$, i.e., when $\triangle$ is isosceles.

17.4 Reflect A in road 1 and let A' be its image.
Likewise B' is the image of B reflected in road 2.
Join A' to B'. If C' is the point where $\overline{A'B'}$ cuts
road 2, and D' is the point where it meets road 1,
then $AD' + D'C' + C'B$ is as short as possible.

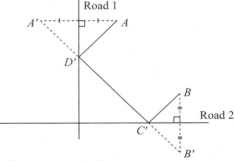

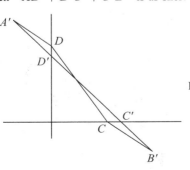

Proof: $AD' = A'D'$ {$\triangle AD'A'$ is isosceles.}

Also $BC' = B'C'$ {as $\triangle BC'B'$ is isosceles.}

$\therefore$ $A'D' + D'C' + C'B' = AD' + D'C' + C'B$

If D and C are other than at D' and C'
the path $A'D + DC + CB' > A'D' + D'C' + C'B'$

$\therefore$ $AD' + D'C' + C'B$ is as short as possible.

17.5 We number the houses H_1, H_2, H_3 and H_4 in such a way that the distances of H_i from the left (west) boundary is x_i km and $0 \leqslant x_1 \leqslant x_2 \leqslant x_3 \leqslant x_4 \leqslant 1$.   Consider two cases:

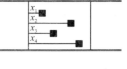
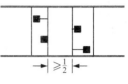
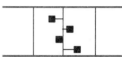

a Suppose $x_3 - x_2 \geqslant \frac{1}{2}$: we construct the driveway as in A:

and its length is $2 + (x_2 - x_1) + (x_4 - x_3)$

$$\leqslant 2 + x_2 + 1 - x_3 \qquad \{\text{as } x_4 - x_1 \leqslant 1\}$$

i.e., $\leqslant 3 + (x_2 - x_3)$

i.e., $\leqslant 2\frac{1}{2} \quad \{x_3 - x_2 \geqslant \frac{1}{2} \quad \Rightarrow \quad x_2 - x_3 \leqslant -\frac{1}{2}\}$

b Suppose $x_3 - x_2 < \frac{1}{2}$: we construct the driveway as in B:

and its length is $1 + (x_2 - x_1) + (x_3 - x_2) + (x_4 - x_2)$

$$\leqslant 1 + x_2 + x_3 - x_2 + 1 - x_2$$

i.e., $\leqslant 2 + x_3 - x_2$

i.e., $\underline{< 2\frac{1}{2}}$

17.6 $\overline{AC}$ is an axis of symmetry of $\triangle$'s APQ and PCQ. Thus $\triangle$'s PNC and QNC are isosceles

$\Rightarrow \quad \underline{PN = NC = QN}$

a Now $\dfrac{p}{2} = AP + PN$

$\therefore \quad \dfrac{p}{2} > AN + NC \quad \{PN = NC \quad \text{and} \quad AP > AN$
$\text{as hypontenuse is } > \text{a 'leg'}\}$

i.e. $\dfrac{p}{2} > d$

$\Rightarrow \quad \underline{p > 2d}$

b $AB + BP > AP$
$PC + CQ > PQ$
$QD + DA > QA \qquad \{\text{triangle inequality}\}$
adding these $\therefore \quad 4a > p \quad \text{or} \quad \underline{p < 4a}.$

c Let the diagonals meet at Y and draw $\overline{PX} \parallel \overline{AY}$
Now $AB + BY = AB + (BX + XY)$
$$= AB + (XP + PN)$$
$$\geqslant (AX + XP) + PN \qquad \{AB \geqslant AX\}$$

$\therefore \quad a + \dfrac{d}{2} \geqslant AP + PN \qquad \{\text{triangle inequality}\}$

$\therefore \quad a + \dfrac{d}{2} \geqslant \dfrac{p}{2}$

$\therefore \quad p \leqslant 2a + d \qquad \{\text{Equality holding when } P \text{ is at } B.\}$

17.7 a The reflections yield $\triangle$'s ABC' and $AB'C$ with X' and X'' being the images of X (as shown).

$\therefore$ perimeter of XYZ
$$= XY + YZ + ZX$$
$$= X''Y + YZ + ZX' \quad \text{which is to be a minimum.}$$
Since X' and X'' are fixed, $X''Y + YZ + ZX'$ is a minimum when X'', Y, Z and X' are collinear.
i.e. $\underline{Y \text{ and } Z \text{ lie on } \overline{X'X''}}.$

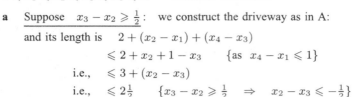
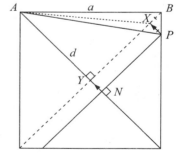
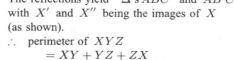
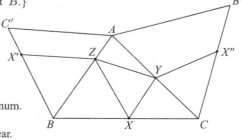

b   Join $\overline{AX}, \overline{AX'}, \overline{AX''}$
$\triangle AX'X''$ is isosceles $\{$as $AX'=AX''=AX=l\}$
and $\angle X'AX'' = 2\alpha + 2\beta$
$\qquad\qquad = 2(\alpha + \beta)$
$\qquad\qquad = 2A$

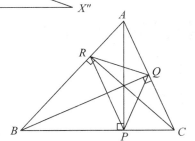

$\therefore \quad \sin A = \dfrac{X'M}{l} = \dfrac{X'X''}{2l}$

$\therefore \quad \underline{X'X'' = 2l \sin A.}$

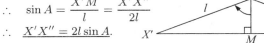

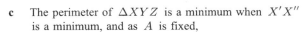

c   The perimeter of $\triangle XYZ$ is a minimum when $X'X''$
is a minimum, and as A is fixed,
$X'X$ is a minimum when $l = AX$ is a minimum.
Thus P must be the foot of the perpendicular from
A to $\overline{BC}$.
Likewise Q from B to $\overline{AC}$, R from C to $\overline{AB}$,
respectively.

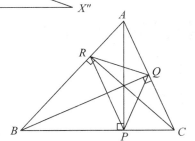

17.8 *Case 1:* right-angled   *Case 2:* obtuse angled.

In cases (1) and (2) the triangles lie
entirely in one half of the circle and
so the sum of the areas of the
segments is obviously more than
half the area of the circle.

Case 3: acute-angled.   In *Case 3*,

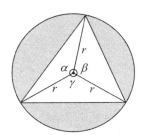

$$\text{Area} \triangle ABC = \tfrac{1}{2}r^2 \sin \alpha + \tfrac{1}{2}r^2 \sin \beta + \tfrac{1}{2}r^2 \sin \delta$$

$$= \tfrac{1}{2}r^2[\sin \alpha + \sin \beta + \sin \delta]$$

$$< \tfrac{1}{2}r^2 . 3 \quad \{\text{max. value of } \sin \theta \text{ is } 1 \text{ when } \theta = 90^o. \text{ This can't be}$$
$$\text{reached as } \alpha, \beta, \delta \text{ can't all be } 90^o \text{ simultaneously.}\}$$

$$\text{i.e. } < \tfrac{3}{2}r^2$$

$$< \dfrac{\pi}{2}r^2$$

$$\therefore \quad \text{sum of segment areas} > \pi r^2 - \dfrac{\pi}{2}r^2$$

$$\text{i.e. } > \dfrac{\pi}{2}r^2, \quad \text{the required result.}$$

17.9 Place coordinate axes through the centre O.
If $\angle POX = \theta$,
P is $(R \cos \theta, R \sin \theta)$.
Let $A(0, r)$ and $B(0, -r)$.

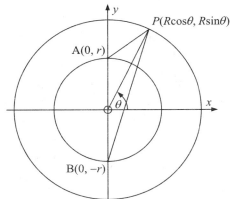

$$\therefore \quad AP \cdot PB = \sqrt{(R\cos\theta)^2 + (R\sin\theta - r)^2} \cdot \sqrt{(R\cos\theta)^2 + (R\sin\theta + r)^2}$$

$$= \sqrt{R^2(\cos^2\theta + \sin^2\theta) - 2Rr\sin\theta + r^2} \cdot \sqrt{R^2(\cos^2\theta + \sin^2\theta) + 2Rr\sin\theta + r^2}$$

$$= \sqrt{R^2 + r^2 - 2Rr\sin\theta} \cdot \sqrt{R^2 + r^2 + 2Rr\sin\theta}$$

$$= \sqrt{(R^2 + r^2)^2 - 4R^2r^2\sin^2\theta} \quad \text{where} \quad 0 \leqslant \sin^2\theta \leqslant 1.$$

$$\therefore \quad AP \cdot PB \leqslant \sqrt{(R^2 + r^2)^2} \qquad \text{i.e.,} \quad \leqslant R^2 + r^2$$

$$\text{and} \quad AP \cdot PB \geqslant \sqrt{(R^2 + r^2)^2 - 4R^2r^2} \geqslant \sqrt{(R^2 - r^2)^2} \geqslant R^2 - r^2$$

$$\therefore \quad R^2 - r^2 \leqslant AP \cdot PB \leqslant R^2 + r^2$$

17.10 If the square is a km by a km,   i.e.

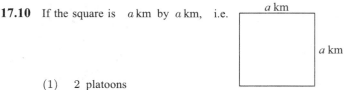

(1)   <u>2 platoons</u>

Divide the square into 2 congruent rectangles.
Place platoons at the centres of these rectangles.

$$d_{\max} = \frac{\sqrt{5}a}{\sqrt{4}} \text{ km}$$

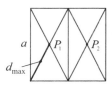

(2)   <u>3 platoons</u>

Divide the square into 3 congruent rectangles
and place platoons at the centres of each.

$$d_{\max} = \frac{\sqrt{5}a}{\sqrt{18}} \text{ km}$$

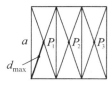

(3)   <u>4 platoons</u>

Divide the square into 4 smaller squares shown.
Place the platoons at the centres of these squares.

$$d_{\max} = \frac{\sqrt{2}a}{4} \text{ km}$$

[Can you find a better arrangement for any of these?]

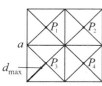

17.11

$$(AP)^2 + (BP)^2 + (CP)^2$$
$$= (x - a)^2 + y^2 + (x - b)^2 + (y - c)^2 + x^2 + y^2$$
$$= x^2 - 2ax + a^2 + y^2 + x^2 - 2bx + b^2 + y^2 - 2cy + c^2 + x^2 + y^2$$
$$= 3x^2 + 3y^2 - 2ax - 2bx - 2cy + a^2 + b^2 + c^2$$
$$= 3\left(x^2 - \frac{2a + 2b}{3}x + \left(\frac{a + b}{3}\right)^2\right) + 3\left(y^2 - \frac{2c}{3}y + \frac{c^2}{9}\right) + a^2 + b^2 + c^2 - 3\left(\frac{a + b}{3}\right)^2 - \frac{3c^2}{9}$$
$$= 3\left(x - \frac{a + b}{3}\right)^2 + 3\left(y - \frac{c}{3}\right)^2 + a^2 + b^2 + \frac{2c^2}{3} - \frac{(a + b)^2}{3}$$

$$\therefore \quad (AP)^2 + (BP)^2 + (CP)^2 \geqslant \left(a^2 + b^2 + \frac{2c^2}{3} - \frac{(a + b)^2}{3}\right), \quad \text{the minimum value}$$

with equality $\iff x = \frac{a + b}{3}, \quad y = \frac{c}{3}$

i.e. $\iff$ <u>P is at the centroid of $\triangle ABC$.</u>

17.12 a   Draw diameter $\overline{CD}$ and join $\overline{BD}$.
$\angle CDB = \angle CAB$ {subtended by arc BC}
and $\angle DBC = 90^{\varrho}$ {angle in semicircle}

$$\therefore \quad \sin A = \frac{BC}{DC} = \frac{a}{2R} \quad .....(1)$$

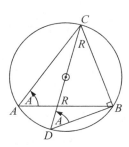
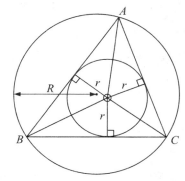

b   Let   area $\triangle ABC = S$

$$\therefore \quad S = \tfrac{1}{2} bc \sin A$$

$$\Rightarrow \quad S = \tfrac{1}{2} bc \left(\frac{a}{2R} \right)$$

$$\therefore \quad \underline{S = \frac{abc}{4R}} \quad .....(2)$$

c   Also $S = \text{area } \triangle OAB + \text{area } \triangle OBC + \text{area } \triangle OCA$

$$= \tfrac{1}{2} cr + \tfrac{1}{2} ar + \tfrac{1}{2} br$$

i.e. $\underline{S = \tfrac{1}{2} r(a + b + c)} \quad .....(3)$

d   The two expressions for S contain a sum and a product of positives which suggests the arithmetic-geometric mean inequality.

i.e. $\dfrac{a + b + c}{3} \geqslant \sqrt[3]{abc}$

$$\therefore \qquad \frac{P}{3} \geqslant [4RS]^{\frac{1}{3}} \qquad \text{\{from (2)\}}$$

$$\therefore \qquad \frac{P^3}{27} \geqslant 4RS \quad \text{i.e.} \quad \geqslant 4R \cdot \frac{rP}{2} \qquad \text{\{from (3)\}}$$

$$\therefore \qquad P^3 \geqslant 54 R r P$$

$$\therefore \qquad P^2 \geqslant 54 R r \qquad \text{\{$P > 0$\}}$$

$$\Rightarrow \qquad P \geqslant \sqrt{54 R r}$$

i.e. $\underline{P \geqslant 3\sqrt{6 R r}}$

17.13 a $\text{Area} = \tfrac{1}{2} ab \sin C$

$$= \tfrac{1}{2} ab \sqrt{1 - \cos^2 C} \quad \text{where} \quad c^2 = a^2 + b^2 - 2ab \cos C$$

$$\therefore \quad A^2 = \frac{a^2 b^2}{4} \left[1 - \left(\frac{a^2 + b^2 - c^2}{2ab} \right)^2 \right]$$

$$= \frac{a^2 b^2}{4} \left[1 + \left(\frac{a^2 + b^2 - c^2}{2ab} \right) \right] \left[1 - \left(\frac{a^2 + b^2 - c^2}{2ab} \right) \right]$$

$$= \frac{a^2 b^2}{4} \left[\frac{2ab + a^2 + b^2 - c^2}{2ab} \right] \left[\frac{2ab - a^2 - b^2 + c^2}{2ab} \right]$$

$$= \tfrac{1}{16} \left[(a + b)^2 - c^2 \right] \left[c^2 - (a - b)^2 \right]$$

$$= \tfrac{1}{16} [a + b + c] [a + b - c] [c + a - b] [c - a + b]$$

$$= \tfrac{1}{16} [2s] [2s - 2C] [2s - 2b] [2s - 2a] \quad \text{where} \quad 2s = a + b + c$$

$$= s(s - a)(s - b)(s - c)$$

$$\therefore \qquad A = \sqrt{s(s - a)(s - b)(s - c)}$$

b If the perimeter is fixed, then s is a constant,

and $\dfrac{A^2}{s} = (s-a)(s-b)(s-c)$, the product of 3 positives.

But $\sqrt[3]{(s-a)(s-b)(s-c)} \leqslant \dfrac{(s-a)+(s-b)+(s-c)}{3}$

{arithmetic-geometric mean inequality with equality when $s-a = s-b = s-c$}

$\therefore \left[\dfrac{A^2}{s}\right]^{\frac{1}{3}} \leqslant \dfrac{3s-(a+b+c)}{3} = \dfrac{s}{3}$

$\therefore \dfrac{A^2}{s} \leqslant \dfrac{s^3}{27}$

$\therefore A^2 \leqslant \dfrac{s^4}{27}$ and so $A \leqslant \dfrac{s^2}{3\sqrt{3}}.$

Thus the maximum area is $\underline{\dfrac{s^2}{3\sqrt{3}}}$ when $s-a = s-b = s-c$ i.e., $a = b = c$

i.e. when the triangle is equilateral.

17.14 We do not lose generality by assuming that $a \leqslant b$.

Case 1.   Sides of mat are parallel to walls.
requires $\underline{b \leqslant c}$

Case 1:
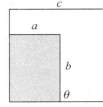

Case 2.   The mat can be laid as shown if $PR \leqslant c$

$\therefore \quad PQ + QR \leqslant c$

$\therefore \quad a\cos 45^\circ + b\cos 45^\circ \leqslant c$

$\therefore \quad \dfrac{a+b}{\sqrt{2}} \leqslant c$

$\therefore \quad a+b \leqslant \sqrt{2}c$

Case 2:
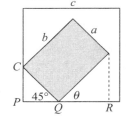

Case 3.   If the mat is placed in any other position it can be translated to
$PQRS$ as shown where $45^\circ < \theta < 90^\circ$.
{Cases (1) and (2) are when $\theta = 90^\circ$ and 45°}
Let $\angle RPS = \alpha$, then $\alpha < 45^\circ$ {as $a \leqslant b$}
If $\theta + \alpha < 90^\circ$ and $45^\circ < \theta < 90^\circ$ {see fig I}
then $45^\circ + \alpha < \theta + \alpha$

$\therefore \quad \sin(45^\circ + \alpha) < \sin(\theta + \alpha)$

$\therefore \quad \sin 45^\circ \cos\alpha + \cos 45^\circ \sin\alpha < \dfrac{RE}{RP} \leqslant \dfrac{C}{RP}$

$\therefore \quad \dfrac{1}{\sqrt{2}}\cdot\dfrac{b}{RP} + \dfrac{1}{\sqrt{2}}\cdot\dfrac{a}{RP} < \dfrac{c}{RP}$ and $\therefore \quad a+b < \sqrt{2}c$

Case 3:
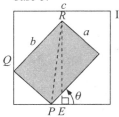

If $\theta + \alpha > 90^\circ$ then $\theta + \alpha < 90^\circ + \alpha$ {see fig II}

$\therefore \quad \sin(\theta + \alpha) > \sin(90^\circ + \alpha)$ {both angles in quad. 2}

$\therefore \quad \sin(180^\circ - [\theta + \alpha]) > \sin 90^\circ \cos\alpha + \cos 90^\circ \sin\alpha$

$\therefore \quad \dfrac{RE}{RP} > \cos\alpha$ i.e., $> \dfrac{b}{RP}$

$\therefore \quad RE > b$ and as $c \geqslant RE$, then $c > b$ or $b < c$

Combining all **3 cases**, the mat can be laid if and only if $\underline{b \leqslant c$ or $a+b \leqslant \sqrt{2}c}$.

17.15 a Place 2 pegs at points F_1 and F_2 and tie the piece of string onto the pegs. Place a pencil against the string and move away from $\overline{F_1 F_2}$ to tighten the string so that $\overline{PF_1}$ and $\overline{PF_2}$ are straight lines. Allow the pencil to move keeping the string tight. In the illustration, the top half of the ellipse will be traced out. Swapping the pencil to the other side of the string we can similarly draw the bottom half.

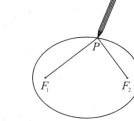

b Let $\overline{F_1 Q}$ meet the ellipse at P.
$$\therefore \quad PF_2 \leqslant PQ + QF_2$$
$$\therefore \quad PF_1 + PF_2 \leqslant PF_1 + PQ + QF_2$$
$$\therefore \quad PF_1 + PF_2 \leqslant (PF_1 + PQ) + QF_2$$
$$\therefore \quad PF_1 + PF_2 \leqslant QF_1 + QF_2$$

where $PF_1 + PF_2$ is fixed, and equality occurs when Q is at T.
$\therefore$ for any point Q, $\underline{QF_1 + QF_2 \text{ is minimised when } Q \text{ is at } T}$.

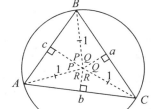

c Let F_2' be the image of F_2 under a reflection in t.
Thus for all Q on t, $QF_2 = QF_2'$
But from (2), $QF_1 + QF_2'$ is minimised when Q is at T
$$\therefore \quad F_1 T F_2' \text{ is a straight line}$$
$$\therefore \quad \alpha_1 = \alpha_2 \qquad \{\text{vertically opposite}\}$$
$$\text{but} \quad \alpha_1 = \alpha_3 \qquad \{\triangle T F_2' F_2 \text{ is isosceles}\}$$
$$\therefore \quad \alpha_2 = \alpha_3$$
Hence, $\underline{n \text{ bisects } \angle F_1 T F_2}$

17.16 a $\cos 2P + \cos 2Q + \cos 2R$
$= \cos 2P + \cos 2Q + \cos 2(180 - P - Q)$
$= \cos 2P + \cos 2Q + \cos (360 - (2P + 2Q))$
$= \cos 2P + \cos 2Q + \cos (2P + 2Q)$
$= 2 \cos (P + Q) \cos (P - Q) + 2 \cos^2 (P + Q) - 1$
$= 2 \cos (P + Q) \{\cos (P - Q) + \cos (P + Q)\} - 1$
$= 2 \cos (P + Q) \, 2 \cos P \cos Q - 1$
$= 4 \cos (180 - R) \cos P \cos Q - 1$
$= -1 - 4 \cos P \cos Q \cos R$

b By the cosine rule, $a^2 = 1^2 + 1^2 - 2.1.1.\cos 2Q$ i.e., $a^2 = 2 - 2 \cos 2Q$
Likewise $b^2 = 2 - 2 \cos 2R$ and $c^2 = 2 - 2 \cos 2P$.
$$\therefore \quad a^2 + b^2 + c^2 = 6 - 2(\cos 2P + \cos 2Q + \cos 2R)$$
$$= 6 - 2(-1 - 4 \cos P \cos Q \cos R) \qquad \{\text{by } \mathbf{a}\}$$
$$= 8 + 8 \cos P \cos Q \cos R$$

Now if the triangle is obtuse angled, one of the three cosine values is negative and the other two are positive. So, $\cos P \cos Q \cos R$ is negative and $\therefore$ $a^2 + b^2 + c^2 < 0$. If the triangle is right-angled, one of the cosine values is 0, and so $a^2 + b^2 + c^2 = 0$. If the triangle is acute angled then all the cosine values are positive and so, by the 'arithmetic-geometric means inequality'

$\dfrac{\cos P + \cos Q + \cos R}{3} \geqslant \sqrt[3]{\cos P \cos Q \cos R}$ with equality occurring when

$\cos P = \cos Q = \cos R$, and this is true only when $P = Q = R = 60°$.

So, $\dfrac{\frac{1}{2} + \frac{1}{2} + \frac{1}{2}}{3} \geqslant \sqrt[3]{\cos P \cos Q \cos R}$ which simplifies to $\cos P \cos Q \cos R \leqslant \frac{1}{8}$.

Thus, $a^2 + b^2 + c^2 \leqslant 8 + 8(\frac{1}{8}) \leqslant 9$.

18. TRIGONOMETRY

18.1 The shaded segment has area $\frac{1}{2}r^2(\theta - \sin\theta)$ where θ is in radians.

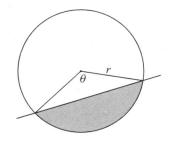

∴   the other portion has area

$$= \tfrac{1}{2}r^2([2\pi - \theta] - \sin[2\pi - \theta])$$

$$= \tfrac{1}{2}r^2(2\pi - \theta - [\underset{0}{\sin 2\pi}\cos\theta - \underset{1}{\cos 2\pi}\sin\theta])$$

$$= \tfrac{1}{2}r^2(2\pi - \theta + \sin\theta)$$

Thus $\tfrac{1}{2}r^2(2\pi - \theta + \sin\theta) = 2.\tfrac{1}{2}r^2(\theta - \sin\theta)$

∴ $2\pi - \theta + \sin\theta = 2\theta - 2\sin\theta$

∴ $3\sin\theta - 3\theta + 2\pi = 0$

where clearly $\dfrac{\pi}{2} < \theta < \pi$,   from the geometry   i.e. $1.571 < \theta < 3.142$

We will solve this equation by 'trial and error'.

θ	$3\sin\theta - 3\theta + 2\pi$
2.0	3.01108
2.50	0.57860
2.60	0.02969
2.61	-0.02609
2.605	$+0.0018168$
2.606	-0.0037624

} clearly the required solution lies between   2.60   and   2.61.

Thus to 4 s.f. $\underline{\theta \doteqdot 2.605}$

18.2 $4a + b + 4c = 100\ldots\ldots(1)$

$3a + b + 2c = \tfrac{1}{4}.(\pi.10^2) = 25\pi\ldots\ldots(2)$

$(1) - (2)$ gives $a + 2c = 100 - 25\pi\ldots\ldots(*)$

Now shaded region R in the diagram below has area

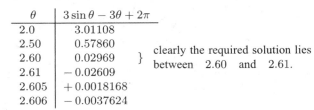

$$2a + b + c = \tfrac{1}{2}.10.10\sin 60^\circ + 2\left(\tfrac{1}{2}10^2\left[\tfrac{\pi}{3} - \sin\tfrac{\pi}{3}\right]\right)$$

$$= \frac{50\sqrt{3}}{2} + 100\left[\frac{\pi}{3} - \frac{\sqrt{3}}{2}\right]$$

$$= 25\sqrt{3} + \frac{100\pi}{3} - 50\sqrt{3}$$

i.e., $2a + b + c = \dfrac{100\pi}{3} - 25\sqrt{3}\ldots\ldots(3)$

Thus $(2) - (3)$ gives $a + c = 25\pi - \dfrac{100\pi}{3} + 25\sqrt{3}\ldots\ldots(**)$

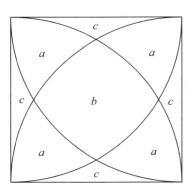

$(*) - (**)$ gives $c = 100 - 25\pi - 25\pi + \dfrac{100\pi}{3} - 25\sqrt{3}$

∴ $c = 100 - \dfrac{50\pi}{3} - 25\sqrt{3}$

$\doteqdot 4\cdot339\,\text{cm}^2$

Thus $a \doteqdot 12\cdot782\,\text{cm}^2$

and $\underline{b \doteqdot 31\cdot515\,\text{cm}^2}.$

18.3   Cut along AB and flatten out
becomes

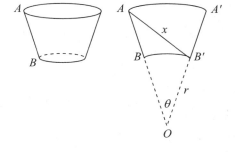

The string line is AB' (the shortest distance).
arc length $AA' = 12\pi$ and   arc length $BB' = 10\pi$.
Now $r\theta = 10\pi$ and $(r + 20)\theta = 12\pi$
Solving these two equations simultaneously

yields $r = \underline{100}$ and $\theta = \dfrac{\pi}{10} = \underline{18^o}$

In $\triangle OAB'$, $x^2 = 100^2 + 120^2 - 2 . 100 . 120 \cos 18^o$
$$\doteqdot 1574.64$$
$$\therefore \quad x \doteqdot 39.68 \, \text{cm}$$
i.e.,   string is $\underline{39.68 \, \text{cm}}$ long.

18.4   **a**   Given $f(a) + f(b) \leqslant 2f\left(\dfrac{a + b}{2}\right)$ for all a, b

with equality when $a = b$.
We notice for $a \leqslant b$ and $f(x)$ is a straight
line between a and b then

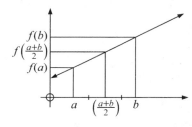

$f(a) + f(b) = 2f\left(\dfrac{a + b}{2}\right)$
Thus for

$f(a) + f(b) \leqslant 2f\left(\dfrac{a + b}{2}\right)$

$f(x)$ must be concave in the interval $a \leqslant x \leqslant b$.

Notice also that if $p > 0$, $q > 0$ then $a < \dfrac{ap + bq}{p + q} < b$

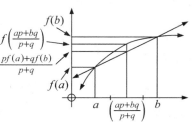

and it is easily checked that $f\left(\dfrac{ap + bq}{p + q}\right) \geqslant \dfrac{pf(a) + qf(b)}{p + q}$ ......(*)

with equality occurring when $a = b$.

Now $f\left(\dfrac{a + b + c}{3}\right) = f\left(\dfrac{2\left(\frac{a+b}{2}\right) + c}{2 + 1}\right)$

$$\geqslant \dfrac{2f\left(\frac{a+b}{2}\right) + f(c)}{2 + 1} \quad \{\text{by } (*)\}$$

i.e., $\geqslant \dfrac{f(a) + f(b) + f(c)}{3}$

with equality occurring when $\dfrac{a + b}{2} = c$ and $a = b$ i.e., $\underline{a = b = c}$.

b $\sin A + \sin B = 2\sin\left(\frac{A+B}{2}\right)\cos\left(\frac{A-B}{2}\right)$.

But, as $\cos\left(\frac{A-B}{2}\right) \leqslant 1$ then $\underline{\sin A + \sin B \leqslant 2\sin\left(\frac{A+B}{2}\right)}$.

with equality $\Longleftrightarrow$ $\cos\left(\frac{A-B}{2}\right) = 1$

$\Longleftrightarrow \quad \dfrac{A - B}{2} = k . 2\pi$

$\Longleftrightarrow \quad A - B = k . 4\pi$

$\Longleftrightarrow \quad A = B$ {all other cases are impossible}

Thus **a** is satisfied by $f(x) = \sin x$

$$\therefore \quad f(A) + f(B) + f(C) \leqslant 3f\left(\frac{A+B+C}{3}\right) \quad \text{with equality} \iff A = B = C.$$

i.e., $\sin A + \sin B + \sin C \leqslant 3\sin\left(\frac{A+B+C}{3}\right)$

with equality $\iff$ the triangle is equilateral

i.e., $\sin A + \sin B + \sin C \leqslant 3 \cdot \sin\frac{\pi}{3} \leqslant \frac{3\sqrt{3}}{2}$

$\therefore$ max. value is $\frac{3\sqrt{3}}{2}$ occurring when the triangle is equilateral.

18.5 $\alpha + 2\alpha + 2\alpha = 180^o$ {sum of angles of $\triangle$ theorem}

$\therefore \quad 5\alpha = 180^o$

$$\underline{\alpha = 36^o}$$

$\triangle ABD$ is isosceles {equal base angles} $\therefore \quad AD = BD = x$ units,   say.

In $\triangle BDC$, $\angle BDC = 2\alpha$. If we let $AB = 2$ units,   say, then

$\qquad AE = BE = 1$ unit   {$\overline{DE}$ bisects $\overline{AB}$

$\qquad\qquad\qquad\qquad\qquad$ - isosceles triangle theorem}

Now $DC = 2 - x$ units   {$\triangle ABC$ is isosceles

$\qquad\qquad\qquad\qquad\qquad$ and $AB = AC$}

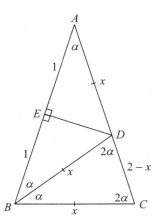

Now $\triangle$'s ABC and BCD are equiangular and $\therefore$ similar.

Hence, $\dfrac{AB}{BC} = \dfrac{BC}{CD}$

i.e. $\dfrac{2}{x} = \dfrac{x}{2-x}$

$\therefore \quad x^2 = 4 - 2x$

$\therefore \quad x^2 + 2x - 4 = 0$

which has solutions $x = -1 \pm \sqrt{5}$.

But, $x > 0$ $\therefore$ $x = \sqrt{5} - 1$.

Now $\cos\alpha = \dfrac{1}{x} = \dfrac{1}{\sqrt{5}-1} = \dfrac{1}{\sqrt{5}-1} \cdot \dfrac{\sqrt{5}+1}{\sqrt{5}+1} = \underline{\dfrac{\sqrt{5}+1}{4}}.$

18.6 Let $ABCD$ be any quadrilateral with diagonals meeting at O, and let θ be the acute angle between them.

Let $OA = a_1$, $OB = b_1$, $OC = a_2$, $OD = b_2$

$\therefore \quad a = a_1 + a_2$,   and $b = b_1 + b_2$

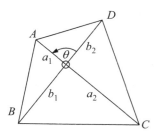

Now   area $ABCD$

$= \text{area}\,OAB + \text{area}\,OBC + \text{area}\,OCD + \text{area}\,ODA$

$= \frac{1}{2}a_1 b_1 \sin(180 - \theta) + \frac{1}{2}a_2 b_1 \sin\theta + \frac{1}{2}a_2 b_2 \sin(180 - \theta) + \frac{1}{2}a_1 b_2 \sin\theta$

$= \frac{1}{2}\sin\theta[a_1 b_1 + a_2 b_1 + a_2 b_2 + a_1 b_2]$ {as $\sin(180 - \theta) = \sin\theta$}

$= \frac{1}{2}\sin\theta(a_1 + a_2)(b_1 + b_2)$

$= \frac{1}{2}ab\sin\theta.$

Hence the ratio of areas is

$\qquad \frac{1}{2}ab\sin 30^o : \frac{1}{2}ab\sin 45^o : \frac{1}{2}ab\sin 60^o$

$= \sin 30^o : \sin 45^o : \sin 60^o$ {as a, b are same in all 3 quadrilaterals}

$= \frac{1}{2} : \frac{1}{\sqrt{2}} : \frac{\sqrt{3}}{2}$

$= \underline{1 : \sqrt{2} : \sqrt{3}}$

18.7 **a**   Let centres be O and C, points of contact A and B.
Draw   radii $\overline{AO}$ and $\overline{BC}$ perpendicular to AB.
Draw $\overline{CD} \parallel \overline{AB}$

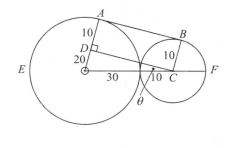

$\quad$ In $\quad \Delta OCD, \quad \sin\theta = \frac{20}{40} = \frac{1}{2}$

$\qquad\qquad \Rightarrow \qquad\quad \theta = 30^o$

$\qquad\qquad \therefore \qquad CD = AB = 20\sqrt{3} \qquad$ {Pythagoras}

$\quad$ Also $\quad \angle BCF = 60^o \quad$ and $\quad \angle AOE = 120^o$

$\quad$ Thus $\quad$ arc $BF = \frac{1}{6} \cdot 2\pi \cdot 10 = \frac{10\pi}{3}$

$\quad$ and $\quad$ arc $EA = \frac{1}{3} \cdot 2\pi \cdot 30 = 20\pi$

$\quad \therefore$ total length $= 2[\text{arc } EA + AB + \text{arc } BF]$

$$= 2\left[20\pi + 20\sqrt{3} + \frac{10\pi}{3}\right]$$

$$= \left[40\sqrt{3} + \frac{140\pi}{3}\right] \text{ cm.}$$

b   In ΔODC,

$\qquad (CD)^2 + (R-r)^2 = (R+r)^2$

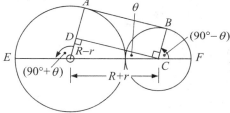

$\quad \therefore \quad (CD)^2 = (R+r)^2 - (R-r)^2$

$\qquad\qquad\qquad = (R+r+R-r)(R+r-R+r)$

$\qquad\qquad\qquad = 2R \cdot 2r$

$\quad \therefore \quad CD = AB = 2\sqrt{Rr}$

$\quad$ Also $\quad$ arc $BF = \left[\dfrac{90^o - \theta}{360^o}\right] \cdot 2\pi r$

$$= \left[\dfrac{\frac{\pi}{2} - \theta}{2\pi}\right] \cdot 2\pi r \quad \text{\{Using circular measure\}}$$

$$= \left(\frac{\pi}{2} - \theta\right) r$$

$\quad$ and $\quad$ arc $EA = \left[\dfrac{\frac{\pi}{2} + \theta}{2\pi}\right] \cdot 2\pi R$

$$= \left(\frac{\pi}{2} + \theta\right) R$$

$\quad$ where $\quad \sin\theta = \dfrac{R-r}{R+r} \quad$ and $\quad \therefore \quad \theta = \arcsin\left(\dfrac{R-r}{R+r}\right)$

$\quad$ Thus $\quad L = 2[\text{arc } EA + AB + \text{arc } BF]$

$$= 2\left[\left(\frac{\pi}{2} + \theta\right) R + 2\sqrt{Rr} + \left(\frac{\pi}{2} - \theta\right) r\right]$$

$$= 2\left[2\sqrt{Rr} + \frac{\pi}{2}(R+r) + \theta(R-r)\right]$$

$\quad$ i.e. $\quad L = 4\sqrt{Rr} + \pi(R+r) + 2(R-r)\arcsin\left(\dfrac{R-r}{R+r}\right)$

18.8 a   Let $AB = AC = a$ units   and let $\angle NAM = \theta$

$\therefore$ $BC = \sqrt{2}a$ units   {Pythagoras}

Draw $\overline{AX} \perp \overline{BC}$.

Now X is the midpoint of $\overline{BC}$ and hence $\overline{MN}$,

and $\overline{AX}$ bisects $\angle NAM$.

Thus $MX = \frac{1}{6}BC = \dfrac{\sqrt{2}a}{6}$ units.

and $AX = BX = \dfrac{\sqrt{2}a}{2}$ units   {$\triangle AXB$ is isosceles}

$\therefore$ $\tan\dfrac{\theta}{2} = \dfrac{MX}{AX} = \dfrac{\sqrt{2}a}{6} \cdot \dfrac{2}{\sqrt{2}a} = \dfrac{1}{3}$

$\therefore$ $\dfrac{\theta}{2} = \arctan\left(\tfrac{1}{3}\right)$

$\therefore$ $\theta = 2\arctan\left(\tfrac{1}{3}\right) \doteq 36 \cdot 87°$

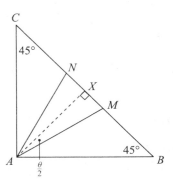

b   Let $BM = MN = NC = x$ units

and $\angle ACB = \theta$

then $AC = 3x\cos\theta$

In $\triangle ANC$, $b^2 = x^2 + [3x\cos\theta]^2 - 2 \cdot x \cdot [3x\cos\theta] \cdot \cos\theta$

$\therefore$ $b^2 = x^2 + 3x^2\cos^2\theta$ ...... (1)

Likewise in $\triangle AMC$,

$a^2 = [2x]^2 + [3x\cos\theta]^2 - 2 \cdot [2x] \cdot [3x\cos\theta] \cdot \cos\theta$

$\therefore$ $a^2 = 4x^2 - 3x^2\cos^2\theta$ ...... (2)

In (1) and (2), equating $3x^2\cos^2\theta$

we get $b^2 - x^2 = 4x^2 - a^2$

thus $5x^2 = a^2 + b^2$

$\therefore$ $x^2 = \dfrac{a^2 + b^2}{5}$

$\therefore$ $x = \sqrt{\dfrac{a^2 + b^2}{5}}$

i.e., $MN = \sqrt{\dfrac{a^2 + b^2}{5}}$

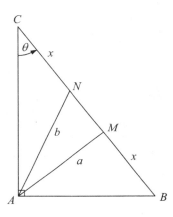

18.9 $OA = 10 - r$, $\sin\theta = \dfrac{r}{10 - r}$ in $\triangle OAB$

Now in $\triangle OAC$, using the Cosine Rule

$(5 + r)^2 = 5^2 + (10 - r)^2 - 2 \cdot 5 \cdot (10 - r) \cdot \cos(90° - \theta)$

$\therefore$ $25 + 10r + r^2 = 25 + 100 - 20r + r^2 - 10(10 - r)\sin\theta$

$\therefore$ $10r = 100 - 20r - 10(10 - r) \cdot \dfrac{r}{(10 - r)}$

$\therefore$ $10r = 100 - 20r - 10r$

$\therefore$ $40r = 100$

$\therefore$ $r = 2\tfrac{1}{2}$ cm.

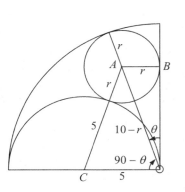

18.10 Using the Cosine Rule:

$$p^2 = \frac{a^2}{4} + \frac{b^2}{4} - 2 \cdot \frac{a}{2} \cdot \frac{b}{2} \cos\theta$$

i.e. $\quad p^2 = \frac{a^2}{4} + \frac{b^2}{4} + \frac{ab\cos\theta}{2} \quad \dots\dots (1)$

Likewise $\quad q^2 = \frac{a^2}{4} + \frac{b^2}{4} - 2 \cdot \frac{a}{2} \cdot \frac{b}{2} \cos(180^\circ - \theta)$

$\therefore \quad q^2 = \frac{a^2}{4} + \frac{b^2}{4} + \frac{ab\cos\theta}{2} \quad \dots\dots (2)$

But $\quad x^2 = p^2 + q^2 \qquad \{\text{Pythagoras}\}$

$\therefore \quad x^2 = \frac{a^2}{2} + \frac{b^2}{2}$

$\therefore \quad x^2 = \frac{a^2 + b^2}{2}$

$\therefore \quad x = \sqrt{\dfrac{a^2 + b^2}{2}} \quad$ as $\quad x > 0.$

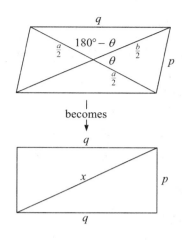

becomes

18.11 By the Sine Rule, $\quad \dfrac{\sin 2\theta}{b} = \dfrac{\sin\theta}{a}$

$\therefore \quad \dfrac{2\sin\theta\cos\theta}{\sin\theta} = \dfrac{b}{a}$

$\therefore \quad \cos\theta = \dfrac{b}{2a} \dots\dots (1) \qquad \{\text{as } \theta \neq 0^\circ,\ 180^\circ, \quad \sin\theta \neq 0\}$

But $\quad a^2 = b^2 + c^2 - 2bc\cos\theta$

$\therefore \quad a^2 = b^2 + c^2 - 2bc\left(\dfrac{b}{2a}\right)$

$\therefore \quad a^2 - c^2 = b^2 - \dfrac{b^2 c}{a}$

$\therefore \quad (a+c)(a-c) = b^2\left(\dfrac{a-c}{a}\right)$

$\therefore \quad a + c = \dfrac{b^2}{a} \qquad \text{p.v.} \quad a - c \neq 0$

$\therefore \quad b^2 = a(a+c) \quad \text{p.v.} \quad a \neq c$

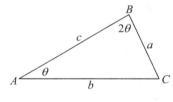

However, if $\underline{a = c}$, $\triangle ABC$ is right-angled isosceles,
as $\quad 4\theta = 180^\circ \quad \Rightarrow \quad \theta = 45^\circ$
and checking, $\quad b^2 = (\sqrt{2}a)^2 = 2a^2$
and $\quad a(a+c) = a(a+a) = a \cdot 2a = 2a^2$
Hence the result holds in this special case also.

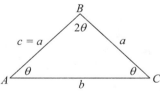

18.12 a In $\triangle ABF$, $\quad \angle AFB = 90^\circ$

$\therefore \quad AF = x\sin 30^\circ = \dfrac{x}{2}$

and $\quad BF = x\cos 30^\circ = \dfrac{x\sqrt{3}}{2}$

In $\triangle BFE$, $\quad \tan 40^\circ = \dfrac{FE}{BF} = \dfrac{FE}{\dfrac{x\sqrt{3}}{2}}$

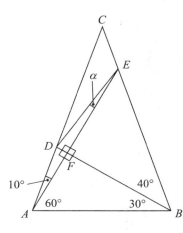

$$\therefore \quad FE = \left(\frac{\sqrt{3}}{2}\tan 40^o\right).x$$

Likewise in $\triangle ADF$, $DF = \left(\frac{1}{2}\tan 10^o\right).x$

Thus in $\triangle DEF$,

$$\tan \alpha = \frac{DF}{FE} = \frac{\left(\frac{1}{2}\tan 10^o\right).x}{\left(\frac{\sqrt{3}}{2}\tan 40^o\right).x} = \frac{\tan 10^o}{\sqrt{3}\tan 40^o}$$

$$\therefore \quad \alpha \doteq 6\cdot 918^o$$

b Since $\triangle ABD$ is right-angled

$$AD = x\sin 30^o = \frac{x}{2}$$

In $\triangle ABE$, $\dfrac{AE}{\sin 60^o} = \dfrac{x}{\sin 80^o}$

$$\Rightarrow \quad AE = \frac{\frac{\sqrt{3}}{2}x}{\sin 80^o}$$

Thus in $\triangle ADE$, $\angle ADE = 90 + (70 - \alpha) = 160 - \alpha$

$$\text{Thus} \quad \frac{\sin(160 - \alpha)}{AE} = \frac{\sin \alpha}{\frac{x}{2}}$$

$$\therefore \quad \frac{\sin(160 - \alpha)}{\sin \alpha} = \frac{\frac{\sqrt{3}}{2}x}{\sin 80^o}\cdot\frac{2}{x} = \frac{\sqrt{3}}{\sin 80^o}$$

$$\therefore \quad \frac{\sin 160\cos \alpha - \cos 160\sin \alpha}{\sin \alpha} = \frac{\sqrt{3}}{\sin 80^o}$$

$$\therefore \quad \sin 20^o \cot \alpha + \cos 20^o = \frac{\sqrt{3}}{\sin 80^o}$$

which simplifies to

$$\tan \alpha = \frac{\sin 20^o \sin 80^o}{\sqrt{3} - \cos 20^o \sin 80^o} \doteq 0\cdot 41757 \qquad \text{and so} \quad \alpha \doteq 22\cdot 66^o.$$

18.13 $\angle c = 180 - 2\alpha - 2\beta$

$\therefore$ each angle at C is $90 - [\alpha + \beta]$.

$\therefore \quad \tan(90 - [\alpha + \beta]) = \cot[\alpha + \beta] = \dfrac{r}{x}$

$\therefore \quad \tan[\alpha + \beta] = \dfrac{x}{r}$

$\therefore \quad x = r\tan[\alpha + \beta]$

$$= r\left[\frac{\tan \alpha + \tan \beta}{1 - \tan \alpha \tan \beta}\right]$$

$$= r\left[\frac{\frac{r}{a} + \frac{r}{b}}{1 - \frac{r}{a}\cdot\frac{r}{b}}\right]\cdot\frac{ab}{ab}$$

$$= \frac{r^2(a + b)}{ab - r^2}$$

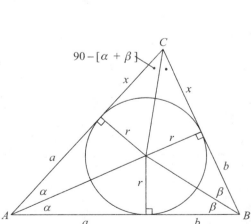

Now   area $\triangle OAB$ = area OAB + area $\triangle OBC$ + area $\triangle OCA$

$$= \tfrac{1}{2}(a+b)r + \tfrac{1}{2}(b+x)r + \tfrac{1}{2}(x+a)r$$

$$= \tfrac{1}{2}r[2a + 2b + 2x]$$

$$= r[a + b + x]$$

$$= r\left[(a+b) + \frac{r^2(a+b)}{ab - r^2}\right]$$

$$= \frac{(a+b)r}{ab - r^2}\left[ab - r^2 + r^2\right]$$

$$= \frac{abr[a+b]}{ab - r^2}$$

18.14 a $\tan A + \tan B + \tan C$

$$= \tan A + \tan B + \tan(180 - [A+B])$$

$$= \tan A + \tan B - \tan[A+B] \qquad \{\tan(180 - \theta) = -\tan\theta\}$$

$$= \frac{\tan A + \tan B}{1} - \frac{\tan A + \tan B}{1 - \tan A \tan B}$$

$$= \frac{(\tan A + \tan B)(1 - \tan A \tan B) - \tan A - \tan B}{1 - \tan A \tan B}$$

$$= \frac{-\tan^2 A \tan B - \tan A \tan^2 b}{1 - \tan A \tan B}$$

$$= -\tan A \tan B \left[\frac{\tan A + \tan B}{1 - \tan A \tan B}\right]$$

$$= -\tan A \tan B \tan[A+B]$$

$$= \tan A \tan B . -\tan[A+B]$$

$$= \underline{\tan A \tan B \tan C} \qquad \{\text{comparing line (1) and line (3) of argument}\}$$

b   If $\tan A + \tan B + \tan C = \tan A \tan B \tan C$

then $\tan A + \tan B = \tan C[\tan A \tan B - 1]$

$\therefore \quad \dfrac{\tan A + \tan B}{1 - \tan A \tan B} = -\tan C \qquad$ p.v. $\tan A \tan B \neq 1 ......(*)$

$\therefore \quad \tan(A+B) = \tan(-C)$

$\qquad \therefore \quad A + B = -C + k.\pi$ where k is an integer $\{\text{equal tan's are } 180^o \text{ apart}\}$

$\therefore \quad A + B + C = k\pi, \quad k\varepsilon Z$

Condition $(*)$ is <u>necessary</u> and is true for all A and B.

Proof: If $\tan A \tan B = 1$

then $\tan A + \tan B + \tan C = \tan C$

$\therefore \quad \tan A + \tan B = 0$

$\therefore \quad \tan B = -\tan A$

$\therefore \quad -\tan^2 A = 1$

$\therefore \quad \tan^2 A = -1 \qquad$ which is absurd, etc.

18.15 By the Cosine Rule, $5^2 = 6^2 + x^2 - 2.6.x.\cos\theta$

i.e. $x^2 + [-12\cos\theta]x + 11 = 0$

Now for the triangle to exist x must be <u>real</u>$_{(1)}$ and <u>positive</u>$_{(2)}$.

$\therefore \quad \Delta \geqslant 0$ <u>and</u> sum and product of roots are positive.

$$144\cos^2\theta - 44 \geqslant 0$$

$$\therefore \quad |\cos\theta| \geqslant \frac{\sqrt{11}}{6}$$

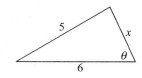

$$\therefore \quad \cos\theta \geqslant \frac{\sqrt{11}}{6}$$

$$\therefore \quad \frac{\sqrt{11}}{6} \leqslant \cos\theta < 1$$

i.e. $\quad 0 < \theta \leqslant \cos^{-1}\left(\frac{\sqrt{11}}{6}\right)$

$$\therefore \quad 0° < \theta \leqslant 56 \cdot 44°$$

18.16 Let $\quad \tan^{-1}\left(\frac{1}{3}\right) = \theta \quad$ and $\quad \tan^{-1}\left(\frac{1}{7}\right) = \phi$

$\therefore \quad \tan\theta = \frac{1}{3} \quad$ and $\quad \tan\phi = \frac{1}{7}$

Now $\quad 2\tan^{-1}\left(\frac{1}{3}\right) + \tan^{-1}\left(\frac{1}{7}\right) = 2\theta + \phi \quad$ and

$$\tan(2\theta + \phi) = \frac{\tan 2\theta + \tan\phi}{1 - \tan 2\theta \,.\, \tan\phi}$$

$$= \frac{\dfrac{2\tan\theta}{1 - \tan^2\theta} + \tan\phi}{1 - \dfrac{2\tan\theta}{1 - \tan^2\theta} \,.\, \tan\phi}$$

$$= \frac{\dfrac{\frac{2}{3}}{1 - \frac{1}{9}} + \frac{1}{7}}{1 - \dfrac{\frac{2}{3}}{1 - \frac{1}{9}} \,.\, \frac{1}{7}}$$

$$= \left[\frac{\frac{3}{4} + \frac{1}{7}}{1 - \frac{3}{4} \cdot \frac{1}{7}}\right] \cdot \frac{28}{28}$$

$$= \frac{21 + 4}{28 - 3}$$

$$= 1$$

$\therefore \quad$ one value of $\quad 2\theta + \phi \quad$ is $\quad \dfrac{\pi}{4}$.

i.e. $\quad$ one value of $\quad 2\tan^{-1}\left(\frac{1}{3}\right) + \tan^{-1}\left(\frac{1}{7}\right) = \dfrac{\pi}{4}$

[actually, $\quad 2\tan^{-1}\left(\frac{1}{3}\right) + \tan^{-1}\left(\frac{1}{7}\right) = \dfrac{\pi}{4} + k\pi, \quad k$ any integer]

18.17 Let O be the centre of the sphere.
Because of the symmetry O lies on $\overline{AG}$
where G is the centroid of $\triangle BCD$.

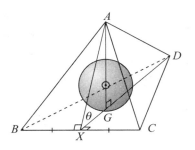

Now $\quad DX = 5\sqrt{3}\,$cm $\quad$ {Pythagoras}

$\therefore \quad DG = \frac{2}{3} \cdot 5\sqrt{3}\,$cm

and $\quad \underline{GX = \frac{1}{3} \cdot 5\sqrt{3}\,\text{cm}} \quad$ {Property of centroid}

Consider $\triangle AXG$:

$$\cos\theta = \frac{\frac{5\sqrt{3}}{3}}{5\sqrt{3}} = \frac{1}{3}$$

But $\quad \cos\theta = 1 - 2\sin^2\left(\frac{\theta}{2}\right)$

$\therefore \quad\quad \frac{1}{3} = 1 - 2\sin^2\left(\frac{\theta}{2}\right)$

$\therefore \quad \sin^2\left(\frac{\theta}{2}\right) = \frac{1}{3}$

$\therefore \quad \sin\left(\frac{\theta}{2}\right) = \frac{1}{\sqrt{3}} \quad$ as $\frac{\theta}{2}$ is acute.

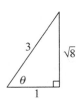

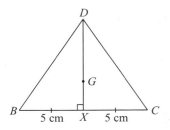

But $\tan\left(\frac{\theta}{2}\right) = \frac{1}{\sqrt{2}} = \frac{r}{\frac{5\sqrt{3}}{3}}$

$\therefore \quad r = \frac{5\sqrt{3}}{3} \cdot \frac{1}{\sqrt{2}} \cdot \frac{\sqrt{2}}{\sqrt{2}} = \frac{5\sqrt{6}}{6}$

Thus the sphere has radius $\frac{5\sqrt{6}}{6}$ cm.

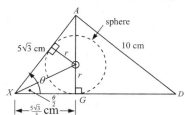

18.18 Let $\triangle ABC$ have sides of length a, b, c units and let $AP = x$ units.

$\therefore \quad BP = c - x$. But $PQRB$ is a parallelogram $\therefore \quad QR = c - x$ units.

Also $\dfrac{PQ}{BC} = \dfrac{AP}{AB}$ {$\triangle APQ$ is similar to $\triangle ABC$}

$\therefore \quad \dfrac{PQ}{a} = \dfrac{x}{c} \quad \Rightarrow \quad PQ = \dfrac{ax}{c}$

Thus the area of $\triangle PQR = \frac{1}{2} PQ . QR . \sin\theta$ where θ is constant.

$= \frac{1}{2} \cdot \dfrac{ax}{c} (c - x) \sin\theta$

$= \dfrac{a\sin\theta}{2c}(cx - x^2)$ {where $\dfrac{a\sin\theta}{2c}$ is positive constant.}

which is a quadratic in x

and the area is a maximum when $x = \dfrac{-B}{2A} = \dfrac{-c}{-2} = \dfrac{c}{2}$,

i.e.,   when P is the midpoint of $\overline{AC}$.

18.19 Centres are at the corners of a regular tetrahedron
with sides 2 cm.

$\therefore$ total height $= 2$ cm $+$ height of the tetrahedron
$= 2 + h$

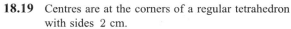

By the Cosine Rule: In $\triangle ABD$,

$2^2 = \left(\sqrt{3}\right)^2 + \left(\sqrt{3}\right)^2 - 2\sqrt{3} . \sqrt{3}\cos\theta$

$\therefore \qquad 4 = 3 + 3 - 6\cos\theta$

$\therefore \qquad 6\cos\theta = 2$

$\cos\theta = \frac{1}{3}$

$\therefore \qquad \sin\theta = \dfrac{2\sqrt{2}}{3} = \dfrac{h}{\sqrt{3}}$

$h = \dfrac{2\sqrt{2}}{\sqrt{3}}$

$\therefore$ total height $= \left(2 + \dfrac{2\sqrt{2}}{\sqrt{3}}\right)$ cm

$= 2\left(1 + \sqrt{\dfrac{2}{3}}\right)$ cm

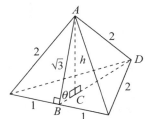

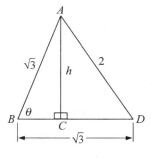

18.20 Using the Cosine Rule

$(AB)^2 = a^2 + d^2 - 2ad\cos\theta$

and $(AB)^2 = b^2 + c^2 - 2bc\cos(180^\circ - \theta)$

$\therefore \quad a^2 + d^2 - 2ad\cos\theta = b^2 + c^2 - 2bc(-\cos\theta)$

$\therefore \quad \cos\theta[2bc + 2ad] = a^2 + d^2 - b^2 - c^2$

$\therefore \qquad \cos\theta = \dfrac{a^2 + b^2 - c^2 - d^2}{2(ad + bc)}$

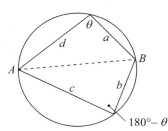

Now   area $= \frac{1}{2}ad\sin\theta + \frac{1}{2}bc\sin(180^\circ - \theta)$

$= \frac{1}{2}ad\sin\theta + \frac{1}{2}bc\sin\theta$

$= \frac{1}{2}\sin\theta(ad + bc)$

$= \dfrac{ad + bc}{2}\sqrt{1 - \left[\dfrac{a^2 + d^2 - b^2 - c^2}{2(ad + bc)}\right]^2}$

$= \sqrt{\left(\dfrac{ad + bc}{2}\right)^2 \cdot \dfrac{[2(ad + bc)]^2 - [a^2 + d^2 - b^2 - c^2]}{4(ad + bc)^2}}$

$= \sqrt{\tfrac{1}{16}(2ad + 2bc + a^2 + d^2 - b^2 - c^2)(2ad + 2bc - a^2 - d^2 + b^2 + c^2)}$

$= \sqrt{\tfrac{1}{16}([a + d]^2 - [b - c]^2)([b + c]^2 - [a - d]^2)}$

$= \sqrt{\tfrac{1}{16}(a + d + b - c)(a + d - b + c)(b + c + a - d)(b + c - a + d)}$

$= \sqrt{\tfrac{1}{16}(2s - 2c)(2s - 2b)(2s - 2d)(2s - 2a)}$

$= \underline{\underline{\sqrt{(s - a)(s - b)(s - c)(s - d)}}}$

18.21   Let $P(a\cos\theta,\ b\sin\theta)$ lie on the ellipse with

equation $\dfrac{x^2}{a^2} + \dfrac{y^2}{b^2} = 1$

and let Q have coordinates (X, Y)

$\therefore$ $\sqrt{(X - a\cos\theta)^2 + (Y - b\sin\theta)^2} = 10$

Thus $(X - a\cos\theta)^2 + (Y - b\sin\theta)^2 = 100$

Also $\dfrac{Y - b\sin\theta}{X - a\cos\theta} = \dfrac{Y}{X}$ {equating slopes of $\overline{QP}$ and $\overline{OQ}$}

$\therefore$ $\dfrac{X}{Y} = \dfrac{a\cos\theta}{b\sin\theta}$

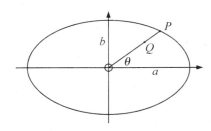

Thus $X = a\cos\theta\, t$ and $Y = b\sin\theta\, t$ for nonzero real number t.

$\therefore$ $(a\cos\theta\, t - a\cos\theta)^2 + (b\sin\theta\, t - b\sin\theta)^2 = 100$

Thus $a^2\cos^2\theta[t - 1]^2 + b^2\sin^2\theta[t - 1]^2 = 100$

$\therefore$ $t = 1 \pm \dfrac{10}{\sqrt{a^2\cos^2\theta + b^2\sin^2\theta}}$ which varies as θ varies.

If Q lies on an ellipse its centre would be $(0, 0)$ and its equation $\dfrac{X^2}{a^2 t^2} + \dfrac{Y^2}{b^2 t^2} = 1$.

But $a^2 t^2$ and $b^2 t^2$ need to be constants, and this is impossible.

$\therefore$ Q does not trace out an ellipse   (although it looks like one.)

18.22   Using the Cosine Rule in $\triangle ABC$,

$(2a)^2 = a^2 + (3b)^2 - 2\,.\,a\,.\,3b\cos(180^\circ - \theta)$

gives $4a^2 = a^2 + 9b^2 - 6ab[\cos 180^\circ \cos\theta + \sin 180^\circ \sin\theta]$

i.e. $3a^2 = 9b^2 - 6ab[-\cos\theta]$

or $a^2 = 3b^2 + 2ab\cos\theta$ ...... (1)

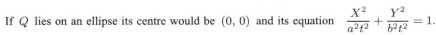

Hence $(CD)^2 = a^2 + b^2 - 2ab\cos\theta$ {Cosine Rule again}

$= a^2 + b^2 - 2ab\left[\dfrac{a^2 - 3b^2}{2ab}\right]$

$$= a^2 + b^2 - (a^2 - 3b^2)$$
$$= a^2 + b^2 - a^2 + 3b^2$$
$$= 4b^2$$
$$\therefore \quad CD = 2b \quad \text{as} \quad b > 0$$

i.e., $\overline{CD}$ is twice as long as $\overline{AD}$.

18.23 By the cosine rule

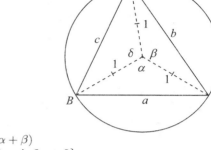

$$a^2 = 2 - 2\cos\delta$$
$$b^2 = 2 - 2\cos\beta$$
$$c^2 = 2 - 2\cos\alpha$$
$$\therefore \quad a^2 + b^2 + c^2 = 6 - 2(\cos\alpha + \cos\beta + \cos\delta) \ldots\ldots (1)$$

We now have to prove $\cos\alpha + \cos\beta + \cos\delta \geqslant -\frac{3}{2}$
for all $\alpha > 0, \quad \beta > 0, \quad \delta > 0, \quad \alpha + \beta + \delta = 2\pi.$

Now $\quad \cos\alpha + \cos\beta + \cos\delta$
$$= \cos\alpha + \cos\beta + \cos[2\pi - (\alpha + \beta)]$$
$$= \cos\alpha + \cos\beta + \cos 2\pi \cos(\alpha + \beta) + \sin 2\pi \sin(\alpha + \beta)$$
$$= \cos\alpha + \cos\beta + \cos(\alpha + \beta) \quad \{\text{as} \quad \cos 2\pi = 1 \quad \sin 2\pi = 0\}$$
$$= \cos(\alpha + \beta) + \cos\alpha + \cos\beta$$
$$= 2\cos\left(\frac{\alpha + \beta + \alpha}{2}\right)\cos\left(\frac{\alpha + \beta - \alpha}{2}\right) + \cos\beta$$
$$= 2\cos\left(\frac{2\alpha + \beta}{2}\right)\cos\left(\frac{\beta}{2}\right) + \cos\beta$$
$$\geqslant -2\cos\left(\frac{\beta}{2}\right) + \cos\beta \quad \text{with equality} \quad \text{when} \quad \cos\left(\frac{2\alpha + \beta}{2}\right) = -1$$
$$\text{i.e.} \quad \frac{2\alpha + \beta}{2} = \pi$$
$$\text{or} \quad 2\alpha + \beta = 2\pi$$

i.e. $\quad \geqslant 2\cos^2\left(\frac{\beta}{2}\right) - 2\cos\left(\frac{\beta}{2}\right) - 1$

i.e. $\quad \geqslant 2\left(\cos^2\left(\frac{\beta}{2}\right) - \cos\left(\frac{\beta}{2}\right) + \frac{1}{4}\right) - 1 - \frac{1}{2}$

i.e. $\quad \geqslant 2\left(\cos\left(\frac{\beta}{2}\right) - \frac{1}{2}\right)^2 - \frac{3}{2}$

i.e. $\quad \geqslant -\frac{3}{2}$

with equality when $\quad \cos\left(\frac{\beta}{2}\right) = \frac{1}{2}$ and $\quad 2\alpha + \beta = 2\pi$

$$\text{i.e.,} \quad \frac{\beta}{2} = \frac{\pi}{3} \quad \text{and} \quad 2\alpha + \beta = 2\pi$$

$$\text{i.e.,} \quad \beta = \frac{2\pi}{3} \quad \text{and} \quad 2\alpha + \beta = 2\pi$$

$$\text{i.e.,} \quad \alpha = \beta = \delta = \frac{2\pi}{3}$$

Thus in (1) $\quad a^2 + b^2 + c^2 \leqslant 6 - 2\left(-\frac{3}{2}\right) \quad \text{i.e.,} \quad \leqslant \underline{9} \quad$ with equality when $\triangle ABC$ is equilateral.

18.24 $\quad \frac{1}{2}ab\sin\theta = 2k$

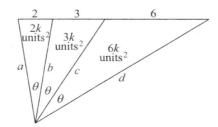

$\frac{1}{2}bc\sin\theta = 3k$

$\frac{1}{2}cd\sin\theta = 6k$

$\frac{1}{2}ac\sin 2\theta = 5k$

$\frac{1}{2}bd\sin 2\theta = 9k$

Thus $\dfrac{a}{c} = \dfrac{2}{3}$, $\dfrac{b}{d} = \dfrac{1}{2}$, $\dfrac{ac}{bd} = \dfrac{5}{9}$

$\therefore$ $a = 2r$, $c = 3r$, $b = s$, $d = 2s$

$\therefore$ $\dfrac{6r^2}{2s^2} = \dfrac{5}{9}$

$\therefore$ $\dfrac{r^2}{s^2} = \dfrac{5}{27}$,   i.e., $\dfrac{r}{s} = \dfrac{\sqrt{5}}{3\sqrt{3}}$

$\therefore$ $r = \sqrt{5}\,k$, $s = 3\sqrt{3}\,k$.

Hence $a = 2\sqrt{5}\,k$, $b = 3\sqrt{3}\,k$, $c = 3\sqrt{5}\,k$, $d = 6\sqrt{3}\,k$

But $\dfrac{\frac{1}{2}ac \cdot 2\sin\theta\cos\theta}{\frac{1}{2}ab\sin\theta} = \dfrac{5k}{2k}$

$\therefore$ $\dfrac{c}{b} \cdot 2\cos\theta = \dfrac{5}{2}$

$\therefore$ $\dfrac{2\sqrt{5}}{\sqrt{3}}\cos\theta = \dfrac{5}{2}$ and hence $\cos\theta = \dfrac{\sqrt{15}}{4}$

and $2^2 = a^2 + b^2 - 2ab\cos\theta$

$\therefore$ $4 = 20k^2 + 27k^2 - 2 \cdot 2\sqrt{5}\,k \cdot 3\sqrt{3}\,k \cdot \dfrac{\sqrt{15}}{4}$

$\therefore$ $4 = 47k^2 - 45k^2$

$\therefore$ $4 = 2k^2$

$k^2 = 2$

$\therefore$ $k = \sqrt{2}$ as $k > 0$

and $a = 2\sqrt{10}$

$\therefore$ $\underline{AB \text{ is } 2\sqrt{10} \text{ cm long.}}$

18.25   Using the Sine Rule:

(1) $\dfrac{a}{\sin 100^o} = \dfrac{PQ}{\sin 40^o}$, $\therefore$ $a = \dfrac{PQ \cdot \sin 100^o}{\sin 40^o}$

(2) $\dfrac{c}{\sin 20^o} = \dfrac{PQ}{\sin 60^o}$, $\therefore$ $c = \dfrac{PQ \cdot \sin 20^o}{\sin 60^o}$

(3) $\dfrac{b}{\sin 100^o} = \dfrac{PQ}{\sin 60^o}$, $\therefore$ $b = \dfrac{PQ \cdot \sin 100^o}{\sin 60^o}$

$b + c - a = PQ\left(\dfrac{\sin 100^o}{\sin 60^o} + \dfrac{\sin 20^o}{\sin 60^o} - \dfrac{\sin 100^o}{\sin 40^o}\right)$

$= PQ \times 0$

$= 0$

$\therefore$ $a = b + c$,   i.e., $\underline{RQ = QS + SP.}$

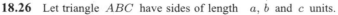

18.26   Let triangle ABC have sides of length a, b and c units.

Let $BP = ar$, $0 < r < 1$ $\therefore$ $PC = a - ar$
$QC = bs$, $0 < s < 1$ $\therefore$ $AQ = b - bs$
$AR = ct$, $0 < t < 1$ $\therefore$ $BR = c - ct$

Now $\dfrac{BP}{BC} = r$, $\dfrac{CQ}{CA} = s$, $\dfrac{AR}{AB} = t$

$\therefore$ $\underline{r = s = t.}$

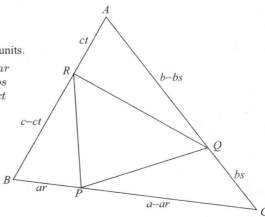

Now   area $\Delta BPR = \frac{1}{2}(ar)(c - ct)\sin\theta$

$$= \frac{1}{2}ac\sin\theta \,.\, r(1-t)$$

$$= r(1-r)\,.\,\Delta \quad \text{where} \quad \Delta = \text{area } \Delta ABC \qquad \{r = t\}$$

Likewise,   area $\Delta ARQ = $ area $\Delta QPC = r(1-r)\Delta$

Thus, $\dfrac{\text{area } \Delta PQR}{\text{area } \Delta ABC} = \dfrac{\Delta - 3r(1-r)\Delta}{\Delta} = 1 - 3r(1-r)$

Thus, $1 - 3r + 3r^2 = r$,   which when solved gives $r = \frac{1}{3}$.

18.27 **a** $P(a\cos\theta,\ b\sin\theta)$ satisfies the equation $\dfrac{x^2}{a^2} + \dfrac{y^2}{b^2} = 1$

as $\dfrac{a^2\cos^2\theta}{a^2} + \dfrac{b^2\sin^2\theta}{b^2} = \cos^2\theta + \sin^2\theta = 1$

Thus for all values of θ, $(a\cos\theta,\ b\sin\theta)$ lies on the ellipse.

> Notice: (1) θ is said to be a parameter,
> (2) $0 \leqslant \theta \leqslant 2\pi$ is sufficient,
> (3) as $\cos\theta$ satisfies the inequality $-1 \leqslant \cos\theta \leqslant 1$,
> then $-a \leqslant a\cos\theta \leqslant a$, $(a > 0)$
> $\Rightarrow \quad -a \leqslant x_p \leqslant a$.
> Likewise, $-b \leqslant y_p \leqslant b$

b **i** Area $PQRS = 4\,.\,a\cos\theta\,.\,b\sin\theta$, $0 < \theta < \dfrac{\pi}{2}$

$$= 4ab\sin\theta\cos\theta$$

$$= 2ab\sin 2\theta$$

which is maximised when $\sin 2\theta = 1$

$$\therefore \quad 2\theta = 90^o$$

$$\therefore \quad \theta = 45^o$$

Thus P is $\left(\dfrac{a}{\sqrt{2}},\ \dfrac{b}{\sqrt{2}}\right)$

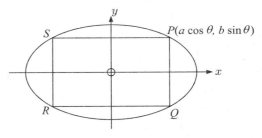

Hence P is located at the point where the diagonal $\overline{LN}$ of the outer rectangle meets the ellipse.

[This line has equation $y = \dfrac{b}{a}x$ and P satisfies it.]

ii The perimeter of $PQRS = 4[a\cos\theta + b\sin\theta]$, $0 < \theta < \dfrac{\pi}{2}$

$$= 4\sqrt{a^2 + b^2}\,.\,\sin(\theta + \alpha) \quad \text{where} \quad \tan\alpha = \dfrac{a}{b}$$

{Auxilliary angle formula}

thus maximum perimeter is obtained when $\sin(\theta + \alpha) = 1$

$$\therefore \quad \theta + \alpha = 90^o$$

$$\therefore \quad \tan\theta = \tan(90 - \alpha) = \cot\alpha = \dfrac{b}{a}$$

$$\therefore \quad \sin\theta = \dfrac{b}{\sqrt{a^2 + b^2}}, \quad \cos\theta = \dfrac{a}{\sqrt{a^2 + b^2}}$$

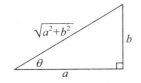

Thus point P is $\left(\dfrac{a^2}{\sqrt{a^2 + b^2}},\ \dfrac{b^2}{\sqrt{a^2 + b^2}}\right)$

18.28   Since $\tan A + 1 = \dfrac{\sin A}{\cos A} + 1$

$$= \frac{\sin A + \cos A}{\cos A}$$

$$= \sqrt{2} \sin \left(A + \frac{\pi}{4} \right) . \sec A$$

Then $\tan A + 1 \leqslant \sqrt{2} \sec A$ $\left\{ \text{as}\ \ \sin \left(A + \dfrac{\pi}{4} \right) \leqslant 1\ \ \text{for all}\ \ 0 < A < \dfrac{\pi}{2}, \ \ \text{given} \right\}$

also $\tan B + 1 \leqslant \sqrt{2} \sec B$

$\therefore$ $\underline{\tan A + \tan B + 2 \leqslant \sqrt{2}\, (\sec A + \sec B)}$ on adding these two inequalities.

18.29 $C = 2\pi r = 2\pi$ $\therefore$ $r = 1$ unit

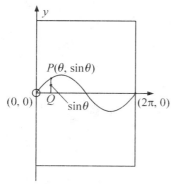
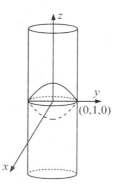
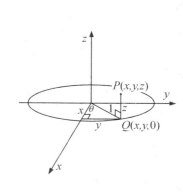

If $P(x, y, z)$ lies on the curve

then $Q(x, y, 0)$ lies in the xoy plane

and $Q(x, y, 0)$ lies on the unit circle.

Thus $x = \cos\theta$, $\quad y = \sin\theta$, $\quad z = PQ = \sin\theta$.

Hence $\underline{y = z}$,   which is the equation of a plane in 3-D coordinate geometry.

$\therefore$ P lies on a plane in space.

Since the plane cuts the cylinder at an angle α where $0 < \alpha < 90^{\circ}$ then $\underline{P \text{ lies on an ellipse.}}$

18.30 $\tan 2\alpha = \dfrac{a}{b}$ and $\tan 3\alpha = \dfrac{2a}{b}$.

$\therefore$ $\tan 3\alpha = 2 \tan 2\alpha$

$\therefore$ $\dfrac{\tan\alpha + \tan 2\alpha}{1 - \tan\alpha \tan 2\alpha} = 2 \tan 2\alpha$

$\therefore$ $\dfrac{t + \dfrac{2t}{1 - t^2}}{1 - t . \dfrac{2t}{1 - t^2}} = 2 . \dfrac{2t}{1 - t^2}$ where $t = \tan\alpha$

$\therefore$ $\dfrac{t - t^3 + 2t}{1 - t^2 - 2t^2} = \dfrac{4t}{1 - t^2}$

$\therefore$ $\dfrac{3t - t^3}{1 - 3t^2} = \dfrac{4t}{1 - t^2}$

$\therefore$ $\dfrac{3 - t^2}{1 - 3t^2} = \dfrac{4}{1 - t^2}$ $\{$as $t = \tan\alpha \neq 0\}$

$\therefore$ $(3 - t^2)(1 - t^2) = 4 - 12t^2$

$\therefore$ $3 - 4t^2 + t^4 = 4(1 - 3t^2)$

$\therefore$ $t^4 + 8t^2 - 1 = 0$

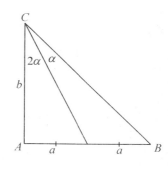

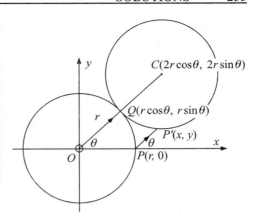

$$\therefore \quad t^2 = \frac{-8 \pm \sqrt{64 - 4(1)(-1)}}{2}$$

$$\text{i.e.} \quad t^2 = \frac{-8 \pm \sqrt{68}}{2}$$

$$\therefore \quad t^2 = \frac{\sqrt{68} - 8}{2} \qquad \{\text{as } t^2 \geqslant 0\}$$

$$\text{i.e.} \quad \tan^2 \alpha = \sqrt{17} - 4$$

$$\therefore \quad \tan \alpha = \sqrt{\sqrt{17} - 4} \qquad \{\text{as } \tan \alpha > 0\}$$

$$\therefore \quad \alpha = \tan^{-1}\left(\sqrt{\sqrt{17} - 4}\right) \qquad \{\doteq 19 \cdot 33^\circ\}$$

18.31

$$\text{arc } QP = \text{arc } QP'$$

$$\therefore \quad QP = QP'$$

$$\text{Thus} \quad (QP)^2 = (QP')^2$$

$$\text{i.e.} \quad (r \cos\theta - r)^2 + (r \sin\theta)^2 = (x - r\cos\theta)^2 + (y - r\sin\theta)^2 \quad \text{which}$$

simplifies to $x^2 + y^2 - 2r[x\cos\theta + y\sin\theta] = r^2[1 - 2\cos\theta] \ldots\ldots (1)$

Also $CP' = r \quad \therefore \quad (x^2 - 2r\cos\theta)^2 + (y - 2r\sin\theta)^2 = r^2$

which simplifies to $x^2 + y^2 - 4r[x\cos\theta + y\sin\theta] + 3r^2 = 0 \ldots\ldots (2)$

$$\therefore \quad 2r^2[1 - 2\cos\theta] - 2x^2 - 2y^2 = -3r^2 - x^2 - y^2 \qquad \{\text{using } (1) \text{ and } (2)\}$$

$$\therefore \quad 2r^2 - 4r^2\cos\theta - 2x^2 - 2y^2 = -3r^2 - x^2 - y^2$$

$$\therefore \quad 5r^2 - 4r^2\cos\theta = x^2 + y^2$$

$$\text{i.e.,} \quad x^2 + y^2 = r^2(5 - 4\cos\theta)$$

Now $\overline{PP'}$ is parallel to $\overline{OC}$. Thus $\tan\theta = \dfrac{y}{x - r}$.

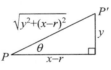

$$\text{i.e.,} \quad PP' = \sqrt{y^2 + (x - r)^2}$$

$$\therefore \quad \cos\theta = \pm\frac{x - r}{\sqrt{y^2 + (x - r)^2}}$$

$$\therefore \quad x^2 + y^2 = r^2\left(5 \pm \frac{4(x - r)}{\sqrt{y^2 + (x - r)^2}}\right)$$

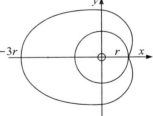

18.32 In $\triangle ABC$,

$$\sin C = \cos A + \cos B$$

$$\therefore \quad \sin(180 - [A + B]) = \cos A + \cos B$$

$$\therefore \quad \sin[A + B] = \cos A + \cos B$$

$$\therefore \quad 2\sin\left[\tfrac{A+B}{2}\right]\cos\left[\tfrac{A+B}{2}\right] = 2\cos\left[\tfrac{A+B}{2}\right]\cos\left[\tfrac{A-B}{2}\right]$$

$$\{\text{Duplication formula and sum to product formula}\}$$

$$\therefore \quad \cos\left[\tfrac{A+B}{2}\right]\left(\sin\left[\tfrac{A+B}{2}\right] - \cos\left[\tfrac{A-B}{2}\right]\right) = 0$$

$$\therefore \quad \cos\left[\tfrac{A+B}{2}\right] = 0 \quad \text{or} \quad \sin\left[\tfrac{A+B}{2}\right] = \cos\left[\tfrac{A-B}{2}\right]$$

$$\therefore \quad \tfrac{A+B}{2} = 90^\circ + k \cdot 180^\circ \quad \text{or} \quad \sin\left[\tfrac{A+B}{2}\right] = \sin\left(90 - \left[\tfrac{A-B}{2}\right]\right) \quad \{\cos\theta = \sin(90^\circ - \theta)\}$$

$$\therefore \quad A + B = 180^\circ + k \cdot 360^\circ \quad \text{or} \quad \tfrac{A+B}{2} = 90^\circ - \left[\tfrac{A-B}{2}\right] + k \cdot 360^\circ$$

$$\text{or} \quad \frac{A+B}{2} + 90^\circ - \left[\tfrac{A-B}{2}\right] = 180^\circ + k \cdot 360^\circ$$

$$\left\{\text{since } \sin\left(90^\circ - \tfrac{A-B}{2}\right) = \sin\left(90^\circ + \tfrac{A-B}{2}\right)\right\}$$

$$\therefore \quad \text{or} \quad \begin{cases} A + B = 180^o + k\,.\,360^o, \quad \text{(which is impossible)} \\ A = 90^o + k\,.\,360^o \\ B = 90^o + k\,.\,360^o \end{cases}$$

$\therefore$ either $A = 90^o$ or $B = 90^o$ (but not both)

Thus, $\triangle ABC$ is right-angled.

18.33 If cone ATC is opened up along AT and flattened,

arc $AC = \frac{1}{2}\,.\,(2\pi r) = \pi r = 2\pi$

$\therefore \quad \angle ATC = 120^o$

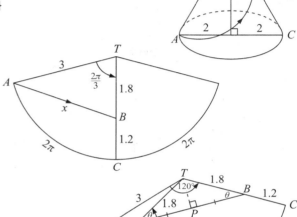

Let $x = AB$, the shortest distance from A to B.

Using the cosine rule,

$$x^2 = 3^2 + (1.8)^2 - 2.3\,.(1.8)\cos 120^o$$

$\therefore \quad x^2 = 9 + 3.24 + 5.4 \quad \{\cos 120^o = -\tfrac{1}{2}\}$

$\therefore \quad x = 4.2\,\text{km}$

$\therefore \quad \underline{AB \text{ is } 4.2\,\text{km}}$

To locate P, where the path is horizontal

Find radius $\overline{TN}$ to cut $\overline{AB}$ at D,

such that $TD = 1.8\,\text{km}$.

$\triangle TDB$ is isosceles.

P, the midpoint of $\overline{DB}$ is the required point.

Using the cosine rule in $\triangle ATB$

$$3^2 = (1.8)^2 + (4.2)^2 - 2(1.8)(4.2)\cos\theta$$

which on simplifying gives $\cos\theta = \frac{11}{14}$

and in $\triangle TPB$, $\cos\theta = \dfrac{BP}{1.8}$

$\therefore \quad BP = 1.8 \times \frac{11}{14} = \frac{99}{70}\,\text{km}.$

18.34 **a**

$$\sin A + \sin B + \sin C$$
$$= \sin A + \sin B + \sin(180^o - [A + B])$$
$$= \sin A + \sin B + \sin[A + B]$$
$$= 2\sin\left[\tfrac{A+B}{2}\right]\cos\left[\tfrac{A-B}{2}\right] + 2\sin\left[\tfrac{A+B}{2}\right]\cos\left[\tfrac{A+B}{2}\right] \quad \begin{array}{l}\{\text{sum to product formula} \\ \text{and duplication formula}\}\end{array}$$
$$= 2\sin\left[\tfrac{A+B}{2}\right]\left(\cos\left[\tfrac{A+B}{2}\right] + \cos\left[\tfrac{A-B}{2}\right]\right)$$
$$= 2\sin\left[\tfrac{A+B}{2}\right]\,2\cos\left(\frac{\frac{A+B}{2} + \frac{A-B}{2}}{2}\right)\cos\left(\frac{\frac{A+B}{2} - \frac{A-B}{2}}{2}\right) \quad \{\text{sum to product formula}\}$$
$$= 4\sin\left[\tfrac{A+B}{2}\right]\cos\left(\tfrac{A}{2}\right)\cos\left(\tfrac{B}{2}\right)$$
$$= 4\sin\left[90^o - \tfrac{C}{2}\right]\cos\left(\tfrac{A}{2}\right)\cos\left(\tfrac{B}{2}\right) \quad \{A + B + C = 180^o\}$$
$$= \underline{4\cos\left(\tfrac{A}{2}\right)\cos\left(\tfrac{B}{2}\right)\cos\left(\tfrac{C}{2}\right)} \quad \{\sin(90 - \theta) = \cos\theta\}$$

b   Now

$$\frac{\sin A \sin B \sin C}{\sin A + \sin B + \sin C} = \frac{2\sin\left(\tfrac{A}{2}\right)\cos\left(\tfrac{A}{2}\right)\,.\,2\sin\left(\tfrac{B}{2}\right)\cos\left(\tfrac{B}{2}\right)\,.\,2\sin\left(\tfrac{C}{2}\right)\cos\left(\tfrac{C}{2}\right)}{4\cos\left(\tfrac{A}{2}\right)\cos\left(\tfrac{B}{2}\right)\cos\left(\tfrac{C}{2}\right)}$$

$$= 2\sin\left(\tfrac{A}{2}\right)\,.\,\sin\left(\tfrac{B}{2}\right)\,.\,\sin\left(\tfrac{C}{2}\right)$$

$$< 2$$

$\{$as maximum value of $\sin\theta$ is 1 when $\theta = 90^o$,   and equality cannot occur, as if

$\dfrac{A}{2} = \dfrac{B}{2} = \dfrac{C}{2} = 90^o$, $\therefore$ $A = B = C = 180^o$,   which is not possible$\}$

thus $\dfrac{\sin A + \sin B + \sin C}{\sin A . \sin B . \sin C} > \tfrac{1}{2}$ {both numerator and denominator are positive $\therefore$ we take reciprocals of both sides}

$\therefore$ $\underline{\sin A + \sin B + \sin C > \tfrac{1}{2}(\sin A . \sin B . \sin C)}$,   the required result.

18.35 **a**   Let $R = M \sin \theta + N \sin \phi$

then $R^2 = M^2 \sin^2 \theta + 2MN \sin \theta \sin \phi + N^2 \sin^2 \phi$......(1)

but $K^2 = M^2 \cos^2 \theta + 2MN \cos \theta \cos \phi + N^2 \cos^2 \phi$...... (2)

adding (1) and (2)

we have $R^2 + K^2 = M^2 + 2MN[\cos \theta \cos \phi + \sin \theta \sin \phi] + N^2$

i.e. $R^2 + K^2 = M^2 + 2MN \cos(\theta - \phi) + N^2$

Thus $R^2 + K^2 \leqslant M^2 + 2MN + N^2$

{Max. value of $\cos(\theta - \phi)$ is 1 when $\theta - \phi = k . 2\pi$}

i.e. $R \leqslant \sqrt{(M+N)^2 - K^2}$

Thus $\underline{\text{Max. } R \leqslant \sqrt{(M+N)^2 - K^2}}$ when $\underline{\theta - \phi = k . 360^\circ}$ $(k \varepsilon Z)$

b   The condition $K \leqslant M + N$ is necessary to ensure that $(M+N)^2 - K^2 \geqslant 0$ for $\sqrt{(M+N)^2 - K^2}$ to exist.

Let the lengths of sides be a, b, c, d and draw in one diagonal. Let angles be θ and $(180 - \phi)$ {as given in the hint}.

$\therefore$ Area $= \tfrac{1}{2}ab \sin \theta + \tfrac{1}{2}cd \sin(180 - \phi)$

$\therefore$ $A = \tfrac{1}{2}ab \sin \theta + \tfrac{1}{2}cd \sin \phi$...... (a)

Now $x^2 = a^2 + b^2 - 2ab \cos \theta = c^2 + d^2 - 2cd \cos(180 - \phi)$

$\Rightarrow$ $2ab \cos \theta - 2cd \cos(180 - \phi) = a^2 + b^2 - c^2 - d^2$

$\Rightarrow$ $\tfrac{1}{2}ab \cos \theta + \tfrac{1}{2}cd \cos \phi = \left[\dfrac{a^2 + b^2 - c^2 - d^2}{4} \right]$ ...... (b)

Also $c + d > x$ and $x + a > b$.

$\therefore$ $c + d > x > b - a$

thus $(c + d)^2 > (b - a)^2$

$\therefore$ $c^2 + 2cd + d^2 > b^2 - 2ab + a^2$

$\therefore$ $2ab + 2cd > a^2 + b^2 - c^2 - d^2$

$\therefore$ $\dfrac{ab + cd}{2} > \dfrac{a^2 + b^2 - c^2 - d^2}{4}$

$\therefore$ $\tfrac{1}{2}ab + \tfrac{1}{2}cd > \left[\dfrac{a^2 + b^2 - c^2 - d^2}{4} \right]$ ...... (c)

i.e.   the condition $M + N > K$ is satisfied.

Thus all conditions (a), (b) and (c) of part (1) are satisfied.

$\therefore$ max. area is $\sqrt{\left(\dfrac{ab}{2} + \dfrac{cd}{2} \right)^2 - \left(\dfrac{a^2 + b^2 - c^2 - d^2}{4} \right)^2}$

occurring when $\theta - \phi = k . 360^\circ$

i.e.   when $\theta - \phi = 0$ {the only sensible solution}

i.e. $\theta = \phi$

i.e.,   angles are θ and $180 - \theta$ $\therefore$ the $\underline{\text{quadrilateral is cyclic.}}$

18.36 The waste is minimum when the area of polygon
$ABCDEFGHKLMN$ is maximum.

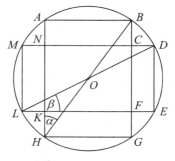

Let $\angle AHB = \alpha$, $\angle DLE = \beta$
$HB = LD = 1$ given
Area polygon
= area $ABGH$ + area $MDEL-$ area $NCFK$
= $\sin \alpha \cos \alpha + \sin \beta \cos \beta - \sin \alpha \sin \beta$
= $\tfrac{1}{2} \sin 2\alpha + \tfrac{1}{2} \sin 2\beta - \sin \alpha \sin \beta$

First we show that only $\alpha < 45^o$, $\beta < 45^o$ need to be
considered. Let $\alpha = 45^o + x$, $\beta = 45^o + y$, $0 < x < 45^o$, $0 < y < 45^o$
then $\sin 2\alpha = \sin(90^o + 2x) = \sin(90^o - 2x)$
$\quad\quad\sin 2\beta = \sin(90^o + 2y) = \sin(90^o - 2y)$
and $\sin(45^o + x) > \sin(45^o - x)$, $\sin(45^o + y) > \sin(45^o - y)$
$\therefore$ the area of the polygon is greater when $\alpha = 45^o - x$, $\beta = 45^o - y$
than when $\alpha = 45^o + x$, $\beta = 45^o + y$

Area = $f(\alpha, \beta)$; let α be constant, β variable.

$$\frac{df}{d\beta} = \cos 2\beta - \sin \alpha \cos \beta$$

$$\frac{df}{d\beta} = 0 \quad \text{when} \quad \cos 2\beta = \sin \alpha \cos \beta ...... (1)$$

similarly $\dfrac{df}{d\beta} = 0$ when $\cos 2\alpha = \sin \beta \cos \alpha ...... (2)$

hence $(1) - (2)$ results in $\cos 2\beta - \cos 2\alpha = \sin(\alpha - \beta)$
$\therefore$ using trig. formula $\therefore$ $2 \sin(\beta + \alpha) \sin(\alpha - \beta) = \sin(\alpha - \beta)$
$\therefore$ $\sin(\alpha - \beta)[2 \sin(\alpha + \beta) - 1] = 0$
$\therefore$ either $\sin(\alpha - \beta) = 0$ or $\sin(\alpha + \beta) = \tfrac{1}{2} ...... (3)$

If $\sin(\alpha + \beta) = \tfrac{1}{2}$ then $\alpha + \beta = 30^o$ as $\alpha + \beta < 90^o$
$(1) + (2)$ results in $\cos 2\beta + \cos 2\alpha = \sin(\alpha + \beta)$
$\therefore$ $2 \cos(\beta + \alpha) \cos(\beta - \alpha) = \sin(\alpha + \beta)$
but $\beta + \alpha = 30^o$
$\therefore$ $2 \cdot \dfrac{\sqrt{3}}{2} \cos(\beta - \alpha) = \dfrac{1}{2}$
$\therefore$ $\cos(\beta - \alpha) = \dfrac{\sqrt{3}}{6}$
$\cos(\alpha - \beta) = \dfrac{\sqrt{3}}{6} ...... (4)$
but $|\alpha - \beta| < 30^o$
$\therefore$ $\cos |\alpha - \beta| > \dfrac{\sqrt{3}}{2}$ contradicting (4)
$\therefore$ $\alpha + \beta \neq 30^o$
hence $\sin(\alpha - \beta) = 0$ (according to (3))

$\therefore$ $\alpha = \beta$ is a necessary condition of $f(\alpha, \beta)$ having a maximum value.

$f(\alpha, \alpha) = \sin 2\alpha - \sin^2 \alpha$

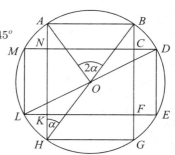

$\dfrac{df}{d\alpha} = 2 \cos \alpha - \sin 2\alpha$, $\dfrac{d^2 f}{d\alpha^2} = -4 \sin \alpha - 2 \cos 2\alpha < 0$ for $\alpha < 45^o$

$\therefore$ $\dfrac{df}{d\alpha} = 0$ when $\tan 2\alpha = 2$.

$\therefore$ $f(\alpha, \alpha)$ has max. value for $\alpha = \tfrac{1}{2}$ arc $\tan 2 < 45^o$

$\angle AOB = 2\alpha$ {angle at centre.... theorem}
$AB^2 = \left(\tfrac{1}{2}\right)^2 + \left(\tfrac{1}{2}\right)^2 - 2 \cdot \tfrac{1}{2} \cdot \tfrac{1}{2} \cos 2\alpha$ {cosine rule}

$AB^2 = \frac{1}{2}(1 - \cos 2\alpha)$

$$\cos^2 2\alpha = \frac{1}{1 + \tan^2 2\alpha} = \frac{1}{1+4} = \frac{1}{5}$$

$$\therefore \quad AB = \sqrt{\frac{1}{2}\left(1 + \frac{1}{\sqrt{5}}\right)}$$

Similarly $\quad AH = \sqrt{\frac{1}{2}\left(1 + \frac{1}{\sqrt{5}}\right)}$

$CD = MN = AN = KH = \frac{1}{2}(AH - AB)$

By the way $\quad \dfrac{AH}{AB} = \dfrac{1 + \sqrt{5}}{2}$ the golden ratio.

[**Note:** for $\alpha = 0$, $f(\alpha, \alpha) = 0$, for $\alpha = 45°$ $f(\alpha, \alpha) = \frac{1}{2}$

<u>When $\tan 2\alpha = 2$,</u> $f(\alpha, \alpha) = \frac{2}{\sqrt{5}} - \frac{1}{2}\left(1 - \frac{1}{\sqrt{5}}\right) = \underline{\dfrac{\sqrt{5}-1}{2}} > \frac{1}{2}$

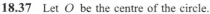

18.37 Let O be the centre of the circle.
$\angle AOB = \angle COD = \angle EOF = 60°$
L, M and N are the midpoints of $\overline{AF}$, $\overline{BC}$, $\overline{DE}$ resp.
Join OL, OM and ON
By the chord theorem, $\overline{OL}, \overline{OM},$ and $\overline{ON}$ meet $\overline{AF}$,
$\overline{BC}$ and $\overline{DE}$ at right angles.

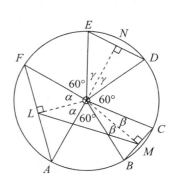

Now $2\alpha + 2\beta + 2\gamma = 360° - 3 \times 60° = 180°$
$\quad \therefore \quad \alpha + \beta + \gamma = 90° \ldots\ldots (1)$

We may take the radius of the circle as 1 unit,
$\quad \therefore \quad OL = \cos\alpha, \quad OM = \cos\beta \quad$ and $\quad ON = \cos\gamma$
Now in $\triangle LOM$, $\angle LOM = \alpha + \beta + 60° = 90° - \gamma + 60°$ (from (1))
$$= 150° - \gamma$$

and by the Cosine Rule, $\quad LM^2 = \cos^2\alpha + \cos^2\beta - 2\cos\alpha\cos\beta\cos(150° - \gamma)$

Similarly in $\triangle LON$, $\quad LN^2 = \cos^2\alpha + \cos^2\gamma - 2\cos\alpha\cos\gamma\cos(150° - \beta)$

$\therefore \quad LM^2 - LN^2$
$= \cos^2\beta - \cos^2\gamma + \cos\alpha[2\cos\gamma\cos(150° - \beta) - 2\cos\beta\cos(150° - \gamma)]$
$= \frac{1}{2} + \frac{1}{2}\cos 2\beta - \frac{1}{2} - \frac{1}{2}\cos 2\gamma + \cos\alpha[\cos(\gamma + 150° - \beta)$
$\quad + \cos(\gamma - 150° + \beta) - \cos(\beta + 150° - \gamma) - \cos(\beta - 150° + \gamma)]$
$\quad$ {Using $\cos^2\theta = \frac{1}{2} + \frac{1}{2}\cos 2\theta$ and $2\cos A\cos B = \cos(A+B) + \cos(A-B)$.}
$= \frac{1}{2}[\cos 2\beta - \cos 2\gamma] + \cos\alpha[\cos(\gamma + 150° - \beta) - \cos(\beta + 150° - \gamma)]$
$= \frac{1}{2}\left[-2\sin\left(\frac{2\beta + 2\gamma}{2}\right)\sin\left(\frac{2\beta - 2\gamma}{2}\right)\right]$
$\qquad + \cos\alpha\left[-2\sin\left(\frac{\gamma + 150° - \beta + \beta + 150° - \gamma}{2}\right)\sin\left(\frac{\gamma + 150° - \beta - \beta - 150° + \gamma}{2}\right)\right]$
$\qquad\qquad$ {using $\cos S - \cos D = -2\sin\left(\frac{S+D}{2}\right)\sin\left(\frac{S-D}{2}\right)$}
$= -\sin(\gamma + \beta)\sin(\beta - \gamma) - 2\cos\alpha[\sin 150°\sin(\gamma - \beta)]$
$= -\sin(90 - \alpha)\sin(\beta - \gamma) - \cos\alpha\sin(\gamma - \beta) \qquad$ {$\sin 150° = \frac{1}{2}$, and using (1)}
$= -\cos\alpha \cdot \sin(\beta - \gamma) - \cos\alpha \cdot -\sin(\beta - \gamma)$
$= \cos\alpha[\sin(\beta - \gamma) - \sin(\beta - \gamma)]$
$= 0$

$\therefore \quad LM^2 = LN^2,$ i.e., $LM = LN$.
Similarly, we can prove $LM = MN,$ $\therefore$ $\underline{\triangle LMN \text{ is equilateral.}}$

18.38
- Let radius $= 1$
- Use sine rule to calculate some lengths.

(1) $AB = 2\cos(180 - 3\alpha) = -2\cos 3\alpha$

(2) $BC = -2\cos 4\alpha$ {in isos. $\triangle BOC$}

$\therefore$ $BX = -2\cos 4\alpha - 1$

$\therefore$ $BW = \frac{1}{2}(-2\cos 4\alpha - 1)$

$\therefore$ $BY = \dfrac{-2\cos 4\alpha - 1}{2\cos \alpha}$

(3) $AZ = \dfrac{\sin(180 - 2\alpha)}{\sin(-180 + 5\alpha)} = \dfrac{\sin 2\alpha}{-\sin 5\alpha}$

Choose α such that $BY + ZA = BA$

i.e. $\dfrac{-2\cos 4\alpha - 1}{2\cos \alpha} + \dfrac{\sin 2\alpha}{-\sin 5\alpha} + 2\cos 3\alpha = 0$

$\therefore$ $2\cos 4\alpha \sin 5\alpha + \sin 5\alpha + 2\sin 2\alpha \cos \alpha - 4\cos \alpha \cos 3\alpha \sin 5\alpha = 0$

$\sin 9\alpha + \sin \alpha + \sin 5\alpha + \sin 3\alpha + \sin \alpha - 2\cos \alpha(\sin 8\alpha + \sin 2\alpha) = 0$

$\sin 9\alpha + 2\sin \alpha + \sin 5\alpha + \sin 3\alpha - \sin 9\alpha - \sin 7\alpha - \sin 3\alpha - \sin \alpha = 0$

    $\sin \alpha + \sin 5\alpha - \sin 7\alpha = 0$

    $\sin \alpha + [2\sin(-\alpha)\cos 6\alpha] = 0$ $\{\sin(-\alpha) = -\sin \alpha\}$

      $\sin \alpha[1 - 2\cos 6\alpha] = 0$

But $\sin \alpha \neq 0$, $\therefore$ $\cos 6\alpha = \frac{1}{2}$ $\{\sin(-\alpha) = -\sin \alpha\}$

$\therefore$ $6\alpha = 300°$ $\{45° \leqslant \alpha \leqslant 60°$ $\therefore$ $270° \leqslant 6\alpha \leqslant 360°$

     $\alpha = 50°$ $\angle BAX = 180 - 3\alpha \geqslant 0$ $\therefore$ $\alpha \leqslant 60$

                 $\angle BCZ = 4\alpha - 180 \geqslant 0$ $\therefore$ $\alpha \geqslant 45\}$

i.e., $\underline{\alpha = 50°}$

18.39   **a** $r^2 = x^2 + y^2$, $\underline{x = r\cos\theta}$, $\underline{y = r\sin\theta}$

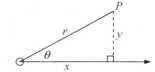

b   **i** $\underline{r = 2, \quad \theta \text{ anything}}$

     ii $r = \dfrac{\theta}{\theta + \pi} = \dfrac{\theta + \pi - \pi}{\theta + \pi} = 1 - \dfrac{\pi}{\theta + \pi}$

$\therefore$ as θ gets very large, r approaches 1.

θ	0	$\frac{\pi}{2}$	π	$\frac{3\pi}{2}$	2π	$\frac{5\pi}{2}$	3π
r	$\frac{1}{\pi}$	$\frac{1}{3}$	$\frac{2}{4}$	$\frac{3}{5}$	$\frac{4}{6}$	$\frac{5}{7}$	$\frac{6}{8}$

.... etc.

spiral, but
approaching a
circle, radius 1
as θ gets very
large

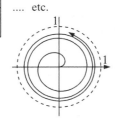

    iii $r = 1 + \cos\theta$

θ	0	$\frac{\pi}{6}$	$\frac{2\pi}{6}$	$\frac{3\pi}{6}$	$\frac{4\pi}{6}$	$\frac{5\pi}{6}$	π	$\frac{7\pi}{6}$	$\frac{8\pi}{6}$	$\frac{9\pi}{6}$	$\frac{10\pi}{6}$	$\frac{11\pi}{6}$	2π
r	2	$1 + \frac{\sqrt{3}}{2}$	$1\frac{1}{2}$	1	$\frac{1}{2}$	$1 - \frac{\sqrt{3}}{2}$	0	$1 - \frac{\sqrt{3}}{2}$	$\frac{1}{2}$	1	$1\frac{1}{2}$	$1 + \frac{\sqrt{3}}{2}$	0

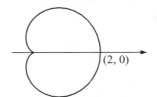

a "cardioid"

(2, 0)

iv $r^2 = 4\sin^2 2\theta$

θ	0	$\frac{\pi}{6}$	$\frac{\pi}{4}$	$\frac{2\pi}{6}$	$\frac{3\pi}{6}$	$\frac{4\pi}{6}$	$\frac{3\pi}{4}$	$\frac{5\pi}{6}$	π
r	0	$\sqrt{3}$	$\sqrt{2}$	$\sqrt{3}$	0	$\sqrt{3}$	2	$\sqrt{3}$	0

.... etc.

$$\Rightarrow r = \begin{cases} 2\sin 2\theta & \text{where} \quad \sin 2\theta \text{ is } +\text{ve.} \\ -2\sin 2\theta & \text{where} \quad \sin 2\theta \text{ is } -\text{ve.} \end{cases}$$

a "four-leaf clover"

c i Using polar coordinates, $r\cos\theta . r\sin\theta = 1$

$$\Rightarrow \quad r^2 = \frac{1}{\sin\theta . \cos\theta} = \frac{2}{\sin 2\theta} \quad ......(1)$$

$$\Rightarrow \quad r^2 \geqslant 2 \quad \text{with equality when} \quad \sin 2\theta = 1 \quad \text{i.e.} \quad \theta = \frac{\pi}{4}, \frac{5\pi}{4}.$$

$\therefore$ The shortest distance to O is $\sqrt{2}$ units.

$$(OQ)^2 = \frac{2}{\sin 2\theta} \qquad \{\text{from } (1)\}$$

The polar equation of ℓ is

$$\left(r^2\right)^2 = 4 . r\cos\theta . r\sin\theta$$

i.e., $r^2 = 4\sin\theta\cos\theta$

$$\therefore \quad (OP)^2 = 2\sin 2\theta$$

Hence $(OP)^2 . (OQ)^2 = 4$

$$\Rightarrow \quad OP . OQ = 2$$

when $\theta = \dfrac{\pi}{4}, \dfrac{5\pi}{4}, \quad OP = OQ$

$$OP \to \infty, \quad OQ \to 0.$$

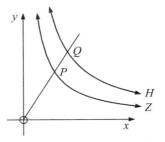

OP	$\frac{1}{4}$	$\frac{1}{3}$	$\frac{1}{2}$	1	2	4	6	8
OQ	8	6	4	2	1	$\frac{1}{2}$	$\frac{1}{3}$	$\frac{1}{4}$

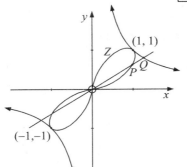

19. PYTHAGOREAN TRIPLES

19.1   **a** $(ax - by)^2 + (ay + bx)^2 = a^2x^2 - 2abxy + b^2y^2 + a^2y^2 + 2abxy + b^2x^2$

$$= a^2x^2 + b^2y^2 + a^2y^2 + b^2x^2$$
$$= a^2(x^2 + y^2) + b^2(x^2 + y^2)$$
$$= \underline{(x^2 + y^2)(a^2 + b^2)}$$

   b   putting $a = 15$, $b = 8$, $x = 5$, $y = 12$ into the identity,

$$\Rightarrow \quad (75 - 96)^2 + (180 + 40)^2 = (25 + 144)(225 + 64)$$
$$\Rightarrow \quad 21^2 + 220^2 = 169 \cdot 289 = 13^2 \cdot 17^2$$
$$\Rightarrow \quad 21^2 + 220^2 = 221^2$$

Thus the lengths are   <u>21 and 220 units</u>.

19.2   If the hypotenuse is 12, then $a^2 + b^2 = 144$ where $1 \leqslant a \leqslant 11$, $1 \leqslant b \leqslant 11$.

a	b^2		a	b^2
1	143		7	95
2	140		8	80
3	135		9	63
4	128		10	44
5	119		11	23
6	108			

and in no case is b a perfect square.
Hence the hypotenuse cannot be 12.

If one of the legs is 12, say, $a = 12$,

then $12^2 + b^2 = c^2$ and $\therefore$ $c^2 - b^2 = 144$

$\therefore$ $(c + b)(c - b) = 144$ where clearly $c + b > c - b$

$\therefore$ $c + b > 12$

$\therefore$ possible factorizations are

$c + b$	$c - b$	$2c$	$2b$	c	b
16	9	25	7	$\times$	$\times$
18	8	26	10	13	5
24	6	30	18	15	9
36	4	40	32	20	16
48	3	51	45	$\times$	$\times$
72	2	74	70	37	35
144	1	145	143	$\times$	$\times$

$\{b, c$ must be integral$\}$

Thus there are 4 such triangles.   <u>$5, 12, 13$; $9, 12, 15$; $12, 16, 20$; $12, 35, 37$</u>

19.3   If a, b, c is the Pythagorean triple and a is prime, $(a \geqslant 3)$,

then $a^2 + b^2 = c^2$

$\Rightarrow \quad a^2 = c^2 - b^2$

$\Rightarrow \quad a^2 = (c + b)(c - b)$

but the only factorization of a^2 possible is $a^2 = a^2 \times 1$.

$\{$as a is prime and $a^2 = a \times a$ $\Rightarrow$ $b = 0$ which is not possible.

$\therefore$ $c + b = a^2$ and $c - b = 1$

Solving these simultaneously, we get

$c = \dfrac{a^2 + 1}{2}$ and $b = \dfrac{a^2 - 1}{2}$,   and each of these is an integer as $a^2 - 1$ is even. $\{a$ is an odd prime$\}$

Since there are infinitely many primes, we may produce <u>infinitely many triples</u>.

3 more examples: <u>$9, 40, 41$; $11, 60, 61$; $13, 84, 85$</u> $(a = 9, 11, 13)$

19.4 a Let the sides be $a - d, \; a, \; a + d, \;$ a is a positive integer.

$$\therefore \quad (a - d)^2 + a^2 = (a + d)^2$$

$$\therefore \quad a^2 - 2ad + d^2 + a^2 = a^2 + 2ad + d^2$$

$$\therefore \quad a^2 = 4ad$$

$$\therefore \quad a(a - 4d) = 0$$

$$\therefore \quad a = 0 \text{ or } 4d$$

but $a \neq 0,$ thus $a = 4d$ and $\therefore \quad \underline{3d, \; 4d, \; 5d} \;$ for d in Z^+.

b Let the sides be $a, \; ar, \; ar^2$ where a and r are positive integers.

$$\therefore \quad a^2 + (ar)^2 = \left(ar^2\right)^2 \quad \text{ and } \quad \therefore \quad 1 + r^2 = r^4$$

$$\therefore \quad r^4 - r^2 - 1 = 0$$

$$\therefore \quad r^2 = \frac{1 \pm \sqrt{1 - 4 \; (1) \; (-1)}}{2}$$

$$\therefore \quad r^2 = \frac{1 + \sqrt{5}}{2} \qquad \{r \text{ is positive}\}$$

where $\dfrac{1 + \sqrt{4}}{2} < \dfrac{1 + \sqrt{5}}{2} < \dfrac{1 + \sqrt{9}}{2}$

i.e. $\frac{3}{2} < r^2 < 2$ which is impossible as r is a positive integer.

Thus the $\underline{3}$ sides cannot be in geometric progression.

19.5 a Now $c^2 = a^2 + b^2$

$$\Rightarrow \quad a^2 = c^2 - b^2$$

$$\Rightarrow \quad a^2 = (c + b)\,(c - b)$$

$$\Rightarrow \quad \left(\frac{c + b}{a}\right)\left(\frac{c - b}{a}\right) = 1$$

$$\Rightarrow \quad \frac{c + b}{a} = \frac{r}{s} \quad \text{ and } \quad \frac{c - b}{a} = \frac{s}{r}, \quad \text{ for positive integers } s \text{ and } r.$$

$$\Rightarrow \quad c + b = \frac{ar}{s} \quad \text{ and } \quad c - b = \frac{as}{r}$$

Adding these produces $2c = a \left(\dfrac{r}{s} + \dfrac{s}{r}\right) = a \left(\dfrac{r^2 + s^2}{rs}\right)$

thus $\dfrac{c}{a} = \dfrac{r^2 + s^2}{2rs} \; \text{......} \; (1)$

Likewise on subtraction, $2b = a \left(\dfrac{r}{s} - \dfrac{s}{r}\right) = a \left(\dfrac{r^2 - s^2}{rs}\right)$

$$\therefore \quad \frac{b}{a} = \frac{r^2 - s^2}{2rs} \; \text{......} \; (2)$$

Thus $a : b : c = \underline{2rs \; : \; r^2 - s^2 \; : \; r^2 + s^2}$

b The area of a right-angled triangle with integral sides $a, \; b, \; c$ (s.t. $a^2 + b^2 = c^2$)

$$= \tfrac{1}{2}ab$$

$$= \tfrac{1}{2}(2rst)\left(r^2 - s^2\right)t \qquad \{t \text{ an integer}\}$$

$$= rst^2\left(r^2 - s^2\right) \quad \text{which is certainly } \underline{\text{an integer}}.$$

c   If a, b, c are Pythagorean integers $(a^2 + b^2 = c^2)$

then $a = 2rst$, $b = (r^2 - s^2)t$ and $c = (r^2 + s^2)t$ for some integers $r, s,$ and t.

Thus $abc = 2rs(r^2 - s^2)(r^2 + s^2)t^3$ and $a + b + c = t[2rs + r^2 - s^2 + r^2 + s^2]$

$$= t[2rs + 2r^2]$$
$$= 2rt[s + r]$$

Since $abc = 2rt(r + s)(r - s)(r^2 + s^2)t^2$ and $a + b + c = 2rt[s + r]$

it is clear that $\underline{a + b + c \text{ is a factor of } abc}$.

19.6 a   From the given examples it appears that such triples have form $a, b, b + 1$

where $(b + 1)^2 = a^2 + b^2$

Thus $a^2 = 2b + 1$ or $b = \dfrac{a^2 - 1}{2}$

Thus if a is chosen to be odd and greater than 1, $a^2 - 1$ is even $\therefore$ b is an integer.
Thus a, b and c are integers.

Also the triple is primitive, since b and $b + 1$ are certainly coprime.

b $a^2 = c^2 - b^2 = (c + b)(c - b)$

If $c - b = p$ (an odd prime)   then p is a factor of a^2

Thus p is a factor of a,   i.e. $a = kp$ for some integer k.

$\therefore$ $(kp)^2 = (c + b)(c - b)$

$\therefore$ $k^2p^2 = (c + b)p$

$\therefore$ $c + b = k^2p$

$\therefore$ p is a factor of $c + b$......(*)

$\therefore$ p is a factor of $(b + p) + b$

$\therefore$ p is a factor of $2b + p$

$\therefore$ p is a factor of b {as $p \neq 2$}

and from $*$ p must be a factor of c also.

This means that p is a factor of a, b and c and so $\underline{a : b : c \text{ is not primitive}}$.

If $c - b = 2$,   then $a^2 = (2b + 2).2 = 4(b + 1)$

$\Rightarrow$ $b + 1$ is a perfect square

$\Rightarrow$ $b + 1 = l^2$,   say, where l is an integer.

thus $a^2 = 4l^2$, $b = l^2 - 1$ and $c = 2 + b = l^2 + 1$.

i.e. $a = 2l$, $b = l^2 - 1$ and $c = l^2 + 1$

and we must choose l to be even, otherwise 2 will be a common factor in a, b and c

l	a	b	c
2	4	3	5
4	8	15	17
6	12	35	37
8	16	63	65
10	20	99	101
12	24	143	145
14	28	195	197
⋮	⋮	⋮	⋮

19.7 **a** **i** Every integer can be expressed in exactly one of the forms $3n$, $3n+1$ or $3n-1$,

and $(3n)^2 = 9n^2 = 3\left(3n^2\right)$

$(3n+1)^2 = 9n^2 + 6n + 1 = 3\left(3n^2 + 2n\right) + 1$

$(3n-1)^2 = 9n^2 - 6n + 1 = 3\left(3n^2 - 2n\right) + 1$

Thus if a is an integer, a^2 leaves remainders of 0 or 1 when divided by 3.

Now if neither x nor y is divisible by 3, then, on division by 3, x^2 and y^2 must have remainder 1 and therefore $z^2 (= x^2 + y^2)$ has remainder $2 (= 1 + 1)\, 2\, (= 1 + 1)$ which is not possible.

Hence, at least one of x, y is divisible by 3.

ii Likewise every integer can be expressed in exactly one of the forms $5n$, $5n \pm 1$, and $5n \pm 2$,   and $(5n)^2 = 25n^2 = 5\left(5n^2\right)$

$(5n \pm 1)^2 = 25n^2 \pm 10n + 1 = 5\left(5n^2 \pm 2n\right) + 1$

$(5n \pm 2)^2 = 25n^2 \pm 20n + 4 = 5\left(5n^2 \pm 4n\right) + 4$

Thus if a is an integer, a^2 leaves remainders of $0, 1$ or 4 when divided by 5......(∗)

Suppose neither x, y nor z is divisible by 5, then on division by 5, z^2 must have the same remainder as $1 + 1$, $1 + 4$,   or $4 + 4$. $\{z^2 = x^2 + y^2\}$

i.e. 2, 0,   or 3

none of which is possible: $2, 3$ by (∗), and 0 by supposition

Therefore at least one of x, y, z is divisible by 5.

iii In a similar manner, every integer can be expressed in exactly one of the forms $16n$, $16n \pm 1$, $16n \pm 2$, $16n \pm 3$, $16n \pm 4$, $16n \pm 5$, $16n \pm 6$, $16n \pm 7$, $16n + 8$.

and $(16n)^2 = 256n^2 = 16\left(16n^2 + 0\right)$

$(16n \pm 1)^2 = 256n^2 \pm 32n + 1 = 16\left(16n^2 \pm 2n\right) + 1$

$(16n \pm 2)^2 = 256n^2 \pm 64n + 4 = 16\left(16n^2 \pm 4n\right) + 4$

$(16n \pm 3)^2 = 256n^2 \pm 96n + 9 = 16\left(16n^2 \pm 6n\right) + 9$

$(16n \pm 4)^2 = 256n^2 \pm 128n + 16 = 16\left(16n^2 \pm 8n + 1\right) + 0$

$(16n \pm 5)^2 = 256n^2 \pm 160n + 25 = 16\left(16n^2 \pm 10n + 1\right) + 9$

$(16n \pm 6)^2 = 256n^2 \pm 192n + 36 = 16\left(16n^2 \pm 12n + 2\right) + 4$

$(16n \pm 7)^2 = 256n^2 \pm 224n + 49 = 16\left(16n^2 \pm 14n + 3\right) + 1$

$(16n + 8)^2 = 256n^2 + 256n + 64 = 16\left(16n^2 + 16n + 4\right) + 0$

Thus if a is an integer, a^2 leaves remainders of $0, 1, 4$, or 9 when divided by 16.

Suppose neither x^2 nor y^2 is divisible by 16.

then $z^2 (= x^2 + y^2)$ on division by 16, has the same remainders

as $1 + 1$, $1 + 4$, $1 + 9$, $4 + 4$, $4 + 9$, $9 + 9$ on division by 16.

i.e. $2, 5, 8, 10$ and 13,   all of which are not possible.

Thus at least one of x^2, y^2 is divisible by 16.

i.e.   at least one of x, y is divisible by 4.

b From **a** parts **i** and **ii**, at least one of x, y is divisible by 3, and one by 4.

Since area $= \frac{1}{2}xy$

$= \frac{1}{2} . 12 . k$ {where k is in Z}

$= 6k$

∴   the area is divisible by 6.

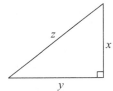

19.8 $d^2 = a^2 + b^2 + c^2$ connects the positive integers a, b, c and d.

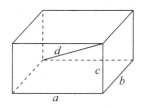

   a If a, b, c, d fall into 2 pairs of consecutive integers,

$$\text{say,} \quad r^2 + (r+1)^2 + s^2 = (s+1)^2$$

$$\text{then} \quad r^2 + r^2 + 2r + 1 + s^2 = s^2 + 2s + 1$$

$$\therefore \quad s = r^2 + r$$

Thus there are infinitely many possibilities of the form

$$r, \quad r+1, \quad r^2 + r, \quad r^2 + r + 1. \qquad \text{\{where the first 3 are in any order.\}}$$

   b If the first 3 are consecutive,

$$\text{then} \quad r^2 + (r+1)^2 + (r+2)^2 = d^2$$

$$\therefore \quad d^2 = 3r^2 + 6r + 5$$

$$\therefore \quad d^2 = 3(r+1)^2 + 2$$

which is impossible as no square leaves a remainder of 2 on division by 3.

If the last 3 are consecutive,

$$\text{then} \quad a^2 + s^2 + (s+1)^2 = (s+2)^2$$

$$\therefore \quad a^2 = s^2 + 4s + 4 - s^2 - s^2 - 2s - 1$$

$$\therefore \quad a^2 = -s^2 + 2s + 3$$

$$\therefore \quad a^2 = (s+1)(3-s) \qquad \text{where} \quad a^2 \geqslant 0$$

Thus $(s+1)(3-s) > 0$ $\therefore$ $s = 0, 1$ or 2.

Hence, $a^2 = 3$ or 4.

Hence $a = 2$ \{the only positive integral solution, when $s = 1$.\}

Thus $a = 2, \quad b = 1, \quad c = 2, \quad d = 3$ is the only solution with this property.

20. MISCELLANEOUS

20.1 A locker will remain open if it has an **odd** number of changes to it. A change occurs when a number is divisible by one or more of 1, 2, 3, 4, ..., 1000. i.e., 1, 2, 3, 4, ..., 1000 are possible factors of the locker number.

Now the only integers having an odd number of factors are the perfect squares; 1, 4, 9, 16, 25, ..., and the last perfect square less than 1000 is $31^2 = 961$. $\therefore$ 31 lockers remain open.

20.2 Form must be '$aab5$', '$aba5$' or '$baa5$'.

   (1) **Case '$aab5$',** $2a + b + 5$ is divisible by 9 and $(a+b) - (a+5)$ is divisible by 11.

            i.e., $2a + b + 5 = 9k$ and $b - 5 = 11l$ (k, l are integers).

            But $0 \leqslant b \leqslant 9$ $\therefore$ $b = 5$ and hence $2a + 10 = 9k$ $\therefore$ $a = 4$.

            i.e., 4455 is a solution.

   (2) **Case '$aba5$'** $2a + b + 5$ is divisible by 9 and $2a - (b+5)$ is divisible by 11.

            i.e., $2a + b + 5 = 9k$ and $2a - b - 5 = 11l$ (k, l are integers)

            $\therefore$ $11(2a + b + 5) + 9(2a - b - 5)$ is divisible by 99.

            i.e., $40a + 2b + 10$ is divisible by 99.

            But, $40a + 2b + 10$ is even and is therefore divisible by 198.

            $\therefore$ $40a + 2b + 10 = 198$ or 396 (can't exceed 388).

            $\therefore$ $40a + 2b = 188$ or 386

            $20a + b = 94$ or 193.

            both of which are impossible for a, b in $\{0, 1, 2, 3, ..., 9\}$

   (3) **Case** '$baa5$' gives the same solution as (1).

            $\therefore$ 4455 is the only solution.

20.3

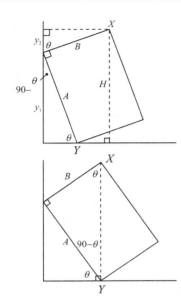

a $\sin\theta = \dfrac{y_1}{A}$ $\therefore$ $y_1 = A\sin\theta$

$\cos\theta = \dfrac{y_2}{B}$ $\therefore$ $y_2 = B\cos\theta$

So, $H = y_1 + y_2$
$$= A\sin\theta + B\cos\theta$$

b H is maximised when XY is parallel to the wall, in which case
$$\text{max } H = \text{diagonal of box}$$
$$= \sqrt{A^2 + B^2}\qquad \{\text{Pythagoras}\}$$

Thus $A\sin\theta + B\cos\theta \leqslant \sqrt{A^2 + B^2}$ with equality occurring

when $\tan\theta = \dfrac{A}{B}.$ {see figure.}

20.4 The tiling is **impossible**.

Every tile covers a black and a while square. Thus 31 tiles cover 31 blacks and 31 whites, leaving one black and one white vacant.

However, opposite corners of the chess board are of the same colour. Hence the impossibility.

20.5 $x(2 - y) = -y^3$

$\therefore\quad x = \dfrac{y^3}{y - 2}$

$$
\begin{array}{r|rrrr}
 & y^2 & + 2y & + 4 \\
\hline
y - 2 & y^3 & + 0y^2 & + 0y & + 0 \\
 & y^3 & - 2y^2 \\
\hline
 & & 2y^2 & + 0y \\
 & & 2y & - 4y \\
\hline
 & & & 4y & + 0 \\
 & & & 4y & - 8 \\
\hline
 & & & & 8
\end{array}
$$

Thus $x = y^2 + 2y + 4 + \dfrac{8}{y - 2}$

But x and y are integers $\therefore$ $y - 2$ is a factor of 8.

$\therefore$ $y - 2 = \pm1, \pm2, \pm4, \pm8.$

So $y = 3, 4, 6, 10, 1, 0, -2$ or -6.

Thus solutions are:

x	27	32	54	125	-1	0	2	27
y	3	4	6	10	1	0	-2	-6

20.6   **a**

diagram 1   diagram 2

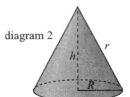

The arc length of diagram 1 $=$ circumference of base circle of diagram 2
$$\therefore\quad r\theta = 2\pi R$$
$$\therefore\quad R = \dfrac{r\theta}{2\pi}$$

b   Cone's volume, $V = \frac{1}{3}\pi R^2 h$ where $h^2 = r^2 - R^2$

$$\therefore \quad V = \frac{1}{3}\pi R^2 (r^2 - R^2)^{\frac{1}{2}}$$

$$\therefore \quad V^2 = \frac{\pi^2}{9} \cdot \frac{r^4 \theta^4}{16\pi^4} \cdot \left(r^2 - \frac{r^2\theta^2}{4\pi^2}\right) = k\theta^4 \left(1 - \frac{\theta^2}{4\pi^2}\right), \quad \text{where } k \text{ is a constant.}$$

$$\therefore \quad \frac{dV^2}{d\theta} = k\left[4\theta^3 \cdot \left(1 - \frac{\theta^2}{4\pi^2}\right) + \theta^4 \cdot \frac{-2\theta}{4\pi^2}\right]$$

$$= k\theta^3 \left[4 - \frac{\theta^2}{\pi^2} - \frac{\theta^2}{2\pi^2}\right]$$

$$= k\theta^3 \left[4 - \frac{3\theta^2}{2\pi^2}\right]$$

$$= k\theta^3 \left(2 + \frac{\sqrt{3}\theta}{\sqrt{2}\pi}\right)\left(2 - \frac{\sqrt{3}\theta}{\sqrt{2}\pi}\right)$$

and the derivative has sign diagram:

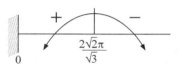

$$\therefore \quad V^2 \text{ is a maximum when} \quad \theta = \frac{2\sqrt{2}\pi}{\sqrt{3}} \text{ radians} \doteqdot 293.4°$$

So, V is a maximum when $\underline{\theta \doteqdot 293.4°}$.

20.7   We notice that if we are to pass through each paddock and go through each gate once only we must have an even number of gates per paddock.

But the two shaded paddocks have an odd number of gates, and I is common to both of these paddocks.

Thus, $\underline{I}$ will be the gate not used.

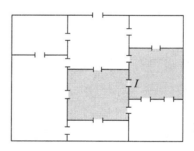

20.8   Let the seating be seen as on a 5 × 5 chess board. There are 25 squares. 13 are black and 12 white, say. If a student is on a black square, he or she must go to a white square, and this is clearly impossible as there is one less white square. Therefore <u>Paula is correct.</u>

20.9   From the points P and Q, draw perpendiculars x_1 and y_1 to FE, x_2 and y_2 to DC.

Let $AM = MB = x$, $PM = a$, $QM = b$.

From similar triangles, $\dfrac{a}{b} = \dfrac{x_1}{y_1} = \dfrac{x_2}{y_2}$.

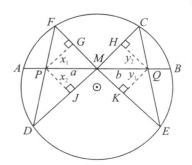

But $\dfrac{x_1}{y_2} = \dfrac{FP}{QC}$ and $\dfrac{x_2}{y_1} = \dfrac{PD}{QE}$

$$\dfrac{a^2}{b^2} = \dfrac{a}{b}\cdot\dfrac{a}{b} = \dfrac{x_1}{y_2}\cdot\dfrac{x_2}{y_1} = \dfrac{FP}{QC}\cdot\dfrac{PD}{QE} = \dfrac{AP \times PB}{BQ \times QA} = \dfrac{(x-a)(x+a)}{(x-b)(x+b)}$$

$$\dfrac{a^2}{b^2} = \dfrac{x^2 - a^2}{x^2 - b^2} = \dfrac{x^2}{x^2} = 1 \qquad \therefore \quad a = b \qquad \text{i.e.,} \quad \underline{PM = MQ}.$$

20.10 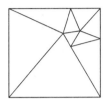   According to VE Hoggatt, American Monthly Magazine, 1961.

20.11 $(10A + B)(10C + D) = (10B + A)(10D + C)$

On expanding and simplifying: $AC = BD$ $\therefore$ $\dfrac{A}{B} = \dfrac{D}{C}$

So, possibilities are:

$\dfrac{A}{B}$	$\dfrac{1}{2}$	$\dfrac{1}{3}$	$\dfrac{1}{4}$	$\dfrac{2}{1}$	$\dfrac{2}{3}$	$\dfrac{2}{4}$	$\dfrac{2}{6}$	$\dfrac{3}{1}$	$\dfrac{3}{2}$	$\dfrac{3}{4}$	$\dfrac{3}{6}$	$\dfrac{4}{1}$	$\dfrac{4}{2}$	$\dfrac{4}{3}$	$\dfrac{6}{2}$	$\dfrac{6}{3}$
$\dfrac{D}{C}$	$\dfrac{3}{6},\dfrac{4}{8}$	$\dfrac{2}{6}$	$\dfrac{2}{8}$	$\dfrac{6}{3},\dfrac{8}{4}$	$\dfrac{4}{6},\dfrac{6}{9}$	$\dfrac{3}{6}$	$\dfrac{3}{9}$	$\dfrac{6}{2}$	$\dfrac{6}{4},\dfrac{9}{6}$	$\dfrac{6}{8}$	$\dfrac{4}{8}$	$\dfrac{8}{2}$	$\dfrac{6}{3}$	$\dfrac{8}{6}$	$\dfrac{9}{3}$	$\dfrac{8}{4}$

These represent 20 solutions.

But, $\dfrac{A}{B}$ and $\dfrac{D}{C}$ could be interchanged. $\therefore$ <u>40 solutions</u> in all.

20.12 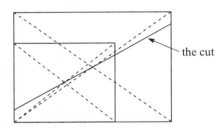 ← the cut

Any line through the centre of symmetry of a rectangle will divide it into equal areas.

So, we locate the centre of symmetry of each rectangle and draw a line passing through each of these centres.

20.13 $a^2 + b^2 = c^2$ {Pythagoras} and $a + b + c = \tfrac{1}{2}ab$ {equating areas}

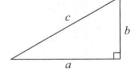

So, $a + b + \sqrt{a^2 + b^2} = \tfrac{1}{2}ab$

$$\sqrt{a^2 + b^2} = \tfrac{1}{2}ab - a - b$$

$$a^2 + b^2 = \tfrac{1}{4}a^2b^2 + a^2 + b^2 - a^2b - ab^2 + 2ab$$

$\therefore$ $\tfrac{1}{4}a^2b^2 - a^2b - ab^2 + 2ab = 0$

$\therefore$ $\tfrac{1}{4}ab(ab - 4a - 4b + 8) = 0$

$\therefore$ $ab - 4a - 4b + 8 = 0$ {as $a \neq 0, \; b \neq 0$}

$\therefore$ $b(a - 4) = 4a - 8$

$$b = \dfrac{4a - 8}{a - 4} = \dfrac{4(a - 4) + 8}{a - 4}$$

So, $b = 4 + \dfrac{8}{a - 4}$

Since b is an integer $a - 4 = \pm 1, \; \pm 2, \; \pm 4, \; \pm 8$.

$\therefore$ $a = 5, b = 12;$ $a = 6, b = 8;$ $a = 8, b = 6;$ $a = 12, b = 5.$

So, we have either the <u>5, 12, 13 triangle</u> or the <u>6, 8, 10 triangle</u>.

20.14

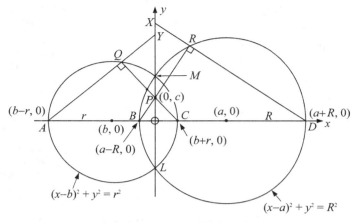

Circles meet where $\quad r^2 - (x-b)^2 = R^2 - (x-a)^2 \quad$ and $\quad x = 0$

$$\therefore \quad r^2 - b^2 = R^2 - a^2 \quad \text{......(1)}$$

Slope of $\overline{CP}$ is $\quad -\dfrac{c}{b+r} \qquad \therefore \quad$ Slope of $\overline{AQ}$ is $\dfrac{b+r}{c}$.

$\therefore \quad$ Equation of $\overline{AQ}$ is $\quad [b+r]x - cy = [b+r][b-r] - 0$

$$\text{i.e.,} \quad [b+r]x - cy = b^2 - r^2$$

$\therefore \quad Y$ is $\left(0, \dfrac{r^2 - b^2}{c} \right) \qquad$ {as it cuts the y-axis when $x = 0$.}

Likewise, slope of $\overline{BP}$ is $\quad -\dfrac{c}{a - R} \qquad \therefore \quad$ slope of $\overline{DR}$ is $\dfrac{a - R}{c}$

$\therefore \quad$ equation of $\overline{DR}$ is $\qquad [a - R]x - cy = [a - R][a + R] - 0$

$$\text{i.e.,} \quad [a - R]x - cy = a^2 - R^2$$

$$\text{i.e.,} \quad [a - R]x - cy = b^2 - r^2 \qquad \text{\{from (1)\}}$$

$\therefore \quad X$ is $\left(0, \dfrac{r^2 - b^2}{c} \right)$

i.e., X and Y are the same point $\qquad \therefore \quad \overline{AQ}, \overline{DR}, \overleftrightarrow{LM}$ are collinear.

> **Note:** • need to discuss case $c = 0$, which is fairly trivial.
> • This proof includes P anywhere on $\overleftrightarrow{LM}$ except P at O, $(c = 0)$.

20.15

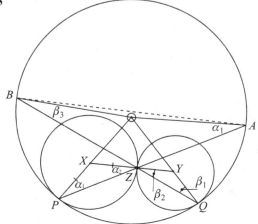

Reminder: The line joining the centres of two touching circles passes through the point of contact:

Proof: Join $\overline{OA}, \overline{OB}$ and $\overline{AB}$.
Join $\overline{OP}, \overline{OQ}, \overline{XY}$.

$$\alpha_1 = \alpha_2 \qquad \{\Delta PXZ \text{ is isosceles}\}$$
$$\alpha_2 = \alpha_3 \qquad \{\Delta POA \text{ is isosceles}\}$$
$$\therefore \quad \alpha_1 = \alpha_3$$
$$\therefore \quad \overline{XZ} \parallel \overline{AO} \qquad \{\text{equal corresponding angles}\}$$

Likewise, $\quad \beta_1 = \beta_2 = \beta_3$

$$\therefore \quad \overline{ZY} \parallel \overline{BO}$$
$$\therefore \quad \overline{OA} \parallel \overline{OB}$$

and as O is common to both B, O and A are collinear. $\quad \therefore \quad \underline{\overline{AB} \text{ is a diameter}}$.

SOLUTIONS
TO COMPETITION PAPERS

THE MASA 1983 SENIOR MATHEMATICS COMPETITION

1 **a** $1 + 2 + 3 + 4 + \ldots\ldots + 30 = \dfrac{30 \times 31}{2}$ $\{1 + 2 + 3 + 4 + \ldots\ldots + n = \dfrac{n(n+1)}{2}\}$

$= 465$

and 465 is not a multiple of 6. $\therefore$ <u>columns cannot</u> have the same sum.

b Since 465 is divisible by 5, it should be possible with each row summing to 93.

A possible arrangement is:

1	2	3	28	29	30
4	5	6	25	26	27
7	8	9	22	23	24
10	11	12	19	20	21
13	14	15	16	17	18

2 Let us suppose that there were n buses, then there are $22n + 1$ tourists.

For $n - 1$ buses there are k passengers per bus, say with no left-overs.

$\therefore$ $22n + 1 = k(n - 1)$ ......(1) where $22 < k < 45$.

Now $22n + 1 = kn - k$

Thus $k + 1 = n(k - 22)$

$\therefore$ $n = \dfrac{k + 1}{k - 22} = \dfrac{k - 22 + 23}{k - 22}$

$\therefore$ $n = 1 + \dfrac{23}{k - 22}$ where $0 < k - 22 < 23$.

and the only way that n can be integral is if $k - 22 = 1$ or 23, as 23 is prime.

Thus, $k = 23$ or 45.

But $22 < k < 45$, and therefore $k = 23$ and $n = 24$, and the number of tourists was <u>529</u>.

Alternatively:

As above until ....(1) then:

As $22n + 1$ is a multiple of $n - 1 = m$, say then $22(m + 1) + 1$ is a multiple of m or $22m + 23$ is a multiple of m.

Thus $22m + 23 = am$ for integer a, and $\therefore$ $m(a - 22) = 23$

So, $m = 1$ or 23.   {Unique factor theorem of integers.}

But the case $m = 1$ is impossible as this would mean that $n = 2$ and by (1), $k = 45$, i.e., 45 on 1 bus.   Thus $m = 23$ $\therefore$ $n = 24$ etc.

3 Any positive integer n, ends in one of the digits   0, 1, 2, 3, 4, 5, 6, 7, 8, or 9.

$\therefore$ n^3 ends in 0, 1, 8, 7, 4, 5, 6, 3, 2, 9.

In table form:

n	0	1	2	3	4	5	6	7	8	9
n^3	0	1	8	7	4	5	6	3	2	9
$n^3 + n$	0	2	0	0	8	0	2	0	0	8
$n^3 - n$	0	0	6	4	0	0	0	6	4	0

Each entry in the table gives the units digit that $n, n^3, n^3 + n, n^3 - n$ ends in.

It is clear that either $n^3 + n$ or $n^3 - n$ ends with digit <u>zero</u>.

4   We must divide the square into 4 congruent squares, as shown:
One of the subsquares must contain 3 points.
Suppose the shaded area is the one containing 3 points.

It has area $\frac{1}{4}$ unit^2.

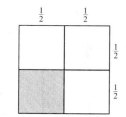

$\therefore$ the maximum possible area for any triangle is $\frac{1}{2} \times \frac{1}{4}$ units$^2 = \frac{1}{8}$ units^2

and this is attainable   e.g.,

Thus the area is $\leqslant \frac{1}{8}$ units^2.

5   Let $\overline{PA}$, $\overline{PB}$ and $\overline{PC}$ be of length a, b and c units respectively.
Without loss of generality, assume $a \leqslant b \leqslant c$.
In $\triangle PBC$,

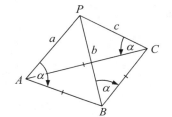

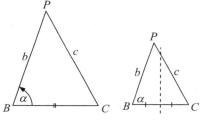

$b \leqslant c \;\;\Rightarrow\;\; m\angle PCB \leqslant \alpha$ ......(1)

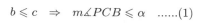

But comparing $\triangle$'s PBC, PAC

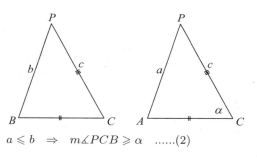

$a \leqslant b \;\;\Rightarrow\;\; m\angle PCB \geqslant \alpha$ ......(2)

From (1) and (2) $m\angle PCB = \alpha$.
$\therefore$ $\triangle PCB$ is isosceles   {equal base angles of α}
which implies that $b = c$.
By similar reasoning $b = a$ and therefore $a = b = c$,
i.e., $AP = BP = CP$.

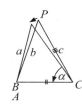

Alternatively:

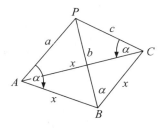

Now $c^2 = b^2 + x^2 - 2bx\cos\alpha$
$b^2 = a^2 + x^2 - 2ax\cos\alpha$ {cosine rule}
$a^2 = c^2 + x^2 - 2cx\cos\alpha$

$\therefore \;\; \dfrac{b^2 + x^2 - c^2}{2bx} = \dfrac{a^2 + x^2 - b^2}{2ax} = \dfrac{c^2 + x^2 - a^2}{2cx} = \cos\alpha$

$\therefore \;\; \dfrac{b^2 + x^2 - c^2}{b} = \dfrac{a^2 + x^2 - b^2}{a} = \dfrac{c^2 + x^2 - a^2}{c} = t, \;\;\text{say}$

Thus $b^2 + x^2 - c^2 = bt,\;\; a^2 + x^2 - b^2 = at,\;\; c^2 + x^2 - a^2 = ct$

$\therefore \;\; c^2 - b^2 + bt = b^2 - a^2 + at = a^2 - c^2 + ct$ {equating x^2's}

$\therefore \;\; a^2 + c^2 - 2b^2 = (a - b)t$

$\therefore \;\; t = \dfrac{a^2 + c^2 - 2b^2}{a - b}$

Thus $b^2 - a^2 + a\left[\dfrac{a^2 + c^2 - 2b^2}{a - b}\right] = a^2 - c^2 + c\left[\dfrac{a^2 + c^2 - 2b^2}{a - b}\right]$

$\therefore \quad (b^2 - a^2)(a - b) + a^3 + ac^2 - 2ab^2 = (a^2 - c^2)(a - b) + a^2c + c^3 - 2b^2c$

$\therefore \quad ab^2 - a^3 - b^3 + a^2b + a^3 + ac^2 - 2ab^2 = a^3 - ac^2 - a^2b + bc^2 + a^2c + c^3 - 2b^2c$

$\therefore \quad a^3 + b^3 + c^3 + ab^2 - 2a^2b - 2ac^2 + bc^2 + ac^2 - 2b^2c = 0$

$\therefore \quad a(a^2 - 2ab + b^2) + b(b^2 - 2bc + c^2) + c(c^2 - 2ca + a^2) = 0$

$\therefore \quad a(a - b)^2 + b(b - c)^2 + c(c - a)^2 = 0$

i.e., the sum of 3 non-negative terms is zero, and $\therefore$ each of them is zero.

$\therefore \quad a - b = b - c = c - a = 0,$ i.e., $\underline{a = b = c}.$

6   **a**   Consider the numbers: $x_1, x_2, x_3, ..., x_{10}$ where $x_1 \leqslant x_2 \leqslant x_3 \leqslant x_4 \leqslant ...... \leqslant x_{10}.$

{i.e., we order them, taking into account that some (or all) could be equal.}

Now $x_1 > x_2 + x_3 + x_4 + ... + x_{10}$ ......(1)

and $x_2 > x_1 + x_3 + x_4 + ... + x_{10}$ ......(2)

$\therefore \quad x_1 + x_2 > x_1 + x_2 + 2(x_3 + x_4 + ... + x_{10})$ {on adding (1) and (2)}

Hence $x_3 + x_4 + ... + x_{10} < 0$

Thus at least one of $x_3, x_4, ..., x_{10}$ must be negative.

b   Since $x_3 \leqslant x_4 \leqslant x_5 \leqslant ...... \leqslant x_{10},$ then, from **a**, $x_3 < 0.$

Since $x_1 \leqslant x_2 \leqslant x_3,$ then x_1 and x_2 are also negative. $\therefore$ at least 3 of them are negative.

c   If $x_1 = x_2 = x_3 = -1,$ and $x_4 = x_5 = x_6 = ... = x_{10} = \frac{1}{10}.$

i	x_i	sum of rest of them
1, 2 or 3	-1	$-1\frac{3}{10}$
4, 5, ..., 10	0.1	$-2\frac{2}{5}$

THE MASA 1984 SENIOR MATHEMATICS COMPETITION

1   **a** $100! = 100.99.98.97......3.2.1$

25, 50, 75 and 100 each contain 2 factors of 5. i.e., 8 in all, and the other 16 multiples of 5 contain 1 factor of 5, i.e., 16 in all, and $\therefore$ there are $8 + 16 = 24$ factors of 5 in 100!

Since there are 50 even numbers in 100!, there are in excess of 24 factors of 2.

$\therefore$ 100! must end in 24 zeros.

b   In 100! there are   10 numbers which end in 1
10 numbers which end in 2

$\vdots$

10 numbers which end in 9.   (We ignore those which end in a 0.)

Thus the last non-zero digit of 100! is the last nonzero digit of $(9.8.7.6.5.4.3.2.1)^{10}.$

Now   5!   has last non-zero digit 2,
$\therefore$ 6!   has last non-zero digit 2,
7!   has last non-zero digit 4,
8!   has last non-zero digit 2,
9!   has last non-zero digit 8,
Thus $(9!)^2$ has last non-zero digit 4,
$(9!)^4$ has last non-zero digit 6,
$(9!)^8$ has last non-zero digit 6,
$(9!)^{10}$ has last non-zero digit $\underline{4}.$

c No solution was forthcoming.

By calculator $100! \approx 9.3326 \times 10^{157}$,   and $\therefore$ $100!$ has <u>158</u> digits.

2 If $a > 0, b > 0$ then $\dfrac{a}{b} + \dfrac{b}{a} \geqslant 2$ ......(1)

Proof: Since $(a - b)^2 \geqslant 0$ for all real a, b, then
$$a^2 + b^2 \geqslant 2ab$$

$\therefore$ $\dfrac{a^2 + b^2}{ab} \geqslant 2$ as $ab > 0$

$\therefore$ $\dfrac{a}{b} + \dfrac{b}{a} \geqslant 2$ for all $a > 0, b > 0$.

Now $(x_1 + x_2 + x_3 + \ldots\ldots + x_n)\left(\dfrac{1}{x_1} + \dfrac{1}{x_2} + \dfrac{1}{x_3} + \ldots\ldots + \dfrac{1}{x_n}\right)$

$= \quad 1 \quad + \quad \dfrac{x_1}{x_2} \quad + \quad \dfrac{x_1}{x_3} \quad + \quad \dfrac{x_1}{x_4} \quad + \quad \ldots\ldots \quad + \quad \dfrac{x_1}{x_n}$

$+ \quad \dfrac{x_2}{x_1} \quad + \quad 1 \quad + \quad \dfrac{x_2}{x_3} \quad + \quad \dfrac{x_2}{x_4} \quad + \quad \ldots\ldots \quad + \quad \dfrac{x_2}{x_n}$

$+ \quad \dfrac{x_3}{x_1} \quad + \quad \dfrac{x_3}{x_2} \quad + \quad 1 \quad + \quad \dfrac{x_3}{x_4} \quad + \quad \ldots\ldots \quad + \quad \dfrac{x_3}{x_n}$

$\vdots$

$+ \quad \dfrac{x_n}{x_1} \quad + \quad \dfrac{x_n}{x_2} \quad + \quad \dfrac{x_n}{x_3} \quad + \quad \dfrac{x_n}{x_4} \quad + \quad \ldots\ldots \quad + \quad 1$

which is an $n \times n$ array of numbers which contains

a n 1's   {along the main diagonal}

b $\dfrac{n^2 - n}{2}$ positive numbers plus their reciprocals   (i.e., $\dfrac{x_i}{x_j} + \dfrac{x_j}{x_i}$)

$\therefore$ the product $\geqslant n.1 + \left(\dfrac{n^2 - n}{2}\right).2$ {as $\dfrac{x_i}{x_j} + \dfrac{x_j}{x_i} \geqslant 2$, from (1)}

$\therefore$ the product $\geqslant n + n(n - 1)$

$\therefore$ the product $\geqslant n + n^2 - n$

$\therefore$ <u>the product $\geqslant n^2$.</u>

3   **a** The factors of $2^n p$ are: $1, 2, 2^2, 2^3, \ldots\ldots, 2^n, p, 2p, \ldots\ldots, 2^{n-1}p, 2^n p$.

Thus, if 2^n is perfect, then
$$[1 + 2 + 2^2 + 2^3 + \ldots\ldots + 2^n] + p[1 + 2 + 2^2 + 2^3 + \ldots\ldots + 2^{n-1}] = 2^n.p$$

$\therefore$ $\left(\dfrac{2^{n+1} - 1}{2 - 1}\right) + p\left(\dfrac{2^n - 1}{2 - 1}\right) = 2^n.p$

$\therefore$ $2^{n+1} - 1 + p.2^n - p = 2^n.p$

$\therefore$ $2^{n+1} - 1 = p$

Thus $2^n p$ is perfect if $2^{n+1} - 1$ is a prime number.

Check: $n = 1,$ $2^2 - 1 = 3$ is prime $\therefore$ $2^1.3 = 6$ is perfect.

$n = 2,$ $2^3 - 1 = 7$ is prime $\therefore$ $2^2.7 = 28$ is perfect.

$n = 3,$ $2^4 - 1 = 15$ is not prime

$n = 4,$ $2^5 - 1 = 31$ is prime $\therefore$ $2^4.31 = 496$ <u>is perfect.</u>

b   For $3^n q$ to be perfect then

$$[1 + 3 + 3^2 + 3^3 + \ldots + 3^n] + q[1 + 3 + 3^2 + 3^3 + \ldots + 3^{n-1}] = 3^n q$$

$$\therefore \quad \left(\frac{3^{n+1} - 1}{3 - 1}\right) + q\left(\frac{3^n - 1}{3 - 1}\right) = 3^n.q$$

$$\therefore \quad 3^{n+1} - 1 + q(3^n - 1) = 2.3^n.q$$

$$\therefore \quad 3^{n+1} - 1 + q.3^n - q = 2.3^n.q$$

$$\therefore \quad 3^{n+1} - 1 = (3^n + 1)q$$

$$\therefore \quad q = \left(\frac{3^{n+1} - 1}{3^n + 1}\right) = \frac{3(3^n + 1) - 4}{3^n + 1}$$

$$\therefore \quad q = 3 - \frac{4}{3^n + 1}$$

$$\therefore \quad 3^n + 1 = 1, 2 \text{ or } 4 \qquad \{\text{as } q \text{ is an integer}\}$$

$$\therefore \quad 3^n = 0, 1 \text{ or } 3$$

$$\therefore \quad n = 0 \text{ or } 1 \qquad \{3^n > 0\}$$

If $n = 0$, $q = 1$ which is not prime.

If $n = 1$, $q = 2$.

Thus $3^1.2 = 6$ is the only perfect number of the form $3^n.q$.

4   **a**

$$\cos 3\phi = \cos(2\phi + \phi)$$
$$= \cos 2\phi \cos \phi - \sin 2\phi \sin \phi$$
$$= [2\cos^2 \phi - 1]\cos \phi - 2\sin^2 \phi \cos \phi \qquad \{\sin 2\phi = 2\sin \phi \cos \phi\}$$
$$= 2\cos^3 \phi - \cos \phi - 2[1 - \cos^2 \phi]\cos \phi \qquad \{\sin^2 \phi = 1 - \cos^2 \phi\}$$
$$= 4\cos^3 \phi - 3\cos \phi$$

$$\therefore \quad 4\cos^3 \phi = 3\cos \phi + \cos 3\phi$$

$$\cos^3 \phi - \tfrac{3}{4}\cos \phi - \tfrac{1}{4}\cos 3\phi = 0 \quad \ldots(1)$$

b   If we let $y = mx$, $x^3 - 3x + 1 = 0$

$$\text{becomes} \quad \left(\frac{y}{m}\right)^3 - 3\left(\frac{y}{m}\right) + 1 = 0$$

$$\text{i.e.,} \quad y^3 - 3m^2 y + m^3 = 0$$

If $y = \cos \phi$ and $m^2 = \tfrac{1}{4}$ then $m = \pm\tfrac{1}{2}$

this equation becomes $\cos^3 \phi - \tfrac{3}{4}\cos \phi \pm \tfrac{1}{8} = 0$

and comparing it with (1), $\cos 3\phi = \pm\tfrac{1}{2}$

If $m = \tfrac{1}{2}$, $\cos 3\phi = -\tfrac{1}{2}$

$$3\phi = 120° \quad \text{or} \quad 240°$$
$$\phi = 40° \quad \text{or} \quad 80°$$

solutions $x = \dfrac{y}{m} = 2\cos 40° \quad \text{or} \quad 2\cos 80°$

If $m = -\tfrac{1}{2}$, $\cos 3\phi = \tfrac{1}{2}$

$$3\phi = 60° \quad \text{or} \quad 300°$$
$$\phi = 20° \quad \text{or} \quad 100°$$

$$x = \dfrac{y}{m} = -2\cos 20° \quad \text{or} \quad -2\cos 100°.$$

$\therefore$ 3 solutions are $-2\cos 20°, \quad 2\cos 40°, \quad 2\cos 80°.$ $\{-2\cos 100° = 2\cos 80°\}$

c Consider $\qquad f(x) = x^3 - 3px + q$

$$\therefore \quad f'(x) = 3x^2 - 3p = 3(x + \sqrt{p})(x - \sqrt{p})$$

Thus $f'(x)$ has sign diagram:

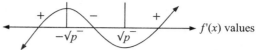

$\therefore$ local max. at $(-\sqrt{p},\ q + 2p^{\frac{3}{2}})$ and local min. at $(\sqrt{p},\ q - 2p^{\frac{3}{2}})$.

3 real roots exist if and only if local max. and min. are not on the same side of the x-axis.

i.e., if and only if $\qquad$ (a) $\quad p \geqslant 0 \quad$ {for $\sqrt{p}$ to exist, $p \geqslant 0$} $\quad$ and

$$\text{(b)} \quad (q + 2p^{\frac{3}{2}})(q - 2p^{\frac{3}{2}}) \leqslant 0 \qquad \text{\{product cannot be positive\}}$$

$$\therefore \quad -2p^{\frac{3}{2}} \leqslant q \leqslant 2p^{\frac{3}{2}}.$$

<u>General procedure</u> for solving $x^3 - 3px + q = 0$.

Let $y = mx \qquad \therefore \quad \left(\dfrac{y}{m}\right)^3 - 3p\left(\dfrac{y}{m}\right) + q = 0$

$$\therefore \quad \frac{y^3}{m^3} - \frac{3py}{m} + q = 0$$

$$\therefore \quad y^3 - 3pm^2y + qm^3 = 0$$

let $y = \cos\phi$ and $m^2 = \dfrac{1}{4p} \quad \therefore \quad m = \pm\dfrac{1}{2\sqrt{p}}.$

$$\therefore \quad \cos^3\phi - \tfrac{3}{4}\cos\phi \pm q.\left(\frac{1}{2\sqrt{p}}\right)^3 = 0$$

[* we need $p > 0$ here for m to be real.]

If $p = 0$, $x^3 + q = 0 \qquad \therefore \quad x = \sqrt[3]{-q}$ is O.K.

$$\therefore \quad \tfrac{1}{4}\cos 3\phi = \pm q\left(\frac{1}{8p^{\frac{3}{2}}}\right)$$

$$\therefore \quad \cos 3\phi = \pm q\left(\frac{1}{2p^{\frac{3}{2}}}\right)$$

and for this to have solutions, $|\cos 3\phi| < 1$

$$\therefore \quad \left| q\left(\frac{1}{2p^{\frac{3}{2}}}\right) \right| < 1$$

$$\therefore \quad \left| \frac{q}{2p^{\frac{3}{2}}} \right| < 1$$

$$\therefore \quad -1 < \frac{q}{2p^{\frac{3}{2}}} < 1$$

$$\therefore \quad -2p^{\frac{3}{2}} < q < 2p^{\frac{3}{2}} \qquad \text{\{as } 2p^{\frac{3}{2}} > 0\}$$

Thus we have solutions $\quad x = \dfrac{y}{m} = \dfrac{\cos\phi}{\pm\dfrac{1}{2\sqrt{p}}} = \underline{\pm 2\sqrt{p}\cos\phi} \quad$ where $\quad \cos 3\phi = \pm\dfrac{q}{2p^{\frac{3}{2}}}.$

5 Call the unit squares U, and the square that bounds the 5 unit squares B.

a

For this arrangement, the length of one side of the bounding square B is $2 + \dfrac{\sqrt{2}}{2}$.

Diagram 1

b Divide the bounding square into 4 equal square regions, and call one of these Q (for quarter). The pigeon-hole principle can be applied to guarantee that at least 2 of the unit squares must have their boundaries inside or on the border of one of the 4 squares Q.

We now show that a square region Q which contains the centres of 2 units squares cannot be smaller than $1 + \frac{1}{4}\sqrt{2}$ on a side.

Put this together with **a** and it follows that **a** is the best possible arrangement.

We begin by considering 2 special cases.

c In diagram 2, the x, y axes represent the boundary of the bounding square B. One of the unit squares touches the x and y axis and the other unit square has its centre along the line $y = x$.

In diagram 2, we have $60° \leqslant \theta \leqslant 90°$.

We begin by estimating the distance between the centre c of one unit square and its distance to P, the nearest corner of the other unit square as indicated on the diagram.

Let the coordinates of c be (x, x).

The coordinates of P are $(\sin\theta, \sin\theta + \cos\theta)$

It follows that $(x - \sin\theta)^2 + (x - \sin\theta - \cos\theta)^2 \geqslant \frac{1}{4}$.

To simplify calculations let $X = x - \sin\theta$ then $X^2 + (X - \cos\theta)^2 \geqslant \frac{1}{4}$

From this it follows that $X \geqslant \frac{1}{2}\cos\theta + \frac{1}{4}\sqrt{2 - 4\cos^2\theta}$

i.e., $x \geqslant \sin\theta + \frac{1}{2}\cos\theta + \frac{1}{4}\sqrt{2 - 4\cos^2\theta}$

$\sin\theta + \frac{1}{2}\cos\theta + \frac{1}{4}\sqrt{2 - 4\cos^2\theta} = \sqrt{1 + \frac{1}{4}}\sin(\theta + \phi) + \frac{1}{4}\sqrt{2 - 4\cos^2\theta}$ where $\tan\phi = \frac{1}{2}$.

For the interval under consideration, $60° \leqslant \theta \leqslant 90°$,

i $\frac{1}{4}\sqrt{2 - 4\cos^2\theta}$ will increase with increasing values of θ,

ii $\sin(\theta + \phi)$ will increase until $\theta + \phi = 90°$, and then decrease.

It follows that $\sin\theta + \frac{1}{2}\cos\theta + \frac{1}{4}\sqrt{2 - 4\cos^2\theta}$ will have its least value either at $\theta = 60°$ or $\theta = 90°$.

A quick calculation shows this to be at $\theta = 90°$.

It follows that $x \geqslant 1 + \frac{\sqrt{2}}{4}$ if $60° \leqslant \theta \leqslant 90°$.

Note that X is the length of the quarter squares Q.

d The same situation as in **c**, but now the angle θ is restricted to lie in the interval $45° \leqslant \theta \leqslant 60°$.

In this case the two unit squares will have an edge in common (see diagram 3.).

The angle ACX is $\theta - 45°$ and the length of AC is $\dfrac{1\frac{1}{2}}{\cos(\theta - 45)} = \dfrac{1\frac{1}{2}}{\sin(\theta + 45)}$.

A is the point where the edge SR of the unit cube meets the line $y = x$.

Let A have coordinates (y, y).

The equation of the line passing through S and R is $y = \sin\theta - (\tan\theta)x$.

The coordinates of A can be found by observing that at A, $y = x$, i.e., $y = \sin\theta - (\tan\theta)y$.

From this $y = \dfrac{\sin\theta}{1+\tan\theta} = \dfrac{\sin\theta\cos\theta}{\sin\theta+\cos\theta} = \dfrac{1}{2\sqrt{2}}\cdot\dfrac{\sin(2\theta)}{\sin(\theta+45)}$

The length of the square Q is $\dfrac{1}{2\sqrt{2}}\cdot\dfrac{\sin(2\theta)}{\sin(\theta+45)} + \dfrac{3}{2}\cdot\dfrac{1}{\sin(\theta+45)}\cdot\dfrac{1}{\sqrt{2}}$

[Remember AC has to be projected on to one of the axes and $\cos(45) = \frac{1}{\sqrt{2}}$.]

i.e., the length of the square Q is $\dfrac{1}{2\sqrt{2}}\dfrac{(3+\sin 2\theta)}{\sin(\theta+45)} \geqslant \dfrac{1}{2\sqrt{2}}(3+\sin 2\theta)$ {as $45^\circ \leqslant \theta \leqslant 60^\circ$}

$$\geqslant \dfrac{1}{2\sqrt{2}}(3+\sin 2\theta)$$

$$\geqslant \underline{1 + \dfrac{\sqrt{2}}{4}}$$

e   The same as in **c** or **d**, but now $0^\circ \leqslant \theta \leqslant 45^\circ$.

By interchanging the x and y axis, this is identical to **c** or **d**. From **c**, **d** and **e**, it follows that if one unit square touches two boundaries of the bounding square B and the other has its centre on the corner of the quarter square A, then the length of the one side of the bounding square $\geqslant 2 + \dfrac{\sqrt{2}}{2}$.

We now show that any other situation is worse than this.

There are essentially only <u>two other situations</u>.

f   **In diagram 4**,   the unit square with its centre on the boundary of A can be moved to have its centre at corner C. The centre C can then slide down the line $y = x$ until the two squares touch as in **c**, **d** or **e**.

g   **In diagram 5**,   one square can move sideways and the other move downwards until both their centres are on the side of a square. This new square is smaller than the square Q which contained the centres of the two unit squares.

We now show that this quarter square with centres C_1 and C_2 on its edges has a length

$$\geqslant \underline{1 + \dfrac{\sqrt{2}}{4}}.$$

Draw a line through C_1 to meet the x-axis at K, and such that $\angle OKG = 45^\circ$. Then either C_2 lies below the line $C_1 K$ or C_2 lies above the line $C_1 K$. If C_2 lies above the line $C_1 K$, interchange the X and Y axes.

We can assume that C_2 lies below the line $C_1 K$.

This means that the unit square which has C_2 as its centre lies within the square with vertices at C_1 and K and with its edges parallel to the x and y axes.

We can apply **c**, **d** or **e** to this square. Hence the length of a side of this square $\geqslant 1 + \dfrac{\sqrt{2}}{4}$.

Diagram 2 $(60^\circ \leqslant \theta \leqslant 90^\circ)$

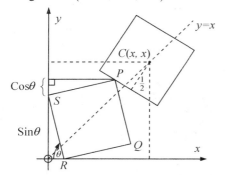

Diagram 3 $(45^\circ \leqslant \theta \leqslant 60^\circ)$

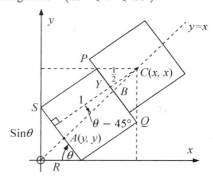

Diagram 4

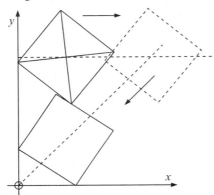

Diagram 5

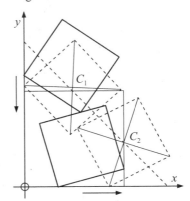

THE MASA 1985 SENIOR MATHEMATICS COMPETITION

1 **a** $1 = 1^2 - 0^2; \quad 3 = 2^2 - 1^2; \quad 5 = 3^2 - 2^2; \quad 7 = 4^2 - 3^2; \quad 9 = 5^2 - 4^2.$

b From the above pattern, guess $2n + 1 = (n + 1)^2 - n^2$

But $(n + 1)^2 - n^2 = n^2 + 2n + 1 - n^2$
$$= 2n + 1$$

Thus every odd integer can be expressed as the difference between two squares.

> Note: This representation is not necessarily unique.
> For example, $9 = 5^2 - 4^2$ or $9 = 3^2 - 0^2.$
> Can you identify all odd numbers for which the representation is unique?

c Suppose a and b are integers such that $2 = a^2 - b^2$
i.e., $2 = (a + b)(a - b)$

Since 1 and 2 are the only factors of 2,

Either $a + b = 2$ and $a - b = 1$ or $a + b = 1$ and $a - b = 2$

In either case $a = \frac{3}{2}$,   which contradicts the condition that a is an integer.

Thus not every even integer can be expressed as the difference between two squares.

Case 1:

However, $4 = 2^2 - 0^2$,   thus some even integers can be expressed as the difference between two squares. In general, every even integer of the form $4n$ can be expressed as the difference between two squares.

If $4n = a^2 - b^2 = (a + b)(a - b)$

You can select $a - b = 2$ and $a + b = 2n$,   which gives
$a = n + 1$ and $b = n - 1.$

Case 2:

Integers of the form $2(2n + 1)$ can not be expressed as the difference between two squares. It is not difficult to show this using the above reasoning.

2 The quick answer is: **minimum 3** since we were given 3, **maximum 4** since a tetrahedron has four triangles as faces.

This is a useful observation but there is more to it. The three given right angles **force** another right angle. The diagram below depicts a piece sliced from a rectangular prism.

From the diagram, it is clear that ADB is also a right angle.

Proof: From Pythagoras' theorem

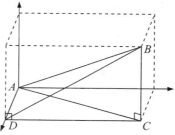

$$AB^2 = AC^2 + BC^2 \quad (\angle ACB = 90°)......(1)$$
$$BD^2 = BC^2 + DC^2 \quad (\angle BCD = 90°)......(2)$$
$$AC^2 = AD^2 + DC^2 \quad (\angle ADC = 90°)......(3)$$

From (2) and (3) $\quad BD^2 = BC^2 + (AC^2 - AD^2)$

i.e., $\quad BD^2 + AD^2 = BC^2 + AC^2$

From (1) $\quad BD^2 + AD^2 = AB^2 \quad$ and $\quad \therefore \quad$ angle ADB is a right angle.

3 **a**
$$\begin{array}{r} 62027 \\ \times \quad 124 \\ \hline 7691348 \end{array}$$

Check: $6 + 2 + 0 + 2 + 7 = 17, \qquad 1 + 7 = 8$
$$1 + 2 + 4 = 7, \qquad\qquad 7$$
$$7 + 6 + 9 + 1 + 3 + 4 + 8 = 38, \qquad 3 + 8 = 11, \qquad 1 + 1 = \underline{2}$$

$8 \times 7 = 56, \quad 5 + 6 = 11, \quad 1 + 1 = \underline{2} \quad$ Check works.

b Any integer m can be written as $\quad m = 9k + r \quad$ where $\quad 0 < r \leqslant 9$.

[0 is a special case, but this causes no problems in simple arithmetic.]

Observe that the process of adding digits amounts to finding the remainder r after dividing by 9. To see this, note that if a is a single digit number, $\quad a \times 10^n = a \times (99......9 + 1)$

which leaves a remainder of a when divided by 9. a is the number used when adding digits.

Consider now the check for multiplication:

Suppose $\qquad\qquad m_1 = 9n_1 + r_1 \qquad$ and $\quad m_2 = 9n_2 + r_2$
$$\therefore \quad m_1 m_2 = (9n_1 + r_1)(9n_2 + r_2)$$
$$= 81n_1 n_2 + 9(n_1 r_2 + n_2 r_1) + r_1 r_2$$
$$= 9(\text{integer}) + r_1 r_2$$

c Suppose $\quad \dfrac{m}{n} = q + \dfrac{r}{n} \quad$ {r is the remainder} $\quad \therefore \quad m = qn + r$

A check can now be based on a multiplication followed by an addition.

For example: $36251 \div 263 = 137 +$ remainder 220

i.e., $\quad 36251 = 137 \times 263 + 220$

$\qquad\qquad\qquad$ _Check:_ $\quad 3 + 6 + 2 + 5 + 1 = 17, \quad 1 + 7 = 8$
Multiplication: $\qquad\qquad 1 + 3 + 7 = 11, \quad 1 + 1 = 2$
$\qquad\qquad\qquad\qquad\qquad 2 + 6 + 3 = 11, \quad 1 + 1 = 2 \quad$ and $\quad 2 \times 2 = 4$
$\qquad$ Addition: $\qquad\qquad 2 + 2 + 0 = 4,$
$\qquad$ Finally $\qquad\qquad\qquad 4 + 4 = \underline{8} \qquad$ which checks with the first number 8.

4 **a** Only ◺ could fit the gap, but ◺ next door is the required tile.

b 6 triminoes have all three digits the same.

6×5 triminoes have one pair the same and the third different.

It should be noted that ◺ and ◺ are **different**, but there are no other

triminoes with the numbers 1, 2 and 3.

So $\quad 2 \times \dfrac{6.5.4}{3.2.1} \quad$ triminoes have three different numbers.

Total number of triminoes is $\quad 6 + 30 + 40 = 76$.

c You can, of course, find the sum by systematically listing the triminoes, but here is a

"Smart Alec's" way: $\dfrac{0+1+2+3+4+5}{6} = \dfrac{15}{6}$

$$\dfrac{15}{6} \times 3 \times 76 = 570$$

The total is 570.

d There are only $7 \times 7 = 49$ tiles in dominoes, which is considerably less than the 76 triminoes.

If the numbers on triminoes were to go from 0 to 6, there would be $7 + 42 + 70 = \underline{119}$ triminoes, which would make the game somewhat unmanageable. For example, the chances of finding a tile which would fit would be considerably reduced.

5

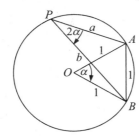

Note that $\angle APB = \frac{1}{2}\angle AOB = 30°$
{"angle at centre" theorem}

In $\triangle APB$, $1^2 = a^2 + b^2 - 2ab\cos 30°$ {cosine rule}

$$\therefore\quad 1^2 = a^2 + b^2 - 2ab \cdot \tfrac{\sqrt{3}}{2}$$
$$\therefore\quad a^2 + b^2 - 1 = ab\sqrt{3}$$
$$\therefore\quad (a^2 + b^2 - 1)^2 = 3a^2b^2$$

Expand and rearrange to obtain $a^4 + b^4 + 1 = a^2b^2 + 2a^2 + 2b^2 \dots\dots(1)$

Starting with $(a^2 + b^2 + 2)^2 = a^4 + b^4 + 2(a^2b^2 + 2a^2 + 2b^2) + 4$
and using (1) $= a^4 + b^4 + 2(a^4 + b^4 + 1) + 4$
$= \underline{3(a^4 + b^4 + 2)}$

We should also consider the possibility of P lying on the arc between A and B when $\angle APB \neq 30°$.

Many **generalisations** are possible. The most obvious one is to make the radius of the circle d, not necessarily 1.

Another generalisation is to allow the point P to be anywhere, not necessarily on the circumference of the circle. In this case, if OP $= c$, then $3(a^4 + b^4 + c^4 + d^4) = (a^2 + b^2 + c^2 + d^2)^2$.

THE MASA 1986 SENIOR MATHEMATICS COMPETITION

1   a $1 = 1^{986}$
$2 = 1^9 \times (8 - 6)$
$3 = (1 + 9 + 8) \div 6$ or $1^9 + 8 - 6$
$4 = -1 - 9 + 8 + 6$ or $(1 - 9) \div (-8 + 6)$
$5 = (1 + 9) \div (8 - 6)$
$6 = -1 + 9 - 8 + 6$
$7 = 1^{98} + 6$
$8 = 1 + 9 - 8 + 6$
$9 = ?$
$10 = -1 + 9 + 8 - 6$
$11 = -1 + ((9 \times 8) \div 6)$
$12 = (1 + 9 - 8) \times 6$ or $1 \times 9 \times 8 \div 6$ or $1 + 9 + 8 - 6$

b The largest number (we think) is $19^{8^6} = (10^{\log 19})^{8^6}$
$= 10^{335217.58397\dots\dots}$
$= 3.8368 \times 10^{335217}$
$\therefore\ \underline{335218 \text{ digits}}$

2   **a**

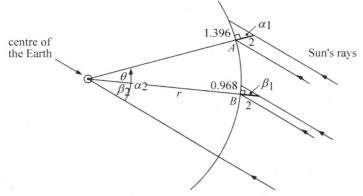

$$\tan \alpha = \frac{1.396}{2} \qquad \tan \beta = \frac{0.968}{2} \quad \text{and} \quad \alpha_1 = \alpha_2, \quad \beta_1 = \beta_2 \qquad \{\text{equal alternate angles}\}$$

Thus $\theta = \alpha - \beta$

$$= \tan^{-1}(0.698) - \tan^{-1}(0.484)$$

$$\doteqdot 9.088^{\circ}$$

But arc $AB = r\theta$ $\{\theta$ in radians$\}$

$$\therefore \quad 1010 \doteqdot r\left(9.088 \times \frac{\pi}{180}\right) \qquad \left\{ \begin{array}{l} \pi^c = 180^{\circ} \\[2mm] \dfrac{\pi^c}{180} = 1^{\circ} \end{array} \right.$$

$$\therefore \quad r \doteqdot \frac{180 \times 1010}{9.088 \times \pi}$$

i.e., $r \doteqdot \underline{6368 \text{ km}}$

b

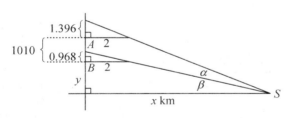

$$\tan \alpha = 0.698 \qquad \doteqdot \frac{1010 + y}{x}$$

$$\tan \beta = 0.484 \qquad \doteqdot \frac{y}{x}$$

Thus $y \doteqdot 0.484x \doteqdot 0.698x - 1010$

$$\therefore \quad 1010 \doteqdot 0.214x$$

$$\therefore \quad x \doteqdot 4720$$

i.e., $\underline{4720 \text{ km from earth.}}$

Note: Clearly the information provided is not sufficient.

3

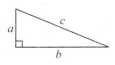

We require   (1) a, b, c integers

(2) $\frac{1}{2}ab = a + b + c$

Now $c^2 = a^2 + b^2$

$$\therefore \quad \tfrac{1}{2}ab - a - b = \sqrt{a^2 + b^2} \qquad \{c > 0\}$$

Thus $(\tfrac{1}{2}ab - a - b)^2 = a^2 + b^2$

$$\therefore \quad \tfrac{1}{4}a^2b^2 + a^2 + b^2 - a^2b + 2ab - ab^2 = a^2 + b^2$$

$$\{\text{as } (x + y + z)^2 = x^2 + y^2 + z^2 + 2xy + 2yz + 2zx\}$$

$$\therefore \quad \tfrac{1}{4}ab(ab - 4a - 4b + 8) = 0$$

$$\therefore \quad ab - 4a - 4b + 8 = 0$$

$$\therefore \quad (a - 4)(b - 4) = 8$$

$$\therefore \quad a = 4 + \frac{8}{b - 4}$$

But a is an integer $\therefore \quad b - 4 = 1, 2, 4$ or 8 i.e., $b = 5, 6, 8$ or 12 and $a = 12, 8, 6$ or 5.

$\therefore$ triangles are: 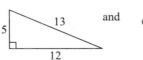   and

4   a

Consider: $n = 5$

Of the $5^2 = 25$ unit squares, 5 will have a diagonal.

Thus $2(1 + 2 + 3 + 4) + 5 = 5^2$

$$2(1 + 2 + 3 + 4) = 5^2 - 5$$
$$= 5(5 - 1)$$
$$1 + 2 + 3 + 4 = \frac{4 \times 5}{2}$$

In general, for an $n \times n$ square, there are n^2 unit squares and n have a diagonal.

Consequently $2(1 + 2 + 3 + 4 + \ldots\ldots + [n - 1]) + n = n^2$

$\therefore$ $2(1 + 2 + 3 + 4 + \ldots\ldots + n - 1 + n) = n^2 + n$

$\therefore$ $1 + 2 + 3 + 4 + \ldots\ldots n = \dfrac{n(n + 1)}{2}$

b   i

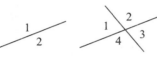   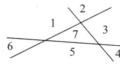   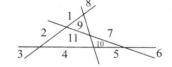

R_n = number of regions for n lines.

$\underline{R_1 = 2}$ $\underline{R_2 = 4}$ $\underline{R_3 = 7}$ $\underline{R_4 = 11}$

$R_2 = R_1 + 2$

$R_3 = R_2 + 3 = R_1 + 2 + 3$

$R_4 = R_3 + 4 = R_1 + 2 + 3 + 4$

$\vdots$

$R_n = R_1 + 2 + 3 + 4 + \ldots\ldots + n$ {by Induction}

The addition of an extra line from r lines to $r + 1$ lines adds $r + 1$ regions.

$\therefore$ $R_n = 1 + (1 + 2 + 3 + \ldots\ldots + n) = 1 + \dfrac{n(n + 1)}{2} = \dfrac{n^2 + n + 2}{2}$

ii   If r_n = number of non-infinite regions for n lines, then $r_1 = 0$, $r_2 = 0$, $r_3 = 1$, $r_4 = 3$, $r_5 = 6$, ...

$r_2 - r_1 = 0$

$r_3 - r_2 = 1$

$r_4 - r_3 = 2$

$r_5 - r_4 = 3$

$\vdots =$

$r_n - r_{n-1} = n - 2$

and adding all of these equations leads to $r_n - r_1 = 1 + 2 + 3 + \ldots\ldots + (n - 2)$

$\therefore$ $r_n = \dfrac{(n - 2)(n - 1)}{2}$

5   **a**   Suppose the rectangles have dimensions $a \times b$ and $c \times d$. If $a > c > d > b$ the two rectangles will not be comparable. Hence there are infinitely many pairs of rectangles which are incomparable.

   b   The statement: *"If two rectangles are not comparable, then one cannot be placed on top of the other without overlapping."* is false. Suppose the rectangles have dimensions $a \times b$ and $c \times d$. If $a > b > c > d$, the two rectangles will not be comparable but the first can be placed on the second without overlap.

   c   Any rectangle cut into two rectangles, produces two comparable rectangles.
   If a rectangle is cut into three rectangles, the first cut produces two rectangles and one of these will have to be cut in two again. These two rectangles are comparable.

   d   When a rectangle is cut into four rectangles, there are two cases:

   Case 1:   If one of the four rectangles contains two corners of the original rectangle, it leaves three rectangles to be cut. We have already proved that two of these are comparable.

   Case 2:   Each of the rectangles contains a corner of the original rectangle, say $ABCD$.

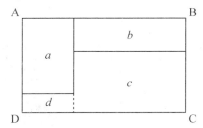

If a and b are comparable, we are finished.

If a and b are not comparable, a situation similar to that shown in the diagram must occur, making the pairs a and d, and b and c comparable.

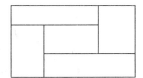

   e   A simple counter-example shows that when a rectangle is divided into five rectangles, no two need to be comparable.

THE MASA 1987 SENIOR MATHEMATICS COMPETITION

1   **a**   The numbers consist of ten digits and a two-digit exponent.
   There are 199 exponents from -99 to $+99$ inclusive.
   Ten digits can be chosen in   2   ×   9   × 10^9 ways.
                                        for $\pm$ (first digit non-zero)   (9 other digits)

   Multiplying by the number of exponents and adding 1 (for zero) gives a total of $2.9.10^9 \cdot 199 + 1$.

   b

```
                    3  3  .  .  .  .  .  .  3  3  3  7
                    3  3  .  .  .  .  .  .  3  3  3  7
   ─────────────────────────────────────────────────────
                 2  3  3  .  .  .  .  .  .  3  3  5  9
              1  0  0  .  .  .  .  .  .  0  0  1  1
           1  0  0  .  .  .  .  .  .  0  0  1  1
        1  0  0  .  .  .  .  .  .  0  0  1  1
                 .  .  .  .  .
                 .  .  .  .  .
                 .  .  .  .  .
        1  0  0  .  .  .  .  .  .  0  0  1  1
     1  0  0  .  .  .  .  .  .  0  0  1  1
   ─────────────────────────────────────────────────────
     1  1  .  .  .  .  .  .  .  1  1  3  5  .  .  .  .  .  .  .  5  5  6  9
```

   $\underbrace{\qquad\qquad\qquad}_{n \text{ ones}}$ ↑ $\underbrace{\qquad\qquad}_{(n-1) \text{ fives}}$ ↑ ↑

                              a three   a six
                                                                          a nine

where n is the number of threes in the given number.

For 1987, the product is 1987 ones, one three, 1986 fives, sixty nine.

2 a "Take $\frac{1}{9}$ of 10, namely $1\frac{1}{9}$ (from 10): $8\frac{8}{9}$ remains.

Multiply $8\frac{8}{9}$ times $8\frac{8}{9}$: it makes $79\frac{1}{81}$.

Multiply $79\frac{1}{81}$ times 10: it makes $\underline{790\frac{10}{81}}$ cubed cubits."

b Volume $= \pi \left(\dfrac{d^2 h}{4} \right)$

The Egyptians used $[(1 - \frac{1}{9})d]^2 . h = \frac{64}{81} d^2 h = \frac{256}{81}(\frac{d^2}{4}h)$.

π is approximated by $\frac{256}{81} = 3\frac{13}{81} \doteqdot \underline{3.1605}$

c Now approximate $(1 - \frac{p}{q})d^2 h$ to $\frac{\pi}{4}d^2 h$.

$$(1 - \frac{p}{q})^2 \doteqdot \frac{\pi}{4}$$

$$1 - \frac{p}{q} \doteqdot \frac{\sqrt{\pi}}{2}$$

$$\frac{p}{q} \doteqdot 1 - \frac{\sqrt{\pi}}{2} \doteqdot \underline{0.1138}$$

$\dfrac{p}{q} = \dfrac{1}{9} \doteqdot 0.1111 = 0.1138 - 0.0027$

Now inspect rational numbers which are larger than $\frac{1}{9}$ but close to it.

$\frac{1}{8} = 0.1250 = 0.1138 + 0.0112$ Worse

$\frac{2}{17} \doteqdot 0.1176 = 0.1138 + 0.0038$ Worse

$\frac{3}{26} \doteqdot 0.1154 = 0.1138 + 0.0016$ Gives a better approximation than $\frac{1}{9}$, (for smallest q).

3 a

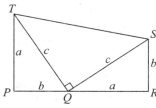

There are many different proofs.
Here is President Garfield's proof (1867).

Area trapezium $PRST$ = area triangles $(TPQ + QRS + TQS)$

$$\frac{1}{2}(a+b)(b+a) = \frac{1}{2}ab + \frac{1}{2}ab + \frac{1}{2}c^2$$
$$a^2 + 2ab + b^2 = 2ab + c^2$$
$$a^2 + b^2 = c^2$$

b Area of equilateral triangle

on side a is $\frac{1}{2}a.a.\sin 60° = \dfrac{\sqrt{3}a^2}{4}$

on side b is $\dfrac{\sqrt{3}b^2}{4}$

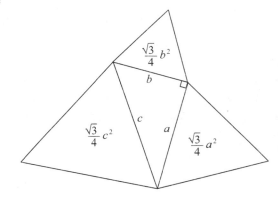

Adding, $\dfrac{\sqrt{3}}{4}(a^2 + b^2) = \dfrac{\sqrt{3}}{4}c^2$ {Pythagoras' theorem}

= area equilateral triangle on the hypotenuse.

c

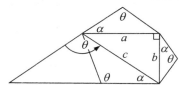

On the hypotenuse, c, are drawn two similar triangles of different area. They cannot both be equal in area to the sum of the areas of the similar triangles on the two smaller sides. The result is **not** necessarily true.

The necessary condition is that the same angle, say θ, must be opposite the side of the right-angled triangle for all three similar triangles. They are then said to be "similarly described".

d Yes. It is true for similar quadrilaterals if they are similarly described.

4 Volume of ball of radius $\dfrac{l}{2} = \dfrac{4}{3}\pi(\dfrac{l}{2})^3 = \dfrac{\pi l^3}{6}$

Volume of cube of edge l is l^3.

$$\dfrac{\text{volume of ball}}{\text{volume of cube}} = \dfrac{(\frac{\pi}{6})l^3}{l^3} = \dfrac{\pi}{6} \doteqdot 0.52 = 52\%$$

Regardless of the size of the cube, there will be 48% wastage when it is cut into a ball. To avoid further waste, l must be a common factor of 66 (6×11), 210 ($6 \times 5 \times 7$), and 462 ($6 \times 7 \times 11$).

For the largest possible balls, we need the highest common factor, which is 6. Make them have diameter 6 cm.

5   **a** Many are possible. For example, ... multiples of 6, 18, 24, 30, 36, ...

b p^k has factors 1, p, p^2, ..., p^{k-1}, (excluding p^k) only.

Adding, $1 + p + p^2 + ... + p^{k-1} = \dfrac{1(p^k - 1)}{p - 1}$

$< p^k - 1$ for $p - 1 \geqslant 1$ which is true.

$< p^k$ since $p > 1$.

Thus p^k cannot be abundant.

c If a number has factors 3, 5, 7, 9, ... then $\dfrac{n}{3}$, $\dfrac{n}{5}$, $\dfrac{n}{7}$, $\dfrac{n}{9}$, ... are also factors of n.

If their sum is greater than n, then n must be abundant since they are not the only factors of n and the true total would exceed n more easily.

$n(\frac{1}{3} + \frac{1}{5} + \frac{1}{7} + \frac{1}{9} + ...) > n$

$\frac{1}{3} + \frac{1}{5} + \frac{1}{7} + \frac{1}{9} + ... > 1$ implies that 3.5.7.9...... is abundant.

In particular

$\frac{1}{3} + \frac{1}{5} + \frac{1}{7} + \frac{1}{9} + \frac{1}{11} + \frac{1}{13} + \frac{1}{15} = \dfrac{46027}{45045} > 1$ by exact calculation,

or $= 1.02180$ by the sum of reciprocals on calculator.

Hence   45045   is an abundant number.

d Two such numbers are   945   (sum 974)
                                   1155   (sum 1163)

Can you find any others?   Is 945 the smallest?

THE MASA 1988 SENIOR MATHEMATICS COMPETITION

1 Let $a + (a+1) + (a+2) + \ldots\ldots + (a + [n-1]) = 1988$ {sum of n consecutive integers}

$\therefore \quad \dfrac{n}{2}(2a + n - 1) = 1988$

$\therefore \quad n(2a + n - 1) = 3976 = 2^3 \times 7 \times 71$

<u>If n is odd,</u>   (1) $n = 7$ $\therefore \quad 2a + 6 = 568$ $\therefore \quad a = 281$ ✓

or (2) $n = 71$ $\therefore \quad 2a + 70 = 56$ which is not possible as $a > 0$

or (3) $n = 7 \times 71$ $\therefore \quad 2a + 496 = 8$ also impossible.

Only solution for n odd is

A: $281 + 282 + 283 + 284 + 285 + 286 + 287 = 1988$

If n is even, $2a + n - 1$ is odd $\therefore \quad 2a + n - 1 = 7, 71$ or 497.

(1) If $2a + n - 1 = 7$,   then $n = 568$ $\therefore \quad a < 0$ which is not possible.
(2) If $2a + n - 1 = 71$,   then $n = 56$ $\therefore \quad a = 8$ ✓
(3) If $2a + n - 1 = 497$,   then $n = 8$ $\therefore \quad a = 245$ ✓

Thus there are 2 solutions for n even;

B: $8 + 9 + 10 + 11 + \ldots\ldots + 63 = 1988$

C: $245 + 246 + 247 + \ldots\ldots + 252 = 1988$

2 Clearly <u>$S = 1$</u>.

Now $3Y = Y$ or $Y + 10$ or $Y + 20$ $\therefore \quad Y = 0, 5$ or 10.

But if $Y = 5$, $3T + 1 = T$, $T + 10$ or $T + 20$,   all of which lead to impossible solutions.

$\therefore \quad$ <u>$Y = 0$</u> and hence $3T = T$ or $T + 10$ or $T + 20$.

$\therefore \quad T = 0, 5$ or 10

$\therefore \quad$ <u>$T = 5$</u>.

Thus the problem becomes: 5 W E N 5 0
                               5 W E N 5 0
                               5 H I R 5 0
                            ―――――――――――――――
                               1 E V E N 5 0

$\therefore \quad 2N + R + 1 = N$ or $N + 10$ or $N + 20$
$\therefore \quad N + R = -1$ or   9   or   19

$\therefore \quad$ <u>$N + R = 9$</u>   which leads to possibilities:

N	2	3	4	5	6	7
R	7	6	5	4	3	2

Thus in 4th column 1 is carried. By identical reasoning in <u>column 4</u>. <u>$E + I = 9$</u>   also.

Now from <u>column 6</u>, $E = 6$ or   7.

Thus possibilities are

	N	R	E	I
a	2	7	6	3
b	3	6	7	2
c	6	3	7	2
d	7	2	6	3

Case a   5 W 6 2 5 0 $\therefore \quad 2W + H + 1 = V + 10$
               5 W 6 2 5 0 $\therefore \quad 2W + H - V = 9$
               5 H 3 7 5 0   where W, H and V are selected from 4, 8 and 9.
            ―――――――――――――――
               1 6 V 6 2 5 0

possibilities are:

	W	H	V	$2W + H - V$
	4	8	9	7
a solution →	4	9	8	9
	8	4	9	11
	8	9	4	21
	9	4	8	14
	9	8	4	22

Case b and **case c** lead to no possible solutions.

Case d leads to the solution $W = 4$, $H = 9$, $V = 8$.

Thus the 2 solutions are:

```
      5 4 6 2 5 0        and        5 4 6 7 5 0
      5 4 6 2 5 0                   5 4 6 7 5 0
      5 9 3 7 5 0                   5 9 3 2 5 0
    ─────────────                 ─────────────
    1 6 8 6 2 5 0                 1 6 8 6 7 5 0
```

3   **a**   Any polygon of n sides can be subdivided into $n - 2$ triangles by drawing in all diagonals from **one** vertex to all other vertices except the 2 adjacent ones.

Thus, the total angle measure for the interior angles of an n-sided polygon is $(n - 2) \times 180^\circ$.

Hence for a regular n-sided polygon each angle measures $\left[\dfrac{(n - 2) \times 180}{n}\right]^\circ$

b

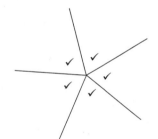

Suppose k equal angles meet at a point.

$$\text{Then} \quad k\left(\frac{(n - 2) \times 180^\circ}{n}\right) = 360^\circ$$

$$\therefore \quad k(n - 2) = 2n$$

$$\therefore \quad k = \frac{2n}{n - 2} = \frac{2(n - 2) + 4}{n - 2} = 2 + \frac{4}{n - 2}$$

$$\therefore \quad n - 2 = 1, 2 \text{ or } 4 \quad \text{as } k \text{ is an integer.}$$

$$\therefore \quad n = 3, 4 \text{ or } 6.$$

$\therefore$ there are 3 and only 3 regular polygons: equilateral triangle, square, regular hexagon.

c

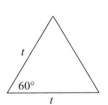

$$\text{Area} = \tfrac{1}{2}.t.t.\sin 60^\circ$$

$$b^2 = \tfrac{1}{2}t^2.\tfrac{\sqrt{3}}{2}$$

$$\therefore \quad t^2 = \frac{4b^2}{\sqrt{3}}$$

$$t \doteqdot 1.5197b$$

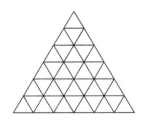

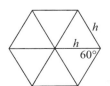

$$\text{Area} = 6.\tfrac{1}{2}h^2\tfrac{\sqrt{3}}{2}$$

$$b^2 = \tfrac{6\sqrt{3}}{4}h^2$$

$$h^2 = \tfrac{2}{3\sqrt{3}}b^2$$

$$h \doteqdot 0.6204b$$

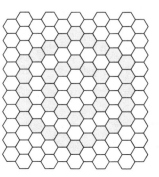

Rows for Δ's	No. of Δ's	Prog. Sum	Number of edges
1	1	$1 = 1^2$	$3 = 3.1 = 3.1$
2	3	$4 = 2^2$	$9 = 3.3 = 3.(1+2)$
3	5	$9 = 3^2$	$18 = 3.6 = 3.(1+2+3)$
4	7	$16 = 4^2$	$30 = 3.10 = 3.(1+2+3+4)$
5	9	$25 = 5^2$	$45 = 3.15 = 3.(1+2+3+4+5)$
6			
$\vdots$			
13		$169 = 13^2$	$3(1+2+3+4+ ...... +13) = 273$

No. of rings	No. of hexagons in ring	Prog. Sum	Number of edges.
1	1	1	3.2
2	6	7	$3.(3+4+3)$
3	12	19	$3.(4+5+6+5+4)$
4	18	37	$3.(5+6+7+8+7+6+5)$
5	24	61	.
6	30	91	.
7	36	127	.
8	42	169	$3.(9+10+11+12+13+14+15+16$ $+ 15+14+13+12+11+10+9)$

Ratio of wax length; $\dfrac{\text{hexagons}}{\text{triangles}} = \dfrac{552h}{273t} \div \dfrac{552h}{273 \times 2.44955h}$ $\{\dfrac{t}{h} \doteq 2.44955\}$

i.e., $\dfrac{\text{hexagons}}{\text{triangles}} \doteq 0.8254 \doteq 82.54\%$

$\therefore$ the hexagon frames use 17.46% less, and the difference is $273t - 552h$
$\doteq$ $273 \times 1.5197b - 552 \times 0.6204b$
$\doteq$ $\underline{72.42b}$

4 $(x^2 - y^2)^2 + (2xy)^2 = x^4 - 2x^2y^2 + y^4 + 4x^2y^2$
$= x^4 + 2x^2y^2 + y^4$
$= \underline{(x^2 + y^2)^2}$

x	y	x^2	y^2	$x^2 - y^2 = m$	$2xy = n$	$x^2 + y^2 = p$	mnp
2	1	4	1	3	4	5	$60 = 60.1$
3	1	9	1	8	6	10	$480 = 60.8$
3	2	9	4	13	12	5	$780 = 60.13$
4	1	16	1	15	8	17	$2040 = 60.34$
4	2	16	4	12	16	20	$3840 = 60.64$
4	3	16	9	7	24	25	$4200 = 60.70$
						etc.	

Observation: It appears that mnp may always be divisible by 60.

Proof: If an integer is divisible by 60, it must be divisible by 3, 5 and 4.

(1) **divisibility by 3:**   If x is any integer then
$$x = 3a, \ 3a + 1, \ 3a + 2 \qquad \{a \text{ is an integer}\}$$
$$\therefore \ \ x^2 = 9a^2, \ \ 9a^2 + 6a + 1, \ \ 9a^2 + 12a + 4$$

Thus x^2 leaves a remainder of 0 or 1 when divided by 3.

If x or y is divisible by 3, then so is n.

If neither x nor y is divisible by 3, then x^2 and y^2 leave a remainder of 1 when divided by 3.

$\therefore \quad m = x^2 - y^2$ is divisible by 3.

(2) **divisibility by 5:**   Any integer x must have one of the following five forms:

$$x = 5b, \qquad\qquad x = 5b \pm 1, \qquad\qquad x = 5b \pm 2,$$
$$\therefore \quad x^2 = 25b^2 \qquad \therefore \quad x^2 = 25b^2 \pm 10b + 1 \qquad \therefore \quad x^2 = 25b^2 \pm 20b + 4$$

$\therefore$ when divided by 5, x^2 leaves a remainder of 0, 1 or 4.

If x or y is divisible by 5, then so is n.

If neither x nor y is divisible by 5, then x^2 and y^2 leave a remainder of 1 or 4.

Table of remainders:

x^2	y^2	$x^2 - y^2 = m$	$x^2 + y^2 = p$
1	1	0	$\cdots$
1	4	$\cdots$	0
4	1	$\cdots$	0
4	4	0	$\cdots$

Thus either m or p is divisible by 5.

(3) **divisibility by 4:**   For $m^2 + n^2 = p^2$,   either   (a)   all 3 of m, n, p are even

or   (b)   one is even and other two are odd.

If case (a); mnp is divisible by 8 (and hence by 4).

If case (b);   (i)   <u>consider m and n to be odd</u>   i.e., $\therefore$ $m = 2a + 1$, $n = 2b + 1$, $p = 2c$

$\therefore \quad 4a^2 + 4a + 1 + 4b^2 + 4b + 1 = 4c^2$

$\therefore \quad 2a^2 + 2a + 2b^2 + 2b + 1 = 2c^2$ which is clearly impossible   {odd = even}

(ii)   <u>consider one of m, n to be odd, the other even</u>

i..e, $m = 2a + 1$, $n = 2b$, $p = 2c + 1$

$\therefore \quad n^2 = 4b^2 = (2c + 1)^2 - (2a + 1)^2$

i.e., $n^2 = (2c - 2a)(2c + 2a + 2)$

i.e., $n^2 = 4(c - a)(c + a + 1)$

Possibilities are:

a	c	$c - a$	$c + a + 1$
odd	odd	even	odd
odd	even	odd	even
even	odd	odd	even
even	even	even	odd

Thus n^2 is divisible by 8.

But n^2 is a perfect square and so must have a factor of 2^4 (at least).

$\therefore \quad n$ must have a factor of 2^2 (at least).

$\therefore \quad n$ is divisible by 4.

5   **a**   If $x = y + k$ then $x^4 + ax^3 + bx^2 + cx + d = 0$ becomes

$(y + k)^4 + a(y + k)^3 + b(y + k)^2 + c(y + k) + d = 0$

$\therefore \quad y^4 + y^3[4k + a] + y^2[\ldots..] + y[\ldots..] + [\ldots..] = 0$

Thus we require $4k + a = 0$,   i.e., $k = -\dfrac{a}{4}$.

b

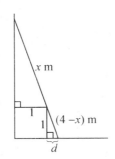

From the similar triangles, $\dfrac{d}{4-x} = \dfrac{1}{x}$ $\therefore$ $d = \dfrac{4-x}{x}$

By Pythagoras' theorem: $(4-x)^2 = 1^2 + \left(\dfrac{4-x}{x}\right)^2$

which when expanded and simplified gives

$$x^4 - 8x^3 + 14x^2 + 8x - 16 = 0 \quad ....(1)$$

Using **a** we let $k = \dfrac{-(-8)}{4} = 2$ and let $x = y + 2$.

Then   (1)   becomes $(y+2)^4 - 8(y+2)^3 + 14(y+2)^2 + 8(y+2) - 16 = 0$ which when expanded gives $y^4 - 10y^2 + 8 = 0$.

$\therefore$ $y^2 = \dfrac{10 \pm \sqrt{100 - 4.1.8}}{2} = 5 \pm \sqrt{17}$

$\therefore$ $y = \pm\sqrt{5 \pm \sqrt{17}}$

$\therefore$ $y \doteqdot \pm\, 3.0204, \pm\, 0.93643$

$\therefore$ $x \doteqdot 5.02044, -1.0204, 2.9364, 1.0636$

Only $x \doteqdot \underline{2.936, 1.064}$ are acceptable.

THE MASA 1989 SENIOR MATHEMATICS COMPETITION

1   If we write $a = 1988$ then the first expression, $F = (a+1)^{a+1}$ and the second expression, $S = a^{a+1} + (a+1)^a$ and the difference

$$\begin{aligned} F - S &= (a+1)^a(a+1) - (a+1)^a - a^{a+1} \\ &= (a+1)^a(a+1-1) - a^{a+1} \\ &= (a+1)^a a - a^a.a \\ &= a[(a+1)^a - a^a] \\ &> 0 \quad \{\text{for } a > 0,\ a+1 > a, \text{ and } \therefore\ (a+1)^a > a^a.\} \end{aligned}$$

Hence $F > S$,   so $1989^{1989} > 1988^{1989} + 1989^{1988}$

2   Suppose that X has travelled for x half hours and Y for y half hours, covering distances $55x$ km and $50y$ km respectively.

Thus, $55x + 50y = 670$ where x and y are integers, one even, one odd.
$11x + 10y = 134$ and $\therefore$ $11x = 134 - 10y$.

The right hand side of this equation has 4 as its last digit and is also a multiple of 11. It must be 44.

$x = 4$	$y = 9$ (different parities)
X travels 2 hours	Y travels $4\frac{1}{2}$ hours
X covers 220 km	Y covers 450 km
X left A at 10 am (SA)	Y left B at 7.30 am (SA) 8.00 am (Vic)

It is just possible, without breaking the speed limits in either state. (Approximate distances only!)

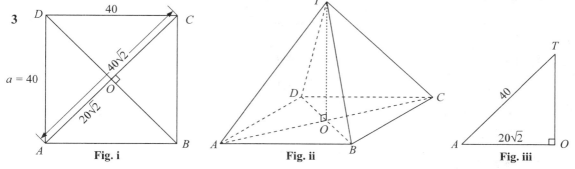

3

Fig. i   Fig. ii   Fig. iii

The top T of the pyramid lies vertically over the intersection, O, of the base diagonals ...... fig (ii)

Denote by a, the common length of the edges TA, TB, TC, TD, AB, BC, CD, DA.

$AO = \frac{1}{2}AC = \frac{\sqrt{2}}{2}a$....... Pythagoras' Theorem, $\triangle ACD$ .... fig (i)

Altitude, OT, $= \sqrt{AT^2 - AO^2}$

$\qquad = \sqrt{a^2 - \frac{a^2}{2}}$

$\qquad = a\sqrt{\frac{1}{2}}$

$\qquad = 40\frac{\sqrt{2}}{2}$

$\qquad = 20\sqrt{2}$ ......fig (iii)

Height of T above ground level $= \underline{20\sqrt{2} \doteq 28.28 \text{ m}}$.   {2 decimal places}

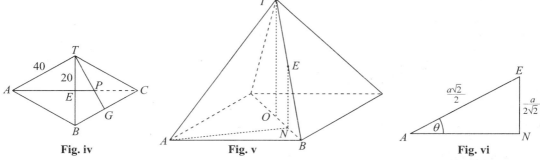

Fig. iv   Fig. v   Fig. vi

To find the shortest length from A to P, along the faces ATB and BTC, unfold into a single plane as shown in fig (iv) and determine the interval AP. (Several methods are now possible. Here is one of them.).

$AE = TG = CE$ {medians of equilateral (and congruent) faces are equal}

$AE \perp TB, \quad CE \perp TB$ {medians of equilateral (and congruent) faces are also altitudes}

$EP = \frac{1}{3}EC$ {concurrence of medians at a point of trisections - theorem}

$\quad = \frac{1}{3}AE$

$AP = AE + EP = \frac{4}{3}AE$

$\qquad\qquad = \frac{4}{3}.(20\sqrt{3})$ using right angled triangle AET.

$\therefore$ length of staircase $= \frac{80}{\sqrt{3}} = 46.19$ {2 decimal places}

Also CP bisects angle TAB, $\angle TAP = 90° - 60° = 30° = \angle BAP = \alpha$

Angle between stairway and AB is 30°.

To find the "steepness" of the stairs at A we need an angle in a vertical plane. Again, there are several possible methods. Here is one of them. E is the midpoint of TB. Its height NE above the ground, N, is half that of

T......fig (v)

$$NE = \tfrac{1}{2}OT = \tfrac{1}{2}\frac{a}{\sqrt{2}}$$

$$AE = AT\sin 60^\circ = \frac{a\sqrt{3}}{2}$$

$$\angle EAN = \theta = \arcsin\frac{NE}{AE}$$

$$= \arcsin\frac{\tfrac{a}{2}\cdot\tfrac{1}{\sqrt{2}}}{\tfrac{a}{2}\cdot\sqrt{3}}$$

$$= \arcsin\left(\tfrac{1}{\sqrt{6}}\right)......\text{fig (vi)}$$

"Steepness" of stairway, $\theta = 24.09^\circ$ {2 decimal places}

Comment:

The stairs from A to E rise,
but those from E to P fall.
Can you see why?
Study figs (vii) and (viii).

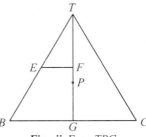

Fig vii Face TBC **Fig viii** Elevation

4

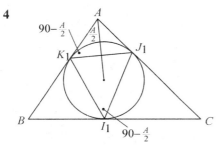

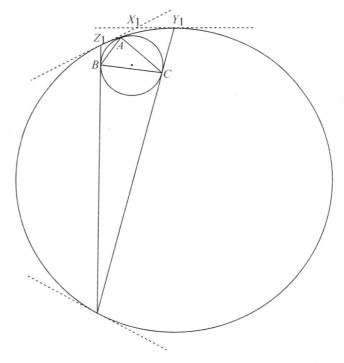

a $\angle K_1 I_1 J = \angle A K_1 J_1$ {angle between tangent and chord theorem}

        $= 90 - \frac{A}{2}$ {diameter bisects angle between tangents}.

For $A = 40^\circ$, $B = 60^\circ$, $C = 80^\circ$,

I_1, J_1, K_1 are $90 - \frac{40}{2}$, $90 - \frac{60}{2}$, $90 - \frac{80}{2} = 70$,   60,   50

I_2, J_2, K_2 are $90 - \frac{70}{2}$, $90 - \frac{60}{2}$, $90 - \frac{50}{2} = 55$,   60,   65

I_3, J_3, $K_3 = 62\frac{1}{2}$, 60, $57\frac{1}{2}$; I_4, J_4, $K_4 = 58\frac{3}{4}$, 60, $61\frac{1}{4}$; I_5, J_5, $K_5 = 60\frac{5}{8}$, 60, $59\frac{3}{8}$

b **i** It would seem that, by continuing this process, the angles would all get closer to $60°$.

    ii This construction is the reverse of construction **a**.

Rearranging $A = 90 - \dfrac{X}{2}$, $X = 180 - 2A$, Y_1, Z_1,   are

$180 - 80$, $180 - 120$, $180 - 160$ $=$ 100, 60, 20

X_2, Y_2, Z_2 are $-20, 60, 140$ not a real triangle.

Outward construction fails if any angle $\geqslant 90°$.
Two sides of the 'triangle' are parallel or diverge.

    iii **Proof:** It is now convenient to use, $A = 60 + \alpha$, $B = 60 + \beta$, $C = 60 + \gamma$,   where α, β and γ are positive, zero or negative, and summation of A, B and C yields $\alpha + \beta + \gamma = 0$.

(i) $I_1 = 90 - \frac{1}{2}(60 + \alpha) = 60 - \frac{1}{2}\alpha$

Angles of $I_1 J_1 K_1$ are: $60 - \frac{1}{2}\alpha$, $60 - \frac{1}{2}\beta$, $60 - \frac{1}{2}\gamma$

$I_2 = 90 - \frac{1}{2}(60 - \frac{1}{2}\alpha) = 60 + (-\frac{1}{2})^2\alpha$ etc.

Angles of $I_2 J_2 K_2$ $= 60 + (-\frac{1}{2})^2\alpha$, $60 + (-\frac{1}{2})^2\beta$, $60 + (-\frac{1}{2})^2\gamma$.

$\vdots$

Angles of $I_n J_n K_n$ $= \underline{60 + (-\frac{1}{2})^n\alpha}$, $60 + (-\frac{1}{2})^n\beta$, $60 + (-\frac{1}{2})^n\gamma$.

(ii) $X_1 = 180 - 2(60 + \alpha) = 60 - 2\alpha$

Angle of $X_n Y_n Z_n = 60 - 2\alpha$, $60 - 2\beta$, $60 - 2\gamma$

$X_2 = 180 - 2(60 - 2\alpha) = 60 + (-2)^2\beta$, ...etc.

Angles of $X_2 Y_2 Z_2$ $= 60 + (-2)^n\alpha$, $60 + (-2)^n\beta$, $60 + (-2)^n\gamma$

$\vdots$

Angles of $X_n Y_n Z_n$ $= \underline{60 + (-2)^n\alpha}$, $60 + (-2)^n\beta$, $60 + (-2)^n\gamma$

If at least two of the differences, α, β, and γ, are non-zero then

    (a) the angles of $I_n J_n K_n$ can be made as close to $60°$ as we please by choosing n large enough (to make $(\frac{1}{2})^n$ sufficiently close to 0).

    (b) for $\angle X_n, Y_n, Z_n$ there will be a finite value of n for which one of the differences will be large enough to produce an angle $\geqslant 180°$, or $\leqslant 0°$. Hence no enclosing triangle.

If $\alpha = \beta = \gamma = 0$, $\triangle ABC$ is equilateral, both sequences **a** and **b** continue indefinitely and all triangles in both sequences are equilateral.

5 **a** Suppose $(n-1)$ students are divided into $(r-1)$ subsets so that each subset has at least one student. This can be done in $S(n-1, r-1)$ ways.

Then we get an extra student, Pat, and an extra subset.

We can **either** put Pat in the extra subset **alone** in $S(n-1, r-1)$ ways, **or** redistribute the $(n-1)$ students into r subsets in $S(n-1, r)$ ways.

To each of these there are r subset choices for Pat, giving $\underline{rS(n-1, r) \text{ ways}}$ of including him/her with others.

Summing, $S(n, r) = S(n-1, r-1) + rS(n-1, r)$ ......*

    b Using this recursion formula to continue the array:

$$S(5, 1) = S(4, 0) + 1.S(4, 1) = 0 + 1.1 = 1$$
$$S(5, 2) = S(4, 1) + 2.S(4, 2) = 1 + 2.7 = 15 \quad ......\text{(required)}$$
$$S(5, 3) = S(4, 2) + 3.S(4, 3) = 7 + 3.6 = 25$$
$$S(5, 4) = S(4, 3) + 4.S(4, 4) = 6 + 4.1 = 10$$
$$S(5, 5) = S(4, 4) + 5.S(4, 5) = 1 + 5(0) = 1$$

This completes the row for $n = 5$.

$$S(6, 1) = S(5, 0) + 1.S(5, 1) = 0 + 1 = 1$$
$$S(6, 2) = S(5, 1) + 2.S(5, 2) = 1 + 2(15) = 31$$
$$S(6, 3) = S(5, 2) + 3.S(5, 3) = 15 + 3(25) = 90 \quad ......\text{(required)}$$

c   By Induction

There is exactly one way of dividing n things into 1 set (or into n sets).

$S(n, 1) = S(n, n) = 1$.

For $n = 1$, $S(n, 2) = S(1, 2) = 0 \qquad 2^0 - 1 = 1 - 1 = 0 \qquad$ True for $n = 1$.

Assume that, for integer $k \geqslant 1 \qquad S(k, 2) = 2^{k-1} - 1$

$$S(k + 1, 2) = S(k, 1) + 2S(k, 2)$$
$$= 1 + 2(2^{k-1} - 1)$$
Applying ......(*)......
$$= 1 + 2^{(k+1)-1} - 2$$
$$= 2^{(k+1)-1} - 1$$

Hence, by Principle of Mathematical Induction $\quad S(n, 2) = 2^{n-1} - 1$.

d   For $n = 2$, $\quad S(n, n - 1) = S(2, 1) = 1$

and $\binom{2}{2} = 1$, $\therefore$ true for $n = 2$.

Assume that, for integer $k \geqslant 1$, $\quad S(k, k - 1) = \binom{k}{2}$.

Applying ...... (*)

$S(k + 1, k) = S(k, k - 1) + kS(k, k)$

$$= \binom{k}{2} + k.1$$

$$= \frac{k(k - 1)}{2} + \frac{2}{2}.k$$

$$= \frac{k^2 - k + 2k}{2}$$

$$= \frac{k(k + 1)}{2}$$

$$= \binom{k+1}{2}$$

Hence ...... etc. $\quad \underline{S(n, n - 1) = \binom{n}{2}}.$

By combinatorial considerations (PREFERRED)

$S(n, 2)$ is the number of ways of dividing a set of n into 2 teams (excluding 0 since then there would be only 1 team).

We can choose the first team in $\quad \binom{n}{1} + \binom{n}{2} + ... + \binom{n}{n-1} \quad$ ways $\quad$ {excluding $\binom{n}{0}$ and $\binom{n}{n}$.}

The sum of a row in Pascal's Triangle is 2^n. $\quad$ Sum above is $\quad 2^n - \binom{n}{0} - \binom{n}{n} = 2^n - 2$

However, each selection is counted twice.

e.g., $ab......cde$ and $cde......ab$ count as one.

$$\therefore \quad S(n, 2) = \tfrac{1}{2}(2^n - 2) = 2^{n-1} - 1.$$

We consider the breaking up of a set of n into $n - 1$ subsets. This can only be done by having one subset of 2 and the rest of one only.

Hence we only have to choose one pair.

This can be done in $\binom{n}{2}$ ways.   Hence $S(n, n - 1) = \binom{n}{2}$.

[**Note:**   The numbers $S(n, r)$ are known as the Stirling numbers of second kind.]

THE MASA 1990 SENIOR MATHEMATICS COMPETITION

1 **a** The number of games each member plays can vary from 1 to 14.

Since there are 15 members, at least two must play the same number of games. (Pigeon-hole principle.)

b Each member plays n games. The total number of games is $\dfrac{15n}{2}$. (Division by 2 avoids

counting the same game twice.) Since $\dfrac{15n}{2}$ is an integer, and 15 is odd, n must be even.

c Each member plays 14 games. The total number is now $\dfrac{15 \times 14}{2} = 105$ which is odd, and cannot be divided equally between the two occasions.

2 Exploring,

Index m	5^m	m	5^m	m	5^m	m	5^m	m	
0	1	4	625	8	390 625	12	244 140 625	16	· · · · · · · · ·
1	5	5	3125	9	1 953 125	13	1 220 703 125	.	
2	25	6	15 625	10	9 765 625	14	6 103 515 625	.	· · · · · · · · 5625
3	125	7	78 125	11	48 828 125	15	30 517 578 125	.	

This table suggests, that for integers $m \geqslant 4$, $5^{m+4} - 5^m$ is divisible by 10 000.

$$5^{m+4} - 5^m = 5^m(5^4 - 1)$$
$$= 5^m.624$$
$$= 5^m.16.39$$
$$= 5^{m-4}.(5^4.2^4).39$$
$$= (39.5^{m-4})10\,000 \qquad \text{as required.}$$

In particular, for $m = 4p + 2$, (p being any positive integer), the remainder on division by 10 000 will always be 5625.

Hence $5^{1990} = 5^{1988+2} = 5^{4(497)+2}$ will end in four digits 5625.

[**Note:** For $m \geqslant k + 2$, $5^{m+2^k} - 5^m$ is divisible by 10^{k+2}. Proof by Induction.)

3

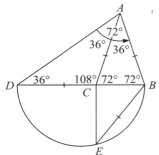

Calculating the angles as shown, we note that triangles ABC and DBA are equiangular, hence similar.

$$\frac{AB}{DB} = \frac{BC}{BA}$$

Since $AB = BA = EB = BE$ we can write

$$\frac{EB}{DB} = \frac{BC}{BE}$$

In triangles EBC and DBE, the angle at B is common, the sides enclosing the angle are proportional, so the triangles are equiangular.

In particular $\angle BCE = \angle BED = 90°$ (since $\angle BED$ is subtended at circumference by diameter.)

Hence EC is perpendicular to BD.

4   **a**   If n, the number of digits, is even, then $(n-1)$ is odd and the leading digit represents $(-2)^{n-1} < 0$.

Let $(-2)^h$ be the number represented by the highest nonzero digit following the leading digit: $h < n-1$.

Let N be the number represented by the nonzero digits following the leading digit.

Then, $N = (-2)^h + \ldots\ldots + (-2)^m$,   where $(-2)^m$ is the last non-zero digit.

Now $N \leqslant 2^h + \ldots\ldots + 2^m$
$$\leqslant 2^h + 2^{h-1} + \ldots\ldots + 1$$
$$\leqslant 2^{h+1} - 1$$
$$\leqslant 2^{n-1} - 1$$
$$< 2^{n-1}$$

Hence $(-2)^{n-1} + N < 0$,   i.e., if the number of digits is even, the number is negative.

b   Some calculations (omitting subscript -2 for convenience)

$[1000] = -8$	$= 0 - 8$
$[1001] = -7$	$= 1 - 8$
$[1010] = -10$	$= -2 - 8$
$[1011] = -9$	$= -1 - 8$
$[1100] = -4$	$= 4 - 8$
$[1101] = -3$	$= 5 - 8$
$[1110] = -6$	$= 2 - 8$
$[1111] = -5$	$= 3 - 8$

$[0] = 0$	$[100] = 4$
$[1] = 1$	$[101] = 5$
$[10] = -2$	$[110] = 2$
$[11] = -1$	$[111] = 3$

$k = 4$
total range -10 to 5
2^4 consecutive integers

successive -2 to 5 successive -10 to -3

Proposition: *"If the number of digits $\leqslant n$, we can represent 2^n consecutive integers."*

[e.g., for $n = 1$ we see two numbers; $n = 2$ yields four; $n = 3$, eight;   and $n = 4$, sixteen ...... etc.]

Assume the proposition is true for some integer k (and that k is even).

The leading digit of a number represented by $(k+1)$ digits adds the term $(-2)^k > 0$ to the number. If we write down all numbers with digit number $\leqslant k$, then, by inductive assumption, there are 2^k consecutive numbers. Adding $(-2)^k$ to these gives another 2^k consecutive numbers. The largest of these is $(-2)^k + M$ (where M is maximum number containing, at most, k digits).

The smallest of the numbers represented by exactly $(k+1)$ digits is then

$((-2)^k + M) - 2^k + 1 = M + 1$ {since there are 2^k consecutive numbers}.

The largest of the numbers with k digits being equal to M, it follows that we obtain sequence of $2^k + 2^k = 2^{k+1}$ consecutive numbers.

Thus when the proposition is true for k it is also true for $(k+1)$.

We reason similarly for odd k. This time the new minimum is $(-2)^k + m$ where m is the minimum for the sequence of 2^k numbers.

Hence for any n, even or odd, we can represent exactly 2^n consecutive integers, using (-2) for base and having at most n digits.

If n is odd, the maximum is $\quad M = \underbrace{[1010......1]}_{n \text{ digits}}{}_{-2}\quad$ omitting digits of negative values,

and if n is even, the minimum is $\quad m = \underbrace{[1010......1]}_{n \text{ digits}}{}_{-2}\quad$ omitting digits of positive values.

Thus if n is odd, numbers range from

$$(-2)^{n-2} + (-2)^{n-4} + ... + (-2) \quad \text{to} \quad (-2)^{n-1} + (-2)^{n-3} + ... + 1.$$

Evaluating the bounds we get for the range,

$$-2\left[\frac{4^{\frac{n-1}{2}} - 1}{3}\right] \quad \text{to} \quad \frac{4^{\frac{n+1}{2}} - 1}{3} \qquad \left(\text{or } -2.\left[\frac{2^{n-1} - 1}{3}\right] \quad \text{to} \quad \frac{2^{n+1} - 1}{3}\right).$$

Similarly, for even n, we get $\quad -2.\left[\dfrac{2^n - 1}{3}\right] \quad$ to $\quad \dfrac{2^n - 1}{3}.$

Clearly the bounds can be as large in absolute values as we wish, hence all integers can be represented as sums of different powers of -2.

c The notation to base (-2) determines each number uniquely, and since all numbers are represented once, and only once, any given number (written in the decimal system) must be fitted into a uniquely determined place.

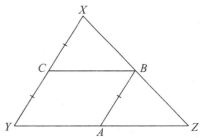

5 **a**
$$\begin{aligned}
BA &= \tfrac{1}{2}XY & \{\text{Midpoint Theorem}\} \\
&= XC \\
&= VC & \{X, Y, Z \text{ coincide at } V\} \\
\text{Similarly,} \quad AC &= VB \\
CB &= VA
\end{aligned}$$

Hence opposite edges of this tetrahedron are equal.

b Let the centres of BA, BC, VA, VC be P, Q, R, S respectively.

$$\left.\begin{aligned}
PQ &= \tfrac{1}{2}AC \quad \text{and is parallel to AC } \{\text{midpoint theorem } \triangle BAC\} \\
RS &= \tfrac{1}{2}AC \quad \text{and is parallel to AC } \{\text{midpoint theorem } \triangle VAC\}
\end{aligned}\right\} \text{ common edge } AC.$$

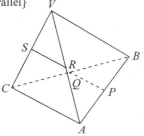

$PQRS$ is a parallelogram. $\qquad$ {one pair of opposite sides equal and parallel}

Similarly $\quad PR = \tfrac{1}{2}BV \qquad$ {midpoint theorem $\triangle ABV$}

$$\begin{aligned}
&= \tfrac{1}{2}AC & \{\text{see } \mathbf{a}\} \\
&= PQ & \{5 \text{ lines above}\}
\end{aligned}$$

$PQSR$ is a rhombus ($\parallel$ gram with adjacent edges equal)

$\therefore$ diagonals PS, QR bisect perpendicularly at O.

$PUST$ is also a rhombus, diagonals PS, UT bisect perpendicularly at O.

Thus the line segments (PS, QR and UT) joining midpoints of opposite edges bisect perpendicularly (at O).

THE MASA 1991 SENIOR MATHEMATICS COMPETITION

1   We are aiming for $2^n + 1 = a^2$ where a is a natural integer.

{We can assume that it is positive since $(-a)^2 = a^2$.}

So, $2^n = a^2 - 1 = (a+1)(a-1)$......(1)

Now, 2^n is a power of 2, so by the Theorem of Unique Prime Factorization, each of its factors, $(a-1)$, $(a+1)$ must be a power of 2.

But the only two powers of 2 which differ by 2 are 2^1 and 2^2.

Hence $a - 1 = 2$, $a + 1 = 4$ and $a = 3$.

From equation (1),   <u>$n = 3$</u>.   This is the only solution.

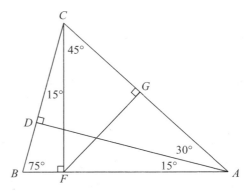

2 $\angle FCA = 90° - \angle FAC$
$= 90° - 45°$
$= 45°$

Thus triangle AFC is isosceles, and right angled, so its altitude FG bisects AC.

A circle with radius $AG = GC$ can be drawn, and it passes through D (since $\angle ADC = 90°$).

<u>$GD = GA = GC$</u>   (as required).

3   Denote $\underbrace{11......1}_{n \text{ digits}}$ by a,   then $\underbrace{22......2}_{n \text{ digits}} = 2a$ and $\underbrace{33......3}_{n \text{ digits}} = 3a$

Also $\underbrace{111......11}_{2n \text{ digits}}$ $=$ $\underbrace{11......1}_{n \text{ digits}} \underbrace{00......0}_{n \text{ digits}}$ $+$ $\underbrace{11......1}_{n \text{ digits}}$

$= a.10^n + a$

$= (10^n + 1)a$

Now we must prove that $\sqrt{(10^n + 1)a - 2a} = 3a$

Note that $10^n - 1 = \underbrace{99......9}_{n \text{ digits}} = 9a$

Under the square root is $(10^n + 1)a - 2a = (10^n - 1 + 2)a - 2a$

$= (10^n - 1)a + 2a - 2a$

$= (10^n - 1)a$

$= 9a.a$

$= (3a)^2$

yielding   <u>$\sqrt{(10^n + 1)a - 2a} = 3a$</u>,   as required.

4   Several solutions are possible.

Construction: Produce QT and RS to meet at X.

Proof: It is easy to show (ASA) that triangles PTQ and STX are congruent.

Hence   (1) $PQ = XS$
        (2) $XT = QT$
              $PQ + SR = QR$ {given}
              $XS + SR = XR = QR$

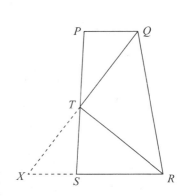

$\therefore$ $\triangle XRQ$ is isosceles

RT bisects base XQ of isosceles $\triangle$ (2)

It does so at right angles $\therefore$ $\underline{\angle QTR = 90^\circ}$.

5 Add the four equations, obtaining $10x_1 + 10x_2 + 10x_3 + 10x_4 = 40$

$$\therefore \quad x_1 + x_2 + x_3 + x_4 = 4.$$

Now subtract equation (1) from (2), obtaining

$$3x_1 - x_2 - x_3 - x_4 = 0$$
$$\therefore \quad 4x_1 - (x_1 + x_2 + x_3 + x_4) = 0$$
$$\therefore \quad 4x_1 - 4 = 0$$
$$\therefore \quad x_1 = 1$$

Similarly, subtracting (2) from (3), (3) from (4) and (4) from (1), yields $\underline{x_2 = x_3 = x_4 = 1}$.

6 Consider $100 > a > b > c > d > e > f > g \geqslant 1$

c is the smallest of the "three largest integers".

The integer nearest to $\frac{100}{7}$, but greater, is 15.

   a either $c > 15$,   in which case $a + b + c \geqslant 18 + 17 + 16 = 51$

   The condition is satisfied.

   b or $c \leqslant 15$,   in which case $d + e + f + g \leqslant 14 + 13 + 12 + 11 = 50$

   i.e., $100 - (a + b + c) \leqslant 50$

   rearranging, $100 - 50 \leqslant (a + b + c)$

   $a + b + c \geqslant 50$ as required.

   Hence the statement is $\underline{\text{true in each case}}$.

THE MASA 1992 SENIOR MATHEMATICS COMPETITION

1 Consider a simpler example such as $(2 - 3x + 4x^2)^{15} = a_0 + a_1 x + a_2 x^2 + a_3 x^3 + \ldots\ldots a_{30} x^{30}$.

Letting $x = 1$ will give $3^{15} = a_0 + a_1 + a_2 + a_3 + \ldots\ldots a_{30}$.

Thus, when $w = x = y = z = 1$, $(w^1 - 9x^9 + 9y^9 - 2z)^{1992}$
$$= (1^1 - 9(1)^9 + 9(1)^9 - 2(1))^{1992}$$
$$= (1 - 9 + 9 - 2)^{1992}$$
$$= (-1)^{1992}$$
$$= 1$$

2 (All values given in seconds or metres unless specified)

$$\left\{ \begin{array}{c} \text{Time for message to reach station,} \quad \frac{4400}{330} = \frac{40}{3}. \\ \text{Time for firefighters to be told} \quad 50(\frac{40}{3}). \end{array} \right\} \quad \text{i.e.,} \quad 51 \times \frac{40}{3} = 680.$$

Time for firefighters to change, $t + (t - 5) + (t - 10) + (t - 15) + (t - 20) = 5t - 50$.

Time to get on the road, $7(t - 15) = 7t - 105$.

Time travelling to the school $= \dfrac{\text{distance}}{\text{speed}} = 4400 \times \dfrac{12}{141}$.

$$\{\text{as,} \quad \text{speed} = 42.3 \text{ kmph} = \frac{42300}{60 \times 60} = \frac{141}{12} \text{ ms}^{-1}\}$$

Total time $= (7{:}06 - 6{:}39)$
$= 27$ mins
$= 1620$ sec.

Adding, $1620 = 680 + (12t - 155) + 4400 \times \dfrac{12}{141}$

$$\therefore \quad t = \frac{1095}{12} - \frac{4400}{141}$$

$$\therefore \quad t \doteqdot 60.04 \text{ sec}$$

Second fire fighter takes <u>55.04 sec.</u> to change.

3 **a** Rearrangement and substitution will "work" but instead consider the following,

Product of equations, $x^2 y^2 z^2 = 1.4.9 = 6^2, \quad xyz = \pm 6$

Dividing this by the 3rd equation yields $x = \dfrac{xyz}{yz} = \pm\dfrac{6}{9} = \pm\dfrac{2}{3}$

Dividing this by the 2nd equation and $y = \dfrac{xyz}{xz} = \pm\dfrac{6}{4} = \pm\dfrac{3}{2}$

and also $z = \dfrac{xyz}{xy} = \pm\dfrac{6}{1} = \pm 6,$

So $(x,\, y,\, z) = \left(\frac{2}{3}, \frac{3}{2}, 6\right)$ or $\left(-\frac{2}{3}, -\frac{3}{2}, -6\right).$

b Likewise, $p^3 q^3 r^3 s^3 = 1.4.9.16 = 1^2.2^2.3^2.4^2.$

$$p^3 = \frac{p^3 q^3 r^3 s^3}{(qrs)^3} = \frac{1^2.2^2.3^2.4^2}{(4^2)^3} = \frac{(3!)^2}{(4^2)^3}; \qquad p = \frac{[(3!)^2]^{\frac{1}{3}}}{4^2}$$

$\left[\begin{array}{l}\text{Note:} \quad \text{that for even } n, \\ \text{solutions are positive} \\ \text{only.}\end{array}\right]$

$q^3 = $ etc.

$$q = \frac{[(3!)^2]^{\frac{1}{3}}}{3^2}$$

$$r = \frac{[(3!)^2]^{\frac{1}{3}}}{2^2}$$

$$s = \frac{[(3!)^2]^{\frac{1}{3}}}{1^2}$$

c Product of n equations

$$(a_1.a_2.a_3......a_n)^{n-1} = 1^2.2^2......n^2 = (n!)^2$$

$$a_1.a_2.a_3......a_n = [(n!)^2]^{\frac{1}{n-1}}, \quad \text{or} \quad \pm((n!)^2)^{\frac{1}{n-1}}, \text{ if } n \text{ is odd.}$$

If we divide by 1st equation we get the first variable.
If we divide by 2nd equation we get the second variable.
If we divide by jth equation we get the jth variable.

$$a_j = \frac{[(n!)^2]^{\frac{1}{n-1}}}{j^2}$$

4 For a quadrilateral with sides of lengths a, b, c, d, Figure (i) shows the position when the diagonals are perpendicular.

Let p, q, r and s be the segments of diagonals so formed.

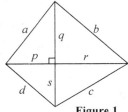

Figure 1

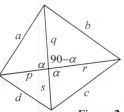

Figure 2

By Pythagoras,
$$a^2 = p^2 + q^2$$
$$b^2 = q^2 + r^2$$
$$c^2 = r^2 + s^2$$
$$d^2 = s^2 + p^2$$

Adding, $a^2 + c^2 = (p^2 + q^2) + (r^2 + s^2)$
$$\therefore \quad a^2 + c^2 = (q^2 + r^2) + (s^2 + p^2)$$
$$\therefore \quad a^2 + c^2 = b^2 + d^2$$

Assume there is an angle $\alpha \neq 90^o$ as shown in Figure (ii); a, b, c, d are unaltered and p, q, r, s are assumed to have changed (at least some) of their values.

$a^2 + c^2 = b^2 + d^2$ as before (it is still the same frame)

By the cosine rule:
$$(p^2 + q^2 - 2pq\cos\alpha) + (r^2 + s^2 - 2rs\cos\alpha) = q^2 + r^2 - 2qr\cos(180 - \alpha) + p^2 + s^2 - 2ps\cos(180 - \alpha)$$
$$\therefore \quad (p^2 + q^2 + r^2 + s^2) - 2(\cos\alpha)(pq + rs) = (q^2 + r^2 + p^2 + s^2) - (2\cos(180 - \alpha))(qr + ps)$$
$$\therefore \quad -2\cos\alpha(pq + rs) = -2\cos(180 - \alpha)(qr + ps)$$
$$\therefore \quad -2\cos\alpha(pq + rs) = +2\cos\alpha(qr + ps)$$
$$\therefore \quad 2\cos\alpha(pq + rs + qr + ps) = 0$$
$$\therefore \quad \cos\alpha = 0 \quad \{\text{since } p, q, r, s \text{ all positive}\}$$
$$\alpha = 90^o$$

5 a

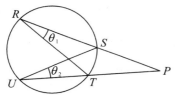

Briefly $\theta_1 = \theta_2$ {angles in same segment theorem}

Triangles PTR, PSU are equiangular and $\therefore$ similar.
$$\frac{PT}{PS} = \frac{RP}{UP}$$
$$PS.PR = PT.PU$$

In particular, if TU is a diameter
$$PS.PR = PT.PU = (PO - r)(PO + r)$$
$$= PO^2 - r^2$$

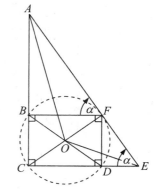

b $\triangle$'s ABF, ACE, FDE equiangular   {since $BF \parallel CD$, $BC \parallel FD$ and right $\angle$'s at B, C and D.}
$$\therefore \quad \frac{AB}{BF} = \frac{AC}{CE} = \frac{FD}{DE} = \tan\alpha \quad .....(1)$$

Since opposite sides rectangle are equal $BF = CD$
$$FD = BC$$
$$\frac{AB}{CD} = \frac{BC}{DE}.$$

Now construct a circle, centre C and radius OB, through vertices of rectangle $BCDF$.

From **a** $EO^2 - OC^2 = ED.EC$
$$AO^2 - OC^2 = AB.AC$$
Since $AO = EO$, $ED.EC = AB.AC$

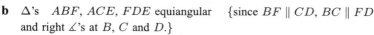

Rearranging, $\dfrac{AC}{CE} = \dfrac{DE}{AB}$

But $\tan\alpha = \dfrac{AC}{CE}$, so substituting in equation (1) (from equiangular Δ's) gives

$\dfrac{AB}{BF} = \dfrac{DE}{AB} = \dfrac{FD}{DE}$ as required.

THE MASA 1993 SENIOR MATHEMATICS COMPETITION

1   **a**   **i** $\dfrac{5.4}{2.1} = 10$ **ii** $\dfrac{10.9}{2.1} = 45$ **iii** $\dfrac{n(n-1)}{2.1} = \dfrac{n^2 - n}{2}$

   b $\dfrac{n(n-1)}{2.1} = 66$ $\therefore$ $n = 12$.

2   Initially there are n buses and $36n + 5$ penguins.
Also, that are $k(n+1)$ penguins where k is a positive integer.

$k = \dfrac{36n + 5}{n+1} = \dfrac{36n + 36 - 31}{n+1} = 36 - \dfrac{31}{n+1}$.

$\therefore$ $n + 1 = 31$ and $\therefore$ $n = 30$

Thus the number of penguins is $36 \times 30 + 5 = 1085$.

3   Let the black balls be B, L, A, C and K, and the white ball be W.

First weighing: $WB\ v\ LA$ Second weighing: $WA\ v\ LC$

$\diagup$ shows the left side is heavier, $\diagdown$ the right is heavier and $\longleftrightarrow$ the balls balance.

If B heavier	$\diagup$	$\longleftrightarrow$	lighter	$\diagdown$	$\longleftrightarrow$
L heavier	$\diagdown$	$\diagdown$	lighter	$\diagup$	$\diagup$
A heavier	$\diagdown$	$\diagup$	lighter	$\diagup$	$\diagdown$
C heavier	$\longleftrightarrow$	$\diagdown$	lighter	$\longleftrightarrow$	$\diagup$

W and two of the black
balls (here L and A) must
be used twice.

K is the different ball if $\longleftrightarrow$ $\longleftrightarrow$

There is no way to tell if K is heavier or lighter than the others in two weighings.

4

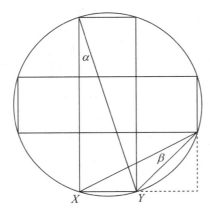

   a   **The elegant solution:**
   Inscribe the rectangle in a circle and complete
   the octagon.
   Chord XY subtends both α and β at the
   circumference.

   b   **A trigonometric proof:**

   $$\tan(\tfrac{\pi}{4} + \beta) = \tfrac{2}{1}$$

   $\therefore$ $$\dfrac{\tan\frac{\pi}{4} + \tan\beta}{1 - \tan\frac{\pi}{4}\tan\beta} = \dfrac{2}{1}$$

   $\therefore$ $$\tan\beta = \tfrac{1}{3} = \tan\alpha$$

5 Since the area is a convex polygon, we can construct a circle within the sides of the polygon.

Let this circle have a radius r, and hence an area πr^2.

If the sides of the polygon each expand 40 m then so does the radius of the enclosed circle.

Hence the new circle has an area of $\pi(r + 40)^2$.

$$\begin{aligned}\text{The difference in area of the two circles is} \quad & \pi\{(r+40)^2 - r^2\} \\ &\geqslant \pi\{80r + 40^2\} \\ &\geqslant 40^2\pi \\ &> 5026 \\ &> 5000 \text{ m}^2.\end{aligned}$$

6 **a** For non-negative integers p and n, if n is even, $n = 2p$

$$\begin{aligned}\text{In } \textbf{modulo 8}, \quad 3^n &= 3^{2p} \\ &= 9^p \\ &\equiv 1^p \\ &\equiv 1\end{aligned}$$

if n is odd, $n = 2p + 1$

$$\begin{aligned}\therefore \quad 3^n &= 3.3^{2p} \\ &\equiv 3(1) \\ &\equiv 3 \qquad \text{(in modulo 8)}\end{aligned}$$

b Let $3^n + 2.17^n = (2q+1)^2$

$$\begin{aligned}&= 4q^2 + 4q + 1 \\ &= 4q(q+1) + 1 \qquad \{\text{where}\quad q(q+1)\quad \text{is even}\} \\ &\equiv 0 + 1 \\ &\equiv 1 \qquad \text{(in modulo 8)}\end{aligned}$$

$$\begin{aligned}\text{But} \quad 3^n + 2.17^n &\equiv 3^n + 2.1 \\ \text{and from } \textbf{a} \qquad &\equiv 1 + 2 \quad \text{or} \quad 3 + 2 \\ &\equiv 3 \quad \text{or} \quad 5\end{aligned}$$

Hence $3^n + 2.17^n$ is never a perfect square.

7 *L*

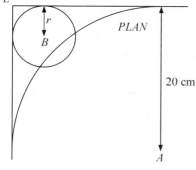

PLAN

20 cm

A

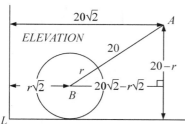

Viewed from above, part of the kitten's ball is hidden. L is the point of intersection of the walls and the floor.

The centres of the kitten's and larger balls lie directly above points B and A respectively, which lie on the floor.

The horizontal distance BL and AL are $\sqrt{2}r$ and $20\sqrt{2}$ respectively.

Using Pythagoras' Rule:

$$\begin{aligned}(20+r)^2 &= (20\sqrt{2} - r\sqrt{2})^2 + (20-r)^2 \\ \therefore \quad 400 + 40r + r^2 &= 3(20-r)^2 \\ \therefore \quad r^2 - 80r + 400 &= 0 \qquad \{\text{on simplifying}\} \\ \therefore \quad r &= (2 - \sqrt{3})20 \text{ cm} \doteqdot 5.4 \text{ cm}\end{aligned}$$

THE MASA 1994 SENIOR MATHEMATICS COMPETITION

1 $9 - 9 + 4 - 1 = 3$ $9 + 9 - 4 - 1 \ = 13$
   $9 + 9 + 4 + 1 = 23$ $(9 + 1) \times 4 - 9 = 31$ etc.

2

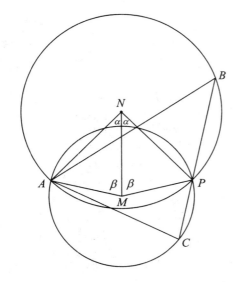

a NM is common
      $AN = NP$ {radii of circle APB}
      $AM = MP$ {radii of circle APC}
      $\therefore$ Δ's ANM, PNM are congruent {SSS}

b $\angle ANP = 2\angle ANM = 2\alpha$
      But $\angle ANP = 2\angle ABP$
      {Angle at centre of circle = twice the
      angle subtended at circumference}

      Similarly $\angle AMP = 2\angle ACP$
      $\therefore$ $\angle ACP = \beta$
      Two angles equal in Δ's PNM and
      ABC implies three angles equal, so
      the triangles are similar.

3 **a**   11, one less than the LCM of 2, 3 and 4.

   b   Observe that $n + 1$ is divisible by 2, 3, 4 ......9.

      The smallest such number $n + 1$ is $2^3.3^2.5.7 = 2520$
      Thus the smallest such n is 2519.

4 Proof by contradiction. Assume opposite is true.
$$\sqrt{2 + \sqrt{2}} + \sqrt{2 - \sqrt{2}} \geqslant 2\sqrt{2}$$
$$\therefore \quad (\sqrt{2 + \sqrt{2}} + \sqrt{2 - \sqrt{2}})^2 \geqslant (2\sqrt{2})^2$$
$$\therefore \quad 2 + \sqrt{2} + 2\sqrt{(2 + \sqrt{2})(2 - \sqrt{2})} + 2 - \sqrt{2} \geqslant 8$$
$$\therefore \quad 4 + 2\sqrt{2} \geqslant 8$$
$$\therefore \quad 2\sqrt{2} \geqslant 4 \quad \text{untrue,} \quad \text{so reverse holds.}$$

5 $f(x + f(y)) = f(f(x)) + y$
   $\therefore$ $f(x + f(0)) = f(f(x)) + 0$ {Substituting $y = 0$}
   $\therefore$ $f(x + c) = f(f(x))$
      $\therefore$ $x + c = f(x)$

6 **a**   For $p \neq 1$,

$$(p - 1)(1 + p + p^2 + ... + p^k) = p + p^2 + p^3 + ... + p^k + p^{k+1} - 1 - p - p^2 - p^3 ..... - p^k$$
$$(p - 1)(1 + p + p^2 + ... + p^k) = p^{k+1} - 1$$
$$1 + p + p^2 + ... + p^k = \frac{p^{k+1} - 1}{p - 1}$$

b $\sigma(p^k q) = (1 + p + p^2 + \ldots p^k) + q(1 + p + p^2 + \ldots + p^k)$

$\qquad\quad = (1 + p + p^2 + \ldots + p^k)(1 + q)$

$\qquad\quad = \sigma(p^k).\sigma(q)$

c $\sigma(p_1{}^{a_1}) = 1 + p_1 + p_1{}^2 + \ldots + p_1{}^{a_1} = \dfrac{p_1{}^{a_1+1} - 1}{p_1 - 1}$ {from **a**}

$\qquad\quad = \sigma(p_1{}^{a_1})\sigma(p_2{}^{a_2})\sigma(p_3{}^{a_3})\ldots\sigma(p_k{}^{k_1})$

$\qquad\quad = \left(\dfrac{p_1{}^{a_1+1} - 1}{p_1 - 1}\right)\left(\dfrac{p_2{}^{a_2+1} - 1}{p_2 - 1}\right)\ldots\left(\dfrac{p_k{}^{a_k+1} - 1}{p_k - 1}\right)$

7

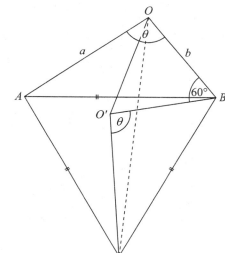

Rotate $\triangle AOB$ through $60°$ about B.
Then $A \to C$;   since $\triangle ABC$ is equilateral.
If $O \to O'$, $\triangle OO'B$ is also equilateral.
{as $O'B = OB = b$,   and $\angle OBO' = 60°$}
$\therefore$ $OO' = b$ and since $AO = CO' = a$,
in $\triangle OO'C$, $OC \leqslant OO' + O'C = b + a$.

We get equality if O, C and O' are
collinear; i.e., if $\angle OO'C = 180°$.
Since $\angle OO'B = 60°$,   then $\theta = 120°$,

when the maximum length of $OC = a + b$.

THE MASA 1995 SENIOR MATHEMATICS COMPETITION

1   **a** $1995 = 3 \times 5 \times 7 \times 19$,   therefore its factors are: 1, 3, 5, 7, 19

$3 \times 5 = 15$, $3 \times 7 = 21$, $5 \times 7 = 35$, $19 \times 3 = 57$, $5 \times 19 = 95$, $7 \times 19 = 133$,

$3 \times 5 \times 7 = 105$, $3 \times 5 \times 19 = 285$, $3 \times 7 \times 19 = 399$, $5 \times 7 \times 19 = 665$,

$1995 = 3 \times 5 \times 7 \times 19$

(16 factors in all)

b   Each factor may consist of between 0 and a factors all p_1, (i.e., $a + 1$ choices).
This argument can be repeated for p_2, p_3, etc., giving the required result.

c $16 = (15 + 1)$

$\qquad = 8 \times 2 = (7 + 1)(1 + 1)$

$\qquad = 4 \times 4 = (3 + 1)(3 + 1)$

$\qquad = 4 \times 2 \times 2 = (3 + 1)(1 + 1)(1 + 1)$

$\qquad = 2 \times 2 \times 2 \times 2 = (1 + 1)(1 + 1)(1 + 1)(1 + 1)$

Numbers of the form $p_1{}^{15}$

$\qquad\qquad\qquad\qquad p_1{}^7 \times p_2$

$\qquad\qquad\qquad\qquad p_1{}^3 \times p_2{}^3$

$\qquad\qquad\qquad\qquad p_1{}^3 \times p_2 \times p_3$

$\qquad\qquad\qquad\qquad p_1 \times p_2 \times p_3 \times p_4$ need to be tested.

2^{15} is much too large.

$$2^7 \times 3 = 384 \qquad 2^3 \times 3 \times 13 = 312 \qquad 2 \times 3^3 \times 5 = 270$$
$$2^3 \times 3^3 = 216 \qquad 2^3 \times 5 \times 7 = 280 \qquad 2 \times 3^3 \times 7 = 378$$
$$2^3 \times 3 \times 5 = 120 \qquad 2 \times 3 \times 5 \times 7 = 210$$
$$2^3 \times 3 \times 7 = 168 \qquad 2 \times 3 \times 5 \times 11 = 330$$
$$2^3 \times 3 \times 11 = 264 \qquad 2 \times 3 \times 5 \times 13 = 390$$

2 If we interchange the chords AB and AD, we will not be changing any lengths, but we produce a trapezoid:

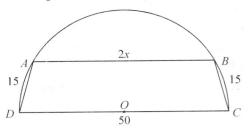 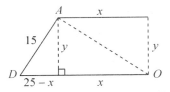

Let $AB = 2x$,

$$\text{Then we see} \qquad y^2 + x^2 = 25^2$$
$$\text{i.e.,} \quad y^2 = 25^2 - x^2$$
$$\text{But} \quad y^2 + (25 - x)^2 = 15^2$$
$$\therefore \quad 25^2 - x^2 + 25^2 - 50x + x^2 = 15^2$$
$$\therefore \quad 2.25^2 - 15^2 = 50x$$
$$\text{Now} \quad AB = 2x$$
$$= \tfrac{1}{25}(2.25^2 - 15^2)$$
$$= 50 - 9$$
$$= 41. \qquad \{= \text{chord } AD \text{ in the original diagram}\}$$

3 Let $a = 2m + 1$

$$N = a^{2^n} - 1$$
$$= (2m + 1)^{2^n} - 1$$
$$= 2^{2^n}.m^{2^n} + \binom{2^n}{1}.2^{2^n - 1}.m^{2^n - 1} + \ldots\ldots + \binom{2^n}{2^n - 2} 2^2 m^2 + \binom{2^n}{2^n - 1} 2m + 1 - 1$$
$$= 2^{2^n}.m^{2^n} + 2^n.2^{2^n - 1}.m^{2^n - 1} + \ldots\ldots + \tfrac{1}{2}2^n(2^n - 1)2^2 m^2 + 2^n.2m$$
$$= 2^{2^n}.m^{2^n} + 2^n.2^{2^n - 1}.m^{2^n - 1} + \ldots\ldots + \tfrac{1}{3.2}2^n(2^n - 1)(2^n - 2)2^3 m^3 + \tfrac{1}{2}2(2^n - 1)2^2 m^2 + 2^n.2m$$

a It is fairly obvious that each term above is divisible by 2^{n+1}.

b It is clear that all the terms except the last two are divisible by 2^{n+2}.

As for the last two terms: $\tfrac{1}{2}.2^n(2^n - 1)2^2 m^2 + 2^n 2.m = 2^{n+1}m[(2^n - 1)m + 1] = s.$

If m is even s is divisible by 2^{n+2}.

If m is odd then $(2^n - 1)m + 1$ is even and $\therefore$ s is divisible by 2^{n+2}.

Hence 2^{n+2} will always divide N.

OR {by induction}

If $n = 1$, the expression becomes $(2m + 1)^2 - 1$
$$= 4m^2 + 4m + 1 - 1$$
$$= 4m(m + 1)$$

Either m or $m+1$ is even, so the expression is clearly divisible by $8 = 2^3 = 2^{n+2}$.

Assuming that the statement is true for $n = k$, then

$$(2m+1)^{2^{k+1}} - 1 = (2m+1)^{2^k \cdot 2} - 1$$
$$= [(2m+1)^{2^k} - 1][(2m+1)^{2^k} + 1]$$

Now the first factor is divisible by 2^{k+2} (provided in **a**) and the second factor is even.

Hence 2^{k+3} is a factor of $(2m+1)^{2^{k+1}} - 1$

Since the statement is true for $n = 1$, and it is true for $n+1$ if it is true for n, the statement is true.

4 In general, we want to know about the divisibility by p.

Look at the sequence modulo p. There are p choices for a remainder. Now consider consecutive remainders.

e.g., in modulo 5: 1, 1, 2, 3, 0, 3, 3, 1, 4, 0, 4, ...

In general, there are only p^2 possibilities for a pair of remainders (x, y) modulo p. Thus after p^2 terms we must have encountered the same pair twice.

e.g., continuing the above: 1, 1, 2, 3, 0, 3, 3, 1, 4, 0, 4, 3, 2, 0, 2, 2, 4, 1, 0, 1, 1, 2, ...

Since each term is obtained by adding the previous two, the same is true of the sequence of remainders. Since the two consecutive terms reappear, the sequence will be periodic. Now it is clear that every fifth number is divisible by 5, (i.e., each fifth remainder modulo 5 is zero).

Similarly: modulo 2: 1, 1, 0, 1, 1, 0, 1, 1, 0, ...   period 3, so every third number in Fibonacci's Sequence is even.

    modulo 3: 1, 1, 2, 0, 2, 2, 1, 0, 1, 1, 2, ... period 8, but every fourth number in Fibonacci's Sequence is divisible by 3.

OR {by induction}

Let $T_n = x$ and $T_{n+1} = y$ be successive terms in the Fibonacci sequence. The terms which follow are $T_{n+2} = x+y$, $T_{n+3} = x+2y$, $T_{n+4} = 2x+3y$, $T_{n+5} = 3x+5y$, $T_{n+6} = 5x+8y$, etc. etc.

Note that if $T_n = x$ is a multiple of 5, then $T_{n+5} = 3x+5y$ is also a multiple of 5.

If we designate $T_{n+5} = 3x+5y$ as x' and $T_{n+6} = 5x+8y$ as y', clearly $T_{n+10} = 3x'+5y'$ and since x' is a multiple of 5, so is $3x'+5y'$.

Now we only need to show that one member of the Fibonacci sequence is a multiple of 5, (and, of course, 5 itself is a member) to show that each fifth term is divisible by 5.

Note that if $T_n = x$ is even and $T_{n+1} = y$ is odd, then $T_{n+2} = x+y$ is odd, $T_{n+3} = x+2y$ is even, $T_{n+4} = 2x+3y$ is odd, as is $T_{n+5} = 3x+5y$.

If we designate $T_{n+3} = x+2y = x'$ and $T_{n+4} = 2x+3y = y'$ we will get a similar sequence of even, odd, odd. Since 2 and 3 are successive Fibonacci terms we can start such a sequence, so every third number on the Fibonacci sequence is even.

Note that if $T_n = x$ is a multiple of 3, then $T_{n+4} = 2x+3y$ is also a multiple of 3.

If we designate $T_{n+4} = 2x+3y$ as x' and $T_{n+5} = 3x+5y$ as y', clearly $T_{n+8} = 2x'+3y'$ and since x' is a multiple of 3, so is $2x'+3y'$.

Now we only need to show that one member of the Fibonacci sequence is a multiple of 3, (and, of course, 3 itself is a member) to show that each fourth term is divisible by 3.

5   **a** $xy + 9x + 9y + 5 = (x+9)(y+9) - 81 + 5 = 1995$

Hence $(x+9)(y+9) = 1995 + 81 - 5$
$= 2071$
$= 19 \times 109$ {both of which are primes.}

Either $x + 9 = 19,$ $y + 9 = 109$ $\therefore$ $x = 10, y = 100$
$x + 9 = 109,$ $y + 9 = 19$ $\therefore$ $x = 100, y = 10$
$x + 9 = 2071,$ $y + 9 = 1$ $\therefore$ $x = 2062, y = -8$
$x + 9 = 1,$ $y + 9 = 2071$ $\therefore$ $x = -8, y = 2062$

The latter answers are unaccaptable as either x or y is negative.

b $$\frac{1}{xy} + \frac{1}{9x} + \frac{1}{9y} + \frac{1}{5} = 1$$
$\therefore$ $45 + 5y + 5x + 9xy = 45xy$
$\therefore$ $36xy - 5x - 5y = 45$
$\therefore$ $36^2 xy - 36.5x - 36.5y = 36.45$
$\therefore$ $(36x - 5)(36y - 5) = 36.45 + 5^2$
$= 1645$
$= 5 \times 7 \times 47$

As in **a**, we try all possibilities, none of which are integral.

6   **a**   Each domino will cover one black and one white square, so if w can cover all squares we must have an equal number of black and white squares. However, removing two opposite corners of an 8×8 board implies that we have removed either two black or two white squares, so we cannot cover the remaining board.

b   We can cover the board whenever we remove one black and one white square. This only happens if one of m and n is even and the other is odd. Then we can cover it as shown in the diagram. If m and n are both even, the argument in **a** shows that it is impossible to cover the board. If m and n are both odd, we would not have an even number of squares left, so 2×1 dominoes could not cover such a board.

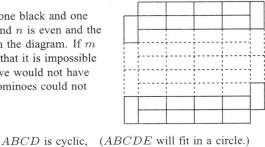

7   **a**

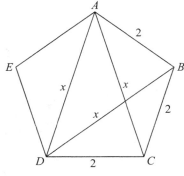

$ABCD$ is cyclic,   ($ABCDE$ will fit in a circle.)

$\therefore$ by Ptolemy's Theorem:

$AC.DB = AB.DC + BC.AD$

i.e., $x^2 = 4 + 2x$

$\therefore$ $x = 1 + \sqrt{5}$ {$x > 0$}
$\therefore$ $x = 2\tau$

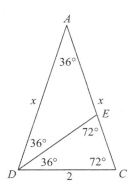

Alternatively: Consider $\triangle ADC$

Bisect $\angle ADC$

$\therefore$ $\triangle EDC$ and $\triangle DEA$ are isosceles

$\therefore$ $AE = DE = DC = 2$ and $EC = x - 2$

Also $\triangle ADC$ and $\triangle DEC$ are similar.

$$\therefore \quad \frac{AC}{DC} = \frac{DC}{EC}$$

i.e., $\dfrac{x}{2} = \dfrac{2}{x-2}$

$$\therefore \quad x^2 - 2x = 4$$
$$\therefore \quad x = 1 + \sqrt{5}$$
$$\quad = 2\tau \quad \{\text{as before}\}$$

b The cube has edges of length 2τ by part **a**.
Consider a cap:

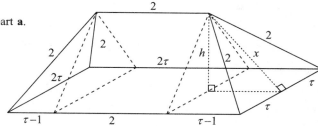

We wish to work out the height h, but first we must find x.

$$2^2 = \tau^2 + x^2 \qquad \{\text{Pythagoras}\}$$
$$x^2 = 4 - \tau^2$$

Now $x^2 = h^2 + (\tau - 1)^2$

i.e., $4 - \tau^2 = h^2 + \tau^2 - 2\tau + 1$

$$\therefore \quad h^2 = 3 + 2\tau - 2\tau^2$$
$$\therefore \quad h^2 = 1 \qquad \{\text{since } \tau^2 = \tau + 1\}$$
$$\therefore \quad h = 1$$

Now the volume of a cap $=$ Volume of

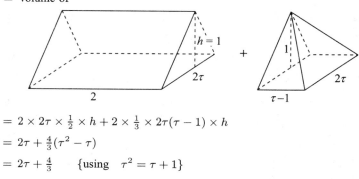

$$= 2 \times 2\tau \times \tfrac{1}{2} \times h + 2 \times \tfrac{1}{3} \times 2\tau(\tau - 1) \times h$$
$$= 2\tau + \tfrac{4}{3}(\tau^2 - \tau)$$
$$= 2\tau + \tfrac{4}{3} \qquad \{\text{using } \tau^2 = \tau + 1\}$$

$\therefore$ volume of dodecahedron $=$ volume of cube $+$ volume of 6 caps

$$= (2\tau)^3 + 6(2\tau + \tfrac{4}{3})$$
$$= 8\tau^3 + 12\tau + 8$$
$$= 8\tau(\tau + 1) + 12\tau + 8 \qquad \{\text{using } \tau^2 = \tau + 1\}$$
$$= 8(2\tau + 1) + 12\tau + 8 \qquad \{\text{using } \tau^2 = \tau + 1\}$$
$$= 28\tau + 16$$
$$= 14(1 + \sqrt{5}) + 16$$
$$= 14\sqrt{5} + 30$$

SENIOR PRIZE WINNERS MASA MATHEMATICS COMPETITIONS

1983

1st	Richard Edward Moore	Yr 12	Prince Alfred College
2nd	James Tanton	Yr 12	Unley HS
3rd	Michael Peake	Yr 11	Prince Alfred College
4th	Andrew Hagger	Yr 12	Pulteney Grammar School
5th	Gary Botha	Yr 12	Stuart HS
	Guy Debelle	Yr 12	St Peters College
	Nicholas Linke	Yr 11	Pulteney Grammar School
	Kenneth Pope	Yr 11	Unley HS
	Michelle Smith	Yr 12	Morialta HS
	Andrew Stobie	Yr 12	Pulteney Grammar School
	Peter Vawser	Yr 11	St Peters College
	Martin Wauchope	Yr 12	Westminster School
	Hin Man Wong	Yr 12	Blackfriars School

Prize for best year 11 entrant   Michael Robert Peake

1984

1st	Michael Peake	Yr 12	Prince Alfred College
2nd	Sepehr Shakib	Yr 12	Norwood HS
3rd	Peter Monk	Yr 11	Pulteney Grammar School
4th	Peter Vawser	Yr 12	St Peters College

Prize for best year 11 entrant   Ian Lundy (Blackwood HS)

1985

1st	Adrian Chen	Yr 11	Prince Alfred College
2nd	Belinda Medlyn	Yr 12	Woodlands CEGGS
3rd	Stephen Loffler	Yr 12	Blackwood HS
4th	Ian Lundy	Yr 12	Blackwood HS
5th	Craig Hutton	Yr 12	Westminster School
6th	Sally Casey	Yr 11	Walford Anglican School

Prize for best year 11 entrant   Adrian Chen

1986

1st	Adrian Chen	Yr 12	Prince Alfred College
2nd	Felicity Smith	Yr 12	Norwood HS
	Terence Tao	Yr 12	Blackwood HS
4th	Mykola Kyrylenko	Yr 12	Pulteney Grammar School
5th	Martin Russell	Yr 12	St Peters College
6th	Stephen Gregory	Yr 12	Westminster School
7th	Surendra Dayal	Yr 12	Pulteney Grammar School
8th	David Wright	Yr 12	Morphett Vale Christian School
9th	Garth Kidd	Yr 12	Pembroke School
10th	Michael Balin	Yr 11	Pulteney Grammar School

Prize for best year 11 entrant   Michael Balin

1987

1st	Michael Balin	Yr 12	Pulteney Grammer School
2nd	Sam Yates	Yr 11	St Peters College
3rd	Woerner Achi	Yr 12	Pembroke School
4th	Khimseng Tew	Yr 12	Norwood HS
5th	Terrence Tao	Yr	Bellevue Heights
6th	Belinda Ward	Yr 12	Scotch College
7th	Nicholas Betts	Yr 12	Pembroke School
	Shane Roberts	Yr 11	Prince Alfred College
	David Standingford	Yr 12	St Peters College
10th	Simon Jenkins	Yr 12	Blackfriars School
11th	David Burgess	Yr 12	Kapunda HS
12th	Jonathan Gill	Yr 12	Prince Alfred College
13th	Faith Jenkins	Yr 12	Concordia College
	Michelle Northcote	Yr 11	Pembroke School
	Trent O'Connor	Yr 12	Pulteney Grammar School
	David Pfitzner	Yr 11	Immanuel College
	Darrin John Smith	Yr 11	Seacombe High
18th	Eric Gerdes	Yr 12	Pembroke School
19th	Jeffrey Balchin	Yr 12	Modbury HS
	Mathew Sorell	Yr 12	St Peters College

Prize for best year 11 entrant   Sam Yates

1988

1st	Sam Yates	Yr 12	St Peters College
2nd	Alexander Hanysz	Yr 12	Blackwood HS
3rd	Katherine Quinn	Yr 12	Scotch College
4th	Shane Roberts	Yr 12	Prince Alfred College
5th	Peter Wiskich	Yr 11	Marryatville HS
6th	Timothy Baldwin	Yr 12	Pulteney Grammar School
	Robert Kennedy	Yr 12	Pembroke School

Prize for best year 11 entrant   Peter Wiskich

1989

1st	Sam Bushell	Yr 12	Scotch College
2nd	Luke Schubert	Yr 12	Concordia College
3rd	Scott Gordon	Yr 12	Blackwood HS
	Simon Ratcliffe	Yr 12	Henley HS
	Andrew Turner	Yr 12	Marryatville HS
	Peter Wiskich	Yr 12	Marryatville HS
7th	Greg Bowering	Yr 11	Westminster School
	Andrew Kleinig	Yr 12	Nuriootpa HS
9th	Carl Stein	Yr 12	Blackwood HS
10th	Ashley Walsh	Yr 12	Prince Alfred College

Prize for best year 11 entrant   Greg Bowering

1990

1st	Greg Bowering	Yr 12	Westminster School
2nd	Daniel Garrard	Yr 12	Faith Lutheran School
	Duncan Richer	Yr 11	The Heights HS
4th	Jiri Baum	Yr 12	Sacred Heart College
	Owen Jepps	Yr 12	Pulteney Grammar School
	Nicole Koenders	Yr 12	Immanuel College
	Brian Ng	Yr 11	Prince Alfred College
	Justin Sawon	Yr 11	Heathfield HS
	Kingsley Storer	Yr 11	Prince Alfred College
	Paul van Wezel	Yr 12	Pembroke School
	Samuel Wee	Yr 12	Prince Alfred College

Prize for best year 11 entrant   Duncan Richer

1991

1st	Brian Ng	Yr 12	Prince Alfred College
2nd	Justin Sawon	Yr 12	Heathfield HS
3rd	Matthew Sherman	Yr 12	Cabra College
4th	Colleen Grady	Yr 12	Walford Anglican School
5th	Duncan Richer	Yr 12	The Heights HS
6th	Christopher Roberts	Yr 12	Scotch College
7th	Kingsley Storer	Yr 12	Prince Alfred College

Prize for best year 11 entrant   Erich Heinzle (St Peters College)

1992

1st	Wing Chung Cheung	Yr 12	Pulteney Grammar School
2nd	Tsen Ling Tan	Yr 12	Pembroke School
3rd	Michael Ashley	Yr 12	Pulteney Grammar School
4th	Chris Wetherell	Yr 12	Norwood HS
5th	Peter Psaltis	Yr 10	St Peters College
6th	Andrew Whitworth	Yr 12	Westminster School
7th	Ern Koh	Yr 12	St Peters College
8th	David Bloustein	Yr 12	Pembroke School
9th	Ian Wong	Yr 12	Prince Alfred College
10th	Julius Wallwork	Yr 12	St Peters College

Prize for best year 11 entrant   Greg Payne (Pembroke School)
Nicholas Tellis (St Ignatius College)

1993

1st	Troy Townsend	Yr 10	Westminster School
2nd	Kirsten White	Yr 12	Seymour College
3rd	Gregory Sherman	Yr 12	Cabra Dominican College
4th	Paul Echermann	Yr 12	Faith Lutheran School
5th	Andrew Bishop	Yr 11	Pulteney Grammar School
6th	Andrew Constantine	Yr 12	Pulteney Grammar School
7th	Kylie Rogers	Yr 12	St Peters Collegiate Girls School
8th	Darren Frith	Yr 12	Henley HS
9th	Tamra Chapman	Yr 12	Craigmore HS
10th	William Campbell	Yr 12	Marryatville HS

Prize for best year 11 entrant   Andrew Bishop

1994

1st	Nigel Tao	Yr 12	Westminster School
2nd	Trevor Tao	Yr 11	Brighton HS
3rd	Martin Sheppard	Yr 11	Marbury School
	Troy Townsend	Yr 11	Westminster School
5th	Andrew Bishop	Yr 12	Pulteney Grammar School
6th	Tat Tsang	Yr 12	Unley HS
7th	Jason Shih	Yr 12	Norwood-Morialta HS
8th	Jeffrey Lim	Yr 12	St Peters College
9th	Tzu Hao Chang	Yr 11	St Peters College
10th	Rodney Polkinghorne	Yr 12	St Peters College

Prize for best year 11 entrant   Trevor Tao

1995

1st	Nigel Tao	Yr 12	Westminster School
2nd	Troy Townsend	Yr 12	Westminster School
3rd	Trevor Tao	Yr 12	Brighton HS
4th	Martin Sheppard	Yr 12	Marbury School
5th	Daniel Noll	Yr 12	Prince Alfred College
6th	Tom Hall	Yr 12	Murray Bridge HS
7th	Andrew McLennan	Yr 12	Pulteney Grammar School
8th	Eric Love	Yr 11	Norwood-Morialta HS
9th	Ben Eckermann	Yr 12	Faith Lutheran School

Prize for best year 11 entrant   Eric Love